The General Exception Clauses of the TRIPS Agreement

Promoting Sustainable Development

The general exception clauses of the TRIPS Agreement of the World Trade Organization permit exceptions to copyrights and to the rights conferred by trademarks, industrial designs and patents. These clauses are intended to facilitate access to diverse forms of proprietary knowledge and therefore foster the interdependent pillars of sustainable development: economic progress, realization of human rights and the conservation of the environment.

In this book Edson Beas Rodrigues Jr. argues that the TRIPS Agreement, in its current configuration, does not hinder the establishment of exceptions to intellectual property rights, devised to promote vital socio-economic interests such as the freedom to carry out creative and inventive activities, freedom of expression, the strengthening of free competition and increased access to educational materials by underprivileged students and to technical knowledge for humanitarian purposes.

EDSON BEAS RODRIGUES JR. is a lawyer based in Brazil. Between 2004 and 2010, he was a Research Fellow at the Instituto de Direito do Comércio Internacional e Desenvolvimento, in São Paulo, Brazil.

The General Exception Clauses of the TRIPS Agreement

Promoting Sustainable Development

Edson Beas Rodrigues Jr.

CAMBRIDGE
UNIVERSITY PRESS

CAMBRIDGE UNIVERSITY PRESS
Cambridge, New York, Melbourne, Madrid, Cape Town,
Singapore, São Paulo, Delhi, Mexico City

Cambridge University Press
The Edinburgh Building, Cambridge CB2 8RU, UK

Published in the United States of America by Cambridge University Press, New York

www.cambridge.org
Information on this title: www.cambridge.org/9781107017481

First published 2012

A catalogue record for this publication is available from the British Library

Library of Congress Cataloguing in Publication data
Rodrigues Jr., Edson Beas (Rodrigues Junior)
The general exception clauses of the TRIPS agreement : promoting sustainable development / Edson Beas Rodrigues Jr.
p. cm.
ISBN 978-1-107-01748-1 (hardback)
1. Agreement on Trade-Related Aspects of Intellectual Property Rights (1994) 2. Intellectual property (International law) 3. Foreign trade regulation. 4. Sustainable development – Law and legislation. I. Title.
K1401.R63 2012
346.04'8 – dc23 2012002688

ISBN 978-1-107-01748-1 Hardback

To my grandmother, Elisa,
my mother, Cida, and
my sister, Keila
for their selfless
and constant support

Isolated knowledge is a lamp to no avail; however, when moving from brain to brain, it turns into science and culture.

Emmanuel and Francisco Cândido Xavier

A hundred times every day I tell myself that my inner and outer life are based on the labors of other men, living and dead, and that I must exert myself in order to give in the same measure as I have received.

Albert Einstein

Contents

List of tables

Acknowledgements

The present work was realized thanks to the cooperation received from various friends, colleagues and institutions. First of all, I would like to thank Jesus Christ, my family and friends for their wide support without which this work would not exist.

I am indebted to the International Development Research Centre (IDRC), Ottawa, Canada, for the grant awarded by its Innovation, Technology and Society Program, which allowed the realization of large portions of this book. In particular I very much appreciate the support provided by Veena Ravichandran, Kim Daley and Louise De Margo. I also thank the Instituto de Direito do Comércio Internacional e Desenvolvimento (IDCID) for the institutional support.

I would like to thank the British Council for the "Researcher Exchange Programme" scholarship which allowed me to carry out research, in early 2009, at the Script Centre, based at the Law School of the University of Edinburgh, Scotland. I am grateful to Professors Abbe Brown and Charlotte Waelde for supporting my research visit.

Especial thanks are due to Professor Richard Gold, McGill University, for encouraging the development of this work. I thank María Teresa La Valle for translating into English portions of this work.

Finally, I would like to thank Cambridge University Press and its staff – notably Kim Hughes, Richard Woodham, Daniel Dunlavey, Laurence Marsh and Leigh Mueller – for their kind attention and for the opportunity to have this work published.

Table of cases

Brazil

Federal Regional Court of the 2nd Region. Civil Appeal no. 2002.51.01.01571 9–6 (Rapporteur: Justice Liliane Roriz. Applicant: Sociedade Brasileira de Autores Teatrais – SBAT. Respondent: Fundação Oswaldo Cruz. Ruling of November 24, 2009. 120

3rd Chamber of the Superior Court of Justice of Brazil. Special Appeal no. 964404. Applicant: Mitra Arquidiocesana de Vitória. Respondent: Escritório Central de Arrecadação e Distribuição – ECAD. Ruling of March 15, 2011. 17–18

Canada

Supreme Court of Canada. Monsanto Canada Inc. *v.* Schmeiser [2004] 1 SCR. 902, 2004 SCC 34. May 21, 2004. 194

CCH Canadian Ltd. *v.* Law Society of Upper Canada [2004] 1 SCR. 339, 2004 SCC. 15

Court of Justice of the European Union (formerly European Court of Justice)

Internationale Handelsgesellschaft mbH *v.* Einfuhr- und Vorrastelle für Getreide und Futtermittel. Reference for a preliminary ruling: Verwaltungsgericht Frankfurt am Main – Germany (Case 1 1–70). Judgment of the Court of December 17, 1970. 83

AB Volvo *v.* Erik Veng (UK) Ltd – Case 238/87. Judgment of the Court of October 5, 1988. 282

United Kingdom of Great Britain and Northern Ireland *v.* Commission of the European Communities. (Case C-180/96). Judgment of May 5, 1998. 83

European Court of Human Rights

France

GATT Panel Reports

India

Inter-American Commission of Human Rights

Inter-American Court of Human Rights

International Court of Justice

Israel

Permanent Court of Arbitration

South Africa

United States of America

World Trade Organization

Treaties, Declarations and Resolutions

Statutes

Abbreviations

ABDR	Brazilian Association of Reprographic Rights
ANFAPE	Brazilian Association of Automotive Parts Manufacturers
BC	Berne Convention for the Protection of Literary and Artistic Works (Paris Act, 1971)
BIRPI	United International Bureaux for the Protection of Intellectual Property
BOC	Brazilian Olympic Committee
CADE	Brazilian Administrative Council for Economic Defense
CJEU	Court of Justice of the European Union
CMO	copyright collective management organization
DNA	deoxyribonucleic acid
DSB	Dispute Settlement Body of the WTO
DSU	WTO Dispute Settlement Understanding
ECAR	European Campaign for the Freedom of the Automotive Parts and Repair Market
ECJ	European Court of Justice
ECHR	Council of Europe's Convention for the Protection of Human Rights and Fundamental Freedoms
ECtHR	European Court of Human Rights
FCB	Federal Constitution of Brazil of 1988
GATS	General Agreement on Trade in Services
GATT	General Agreement on Tariffs and Trade
GPOPAI	University of São Paulo's Research Group on Public Policy for Access to Information
ICCPR	International Covenant on Civil and Political Rights
ICESCR	International Covenant on Economic, Social and Cultural Rights
ICHR	Inter-American Court of Human Rights
ICJ	International Court of Justice

ICSID	International Centre for Settlement of Investment Disputes
IDCID	Institute for International Trade Law and Development
IMASPs	Independent Manufacturers of Automotive Spare Parts
INPI	Brazilian Institute of Industrial Property
IPRs	intellectual property rights
LDA	Copyright Act of Brazil – Law no. 9.610/98
LPI	Industrial Property Act of Brazil – Law no. 9.279/96
MEAs	multilateral environmental agreements
MPF	Federal Public Prosecution Office (Brazil)
NGO	non-governmental organization
NIH	United States National Institutes of Health
OECD	Organization for Economic Co-operation and Development
OHCHR	Office of the High Commissioner for Human Rights
PCH	patent clearing house
PCR	polymerase chain reaction
PROCADE	Office of CADE's Attorney General
R&D	research & development
SACGHS	Secretary's Advisory Committee on Genetics, Health and Society
SCLP	WIPO Standing Committee on the Law of Patents
SDE	Secretariat of Economic Law of the Ministry of Justice of Brazil
STJ	Superior Court of Justice of Brazil
TGI	Tribunal de grande instance (High Court of Paris)
TRIPS	Agreement on Trade-Related Aspects of Intellectual Property Rights
UDHR	Universal Declaration of Human Rights
UNDP	United Nations Development Programme
UNEP	United Nations Environment Programme
UNESCO	United Nations Educational, Scientific and Cultural Organization
UNFCCC	United Nations Framework Convention on Climate Change
UNGA	United Nations General Assembly
USP	University of São Paulo
USPTO	United States Patent and Trademark Office
USTR	United States Trade Representative
VCLT	Vienna Convention on the Law of Treaties
WCT	WIPO Copyright Treaty

WHO	World Health Organization
WIPO	World Intellectual Property Organization
WPPT	WIPO Performances and Phonograms Treaty
WTO	World Trade Organization

1 Introduction

1.1 Relationship between sustainable development and access to knowledge

Sustainable development consists of a type of development that rests on three interdependent pillars: economic, social and environmental. The economic pillar refers to the need to expand business activity and the capacity of this sector to produce goods and services that meet the demands of society.[1] The social pillar refers to the realization of the human right to development,[2] defined as the right to all fundamental freedoms and human rights guaranteed to all individuals by the International Bill of Human Rights, comprising the Universal Declaration of Human Rights (UDHR), the International Covenant on Civil and Political Rights (ICCPR) and the International Covenant on Economic, Social and Cultural Rights (ICESCR).[3] Finally, the environmental pillar refers to the protection of the environment and its resources for present and future generations.[4] Or, in the words of the 1987 Brundtland Report prepared by the World Commission on Environment and Development, "[s]ustainable development requires meeting the basic needs of *all* and

[1] See principles 8, 9 and 11 of the Stockholm Declaration of the United Nations Conference on the Human Environment 1972 (Stockholm Declaration).

[2] Principle 3 of the Rio Declaration on Environment and Development 1992 (Rio Declaration) reads: "The right to development must be fulfilled so as to equitably meet developmental and environmental needs of present and future generations."

[3] Art. 1(1) of the United Nations Declaration on the Right to Development (UNGA, Resolution 41/128) defines the right to development as "an inalienable human right by virtue of which every human person and all peoples are entitled to participate in, contribute to, and enjoy economic, social, cultural and political development, in which all human rights and fundamental freedoms can be fully realized." Art. 6 of the Declaration reaffirms the interdependence of human rights and the duty of states to engage in the realization of all fundamental freedoms and human rights. This implies that the right to development is not observed if a certain State gives priority to the realization of economic, social and cultural rights, while neglecting the observance of civil and political rights, or vice versa.

[4] See, e.g., principles 2, 3, 4 and 5, Stockholm Declaration.

extending to *all* the opportunity to satisfy their aspirations for a better life . . . In essence, sustainable development is a process of change in which the exploitation of resources, the direction of investments, the orientation of technological development, and institutional change are all in harmony and enhance both current and future potential to meet human needs and aspirations."[5]

In harmony with the definition adopted by this study, the 2002 Convention for Cooperation in the Protection and Sustainable Development of the Marine and Coastal Environment of the Northeast Pacific adopts a definition of sustainable development which outlines its three interdependent pillars of support:

> "Sustainable development" means the process of progressive change in the quality of life of human beings, *which places it as the centre and primordial subject of development*, by means of economic growth with *social equity* and the transformation of methods of production and consumption patterns, and which is *sustained in the ecological balance and vital support of the region*. This process implies respect for regional, national and local *ethnic and cultural diversity*, and the full participation of people in peaceful *coexistence and in harmony with nature*, without prejudice to and ensuring the *quality of life of future generations* (art. 1(a)). (emphasis added)

In a scenario marked by the absence of industrial and commercial activity, there are no jobs, just subsistence farming and over-exploitation of natural resources as a way to temporarily relieve the evils of material poverty in which large segments of the population live. Economic progress is therefore a condition for poverty eradication and, hence, sustainable development;[6] however, it does not automatically lead to social welfare. There are cases of materially rich countries, which still retain large parts of their populations living in subhuman conditions. That is the reason why sustainable development requires that economic progress be channeled to enhance the well-being of mankind, by creating conditions that allow the full realization of all human rights guaranteed to all individuals.

But sustainable development requires not only that economic progress goes hand in hand with human rights. In addition, it requires strict observance of the limits imposed by the laws of nature, for a serious but neglected reason: the future of humanity is closely linked to the fate of the biosphere. This requirement is summarized in the award in the *Ijzeren Rijn* case, delivered by the Permanent Court of Arbitration:

[5] World Commission on Environment and Development 1987, cap. 2, paras. 4 and 15.

[6] See principle 5, Rio Declaration.

Since the Stockholm Conference on the Environment in 1972 there has been a marked development of international law relating to the protection of the environment. Today, both international and EC law require the integration of appropriate environmental measures in the design and implementation of economic development activities. Principle 4 of the Rio Declaration on Environment and Development, adopted in 1992 . . . which reflects this trend, provides that "environmental protection shall constitute an integral part of the development process and cannot be considered in isolation from it." Importantly, these emerging principles now integrate environmental protection into the development process. Environmental law and the law on development stand not as alternatives but as mutually reinforcing, integral concepts, which require that where development may cause significant harm to the environment there is a duty to prevent, or at least mitigate, such harm . . . This duty, in the opinion of the Tribunal, has now become a principle of general international law. This principle applies not only in autonomous activities but also in activities undertaken in implementation of specific treaties between the Parties.[7]

Along the same line, Judge Weeramantry, from the International Court of Justice (ICJ), in a separate opinion concerning the *Gabčíkovo-Nagymaros* case, points out that sustainable development is already a principle of international law whose function is to reconcile norms in collision. The only aspect of the opinion open to criticism is that it seems to have considered that sustainable development relies on two pillars – economic development and environmental conservation – while, at present, the international community considers that sustainable development relies on three interdependent pillars. Possibly this oversight (or omission) is due to the fact that the dispute involved a potential conflict between environmental and economic issues:

The problem of steering a course between the needs of development and the necessity to protect the environment is a problem alike of the law of development and of the law of the environment. Both these vital and developing areas of law require, and indeed assume, *the existence of a principle which harmonizes both needs.*

To hold that no such principle exists in the law is to hold that current law recognizes the juxtaposition of two principles which could operate in collision with each other, without providing the necessary basis of principle for their reconciliation. The untenability of the supposition that the law sanctions such a state of normative anarchy suffices to condemn a hypothesis that leads to so unsatisfactory a result.

Each principle cannot be given free rein, regardless of the other. *The law necessarily contains within itself the principle of reconciliation. That principle is the principle of sustainable development* . . . The components of the principle [of sustainable

[7] Permanent Court of Arbitration, award in the arbitration regarding the Iron Rhine ("Ijzeren Rijn") railway between Belgium and the Netherlands, para. 59.

Table 1.1 *Types of growth*

Types of growth	Economic	Human	Ecological
Wild	Positive effects	Negative effects	Negative effects
Socially benign	Positive effects	Positive effects	Negative effects
Stable	Positive effects	Negative effects	Positive effects
Sustainable development	Positive effects	Positive effects	Positive effects

Source: Based on the typology developed by Sachs (2007, 269).

development] come from well-established areas of international law – human rights, State responsibility, environmental law, economic and industrial law, equity, territorial sovereignty, abuse of rights, good neighbourliness – to mention a few. It has also been expressly incorporated into a number of binding and far-reaching international agreements, thus giving it binding force in the context of those agreements. It offers an important principle for the resolution of tensions between two established rights.[8] (emphasis added)

In other words, sustainable development aims to channel most of the fruits of economic growth policies into the implementation of all human rights and fundamental freedoms and into the preservation of the environment for present and future generations. Therefore, policies that pursue, in an isolated and conflicting manner, any of these goals,[9] e.g. a policy that generates socio-economic progress and environmental destruction as a side-effect, or a policy which pursues the preservation of the environment in a manner that neglects the demands of society and economy are not policies that can lead to sustainable development. In this sense, the Rio Declaration on Environment and Development 1992 (Rio Declaration) puts human beings "at the centre of concerns for sustainable development," and states that "they are entitled to a healthy and productive life in harmony with nature" (principle 1), and stresses that "[t]he right to development must be fulfilled so as to equitably meet developmental and environmental needs of present and future generations" (principle 3). Table 1.1 on types of growth sets out the tripod on which rests the ideal of sustainable development and clarifies the differences between this and the other types of growth. The table also facilitates the understanding that sustainable development should not be confused with economic growth at any cost or with environmental preservation detached from socio-economic progress. However, the table does not

[8] Separate opinion of Weeramantry. *Gabčíkovo-Nagymaros Project* (Hungary v. Slovakia), Judgment of September 25, 1997. The Hague: ICJ Reports 1997), pp. 95–99.
[9] See principle 4, Rio Declaration.

make clear that policies directed at promoting sustainable development shall be able to generate positive effects worldwide.

The goal of sustainable development has gained ground on the political agenda of the international community since the United Nations Conference on the Human Environment, which took place in Stockholm in 1972, and from then onwards the international community has been committed to make it a reality.

In the 1980s, the United Nations (UN) commissioned from an independent commission – the World Commission on Environment and Development – a comprehensive study whose aim was to identify the causes of the rapid deterioration of the environment in the second half of the twentieth century and to propose solutions to prevent the installation of global environmental chaos. The work carried out by the World Commission on Environment and Development, known as the Brundtland Report, was published in 1987. In response to the report, the UN bestowed on sustainable development the status of a governing principle in its programs[10] and specialized agencies, and in 1992 it convened in Rio de Janeiro the UN Conference on Environment and Development. During the conference, the international community undertook binding and political obligations aimed at implementing the goal of sustainable development, these being crystallized in, inter alia, the Convention on Biological Diversity, the United Nations Framework Convention on Climate Change, the Rio Declaration on Environment and Development and Agenda 21.

In 2000, the UN Member States committed to achieving by 2015 the so-called Millennium Development Goals: to eradicate extreme poverty and hunger; ensure universal access to primary education; promote gender equality and empower women; reduce child mortality; improve maternal health; combat HIV/AIDS, malaria and other serious diseases; ensure environmental sustainability; foster a global partnership for development through, amongst other measures, the development of an open and non-discriminatory trading system; meet the material needs of poor countries and promote access to medicines.[11] There is no doubt that the achievement of this set of goals will promote sustainable development.

In 2002, during the World Summit on Sustainable Development, the international community reaffirmed a collective commitment "to advance and strengthen the interdependent and mutually reinforcing pillars of sustainable development – economic development, social development and environmental protection – at the local, national, regional

[10] See UNGA, Resolution 42/187.
[11] See UNGA, United Nations Millennium Declaration (Resolution A/RES/55/2).

and global levels"; "to act together, united by a common determination to save our planet, promote human development and achieve universal prosperity and peace"; and "to ensure that our collective hope for sustainable development is realized."[12]

Sustainable development is also listed as one of the objectives of the multilateral trading system: in 1994, at the end of the GATT Uruguay round of negotiations, which culminated in the creation of the World Trade Organization (WTO), the participating States decided to include sustainable development in the list of objectives pursued by the nascent organization.[13] The inclusion of this objective in the preamble of the Marrakesh Agreement establishing the WTO was not trifling. The preamble of this agreement was based substantially on the preamble of the General Agreement on Tariffs and Trade 1947 (GATT 1947), however, there is a remarkable difference between them and, therefore, their goals. While the preamble of the GATT 1947 named as one of its objectives the promotion of "the full use of the resources of the world," which could lead to the over-exploitation of these resources, the preamble of the Marrakesh Agreement states as one of its goals the promotion of "the optimal use of the world's resources in accordance with the objective of sustainable development, seeking to protect and preserve . . . the environment . . . "[14] This change in approach should be reflected in the approach used to interpret and apply the rules of the WTO legal framework. In order to confirm that the replacement of the GATT 1947 regime by the WTO regime involved a real change of goals, the 1994 Declaration on Trade and Environment, adopted by ministers at the meeting of the Uruguay Round Trade Negotiations Committee in Marrakesh, stresses "that there should not be, nor need be, any policy contradiction between safeguarding and upholding an open, non-discriminatory and equitable multilateral trading system on the one hand, and acting for the protection of the environment, and the promotion of sustainable development on the other."[15]

The 2002 Johannesburg Declaration reaffirmed as essential prerequisites for achieving the goal of sustainable development, amongst others, poverty eradication, changing consumption and production patterns, protecting and managing the natural resource base, the substantial reduction of the socio-economic gap that sets industrialized countries apart

[12] Johannesburg Declaration on Sustainable Development, 2002, paras. 5, 35 and 37.

[13] In *US – Shrimp*, the WTO Appellate Body rightly upheld the widespread view that sustainable development is a type of development that integrates economic and social development and environmental protection (WTO, WT/DS58/AB/R, Report of the Appellate Body, para. 129, footnote 107).

[14] See Hu 2004, 150.

[15] WTO, Decision on Trade and Environment, 1994, preamble.

from developing countries and the equitable distribution of the fruits and costs of economic globalization.[16] The fulfillment of these requirements depends on, inter alia, easier access to modern technologies and other forms of knowledge; capacity building of human resources and improvement of the quality of education.[17] There is therefore a direct relationship between sustainable development and wider access to knowledge.[18]

It is a mistake to believe that scientific, technological and cultural advances depend exclusively on the intellectual sharpness of creators and massive investments in creative and inventive activities. Scientific, technological and cultural development is not a stand-alone, isolated process. Quite the contrary. The development of new knowledge, technologies, processes and products stem from the application of previous information, knowledge and technologies.[19] Briefly, the generation of knowledge is a cumulative process; it is in line with this understanding that Isaac Newton said in a letter written in 1676, addressed to Robert Hooke: "If I have seen further it is by standing on the shoulders of Giants." In this same vein, Judge Story in *Emerson* v. *Davies* underscored that "in literature, in science and in art, there are, and can be, few, if any, things, which, in an abstract sense, are strictly new and original throughout. Every book in literature, science and art, borrows, and must necessarily borrow, and use much which was well known and used before . . . No man writes exclusively from his own thoughts, unaided and uninstructed by the thoughts of others. The thoughts of every man are, more or less, a combination of what other men have thought and expressed, although they may be modified, exalted, or improved by his own genius . . . Virgil borrowed much from Homer; Bacon drew from earlier as well as contemporary minds; Coke exhausted all the known learning of his profession; and even Shakespeare and Milton, so justly and proudly our boast as the brightest originals, would be found to have gathered much from the abundant stores of current knowledge and classical studies in their days."[20]

[16] Johannesburg Declaration on Sustainable Development, paras. 11–14.

[17] *Ibid.*, paras. 18 and 28.

[18] The term "knowledge" entails data, information and knowledge in the strict sense. The elements that make up the notion of knowledge were defined by Elinor Ostrom and Charlotte Hess (2007, 8), based on Machlup, as follows: "Machlup . . . introduced this division of data-information – knowledge, with data being raw bits of information, information being organized data in context, and knowledge being the assimilation of the information and understanding of how to use it. Knowledge . . . refers to all types of understanding gained through experience or study, whether indigenous, scientific, scholarly, or otherwise nonacademic."

[19] See Scotchmer 1991.

[20] *Emerson* v. *Davies*, 8 F. Cas. 615, 619 (CCD Mass. 1845).

As will be seen below, continuous access to a robust stock of different forms of knowledge is the fuel for endogenous capacity building in any country. Furthermore, wider and more facilitated access to knowledge frees developing countries and least developed countries (jointly referred to hereafter as developing countries) from the need to import "ready-made solutions" for their social and environmental challenges[21] and the endless waiting for transfer of knowledge from industrialized countries on favorable terms.[22]

Access to technologies

New technologies are important tools for the efficient implementation of multilateral environmental agreements (MEAs) at the domestic level. In this sense, it should be noted that the UN Convention on Biological Diversity states that compliance by developing countries with their obligations will depend, inter alia, on facilitated access to technologies owned by industrialized countries (art. 20(4)).

Access to technologies and to technological inputs is essential to the development of new products and processes whose aim is to: improve production processes and reuse of industrial waste; be less dependent on energy resources and materials (decarbonization of production processes); facilitate the diagnosis of emerging environmental problems; enable the sustainable exploitation of natural resources; rehabilitate sick ecosystems of the Earth; allow the conservation of natural resources for future generations; prevent risks to the natural environment, produced by human activities, from causing serious or irreversible environmental damage; generate new drugs and therapies to benefit the health of humans and animals; expand substantially the production of food using fewer natural resources, notably water, land and chemical inputs;[23] improve the nutritional quality of foods; develop pesticides that do not poison

[21] See principle 9, Rio Declaration.

[22] For the sake of illustration, it is worth mentioning the results of a recent joint survey conducted by the European Patent Office, the United Nations Environment Programme and the International Centre for Trade and Sustainable Development (ICTSD) (Simmons 2010). According to the survey, patents covering clean energy occupy a prominent place in the portfolio of intangible assets of a growing number of companies in the US, Europe and Japan. Nevertheless, these technologies are transferred, very rarely, to developing countries: out of the 150 companies participating in the poll, 58 percent said they never transferred their clean technologies to developing countries; only 5 percent of the companies surveyed reported having frequently transferred clean technologies to developing countries. The licensed technologies have as targets a small number of developing countries: Brazil, China, India and Russia and, to a lesser extent, Malaysia, Thailand and South Africa.

[23] See De Schutter 2009, 15–16.

human beings and their environment; develop less polluting means of transport; increase access to safe drinking water.[24] Access to technologies is also essential to strengthen the business community, to promote free competition and to release human beings from unhealthy and poorly paid labor.

In other words, access to technologies is indispensable to: guaranteeing the rights to health and to food of all individuals; preventing the phenomenon of the tragedy of the commons, marked by the over-exploitation of natural resources, followed by their deterioration or extinction[25]; stimulating the development of clean energy; generating new jobs, especially in emerging sectors of the economy (biotechnology, nanotechnology, agro-biotechnology and software); promoting the development of new products and new enterprises; reducing the prices of goods and services and expanding access to goods and services by less affluent sectors of society. It is no accident that principle 20 of the Stockholm Declaration on the Human Environment states that:

> Scientific research and development in the context of environmental problems, both national and multinational, must be promoted in all countries, especially the developing countries. In this connection, the free flow of up-to-date scientific information and transfer of experience must be supported and assisted, to facilitate the solution of environmental problems; environmental technologies should be made available to developing countries on terms which would encourage their wide dissemination without constituting an economic burden on the developing countries

[24] There is a great number of international and national instruments that recognize the symbiotic relationship between access to technology and to knowledge and preservation of the environment. See, e.g., principles 18 and 20, Stockholm Declaration 1972; principle 9, Rio Declaration 1992; arts. 16–17, Convention on Biological Diversity; arts. 244, 266 *et seq.*, United Nations Convention on the Law of the Sea; Chapter 34, Agenda 21; art. 1(c) and (h) and art. 4(5), UNFCCC; art. 10 (c), Kyoto Protocol on Climate Change; art. 22, Cartagena Protocol on Biosafety to the Convention on Biological Diversity; art. 5(1)(e) and art. 13(2)(a) and (b), International Treaty on Plant Genetic Resources for Food and Agriculture; UNFCCC Copenhagen Accord, paras. 4, 5, 8, 10.

[25] According to Hardin (1968, 1243–1244), "[t]he tragedy of the commons develops in this way. Picture a pasture open to all. It is to be expected that each herdsman will try to keep as many cattle as possible on the commons . . . As a rational being, each herdsman seeks to maximize his gain. Explicitly or implicitly, more or less consciously, he asks, 'What is the utility *to me* of adding one more animal to my herd?' . . . [T]he rational herdsman concludes that the only sensible course for him to pursue is to add another animal to his herd. And another; and another . . . But this is the conclusion reached by each and every rational herdsman sharing a commons. Therein is the tragedy. Each man is locked into a system that compels him to increase his herd without limit – in a world that is limited. Ruin is the destination toward which all men rush, each pursuing his own best interest in a society that believes in the freedom of the commons. Freedom in a commons brings ruin to all."

and that principle 9 of the Rio Declaration provides:

> States should cooperate to strengthen endogenous capacity-building for sustainable development by improving scientific understanding through exchanges of scientific and technological knowledge, and by enhancing the development, adaptation, diffusion and transfer of technologies, including new and innovative technologies.

Access to knowledge condensed into literary and scientific works

Even if a State has guaranteed free access to all technologies that may be required for its economic development, if its population is not technically enabled to master and apply them productively, access to the advances of science and technology will be meaningless.[26] For this reason, facilitated access to publications in general – literary, artistic and scientific works – plays a central role in scientific and technological progress and in the technical qualification of populations, with a view to enable them to: diagnose new environmental challenges and devise solutions to face them; generate new scientific knowledge on how to extract greater benefits from natural resources, without exhausting them; recover damaged biomes; manage and apply new scientific and technological knowledge for the well-being of humanity.

Access to books and other publications is also essential for the formation of proactive, conscious and responsible citizens, enabled: to act politically; to claim and defend their rights; to distinguish between environmentally sustainable companies and those that degrade the environment; and to make conscious consumer choices. Access to scientific and literary works is equally indispensable to improve the living conditions of individuals. At present, there is no doubt that the higher the qualifications of an individual, the greater his chances of taking a well-paid post. Economically independent individuals are more likely to achieve a happy and fulfilling life. Finally, access to literary and scientific works provides fuel to the process of generating new intellectual productions, resources which are urgently needed for the preservation and continued expansion of cultural diversity.[27]

[26] See Commission on Intellectual Property Rights 2002, 103.

[27] It is worth reproducing here the wording of art. 2(6) of the Convention on the Protection and Promotion of the Diversity of Cultural Expressions 2005, as this provision considers cultural diversity "as a rich asset for individuals and societies" and its "protection, promotion and maintenance . . . an essential requirement for sustainable development for the benefit of present and future generations."

Access to the ornamental plastic form of durable goods

Increased longevity of consumer goods is one way to reduce the carbon footprint of humanity. Increased longevity of durable goods, notably cars, depends on consumer access to, among other things, must-match spare parts, i.e. those directed at restoring the original appearance of the damaged body of these goods. The free production of these parts promotes free competition in the repairs market. In the context of a society increasingly concerned with environmental sustainability, the introduction of free competition in the market for spare parts encourages economic actors to use new tools to entice consumers.[28] Instead of focusing their marketing strategy on the commercialization of poor-quality and inexpensive products, it is conceivable that there will be a move to win over well-informed and socially responsible consumers with more durable and environmentally sustainable products. The expansion of free competition also reduces the maintenance costs of durable goods, which, in turn, extends their life span and reduces their replacement rate. The lower this rate is, the lower the industry demand is for scarce natural resources. The reduction of maintenance costs of durable goods still allows consumers to invest the saved resources in their quality of life through the purchase of environmentally sustainable goods, which, as a rule, are still more expensive than the environmentally degrading ones.

Access to the identification signs used by companies and their products and services

Companies and their products and services are identified, in trade, by distinctive identification signs known as trademarks. Publicity about the antisocial practices committed by the business sector may involve the appropriation of their trademarks. Critical messages disseminated by civil society organizations and the media are instruments that can instigate the public to change their consumer habits. This shift in habits, in turn, exerts strong pressure on the business sector as a whole to adopt more socially and environmentally responsible policies. Such critical messages also serve to instigate consumers, civil society organizations and public prosecutors to sue private organizations for allegedly illicit antisocial actions. In short: consumers' demands fuel the manufacture of products

[28] See UNEP 2010, 1–2 (the study conducted by the UNEP based on empirical research, points out that a growing number of consumers worldwide have been opting to purchase environmentally friendly products and rejecting products and services provided by companies that flout the environment).

and services. It is therefore their responsibility to encourage, through sustainable consumer habits, the recasting of the policies followed by the private sector. And in order to catalyze changes in consumer habits, it is essential to guarantee media and civil society organizations the right to appropriate famous trademarks, with the specific aim of informing the public.

1.2 Role of intellectual property rights in restricting access to knowledge

Knowledge is a public good in the economic sense of the term, as it can be used simultaneously by an infinite number of individuals and institutions. Unlike private goods – e.g. natural resources in general, tangible assets – the use of knowledge by an individual does not impose any restriction on the freedom of others to enjoy it simultaneously.[29] In other words, knowledge is not subject to a tragedy of the commons. In fact, the simultaneous use of knowledge by many individuals leads to the faster generation of new knowledge, since each individual is endowed with intellectual capacity of his or her own.

To date, intellectual property rights (IPRs) are considered as the main mechanism for protecting intellectual goods.[30] Artificially, IPR regimes turn public goods into private goods, and therefore scarce ones, by according to right holders the right to exclude third parties from the enjoyment of the protected objects.

Nowadays, the various forms of knowledge required for the attainment of sustainable development are very often protected by IPRs: a growing number of technologies and socially valuable products and processes are under patent protection; literary, artistic and scientific works are under copyright protection, which can last for up to 100 years after the death of the authors;[31] the ornamental plastic form of complex products such as cars is usually protected as an industrial design; identification signs, used by businesses in commercial operations, are protected as trademarks. Patents, copyrights, industrial designs and trademarks give their holders a powerful right to exclude others from unauthorized enjoyment of the protected intangible assets. IPRs, by preventing the free movement of

[29] Ostrom and Hess (2003) argue that knowledge is a non-rival good, as it can be consumed by an infinite number of people, and is a non-excludable good, as the process of excluding unauthorized third parties from its enjoyment is technically impossible or too costly.

[30] See Rodrigues Jr. 2010, 57.

[31] This is the case of Mexico. See art. 29, I, Ley Federal de Derecho de Autor, amended on July 23, 2003.

knowledge, create serious barriers to achieving sustainable development, affecting developing countries in particular. The problem of providing the holders of IPRs with a broad right of exclusion is the fact that there are no guarantees that they will exercise it in ways that reconcile their individual interests with the legitimate interests of society.

Today's main international treaty on intellectual property is the WTO Agreement on Trade-Related Aspects of Intellectual Property Rights (TRIPS Agreement or TRIPS). This agreement has as its foundations the main international treaties devoted to the protection of IPRs, i.e. the Paris Convention for the Protection of Industrial Property of 1967 (Paris Convention), the Berne Convention for the Protection of Literary and Artistic Works of 1971 (Berne Convention or BC), the International Convention for the Protection of Performers, Producers of Phonograms and Broadcasting Organizations of 1961 (Rome Convention) and the Treaty on Intellectual Property in Respect of Integrated Circuits of 1989. TRIPS, however, goes beyond these treaties, as it guarantees broader rights to the holders of IPRs and, more importantly, because it relies on the highly effective WTO dispute settlement mechanism.

This means that if a WTO Member fails to secure any of the minimum rights guaranteed by the TRIPS, the aggrieved Member can always require the set up of a panel, a sort of ad hoc first instance court, composed of experts in international trade, charged with the duty of investigating whether the defendant breached any of the provisions of the TRIPS Agreement. The losing party may appeal to the Appellate Body of the WTO in order to try to reverse the decision of first instance (the panel report). In any event, the losing party must comply with the determinations set by the panel or the Appellate Body, because the reports rendered by these bodies are adopted by negative consensus by the WTO Dispute Settlement Body (DSB)[32], i.e. these reports will only be non-binding, when all members of the WTO decide not to adopt them. After the adoption of the report rendered by a panel or the Appellate Body, it must be fully observed by the losing party, otherwise it will bear heavy trade sanctions applicable by the prevailing party.

At least formally, the TRIPS Agreement does not limit itself to pursue a commercial goal, i.e. strengthening IPRs at any cost. TRIPS, one of the fundamental pillars of the WTO system, also aims to safeguard interests that overlap with those protected by international human rights treaties and MEAs, notably: sustainable development, environmental protection, raising standards of living of individuals, full employment, transfer and dissemination of technical knowledge, social and economic

[32] At the DSB, all the Members of the WTO are represented.

welfare, the balance between IPRs and the obligations of right holders towards society.[33] In other words, at least in theory, the TRIPS Agreement seeks to protect, inter alia, many of the interests guaranteed by the UDHR, the ICCPR and the ICESCR, and the central underlying objectives pursued by the MEAs. The great difficulty in giving shelter to all those legitimate interests is that while IPRs provide their holders with the right to prevent the spread of proprietary intangible goods, the realization of various human rights and environmental protection depend on, inter alia, the wide dissemination of knowledge, science and culture.

In order to harmonize these disparate interests, at the same time TRIPS grants to the owners of IPRs a wide range of minimum rights that must be enforced by all WTO Members; it offers to its parties some "flexibilities," which *may* be employed to safeguard the interests of public nature. However, the terms of the TRIPS Agreement have been interpreted and its provisions applied by WTO Members and the WTO itself as if it had been designed to maximize exclusively economic interests of the holders of IPRs. Consequently, the WTO's social and environmental goals remain neglected, and sustainable development remains as a distant goal to be achieved. For this reason, the United Nations Development Programme's Human Development Reports of 1999 and 2000 characterized the TRIPS Agreement as a highly unbalanced agreement, which sets barriers to the eradication of poverty, to the realization of various human rights and to the transfer of technology to developing countries;[34] the Sub-Commission on Human Rights resolutions 2000/7 and 2001/21 stressed that TRIPS potentially conflicts with the set of human rights; a report by the UN Commmission on Human Rights argued that the TRIPS Agreement promotes the economic interests of the holders of IPRs, rather than the realization of the rights to health, food and education;[35] the UN High Commissioner for Human Rights held that the protection of human rights is at best a secondary interest to the TRIPS Agreement;[36] and Olivier De Schutter, UN Special Rapporteur on the Right to Food, considered IPRs harmful to the right to food, once it suppresses the right of farmers to save, re-use and exchange seeds and stimulates the replacement of agro-biodiversity by homogeneous

[33] See the preamble of the Marrakesh Agreement Establishing the World Trade Organization (Marrakesh Agreement) and art. 7 TRIPS.

[34] See UNDP 1999, 35. See also UNDP 1999, 6–10, 35, 68, 72–76, 108; UNDP 2000, 83–85.

[35] Commission on Human Rights, E/CN.4/Sub.2/2001/10, paras. 20, 21, 29 and 31.

[36] OHCHR 2001, para. 38.

plant varieties and seeds.[37] Because of the alleged intrinsic imbalances of TRIPS, harmonization between the economic interests of the holders of IPRs and those of a socio-environmental nature would depend on the substantial reform of this agreement.[38]

But before it can be said that TRIPS is actually an unbalanced treaty, incapable of safeguarding human rights and environmental concerns, it is necessary to identify the general exception clauses thereof, and to investigate whether these provisions ensure to WTO Members the legitimacy to adopt vigorous exceptions to IPRs.

1.3 Purpose and plan of the work

Exceptions to IPRs allow third parties to use protected subject matter in certain circumstances and for certain socially relevant purposes, regardless of any authorization granted by the right holders and, often but not always, without the payment of any fee.[39] Despite its name, exceptions are *user's rights* held by the consumers of proprietary intangible goods.[40] Accordingly they are enforceable against third parties, including holders of IPRs. Their function is to reconcile the economic interests of IPR holders with the interest of various sectors of society to access, with the utmost ease possible, protected intellectual products, in order to meet the needs of important individual and collective interests.

Exceptions to IPRs play a unique role in the realization of the cultural rights guaranteed under the ICESCR – notably, the freedom to conduct scientific research and creative activities – by creating conditions that

[37] De Schutter 2009, 3. Similarly, Then and Tippe (2009), 29, criticize the recent and growing trend of granting patents for plants, seeds and animals developed with conventional techniques (i.e. essentially biological), because these patents stimulate business concentration; reduce competition; lead to arbitrary increases in the prices of seeds; cause farmers to become increasingly dependent on patented inputs; affect the pace of innovation due to the privatization of trivial techniques and products; stimulate the increase in food prices.

[38] See, e.g., Byström and Einarsson 2002, 9–10; OHCHR 2001, para. 68; UNDP 1999, 74, 108; UNDP 2000, 85.

[39] See Bently 2010, 7.

[40] See Geiger 2006a, 371. The view that exceptions to IPRs are in actual fact user's rights was endorsed by the Supreme Court of Canada in *CCH Canadian Ltd* v. *Law Society of Upper Canada*. The consequence arising from this understanding is not negligible, as noted by the Supreme Court of Canada, in the context of the local Copyright Act: "The fair dealing exception, like other exceptions in the *Copyright Act*, is a user's right. In order to maintain the proper balance between the rights of a copyright owner and users' interests, it *must not be interpreted restrictively*. As Professor Vaver . . . has explained . . . : 'User rights are not just loopholes. Both owner rights and user rights should therefore be given the fair and balanced reading that befits remedial legislation" (*ibid.*, p. 48) (emphasis added). I thank Jeremy de Beer for bringing this case to my attention.

allow for the conservation, development and diffusion of science and culture (art. 15(2) and (3)). Also in the field of human rights, exceptions to IPRs are levers for the promotion of the rights to education, health, life, food, freedom of expression and work. In the business arena, exceptions to IPRs serve to promote free competition, as they facilitate access to intellectual inputs for a large number of productive and scientific institutions, regardless of any case-by-case governmental intervention.[41] In the environmental sphere, exceptions promote the efficient use of natural resources and the restoration and conservation of ecosystems, through the dissemination of technologies. In summary, the exceptions to IPRs promote their socio-environmental function.

However, the scope available for the adoption of measures directed at restricting the scope of IPRs on behalf of public interests are not easily measurable. From this perspective, the TRIPS Agreement creates monumental problems for WTO Members, especially for the most vulnerable, in terms of mastering the complex rules of the multilateral trading system.

Among the opportunities provided by the TRIPS Agreement, deserving special attention from academics, policy makers, lawyers and judges, are those provided by its general exception clauses, which allow the making of exceptions to the exclusive rights granted to the holders of copyright (art. 9(2) BC[42] and art. 13 TRIPS), industrial designs (art. 17), trademarks (art. 26.2) and patents (art. 30).[43] Such provisions can be used primarily by legislators in the process of assessing the legitimacy of bills that propose the adoption of exceptions to any of these IPRs. In addition, the general exception clauses of the TRIPS Agreement may be employed by judicial bodies – and by governmental antitrust and administrative organs vested with the competence to hear cases involving IPRs – for two other functions related to the settlement of private disputes.

The first function is to clarify the scope of the exceptions expressly provided for in legal texts, especially when they incorporate polysemic terms. The second function is performed in the process of assessing the legitimacy of uses of proprietary intellectual products which are not expressly backed by any exception enshrined in a statute. That is, the general

[41] See Max Planck Institute and Queen Mary, University of London 2008, 2.

[42] Pursuant to art. 9 (1) TRIPS Agreement, arts. 1 to 21 and the Appendix to the Berne Convention (with the exception of art. 6bis) are integral parts of the TRIPS Agreement.

[43] The general exception clauses do not specify the objectives to be pursued by the exceptions adopted under their protection, or they indicate a wide array of goals that can be pursued by the limitations. Special exception clauses, in turn, exhaustively specify the goals that the exceptions must necessarily promote. An example of a special exception clause can be seen in art. 10(2) of the Berne Convention.

exception clauses of TRIPS authorize the establishment of limitations to IPRs by judicial or administrative organs, on a case by case basis. In this sense, a recent ruling delivered in March 2011 by the Superior Court of Justice of Brazil (STJ) (Special Appeal no. 964404) stands out. Although this ruling refers only to art. 9(2) BC and to art. 13 TRIPS, the rationale introduced thereby is applicable to the other general exception clauses of TRIPS. Reproduced below are the main points in the judgment delivered by Justice Paulo de Tarso Sanseverino, rapporteur of the Special Appeal no. 964404:

The case concerns the duty of the applicant to pay royalties to the ECAD (Central Bureau of Collection and Distribution of Royalties) for the amplification of music broadcasts during the celebration of the opening of the Vocational Year at School, a religious, non-onerous and not-for-profit event. In my view the special appeal should be allowed.

At first sight, the isolated reading of the normative statement enshrined in art. 68 of Law no. 9.610/98 would indicate that the organization responsible for the above referred event should pay royalties, once it amplified music broadcasts in a public place...

Nonetheless, the rules enshrined in the chapeau and in the paragraphs of art. 68 just set the prima facie scope of exclusive rights held by copyright holders; their effective scope only emerges after the identification of the exceptions and limitations applicable to these exclusive rights, set by the Brazilian Copyright Act.

Arts. 46, 47 and 48 of Law no 9.610/98 regulate the exceptions to the exclusive rights held by copyright holders. The point under discussion is whether these exceptions are only illustrative or have an exhaustive character.

Leonardo Macedo Poli notes that... "each of the exceptions enshrined in the Brazilian Copyright Act aims at safeguarding a constitutionally guaranteed principle," relating to, for example, the "right to privacy and private life," "the right to national development," "the right to culture, education and science."

I recall at this point that the fundamental rights and freedoms have direct and immediate application in Brazil (art. 5 §1, Federal Constitution), binding the Government as a whole – the executive, the legislative and the judicial powers – to a duty to confer, in the words of Paulo Gustavo Gonet... "the maximum possible efficacy" to these rights. As emphasized by Ingo Wolfgang Sarlet, these rights are not, therefore, "in the sphere of availability of government"; the government, in reverse, has "the obligation to do everything in order to promote the realization of the fundamental rights."

As the copyright exceptions enshrined in arts. 46, 47 and 48 of Law 9.610/98 represent the appreciation by the legislator of fundamental rights and guarantees vis-à-vis author's rights, which are also fundamental rights in Brazil (art. 5, XXVII Federal Constitution), these exceptions are the result of a weighing-up process between conflicting values, and therefore should not be seen as the only existing exceptions to the exclusive rights held by copyright holders.

. . .

I stress that adopting a view in the opposite direction would, in case of omission by the legislator, lead to the breach of a fundamental right or freedom which, in certain concrete circumstances, should trump an author's rights. Furthermore, an opposite view would lead to the breach of the duty of optimization of fundamental rights and freedoms (art. 5 § 1 FC), which binds not only the legislature but also the judiciary.

Therefore, the effective scope of the exclusive rights held by copyright holders stands out after consideration of the exceptions contained in arts. 46, 47 and 48 of Law 9.610/98, interpreted and applied in accordance with the fundamental rights and guarantees, and after considering the individual rights and guarantees *per se*.

Values such as culture, science, intimacy, privacy, family, national development, freedom of press, of religion and worship should be considered when ascertaining the scope of the exclusive rights held by copyright holders. This weighing-up process [between conflicting values] cannot, however, occur in an arbitrary manner and shall observe strict criteria. [In this sense], [t]he Berne Convention for the protection of literary, artistic and scientific works (1886) and the WTO TRIPS Agreement . . . both in force in Brazil, regulate, among other things, the exceptions to copyright. Art. 13 of the TRIPS Agreement, which reproduces to a great extent the text of art. 9(2) of the Berne Convention, reads as follows: "Members shall confine exceptions or exceptions to exclusive rights to certain special cases which do not conflict with a normal exploitation of the work and do not unreasonably prejudice the legitimate interests of the right holder."

. . .

The objective of the event in the instant case – not-for-profit, non-onerous and religious – does not conflict with the normal commercial exploitation of the work (music or background music), and does not unreasonably prejudice the legitimate interests of authors, since it is not an event of major proportions.

. . .

Also the first requirement is present in the instant case, as the event can be considered, in the words of the law, "special," provided it took place within a school and it consists of a not-for-profit event, with free admission and exclusively religious purposes. In this specific case, the fundamental right to freedom of worship and religion prevails over copyright. (notes omitted)

The view taken by the STJ, which ensures direct applicability to art. 13 of TRIPS, is reasonable vis-à-vis the wording of the general exception clauses of TRIPS – which are addressed to the WTO Members – since courts and organs of the executive power represent WTO Members as much as their national parliaments.

The TRIPS Agreement features five general exception clauses that are similar in structure, substance and function; they are popularly known as "three-step tests." These provisions allow WTO Members to adopt exceptions to copyright and to the rights conferred by trademarks, patents and industrial designs, as long as the conditions set by them are cumulatively met[44] (Table 1.2). Those exceptions and uses not expressly backed by law that fail to pass the scrutiny of such tests shall be discarded.

The origin of the tests shown in Table 1.2 goes back to the Review Conference of the Berne Convention for the Protection of Literary and Artistic Works, which took place in Stockholm in 1967.[45] One of the most notable achievements of the Conference was the introduction of art. 9(2), which contains a test whose function is to control the legality of the exceptions to the right of reproduction of works. The wording of the test is flexible enough to harmonize public and private interests and offers broad scope for the policy actions of States. So much so, that the test allows countries within the Roman-German system to adopt *numerus clausus* exceptions to copyright, whilst countries within the Common Law system may adopt more flexible exceptions, known as "fair use."

On the one hand, the ambiguous wording of the general exception clauses of the TRIPS Agreement makes it hard to determine its scope; on the other hand, precisely because of that, if exploited correctly, it offers to WTO Members room to adopt exceptions capable of neutralizing the harmful effects produced by the main branches of IPRs. However, in the opportunities it has had, the WTO has construed the terms of three of the general exception clauses (arts. 13, 17 and 30) in a way that exclusively favored the private interests of copyright, trademarks and patents holders. Thus in *Canada – Pharmaceutical Patents*, according to the view taken by the panel, art. 30 offers too limited an opportunity, which can only be legitimately used for the adoption of exceptions affecting in an insignificant manner the economic interests of patent holders. A similar view was adopted in *United States – Section 110 (5) of US Copyright Act* and in *EC – Trademarks and Geographical Indications*.

[44] In the opposite direction, as regards the conditions laid down by the general exception clauses of TRIPS, Kur 2008, 41, and the Declaration on the Three-Step Test in Copyright Law, put together by the Max Planck Institute and Queen Mary at the University of London (2008), seem to hold that these conditions would not be cumulative.

[45] See Bergström 1967, 291 ff.

Table 1.2 *The general exception clauses of the TRIPS Agreement*

Subject matter	1st step	2nd step	3rd step
Copyright (Art. 9(2) BC)	States may adopt exceptions to the right of reproduction "in certain special cases"	"provided that such reproduction does not conflict with a normal exploitation of the work"	"and does not unreasonably prejudice the legitimate interests of the author."
Copyright (Art. 13 TRIPS)	"Members shall confine limitations or exceptions to exclusive rights to certain special cases"	"which do not conflict with a normal exploitation of the work"	"and do not unreasonably prejudice the legitimate interests of the right holder."
Trademark (Art. 17 TRIPS)	"Members may provide limited exceptions to the rights conferred by a trademark"	There is no step similar to "step 2" in the other tests.	"provided that such exceptions take account of the legitimate interests of the owner of the trademark and of third parties."
Industrial design (Art. 26(2) TRIPS)	"Members may provide limited exceptions to the protection of industrial designs"	"provided that such exceptions do not unreasonably conflict with the normal exploitation of protected industrial designs"	"and do not unreasonably prejudice the legitimate interests of the owner of the protected design, taking account of the legitimate interests of third parties."
Patent (Art. 30 TRIPS)	"Members may provide limited exceptions to the exclusive rights conferred by a patent"	"provided that such exceptions do not unreasonably conflict with a normal exploitation of the patent"	"and do not unreasonably prejudice the legitimate interests of the patent owner, taking account of the legitimate interests of third parties."

In theory, the adopted reports handed down by the organs of the DSB (panels and the Appellate Body) do not bind all the WTO Members, but only the litigants, because the exclusive competence to adopt binding interpretations to the covered agreements is vested in the WTO Ministerial Conference and in the WTO General Council.[46] However,

[46] See art. IX(2) Marrakesh Agreement.

in practice, these materials are treated as legal precedents, serving as a guideline for the solution of similar cases.[47] Nevertheless, in *US – Stainless Steel*, the Appellate Body of the WTO held that it is possible to set aside the interpretations condensed in the adopted reports, so long as there are "cogent reasons" to do so.[48]

Undoubtedly, there are cogent reasons why the organs of the WTO dispute settlement system and its members should set aside, *to a large extent*, the interpretations proposed by the WTO in *Canada – Pharmaceutical Patents*, *US – Section 110 (5) Copyright Act* and *EC – Trademarks and Geographical Indications*. As this study will strive to demonstrate, the interpretations put forward in such cases substantially breach art. 3(2) of the Understanding on Rules and Procedures Governing the Settlement of Disputes at the WTO (WTO Dispute Settlement Understanding or DSU), which provides that the function of the dispute settlement system of the WTO is "to preserve the rights and obligations of Members under the covered agreements, and to clarify the existing provisions of those agreements in accordance with customary rules of interpretation of public international law," which are codified in arts. 31 and 32 of the Vienna Convention on the Law of Treaties (VCLT).[49] As a result, the interpretations proposed for the terms of the exception clauses, inscribed in Articles 13, 17 and 30 of the TRIPS Agreement, breached articles 3(2)[50] and

47 In *US – Stainless Steel*, the WTO Appellate Body noted: "Dispute settlement practice demonstrates that WTO Members attach significance to reasoning provided in previous panel and Appellate Body reports. Adopted panel and Appellate Body reports are often cited by parties in support of legal arguments in dispute settlement proceedings, and are relied upon by panels and the Appellate Body in subsequent disputes. In addition, when enacting or modifying laws and national regulations pertaining to international trade matters, WTO Members take into account the legal interpretation of the covered agreements developed in adopted panel and Appellate Body reports. Thus, the legal interpretation embodied in adopted panel and Appellate Body reports becomes part and parcel of the *acquis* of the WTO dispute settlement system" (WTO, WT/DS344/AB/R, para. 160).

48 *Ibid.*

49 The approach taken by the DSB is that "the customary rules of interpretation of public international law" are those established in arts. 31 and 32 of the Vienna Convention on the Law of Treaties (VCLT). See *US – Section 301 Trade Act* (WTO, WT/DS152/R, para. 7.21): "Evaluating the conformity of Sections 30 1–310 with US obligations under the WTO requires interpretation of several provisions of the covered agreements. Article 3.2 of the DSU directs panels to clarify WTO provisions 'in accordance with customary rules of interpretation of public international law.' Articles 31 and 32 of the Vienna Convention on the Law of Treaties ('Vienna Convention') have attained the status of rules of customary international law." See also WTO, WT/DS62/AB/R, WT/DS67/AB/R, WT/DS68/AB/R (*EC – Computer Equipment*), Appellate Body Report, paras. 84–86.

50 Art. 3(2) DSU provides that "recommendations and rulings of the DSB cannot add to or diminish the rights and obligations provided in the covered agreements."

19(2)[51] of the DSU, as they unduly increased the scope of the exclusive rights provided by TRIPS to the holders of copyright, trademarks and patents, as well as breached art. 3(5), also of the DSU, because such interpretations set barriers for the achievement of the socio-environmental objectives pursued by the WTO system. Therefore, the assessment of the actual space afforded by the general exception clauses of the TRIPS Agreement to adopt exceptions to IPRs should not be affected by the reports of such cases adopted by the DSB of the WTO. For these reasons, the present study seeks to demonstrate that the TRIPS Agreement, by its nature, does not engender conflicts between, on the one hand, IPRs and, on the other hand, the exceptions aimed at protecting human rights and the environment, since the general exception clauses of this agreement, when properly interpreted, offer to WTO Members broad scope for the adoption of robust exceptions to IPRs.

Part I of this study is dedicated to investigating the correct normative meaning of the prescriptions contained in the general exception clauses of the TRIPS Agreement, indicated in Table 1.2, in light of the customary rules of treaty interpretation, codified by the VCLT. The competence vested in the interpretation rules of the VCLT is to single out, from the possible interpretations for a provision, the most suitable one.[52] Chapter 2 starts by clarifying the complex customary rules of treaty interpretation, condensed in arts. 31 and 32 VCLT, and identifies, specifically, the elements against which the general exception clauses of TRIPS should be interpreted. Chapter 3 is devoted to clarifying the normative meaning of art. 30 TRIPS Agreement, as well as arts. 17 and 26(2), since the wording of these provisions is quite similar. Chapter 4 investigates the correct normative meaning of art. 9(2) BC and art. 13 TRIPS, i.e. the two general exception clauses of copyright, the wording of the latter provision being inspired substantially by the text of the former.

At this point it is important to warn that the interpretations proposed in this study for the general exception clauses of TRIPS are not necessarily the only ones that can be considered correct. Certainly, there are interpretations that are legally unsustainable and therefore must be discarded. However, the ambiguities contained in those provisions of TRIPS allow other interpretations, as long as they are built in light of the customary rules of treaty interpretation. Among other valuable previous works that propose innovative interpretations for some of the general

[51] Art. 19(2) DSU reads: "In accordance with paragraph 2 of Article 3, in their findings and recommendations, the panel and Appellate Body cannot add to or diminish the rights and obligations provided in the covered agreements."

[52] Lauterpacht 1949, 82.

exception clauses of TRIPS one can cite in particular studies by Martin Senftleben (2004), Rochelle Dreyfuss and Graeme Dinwoodie (2004), Christophe Geiger (e.g. 2007a), Annette Kur (2008) and Henning Ruse-Khan (2008); and the "Declaration: A Balanced Interpretation of the 'Three-Step Test' in Copyright Law," developed by researchers from the Max Planck Institute and Queen Mary, University of London (2008). Although I do not agree with all the points that are made in these works, they along with other studies have certainly inspired and helped in the development of the interpretations proposed in the present book.

Part II of this study is dedicated to investigating whether the general exception clauses of TRIPS, when properly interpreted, can actually be applied to reconcile important social, economic and environmental pressing interests, through the adoption of robust exceptions to the exclusive rights conferred by copyrights, patents, industrial designs and trademarks. With this purpose in mind, in separate chapters, some of the real problems engendered by these branches of intellectual property law that undermine the realization of the sustainable development ideal will be identified. Proposals for hypothetical exceptions are featured, each one tailored to overcome the specific problems previously identified. Finally, the legality of the hypothetical exceptions vis-à-vis the general exception clauses of the TRIPS is investigated.[53]

Chapter 5 addresses the problems created by biotechnology patents and investigates the legality of a Research & Development (R&D) exception and a genetic diagnostic test exception, which authorize the development and commercialization of new technologies (products and processes) and genetic diagnostic tests. Chapter 6 deals with the conflict between trademark law and the right to freedom of expression and evaluates the legality of a parody and criticism exception, designed to reconcile the legitimate interests of trademark owners to keep the magnetism of their commercial distinctive signs with the right to free speech of third parties. Chapter 7 addresses competition and consumerism problems created by protected industrial designs, and also investigates the legality of a repair exception as proposed in the European Union, which authorizes the manufacture and marketing of spare parts for complex goods. Chapter 8 deals with the obstacles created by copyright for the realization of the right of access to knowledge, education and culture, and assesses the legality of an education exception, aimed at increasing access

[53] The idea of assessing the legality of each of the proposed hypothetical exceptions vis-à-vis the pertinent general exception clause was inspired by Senftleben (2004), as well as by Dinwoodie and Dreyfuss (2004).

to literary and artistic works by the marginalized sectors of developing countries.

1.4 Methodological approach

The methodological approach used in this work is positivist. I have opted for this approach for an eminently practical reason: even though from a moral viewpoint it is justifiable to consider that, in case of conflict, human and environmental rights should outweigh the legitimate interests of the holders of IPRs,[54] one should not neglect to note that all 153 WTO Members are obliged to observe strict rules for the protection of wider public interests that may conflict with IPRs. The correct determination of the normative meaning of the general exception clauses of the TRIPS Agreement, in light of the customary rules of treaty interpretation, is therefore of vital importance to any of the WTO Members wishing to adopt robust exceptions to IPRs because, in case of dispute, the respondent will have the burden of proving that the WTO legal framework backs the challenged exceptions.[55] In other words, it would not make sense to propose interpretations for the general exception clauses to the TRIPS Agreement which did not have immediate legal application.

The legal points of reference adopted are the same as those that the WTO Members and the organs of the DSB (panels and Appellate Body) are required to consider in the process of construing the general exception clauses of the TRIPS Agreement, namely: the customary rules of treaty interpretation, condensed in arts. 31 and 32 of the VCLT, and all other rules authorized by the CVDT, e.g. the provisions enshrined in the covered agreement of the WTO, the case law of the WTO, rules of international law (general legal principles and international customary law) and other canons of interpretation. Briefly, the general rule of interpretation codified by the VCLT provides that the terms of a treaty should be interpreted according to the ordinary meaning attributed to them in context. The context of a treaty not only comprises its text (provisions, preamble, annexes), but also: (i) "any agreement relating to the treaty which was made between all the parties in connection with the conclusion of the treaty"; (ii) "any instrument which was made by one or more

[54] See, e.g., the UN Sub-Commission on Human Rights resolution 2001/21, para. 3: "*Reminds* all Governments of the primacy of human rights obligations under international law over economic policies and agreements, and requests them, in national, regional and international economic policy forums, to take international human rights obligations and principles fully into account in international economic policy formulation." See also Simma and Paulus 1999, 308.

[55] See, e.g., WTO, S/WPDR/W/27, para. 7.

parties in connection with the conclusion of the treaty and accepted by the other parties as an instrument related to the treaty"; (iii) "any subsequent agreement between the parties regarding the interpretation of the treaty or the application of its provisions"; (iv) "any subsequent practice in the application of the treaty which establishes the agreement of the parties regarding its interpretation"; (v) "any relevant rules of international law applicable in relations between the parties" (art. 31(2) and (3)). If the application of general rule of treaty interpretation leads to an "ambiguous," "obscure" or "manifestly absurd or unreasonable" meaning, the interpreter may have recourse to supplementary means of interpretation, e.g. canons of interpretation, the preparatory work of the treaty or the circumstances surrounding the conclusion of the treaty (art. 32), in order to identify the correct meaning of the provision.

Part I

Determining the normative meaning of the general exception clauses of the TRIPS Agreement

Don't you know that a little yeast leavens the whole lump? Purge out the old yeast, that you may be a new lump

St. Paul (First Letter to the Corinthians, 5: 6–7)

2 The customary rules of treaty interpretation and the elements in light of which the general exception clauses of TRIPS should be interpreted

Introduction

The WTO is a self-contained regime, insofar as it is made up of special primary rules, i.e. substantive rules, aimed at legislating specifically for the liberalization of international trade, and special secondary rules, i.e. rules that govern the solution of interstate controversies. These sets of rules differ from the standing rules and mechanisms of general international law.[1]

The Dispute Settlement Body of the WTO (DSB) has exclusive competence to solve litigation that involves infringements of the rules covered by the legal framework of the WTO. It is not empowered to solve disputes relating to rules external to the WTO.[2] As the central role of the DSB is to "preserve the rights and obligations of members under the covered agreements," in the sense that it cannot increase or reduce "the rights and obligations provided in the covered agreements,"[3] art. 7 of the DSU established, as a general rule, that the terms of reference of disputes brought to the DSB only include provisions that constitute the legal system of the WTO.[4]

Nevertheless, that does not mean, as acknowledged by the Appellate Body in *US – Gasoline*, that the rules of the covered agreements of the WTO are to be "read in clinical isolation from public international law."[5] By granting the DSB the right to interpret the provisions of the WTO agreements in accordance with customary rules of interpretation of treaties, art. 3(2) DSU opened the door for other rules of international

[1] Koskenniemi 2006, paras. 128–135. [2] Arts. 1(1) and 7 DSU.

[3] Art. 3 (2) DSU.

[4] Art. 7 (3) of DSU allows the parties in litigation to add to the terms of reference of the litigation norms external to the WTO legal framework. This means that when the parties to the litigation expressly agree, rules outside the WTO framework may be applied in the solution. Otherwise, only WTO rules may be applied (Hestermeyer 2007, 217).

[5] WTO, WT/DS2/AB/R, Appellate Body Report, p. 12.

law to be taken into account in the process of interpretation and application of WTO rules. Those customary rules are included in arts. 31 and 32 of the VCLT:

Article 31
General rule of interpretation
1. A treaty shall be interpreted in good faith in accordance with the ordinary meaning to be given to the terms of the treaty in their context and in the light of its object and purpose.
2. The context for the purpose of the interpretation of a treaty shall comprise, in addition to the text, including its preamble and annexes:
   (a) any agreement relating to the treaty which was made between all the parties in connection with the conclusion of the treaty;
   (b) any instrument which was made by one or more parties in connection with the conclusion of the treaty and accepted by the other parties as an instrument related to the treaty.
3. There shall be taken into account, together with the context:
   (a) any subsequent agreement between the parties regarding the interpretation of the treaty or the application of its provisions;
   (b) any subsequent practice in the application of the treaty which establishes the agreement of the parties regarding its interpretation;
   (c) any relevant rules of international law applicable in the relations between the parties.
4. A special meaning shall be given to a term if it is established that the parties so intended.

Article 32
Supplementary means of interpretation
Recourse may be had to supplementary means of interpretation, including the preparatory work of the treaty and the circumstances of its conclusion, in order to confirm the meaning resulting from the application of article 31, or to determine the meaning when the interpretation according to article 31:
(a) leaves the meaning ambiguous or obscure; or
(b) leads to a result which is manifestly absurd or unreasonable.

Customary rules of interpretation of treaties operate as tools of discovery and selection of the most appropriate meaning of a legal rule among the many possible ones. Even if the content of a provision may seem clear, certainty will only come after applying the rules for the interpretation of treaties.[6]

Art. 31 VCLT covers only one rule of interpretation, whose multiple components are interconnected.[7] That accounts for its title: "general rule of interpretation." That general rule seems to suggest an order in the process of interpretation. The starting point of the interpretation process of the provisions in a treaty is its own text and the ordinary sense

[6] See Sinclair 1984, 116. [7] International Law Commission 1966, 219–220.

that can be attributed to its terms insofar as the writing crystallizes the genuine expression of the will of the parties.[8] In a second phase, the terms in the provisions must be interpreted within the context of the treaty to which they are linked (immediate context). Thirdly, the provisions must be interpreted in the light of the object and purpose of the treaty to which they belong, which will be identified through an analysis of the text of the treaty. Lastly, the provisions must be interpreted within the wider context of the relevant norms of international law. All these phases are governed by the principle of good faith. This order, though not mandatory, reflects a logical process: the interpreter starts with the text of the provision and goes to its immediate context; from the immediate context he proceeds to the goals of the treaty, and from its aims to the relevant norms in international law.[9]

The order of the phases in the process of interpretation may not be identical to the one described but, naturally, the starting point should always be the text of the provision, be it ambiguous or seemingly clear.[10] Be that as it may, those phases are compulsory in the process of interpretation of treaties, as they reject any meanings that do not reconcile, *simultaneously*, with the principle of good faith, the immediate and the wider contexts of the provision and with the purposes of the treaty in which they belong. Consequently, the correct meaning of a treaty is not necessarily the one that reflects the natural, ordinary meaning of its terms.

Art. 32 VCLT, on the other hand, adds a relevant aspect to the process of interpretation. It applies whenever the application of the general rule of interpretation leads to an ambiguous, obscure, absurd or unreasonable result. In such cases, the interpreter may resort to supplementary means of interpretation, – e.g. the conditions in which the treaty was signed, preparatory work – in order to better understand the meaning of the controversial provision. Supplementary means of interpretation may also be used to confirm the result arrived at after applying the general rule of interpretation. Consequently, if the interpreter finds a reasonable meaning of the provision through the application of the general rule of interpretation, he is not obliged to resort to the supplementary means of interpretation in order to confirm his interpretation.

Briefly, arts. 31 and 32 of the Vienna Convention describe four methods of interpretation: (i) textual or literal method: determination of the ordinary meaning attributed to the terms of the provision; (ii) contextual method: the terms of the provision are interpreted in their immediate

[8] *Ibid.*, 220. [9] Koskenniemi 2006, para. 463.
[10] International Law Commission 1966, 220.

context (the treaty) and the wider context (the relevant rules of international law); (iii) teleological method: the terms of a treaty are interpreted in the light of the object and purpose of the treaty, expressed in its text; and (iv) intentional method, which tries to express the intention of the parties behind the text.[11]

The following sections will examine arts. 31 and 32 VCLT in more detail. They will also identify simultaneously the points that must be considered by the DSB and any WTO Member in the process of interpretation of any of the general exception clauses of the TRIPS Agreement (arts. 9(2) BC and arts. 13, 17, 26(2) and 30 TRIPS). These data will be important for determining the correct meaning of these provisions in the remaining chapters of Part I.

2.1 Ordinary meaning attributable to the terms of the treaty

An interpreter usually begins the process of interpretation of the provisions of a treaty on the basis of the ordinary meaning of its terms, registered in dictionaries, technical literature or even in international instruments, which may be binding or otherwise.[12] Although the text of a treaty must be read as the expression of the genuine will of the parties to the treaty, the process of interpretation is not restricted to an investigation of the *abstract* meaning of its terms, in dictionaries or international instruments.[13] The interpreter would err if he limited his task to drawing up a list of the ordinary meanings attributed to the terms in a given provision or to choose the meaning he personally judges more reasonable.[14] In

[11] Yambrusic 1987, 174–175, 203.

[12] In *EC – Biotech Products*, the WTO has already accepted the use of international instruments as a resource to be used in investigations on the ordinary meaning of the terms used in WTO agreements: "The ordinary meaning of treaty terms is often determined on the basis of dictionaries. We think that, in addition to dictionaries, other relevant rules of international law *may* in some cases aid a treaty interpreter in establishing, or confirming, the ordinary meaning of treaty terms in the specific context in which they are used. *Such rules would not be considered because they are legal rules, but rather because they may provide evidence of the ordinary meaning of terms in the same way that dictionaries do.* They would be considered for their informative character" (emphasis added) (WTO, WT/DS291/R, WT/DS292/R, WT/DS293/R, para. 7.92). "[T]he mere fact that one or more disputing parties are not parties to a convention does not necessarily mean that a convention cannot shed light on the meaning and scope of a treaty term to be interpreted" (*ibid.*, para. 7.94). In the same sense, in *US – Shrimp*, the WTO Appellate Body used as aids, inter alia, the Convention on Biological Diversity, Agenda 21 and the Convention on the Law of the Sea to clarify the meaning of the expression "exhaustible natural resources" (WTO, WT/DS58/AB/R, para. 128–134).

[13] Gardiner 2008, 145.

[14] See, e.g., the understanding held by the WTO Appellate Body in *US – Gambling*: "Article 31(1) of the Vienna Convention requires a treaty to be interpreted 'in good faith in accordance with the ordinary meaning to be given to the terms of the treaty in their context and in the light of its object and purpose.' In order to identify the

fact, the general rule of interpretation does not simply determine that "a treaty shall be interpreted in good faith in accordance with the ordinary meaning to be given to the terms of the treaty."[15] Even if the interpreter wished to limit his task to research in dictionaries, which meaning would he choose for a term that has two or more dictionary meanings?

That is why the general rule of interpretation establishes that the immediate and wider context of the treaty and its purposes and the requirements set by the principle of good faith will guide the interpreter in the identification of the terms used in it. In other words, the interpreter must find the *relative* meaning of the terms in a treaty, i.e. the sense that best coincides with the subject matter of the treaty, with the immediate and wider contexts where the terms are used, the purposes of the treaty, the principle of good faith and, lastly, he must make sure it does not prove unreasonable or absurd.[16] Even in a provision with terms whose meaning seems obvious, one must go through a process of interpretation, as established in the VCLT general rule of interpretation in order to identify its true meaning.[17] This may be more fully understood with an example used by McNair that illustrates how inappropriate it is to interpret a provision on the basis of an abstract, out of context meaning of its terms:

> A man, having a wife and children, made a will of conspicuous brevity consisting merely of the words 'All for mother'. No term could be 'plainer' than 'mother', for a man can only have one mother. His widow claimed the estate. The court, having admitted oral evidence which proved that in the family circle the deceased's wife was always referred to as 'mother', as is common in England, held that she was entitled to apply for administration with the will annexed, which in effect meant that she took the whole estate. 'Mother', is, speaking abstractly, a 'plain term', but, taken in relation to the circumstances surrounding the testator at the time when the will was made, it was anything but a 'plain term'.[18]

2.2 Principle of good faith

Art. 31(1) VCLT states that treaties must be interpreted in good faith. This means that good faith must permeate the entire interpretation process. In accordance with the principle of good faith, whoever interprets a treaty must follow to the letter the general rule of interpretation, as a way to ensure the fullest possible compliance with the aims of the treaty.[19] It

ordinary meaning, a Panel may start with the dictionary definitions of the terms to be interpreted. But dictionaries, alone, are not necessarily capable of resolving complex questions of interpretation, as they typically aim to catalogue *all* meanings of words – be those meanings common or rare, universal or specialized" (WTO, WT/DS285/AB/R, para. 164).

[15] Yambrusic 1986, 186.

[16] See, e.g., Gardiner 2008, 166; McNair 1961, 380; Sinclair 1984, 12.

[17] See Gardiner 2008, 169. [18] McNair 1961, 367. [19] See Gardiner 2008, 152.

is important to recall that within the context of the general rule of interpretation, the principle of good faith does not operate as an autonomous source of rights and duties, but only as a tool to determine the meaning of the terms in the treaty.[20]

The core notion of the principle of good faith is the "idea of social solidarity" and honesty[21] and its ultimate end is to contribute to cooperation between States. There can be no doubt that it would prove impossible to forge peaceful and predictable international relations if the word given by States and established in treaties were not credible. Kolb identified many guises or expressions of the principle of good faith, as for example: the prohibition to deprive treaties of their object and purposes; the obligation to emphasize the spirit of the treaty rather than its wording in the process of interpretation; responsibility for the appearances created (theory of appearance); prohibition of abuse of rights; the rule that forbids anyone from benefitting from his own turpitude.[22] As to the interpretation of treaties, two of the actual concretizations of the principle of good faith are particularly relevant: the principle of effectiveness in the interpretation of treaties and the principle of prohibition of abuse of rights (doctrine of abuse of rights), which will be addressed below.

2.2.1 Principle of effectiveness in the interpretation of treaties

The principle of effectiveness in interpretation (*ut res magis valeat quam pereat*) – also known as the principle of *effet utile* – stands as the corollary to *pacta sunt servanda*.[23] Its purpose is to maximize the goals set by treaties, through ensuring the integrity of the rights and duties of the parties.[24] Within this context, whenever a provision or ambiguous terms thereof may be interpreted in two or more different ways, the interpreter must choose the interpretation that guarantees the harmonious observance of *all* the terms of the treaty, purposes included.[25]

The limit to the principle of effectiveness is the space offered by the text of the treaty and its goals, banning an interpretation that, if on one side it maximizes the effectiveness of its purposes, it violates its text on the other.[26] If the mutilation of the text were allowed, the interpreter would

[20] See Zeitler 2005, 757. [21] See Kolb 2006, 18–29. [22] *Ibid.*, 19–20.

[23] See International Law Commission 1966, 221. The principle of *pact sunt servanda* is included in art. 26 VCLT: "Every treaty in force is binding upon the parties to it and must be performed by them in good faith."

[24] See Bederman 2001, 197; McNair 1961, 385.

[25] See Zeitler 2005, p. 729; WTO, WT/DS103/AB/R, WT/DS113/AB/R (*Canada – Dairy*), Appellate Body Report, para. 133.

[26] Bederman 2001, 197; Waldock 1964, 60.

transform the treaty into an unstable set of rights and duties. This does not mean that the text of a treaty will be infringed if the interpreter infers terms that are not mentioned in order to maximize the effectiveness of the purposes of the treaty, provided the terms inferred do not make parts of the treaty redundant or useless.[27] Along a similar line, in *Canada – Pharmaceutical Patents*, the Panel understood that the exclusive rights granted by the patent extend along a "more or less brief" period, beyond the twenty years established by law. Such additional period would be a logical consequence of the rights to exclude third parties from using and producing the patented innovation, during the period of validity of the patent.[28] The Panel, however, applied the principle of effectiveness wrongly since it openly breached the terms in TRIPS (i.e. the term of validity of a patent is expressly pre-established in the TRIPS Agreement), including the WTO goals.[29] Briefly, once the limits established by the terms of the treaty to be interpreted have been observed, the principle of effectiveness in interpretation can fill loopholes by identifying the will of the parties, expressed in the words of the treaty.[30]

The fact that the principles of effectiveness in interpretation and of *pacta sunt servanda* are corollaries to the principle of good faith points to the intimate connection between interpreting and applying a treaty, keeping in mind that interpretation necessarily occurs prior to application.[31] In view of the connection between interpretation and application of a treaty, it is the interpreter's responsibility to take note of the consequences that would ensue from each possible interpretative option and choose the one that, besides being consistent with the wording of the treaty, fulfils most efficiently the objectives of the treaty.[32]

Treaties must be observed not only in their words, but also in their spirit. Even if the terms of a treaty have been written in an ambiguous manner to reflect the lack of consensus among the parties, it is the duty of the interpreter to make sense of them in light of the objectives of the treaty.[33] The interpretation and application of a treaty in ways that would defeat its purposes, even if it formally follows its wording to the letter, is a breach of the *pacta sunt servanda* principle,[34] and, consequently, of the principle of good faith.[35] On this subject, in *US – Shrimp*, a WTO

[27] Waldock 1964, 61.
[28] WTO, WT/DS114/R (*Canada – Pharmaceutical Patents*), Panel Report, para. 7.35
[29] As will be seen in sections 2.3.1 and 2.3.2, neither TRIPS nor OMC pursue exclusively commercial goals.
[30] See Lauterpacht 1949, 74.
[31] See Sinclair 1984, 119; Waldock 1964, 8.
[32] See Mitchell 2007, 811–812.
[33] See Lauterpacht 1949, 78–79.
[34] See WTO, WT/DS163/R (*Korea – Procurement*), Panel Report, paras. 7.93 and 7.94.
[35] For instance, in *US – Offset Act*, the Panel noted that "Good faith requires a party to a treaty to refrain from acting in a manner which would defeat the object and purpose

panel added that "the principle of international law according to which international agreements must be applied in good faith, in light of the *pacta sunt servanda* principle . . . is explained in Article 18 of the Vienna Convention which states that '[a] State is obliged to refrain from acts which would defeat the object and purpose of a treaty.'"[36]

Briefly, the principles of effectiveness in interpretation imposes on the interpreter the obligation to opt for the interpretation which gives meaning and function to the interpreted provision, ensures the integrity of the text of the treaty[37] and enables the realization of the object and purpose of the treaty to the greatest extent possible.[38]

2.2.2 *Doctrine of abuse of rights*

The Latin maxim *summum jus summa injuria* well summarizes the understanding that there shall be no absolute rights. Every right is limited by its social function and the rights of third parties. Any infringement of these limits turns the exercise of a legal right into an abuse of rights, which will have harmful social effects. There is, therefore, *interdependence* between rights and duties in the sense that the rights granted to a State must be exercised in a way that is consistent with its social function, as well as with duties to third parties, derived from treaties or from general international law.[39] Along the same line, in the context of human rights, the Inter-American Convention on Human Rights establishes that "[t]he rights of each person are limited by the rights of others, by the security of all, and by the just demands of the general welfare, in a democratic society" (art. 32(2)).[40] In a more general sense, in *US – Shrimp*, the WTO Appellate Body stated the same understanding on the contents of the doctrine of abuse of rights:

of the treaty as a whole or the treaty provision in question" (WTO, WT/DS217/R, WT/DS234/R, para. 7.64)

36 WTO, WT/DS58/AB/R, Panel Report, para. 7.41.

37 In this sense, in *US – Gasoline*, the WTO Appellate Body acknowledged "[o]ne of the corollaries of the 'general rule of interpretation' in the Vienna Convention is that interpretation must give meaning and effect to all the terms of a treaty. An interpreter is not free to adopt a reading that would result in reducing whole clauses or paragraphs of a treaty to redundancy or futility" (WTO, WT/DS2/AB/R, p. 27). In the same sense, in *Korea – Dairy* the WTO Appellate Body repeated the understanding that "In light of the interpretive principle of effectiveness, it is the *duty* of any treaty interpreter to 'read all applicable provisions of a treaty in a way that gives meaning to *all* of them, *harmoniously*" (emphasis added) (WTO, WT/DS98/AB/R, para.81).

38 See Gardiner 2008, 148. 39 See Iluyomade 1975, 91.

40 The doctrine of abuse of rights was enshrined in several international conventions, including ICESCR (art. 5(1)), ICCPR (art 5(1)) and UDHR (art. 30). For an in-depth analysis of this subject see Byers 2002.

> This principle [of good faith], at once a general principle of law and a general principle of international law, controls the exercise of rights by states. One application of this general principle, the application widely known as the doctrine of *abus du droit*, prohibits the abusive exercise of a state's rights and enjoins that whenever the assertion of a right "impinges on the field covered by [a] treaty obligation, it must be exercised *bona fide*, that is to say, reasonably." An abusive exercise by a member of its own treaty right thus results in a breach of the treaty rights of the other members and, as well, a violation of the treaty obligations of the member so acting.[41]

The purpose of the doctrine of abuse of rights is to set limits to the exercise of rights. It is particularly useful to establish the limits of those rights whose scope is not strictly determined and which, when exercised, may impinge on the realization of rights of third parties.[42] Even in cases where the limits to rights seem clear, the doctrine of abuse of rights may need to be applied in view of the fact that the rules of international law are produced by organizations that pursue different and, not unusually, conflicting goals. In order to guarantee consistency within the international legal order, the doctrine of abuse of rights specifically prohibits the following actions:[43]

- The arbitrary exercise of a right, in ways that may harm the interests of third parties. Every right was conceived in order to comply with a specific end, which may be called its social function, because even if the right protects private interests directly, its ultimate aim is social. On this account, the Law on Introduction to the Brazilian Law establishes that "when applying the law, the judge will focus on the social ends it serves and the requirements of the common good."[44] Rights must be exercised with the purpose of realizing in formal and material terms the legitimate interests they protect.[45] An arbitrary exercise of rights runs counter to compliance of its legitimate purposes. Harm experienced by third parties due to the arbitrary exercise of rights is due to non-compliance with the social purpose of the right in question;[46]
- exercise of a right to cover up an illegal action;[47]
- exercise of discretionary power for an end different from the one authorized by the law (*détournement du pouvoir*).[48] For example, if the legal order of a given country only permits local authorities to expropriate private property to protect a public interest, should an expropriation

[41] WTO, WT/DS58/AB/R, Report of the Appellate Body, para. 158.
[42] See García Amador 1961, 57. [43] See D'Amato 1992, 600.
[44] Art. 5, Decree-Law no. 4657/1942. [45] See Cheng 1953, 122.
[46] See Kiss 2009, para. 6. [47] See Iluyomade 1975, 82.
[48] See, e.g., Kiss 2009, para. 5; Taylor 1972, 341–342.

be done for commercial purposes, albeit tacit, the State will have made an abusive use of its discretion;

- exercise by a State of a valid right in ways that will negatively interfere in the possibility of another State to exercise its own rights; that is, a State exercises its rights in a way that contravenes its obligations;[49]
- unreasonable, disproportionate exercise of a right in the sense that its anti-social effects outweigh the benefits obtained.[50] Right holders should always pay attention to the negative and positive effects that may ensue from the exercise of their rights and abstain from exercising them when damages disproportionately outweigh benefits.[51]

The assessment of the correct exercise of a right is not restricted to an evaluation of the formal aspects of the legal action, since abusive actions are often concealed in legal guise and their proponents are sufficiently cunning to avoid public declarations that would put those actions in the limelight.[52] Characterizing an action as an abuse of rights is based on the presence of two features: the exercise of a right in ways that are detrimental to its social function; and the existence of damage caused to third parties, in view of the non-realization of the social function of the right in question.[53] The unlawful intentions of the agent of an abuse can be inferred from the objective circumstances in which the right was exercised and from the effects produced by the act.[54] According to the understanding upheld by the WTO Appellate Body in *Japan – Alcoholic Beverages*, the most usual way to infer objectively the abusive intention of the agent is by means of an assessment of the "design, architecture and the revealing structure of a [challenged] measure."[55]

Originally, the abuse of rights doctrine was conceived to govern the exercise of the rights conferred on States. In view of the inextricable link between the interpretation and application of a treaty, there is no doubt about its applicability in the process of interpretation of treaties. In that field the interpreter is bound to dismiss any interpretation that, despite seeming formally appropriate, if applied would:

[49] On this point, Cheng (1953, 130) notes: "Every right is subject to such limitations as are necessary to render it compatible both with a party's contractual obligations and with his obligations under the general law."

[50] Friedmann (1963, 288) classifies the principle of abuse of rights as a principle of interpretation of the law: "This [the abuse of rights principle] does not say anything on the specific content and extent of certain rights, such as ownership of land or territory, the use of waters, fishing and the like; it merely says that whatever these rights are, they must not be used in such a manner that its anti-social effects outweigh the legitimate interests of the owner of the right."

[51] See International Law Commission 2006, para. 203.

[52] See Kolb 2006, 28.

[53] See, e.g., Iluyomade 1975, 75–76; D'Amato 1992, 509.

[54] See, e.g., Byers 2002, 412; Cheng 1953, 134; Weber 2004, 52.

[55] WTO, WT/DS8/AB/R, WT/DS10/AB/R, WT/DS11/AB/R, p. 34.

(i) prevent the realization of the purposes of the treaty which contains the provision under interpretation or the actual aims of the provision; and/or

(ii) have anti-social consequences that outweigh the benefits achieved by compliance with the law; and/or

(iii) affect the exercise of rights by third parties, granted by the same treaty or by other sources of international law. As far as possible, the interpreter must envisage interpretations that harmonize potentially conflictive provisions, ensuring they all remain valid. That is a tool in public international law to ensure the presumption against conflict, which "rests on the assumption that the new rule is compatible with international law in force until then, because it is reasonable to assume that States would want harmony between the old and the new law . . . and also that States would not strive to produce contradictory rules that could compromise hard-won diplomatic achievements."[56] If all the various rights can be observed and can maintain all their terms, then there is no conflict.[57]

It is only possible to hold confidently that one of the interpretative options in particular is the most appropriate among all those that are possible after certifying that the *effects* that will ensue from its application contribute to the realization of the purposes of the treaty and that they are consistent with the context of the ruling and the relevant rules of international law.[58]

2.3 Object and purposes of the WTO system and the TRIPS Agreement

The Doha Declaration on the TRIPS Agreement and Public Health reaffirms the VCLT general rule of interpretation by establishing that each provision of the TRIPS Agreement is to be read in the light of its objectives and principles: "In applying the customary rules of interpretation of public international law, each provision of the TRIPS Agreement shall be read in the light of the object and purpose of the Agreement as expressed, in particular, in its objectives and principles."[59]

In the process of interpretation of treaties, the purposes of a treaty serve to confirm the meaning suggested for its provisions through the attribution of the ordinary meaning to its terms, as well as to alter its meaning whenever the meaning suggested contradicts them. In other words, the meaning given to the provisions in a treaty must be drawn up

[56] See Amaral Jr. 2011, 294–295 (free translation). [57] See McBrady 2009, 17.
[58] See Mitchell 2007, 811–812. [59] See WTO, WT/MIN(01)/DEC/2, para. 5(a).

in ways that will promote its aims, instead of blocking their realization or attacking them.[60]

The aims of a treaty operate in the space left open by the ambiguous wording of its provisions. The more ambiguous and indeterminate the terms of a treaty, the more scope there is to use the treaty's aims to adjust the meaning that would ordinarily be attributed to its terms; contrariwise, a provision with a clear and objective meaning will offer fewer chances for the objectives of a treaty – as well as the other elements indicated in the general rule of interpretation – to have any influence on determining its meaning.[61] Consequently, if a provision provides a truly unequivocal meaning, no State can refrain from observing it by alleging that its enforcement contradicts the purposes of the treaty.[62] Should that type of conduct be permitted, States that are parties to a treaty would never know with any certitude which obligations are actually valid.

The objectives of a treaty should be inferred from its text since it is the expression of the genuine will of the parties.[63] The Marrakesh Agreement that established the WTO states in its art. II(2) that "The agreements and associated legal instruments included in Annexes 1, 2 and 3 (hereinafter referred to as 'Multilateral Trade Agreements') are integral parts of this Agreement, binding on all Members." This means that the Marrakesh Agreement and *all* the multilateral trade agreements make up a single undertaking, i.e. a sole and harmonious set of rights and duties that binds all WTO Members. In this sense, in *Korea – Dairy*, the WTO Appellate Body held that "[a]rticle II:2 of the WTO Agreement expressly manifests the intention of the Uruguay Round negotiators that the provisions of the WTO Agreement and the Multilateral Trade Agreements included in its Annexes 1, 2 and 3 must be read as a whole."[64]

As the TRIPS Agreement is included as Annex 1(C) of the Marrakesh Agreement, its aims must be inferred not only from its own preamble but also from the preamble and the text of the Marrakesh Agreement. In the case of *US – Shrimp*, the Appellate Body recognized that the aims included in the preamble to the Marrakesh Agreement inform all the multilateral agreements that make up the WTO legal framework:

> The preamble of the *WTO Agreement* – which informs not only the GATT 1994, but also the other covered agreements – explicitly acknowledges "the objective of *sustainable development*".

[60] See, e.g., Gardiner 2008, 189; Waldock 1964, 53.
[61] See Ruse-Khan 2008, 60–61. [62] See Mitchell 2007, 806.
[63] See Sinclair 1984, 134. [64] WTO, WT/DS98/AB/R, para. 81.

It is proper for us to take into account, as part of the context of the chapeau, the specific language of the preamble to the *WTO Agreement*, which, we have said, gives colour, texture and shading to the rights and obligations of Members under the *WTO Agreement*, generally, and under the GATT 1994, in particular.[65]

2.3.1 *General objectives of the WTO system*

From the analysis of the weighty preamble to the Marrakesh Agreement, it is possible to identify a substantial number of objectives pursued by the WTO legal system (including by the TRIPS), many of which are potentially conflicting, namely:[66]

- raising the standards of living of the population of all the members of the Organization;
- ensuring full employment;
- steadily increasing real income and effective demand for services and goods;
- expanding the production of and trade in goods and services;
- promoting the use of natural resources in accordance with the objective of sustainable development;
- protecting and preserving the environment;
- enhancing the means to protect and preserve the environment, in a manner consistent with the needs and interests of WTO Members and in accordance with the different levels of economic development;
- promoting "positive efforts designed to ensure that developing countries, and especially the least developed among them, secure a share in the growth in international trade commensurate with the needs of their economic development";
- substantially reducing tariffs and non-tariff barriers to international trade; and
- creating a multilateral secure and predictable trade system.

Despite being criticized as a biased organization that over-protects the commercial interests of industrialized countries, the WTO also strives to contribute to the realization of the economic, human and environmental interests of all Members of the organization. Such purposes are not empty rhetoric. In fact, art. III(1) of the Marrakesh Agreement states that "The WTO shall facilitate the implementation, administration and operation, and further the objectives of this Agreement and of the Multilateral Trade Agreements."

65 WTO, WT/DS58/AB/R, Report of the Appellate Body, paras. 155 and 129, respectively.

66 The objectives identified are listed in the first four paragraphs of the preamble to the Marrakesh Agreement.

2.3.2 *Specific objectives of the TRIPS Agreement*

Besides the objectives listed in the preamble to the Marrakesh Agreement, the TRIPS Agreement pursues other complementary aims, mentioned in its preamble and in articles 7 and 8, which respectively establish its objectives and guiding principles. At least two objectives may be identified in the preamble to the TRIPS Agreement: to reduce distortions and obstacles to international trade. Art. 7 of the TRIPS Agreement, in its turn, establishes that "the protection and enforcement of intellectual property rights should":

- contribute to the promotion of technological innovation;
- contribute to the transfer and dissemination of technology. Transfer and dissemination of technology should not be confused.[67] Transfer of technology denotes a contractual relationship, namely payment of a fee against the transfer of a protected technology. Dissemination of technology denotes a wide circulation of technology, independently from any agreement between the owners of protected technology and its users[68];
- contribute to the *mutual* advantage of producers and users of technological knowledge;
- lead to social and economic welfare. In view of the goals set forth in the preamble to the Marrakesh Agreement, "social and economic welfare" implies the observance of the human rights guaranteed, for example, by the International Covenants on Human Rights of 1966;
- establish a *balance* of rights and obligations between IPRs and the duties of the owners of those rights towards society. This objective supports full compliance with art. 15 of the ICESCR, which determines the alignment of moral and economic rights resulting from any scientific, literary or artistic production held by the holders of IPRs with: the right to "take part in cultural life," the right to "enjoy the benefits of scientific progress and its applications" and with the right to "the freedom indispensable for scientific research and creative activity." The expression "balance of rights and obligations" used in art. 7 of the TRIPS Agreement stands as an entrance door for the doctrine of abuse of rights[69] and for the principle of

[67] See Correa 2007, 99.

[68] The *Cambridge Advanced Learner's Dictionary* defines the noun "dissemination" as follows: "to spread or give out something, especially news, information, ideas, etc., to a lot of people" (Cambridge University Press 2011).

[69] In *US – Section 211 Appropriations Act*, the Panel stressed: "We are very cognizant of the potential abuse that might arise in connection with any national legislation that seeks to arbitrarily regulate the ownership of intellectual property. The TRIPS Agreement,

> proportionality.[70] This implies that the rules authorizing WTO Members to institute exceptions to IPRs must be interpreted in ways that guarantee as far as possible the enactment of *all* the objectives in the TRIPS Agreement and the WTO, including those connected to socio-environmental concerns. *A contrario sensu*, it violates art. 7 of the TRIPS Agreement when it grants a wide scope of rights to IPR holders by way of interpretations that restrict or cancel the political leeway provided to WTO Members by the general exception clauses of the agreement for them to implement exceptions to IPRs. It should be recalled that it is especially through the exceptions that the social and environmental objectives of the WTO system may be realized.

In broad lines, art. 7 includes two potentially conflicting interests. They articulate the opposing stances of the groups that forged the TRIPS Agreement, i.e. the desire of industrialized countries to guarantee protection for their intellectual production on a global scale. Their rationale was that IPRs are tools for the promotion of innovation and creativity. On the other hand, developing countries held that the free dissemination of knowledge and an easier transfer of technology are the most efficient way to promote innovation, human well-being and economic development.[71]

The TRIPS Agreement does not establish that its potentially conflicting objectives must be reconciled in order to attain a 'zero-sum game'.[72] Neither does it place commercial interests on a higher hierarchical rung than public interests. Quite the opposite. Its Art. 7 establishes that IPRs must be drawn and implemented in *mutually* beneficial ways for IPR holders and users of intellectual productions, as a means of promoting general well-being.[73] As neither the Marrakesh Agreement nor the TRIPS Agreement established a hierarchy among the objectives set, WTO Members are obliged to work out their rules for the protection of intellectual property in ways that may optimize the realization of *all* of

however, is not without safeguards against potential abuse . . . Article 7 of the TRIPS Agreement states that one of the objectives is that '[t]he protection and enforcement of intellectual property rights should contribute . . . to a balance of rights and obligations.' We consider this expression to be a form of the good faith principle. The Appellate Body in *United States – Shrimps* stated that this principle 'controls the exercise of rights by states. One application of this principle, the application widely known as the doctrine of *abus de droit*, prohibits the abusive exercise of a state's rights and enjoins that whenever the assertion of a right 'impinges on the field covered by [a] treaty obligation, it must be exercised bona fide, that is to say reasonably.' . . . Members must therefore implement the provisions of the TRIPS Agreement in a manner consistent with the good faith principle enshrined in Article 7 of the TRIPS Agreement" (WTO, WT/DS176/R, para. 8.57).

70 On the principle of proportionality see sections 2.3.3.2.1 and 2.4.2.1.

71 See Correa 2007, 92; Frankel 2005, 393.

72 See Taubman 2007, 94.

73 *Ibid.*, 107.

them.[74] Although IPRs are private rights, their protection may not occur at the expense of the public interest pursued by the TRIPS Agreement and the WTO. Briefly put, IPRs are private rights designed to promote public policies.

Consequently, art. 7 serves to clarify that IPRs must not be treated as a sort of natural right of innovators and creators, with unlimited scope, but rather as rights granted by States for the realization of social, economic and technological objectives for the benefit of society as a whole, and not exclusively industrialized societies.[75] Interpreting and applying TRIPS rules on the basis of its objectives results in building legitimate and, consequently, balanced legal regimes.[76]

2.3.3 Article 8 of the TRIPS Agreement and the guiding principles of the general exception clauses

Art. 8 of the TRIPS Agreement is vested with the competence of harboring the informing principles of the general exception clauses of the Agreement. Its full compliance is indispensable to realize the objectives of the TRIPS Agreement and of the WTO system. Bandeira de Mello adopts a comprehensive definition of principle, which brings out the importance of art. 8 to the whole TRIPS edifice:

> [Principle is] a nuclear command of a system; the real foundation thereof; a fundamental provision that radiates on the different rules that make up the system, by composing their spirit and serving as a criterion for its correct understanding and intelligence, provided it defines the logic and rationale of the whole system and guarantees . . . its [internal] harmony. It is the knowledge of the principles that governs the intellection of the various component parts of the unitary whole called legal system. [Because of its fundamental importance] inattention to a particular principle implies offence not only to a specific command, but to the whole system of commands. It is the most serious form of illegality . . . because it represents an insurgency against the whole system, a subversion of its core values, unpardonable insult to its logical framework and corrosion of its infra-structure.[77]

In other words, the principles are the legal foundations of the legal system; from them stem the rules of law directly applicable to settle disputes.[78] The central role of the principles is to arrange the norms that make up the legal system, making them a coherent whole.[79]

Art. 8 recognizes that the achievement of several of the social, environmental and economic goals pursued by the WTO and by TRIPS

[74] See Frankel 2005, 391. [75] See The Royal Society 2003, paras. 1.7 and 3.4.
[76] See Taubman 2007, 104. [77] Bandeira de Mello 2004, 841–842.
[78] See, e.g., Mitchell 2007, 797; Virally 2000, 173.
[79] See Andenas and Zleptnig 2007, 377–378.

may depend on the restriction of the scope of IPRs. Art. 8 provides WTO Members with the discretion to implement "necessary" measures in order to realize important public interests that are crucial to members' development, provided they are "consistent" with the provisions of the TRIPS Agreement. This provision formulates the general guidelines to be observed by WTO Members when they adopt exceptions to the exclusive rights conferred by IPRs. Whereas art. 8 formulates the general rule on exceptions to IPRs, the general exception clauses of TRIPS establish the specific rules for the establishment of exceptions to the rights granted to holders of copyright, industrial designs, trademarks and patents. The interpretation of the TRIPS norms – notably its general exception clauses – in light of the principles of TRIPS is a *sine qua non* for the full realization of the various objectives pursued by this agreement and by the WTO system.

Art. 8 provides: (1) the political objectives that may be pursued by measures that limit the scope of IPRs; (2) the means to determine the "necessity" of measures promoting legitimate objectives; and (3) assessment of the "consistency" of the measures with the provisions of the TRIPS Agreement. The following sections will examine these points in detail.

2.3.3.1 Objectives pursued by the exceptions to IPRs Art. 8 provides a non-exhaustive list of the objectives that may be pursued by measures limiting the scope of IPRs, namely:

- "protect public health and nutrition." The WTO Members are allowed to adopt measures dedicated to the realization of "the right of everyone to the enjoyment of the highest attainable standard of physical and mental health" (art. 12(1), ICESCR) and the right to food (art. 11(1), ICESCR);
- "prevent the abuse of intellectual property rights by right holders";
- "prevent the resort to practices which unreasonably restrain trade";
- prevent practices that "adversely affect the international transfer of technology"; and
- "promote the public interest in sectors of vital importance for their socio-economic and technological development." The WTO Members enjoy wide autonomy to elect the goals pursued by exceptions to IPRs, as long as they are designed to promote a "public interest in sectors of vital importance to their socio-economic and technological development."

There can be no doubt that the objectives set by the WTO and listed in the preamble to the Marrakesh Agreement may be promoted through exceptions to IPRs, as it does not fall within the sphere of the WTO to assess the convenience of their adoption.[80] WTO Members are thus authorized to take measures designed to fulfill their obligations under, inter alia, the UDHR, the ICCPR, the ICESCR and multilateral environmental agreements, given that the protection and promotion of fundamental freedoms, human and environmental rights are conditions for the socio-economic progress of any state.

Additionally, WTO Members enjoy the exclusive right to demarcate the *level of protection of the objective pursued* by exceptions to IPRs, according to their national interests. The WTO is not entitled to give its opinion on the subject,[81] even if the level of protection chosen causes dramatic detrimental effects on the commercial interests of IPR holders.[82]

Should litigation be filed to assess the legitimacy of a given exception to an intellectual property right, the State against which a suit has been brought may hold that the measure that is challenged pursues legitimate objectives. That notwithstanding, in order to identify beyond any doubt the objectives pursued by the measure, the panel concerned will probably study its political purposes based on official State documents, the architecture of the measure and its actual or potential effects.[83]

2.3.3.2 The necessity standard As highlighted by a number of commentators, the adjective "necessary" used to qualify the measures aimed at meeting public interest has a particular meaning in the WTO context, developed in the realm of the GATT 1994.[84] Since both the TRIPS and the GATT 1994 are *integral parts* of the Marrakesh Agreement establishing the WTO, the meaning given to that adjective in the realm of the GATT 1994 must be considered in the process of construing the necessity standard of art. 8 of the TRIPS, provided the GATT 1994 is

[80] Within the context of art. XX GATT 1994, in *US – Gasoline* the WTO Appellate Body confirmed the autonomy of WTO members to espouse measures aimed at promoting any of the legitimate interests mentioned in art. XX (WTO, WT/DS2/AB/R, Appellate Body Report, 30–31).

[81] Within the context of GATT 1994, the WTO avowed such prerogative in *EC – Asbestos*: "As to Canada's third argument, relating to the level of protection, we note that it is undisputed that WTO Members have the right to determine the level of protection of health that they consider appropriate in a given situation" (WTO, WT/DS135/AB/R, Appellate Body Report, para. 168). The existence of this prerogative was confirmed in *Korea – Beef* (WT/DS161/AB/R, WT/DS169/AB/R, para. 176) and in *Dominican Republic – Cigarettes* (WT/DS302/AB/R, para. 72). As is the case with the GATT, the TRIPS Agreement grants the same prerogative to WTO Members.

[82] In the context of the GATT 1994, in *EC – Asbestos*, the Appellate Body confirmed the autonomy of the European Community to protect the lives of its citizens at the highest possible level through a full ban of the asbestos trade (WTO, WT/DS135/AB/R, Appellate Body Report, para. 174).

[83] See McGrady 2009, 4.

[84] See, e.g., McGrady 2009; Neumann and Turk 2003; Ruse-Khan 2008, 20–24; WTO, S/WPDR/W/27, paras. 27–36; WTO 2005.

part of the context in which the provisions of TRIPS should be read, as noted by Kur (2008). In keeping with this understanding and also based on *US – Section 110 (5) Copyright Act*,[85] *US – Section 211 Omnibus Appropriations Act*[86] and *EC – Trademarks and Geographical Indications*,[87] it may be argued that when the wording of a TRIPS provision is similar to the wording of a provision from another WTO agreement, it is possible to resort to the case law regarding the latter to clarify the meaning of the former, provided the interpreter takes note of the relevant differences.[88] That said, to clarify the meaning of the necessity standard embedded in art. 8 of the TRIPS Agreement, it is useful to have recourse to the reports, adopted under the GATT and the WTO systems, dedicated to clarify its meaning in the context of art. XX of the GATT (1947 and 1994).[89]

Art. XX of the GATT 1994 and of its predecessor, GATT 1947, focuses on regulating the extent to which Contracting Parties can establish exceptions to the GATT rules, based on non-commercial objectives. Paragraphs (a), (b) and (d) in art. XX allow Contracting Parties to the GATT to enact measures inconsistent with GATT terms and, consequently, detrimental to free trade, provided they are "necessary" to realize the objectives referred to above, and are applied in a non-discriminatory manner (chapeau art. XX).[90]

Article XX
General Exceptions
Subject to the requirement that such measures are not applied in a manner which would constitute a means of arbitrary or unjustifiable discrimination between countries where the same conditions prevail, or a disguised restriction on international trade, nothing in this Agreement shall be construed to prevent the adoption or enforcement by any contracting party of measures:
(a) necessary to protect public morals;
(b) necessary to protect human, animal or plant life or health;
(c) necessary to secure compliance with laws or regulations which are not inconsistent with the provisions of this Agreement, including those relating to customs enforcement, the enforcement of monopolies operated under paragraph 4 of Article II and Article XVII, the protection of patents, trademarks and copyrights, and the prevention of deceptive practices.

[85] See WTO, WT/DS160/R, Panel Report, para. 6.185.
[86] See WTO, WT/DS176/AB/R, Appellate Body Report, para. 242.
[87] See WTO, WT/DS174/R, Panel Report, para. 7.135. [88] See Frankel, 2010.
[89] Pursuant to art. II(4) of the Marrakesh Agreement, "The General Agreement on Tariffs and Trade 1994 as specified in Annex 1A (hereinafter referred to as 'GATT 1994') is legally distinct from the General Agreement on Tariffs and Trade, dated 30 October 1947 . . . (hereinafter referred to as 'GATT 1947')." Nevertheless, the wording as art. XX of GATT 1947 has the same wording as art. XX of GATT 1994, and for that reason, the case law regarding the meaning of the terms of the former is applicable to understand the meaning of the terms of the latter.
[90] See WTO, WT/CTE/W/203, paras. 12 and 21.

The meaning of "necessary" was first analyzed in 1989, within the sphere of the GATT system. The Panel Report in *US – Section 337 of the Tariff Act*, that examined the legitimacy of a provision in a US law in the light of paragraph (d) of art. XX of the GATT 1947, held that a measure inconsistent with the terms of this agreement could only be deemed necessary if: (1) it pursued one of the legitimate objectives authorized by paragraph (d) of art. XX; (ii) the measure contested was genuinely suitable for the realization of the objectives that justified its implementation; and (iii) the respondent State did *not* have an alternative measure to that which was challenged, which would serve to attain the same policy objective and with the same level of protection, as well as being consistent with the terms of the GATT 1947 or, should it contradict them, less inconsistent than the measure challenged.

In 2000, already under the auspices of the WTO, in *Korea – Beef*, the WTO Appellate Body introduced a substantial change in the meaning of the necessity standard. The first clarification mentioned was that for a measure to be necessary it does not need to be indispensable for the realization of the objective that grounds it. Within the context of art. XX, a measure will be "necessary" if it is close to the category of indispensable:

> As used in Article XX (d), the term "necessary" refers, in our view, to a range of degrees of necessity. At one end of this continuum lies "necessary" understood as "indispensable"; at the other end, is "necessary" taken to mean as "making a contribution to". We consider that a "necessary" measure is, in this continuum, located significantly closer to the pole of "indispensable" than to the opposite pole of simply "making a contribution to."[91]

The Appellate Body confirmed the understanding that a measure inconsistent with the GATT 1994 will be necessary if the State that has been challenged cannot provide a "reasonably available" alternative with fewer detrimental effects on free trade.[92] It is worth emphasizing that the alternative measure must be reasonably available to the State proposing it, in technical and economic terms.[93] This means that an alternative measure that, if adopted, will create excessive costs to an impoverished State facing huge social challenges and a meager budget or limited technological or institutional capacity, cannot qualify as a reasonably available alternative because, in view of its costs, the State would eventually stop pursuing the public interest concerned.[94] In addition, the Appellate Body established

[91] WTO, WT/DS161/AB/R, WT/DS169/AB/R, Appellate Body Report, para. 161.

[92] *Ibid.*, para. 163 *in fine*.

[93] See WTO, WT/DS285/AB/R (*US – Gambling*), Appellate Body Report, para. 308; WTO, Appellate Body Report, WT/DS332/AB/R (*Brazil – Retreaded Tyres*), para. 207.

[94] GATT, L/6439 – 36S/345, Panel Report, para. 5.26.

that measures feasible in technical and economic terms in view of the reality of the State challenged, but that would interfere significantly less with free trade, would be the only ones to qualify as alternative measures.[95] If the alternative measure is able to promote the same interest and to exactly the same extent but, when compared to the measure challenged, would cause a minimal decrease in the level of free trade restrictions, it should be rejected. The purpose of this change is to guarantee a certain margin of appreciation for WTO Members and thus respect their sovereignty.

Nevertheless, the main innovation contributed by *Korea – Beef* is the indication that the process involved in determining the necessity of a measure implies "weighing and balancing a series of factors":

> In sum, determination of whether a measure, which is not "indispensable," may nevertheless be "necessary" within the contemplation of Article XX(d), involves in every case a *process of weighing and balancing a series of factors* which prominently include the contribution made by the compliance measure to the enforcement of the law or regulation at issue, the importance of the common interests or values protected by that law or regulation, and the accompanying impact of the law or regulation on imports or exports.[96] (emphasis added)

In other words, before assessing the availability of alternative measures that are less trade-restrictive, the interpreter must revise another couple of aspects. In the first place, he must verify whether the challenged measure is, in fact, suitable for the purpose of attaining the objectives theoretically pursued. This will prevent the enactment of measures inconsistent with the GATT, which, under the guise of aiming at legitimate ends, actually create a new trade distortion:

> There are other aspects of the enforcement measure to be considered in evaluating that measure as "necessary." One is the extent to which the measure contributes to the realization of the end pursued, the securing of compliance with the law or regulation at issue. The greater the contribution, the more easily a measure might be considered to be "necessary."[97]

Secondly, the relative social importance of the interests promoted by the inconsistent measure must also be evaluated, i.e. the importance of the social interest promoted by the measure as opposed to the commercial

[95] See Neumann and Turk 2003, 214. In a 2002 report, the WTO recognized this change by noting: "It may be possible to say that there has been some evolution in the interpretation of the necessity requirement of Article XX (b) and (d). It has evolved from a least-trade restrictive approach to a less-trade restrictive one . . . ." (WTO, WT/CTE/W/203, para. 42)

[96] WTO, WT/DS161/AB/R, WT/DS169/AB/R, Appellate Body Report, para. 164.

[97] *Ibid.*, para. 163.

interests harmed. The more relevant the interests promoted, the higher the chances of the measure being deemed to be necessary:

> Clearly, Article XX(d) is susceptible of application in respect to a wide array of "laws and regulations" to be enforced. It seems to us that a treaty interpreter assessing a measure claimed to be necessary to secure compliance of a WTO-consistent law or regulation may, in appropriate cases, take into account the *relative* importance of the common interests or values that the law or regulation to be enforced is intended to protect. *The more vital or important those common interests or values are, the easier it will be to accept as 'necessary' a measure designed as an enforcement instrument.* (emphasis added)[98]

In 2001, in *EC – Asbestos*, in 2005, in *Dominican Republic – Cigarettes*, and in 2007, in *Brazil – Retreaded Tyres*, the WTO Appellate Body confirmed the understanding of the sense of the necessity standard, introduced in *Korea – Beef.*[99] The adopted report on the *Brazil – Retreaded Tyres* case is worth noting as it includes some interesting explanations on the interpretation and application of the necessity standard.[100] The case dealt with the legality of a measure enacted by Brazil in connection with paragraph (b) in art. XX of the GATT 1994, which was challenged by the European Community (EC). The challenged measure banned imports of retreaded tyres from all over the world with the exception of MERCOSUR. Its political purpose was to reduce health risks for humans, plant and animal life ensuing from large stocks and burning of retreaded tyres by means of prohibiting imports of these tyres from several regions of the world.

At first instance, the initial step taken by the Panel in the process of evaluation of the necessity of the measure challenged was to examine the social relevance of the political purposes pursued by the measure. The Panel came to the conclusion that the various non-commercial objectives envisaged by the measure – i.e. protection of human and animal health and of plant resources – were of great importance for society and, consequently, higher than the commercial interests harmed.[101] Despite the uncontested relevance of the aims pursued by the Brazilian measure, this was not sufficient for it to qualify as necessary.[102] The Panel proceeded with its assessment and analyzed whether the measure could adequately fulfill its purposes and, lastly, whether there were alternative measures

98 *Ibid.*, para. 162.

99 See WTO, WT/DS135/AB/R, paras. 171–174; WT/DS302/AB/R, para. 70; WTO, WT/DS332/R.

100 For an in-depth analysis about this case see McGrady 2009.

101 *Ibid.*, paras. 7.11 1–7.112.

102 *Ibid.*, para. 7.210.

reasonably available for Brazil, that could comply with the same objectives but without such a hard impact on free trade in tyres.

As to the evaluation of the suitability of the measure selected, the Panel established that the measure would be deemed appropriate if it was able to promote the objectives proposed; that is, if there was a causal relation between the realization of proposed objectives and the measure challenged.[103] Lastly, the Panel enquired whether there was an alternative to the Brazilian measure able to fulfill the same specific objectives, albeit with a smaller restriction on free trade. The Panel concluded that although the Brazilian measure was overly restrictive of tyre-trade, there were no alternative measures reasonably available for Brazil.[104]

The report of the Panel includes two points worth mentioning, which were confirmed by the WTO Appellate Body: firstly, the conclusion that a measure that is extremely trade-restrictive must not be judged unnecessary, a priori. And equally relevant, the fact that an overly trade-restrictive measure aimed at fulfilling an objective of major social significance proves "necessary" insofar as there is no alternative less restrictive measure able to attain the same aim.[105]

The EC was not satisfied with the result of the litigation so it appealed to the Appellate Body. The Appellate Body, in a more organized manner, clarified that the process of assessing the necessity of a measure includes two phases. The first phase requires the following:

- to identify the political objectives pursued by the challenged measure and verify if they are legitimate, on the basis of being permitted by art. XX, paragraphs (a), (b) or (d);
- to assess the capacity of the disputed measure to actually contribute substantially to the realization of its political objectives, e.g. whether a reduction in the volume of discarded tyres is really a measure with the capacity to diminish risks to health and the environment;
- to assess the social relevance of the political objectives pursued by the measure and to identify the level of trade restrictions caused by the measure challenged; and
- to compare the social benefits generated by the measure with the damage produced to trade, in order to assess whether the social benefit is greater than the negative side effects.

If the measure is pronounced adequate for the promotion of legitimate objectives and if the social benefits it promotes surpass the harms to trade, the measure will be deemed preliminarily necessary.[106] In view of that

[103] *Ibid.*, para. 7.119. [104] *Ibid.*, para. 7.212.
[105] *Ibid.*, para. 7.211; ICTSD 2010, 4–7.
[106] WTO, WT/DS332/AB/R, Appellate Body Report, paras. 178–179.

preliminary result, it is necessary to confirm the necessity of the measure with a final test. It would assess the existence of alternative measures to the one challenged with the capacity to cause lesser restrictions to trade than the challenged measure:

> If this analysis yields a *preliminary* conclusion that the measure is necessary, this result must be confirmed by comparing the measure with possible alternatives, which may be less trade restrictive while providing an equivalent contribution to the achievement of the objective. This comparison should be carried out in the light of the importance of the interests or values at stake."[107]

The Appellate Body considered that it was reasonable that, in the course of the process of evaluation of potentially alternative measures, they might be assessed either individually or collectively.[108] In other words, it is possible to associate two or more complementary measures and treat them as one. This is done in order to assess its capacity to promote a given political objective – the same interest pursued by the challenged measure, with the same level of protection – but causing fewer detrimental effects on trade.[109] Finally, the contested measure will be judged "necessary" if there is no less trade-restrictive alternative reasonably available to the State that has been challenged.

Presumably the current meaning attributed by the WTO Appellate Body to the necessity standard has been influenced by the case law on human rights. In the context of the Inter-American system of human rights, art. 13 of the American Convention on Human Rights guarantees all individuals the right to freedom of thought and expression, but it also sets limits. The exercise of the right to freedom of expression "shall not be subject to prior censorship but shall be subject to subsequent imposition of liability." The reasons for liability "shall be expressly established by law to the extent *necessary* to ensure: (a) respect for the rights or reputations of others; or (b) the protection of national security, public order, or public health or morals" (art. 13(2)).

The Inter-American Court of Human Rights (ICHR) referred to the jurisprudence of the European Court of Human Rights (ECtHR) relevant to the specification of the term "necessary," used in art. 10(2) of the European Convention on Human Rights (ECHR), in order to clarify by analogy the meaning of the same term, employed in art. 13(2) of the American Convention on Human Rights.[110] According to the ICHR, both the right to freedom of expression and the other interests

[107] *Ibid.*, para. 178. [108] See McGrady 2009.
[109] WTO, WT/DS332/AB/R, Appellate Body Report, paras. 180–181.
[110] Corte Interamericana de Derechos Humanos, 1985, paras. 43–46.

protected by art. 13(2) of the American Convention are relevant in building a democratic society. Measures for the imposition of liabilities will be "necessary" to protect the rights of others, national security, public order, public health or morals, provided they are proportionate, in the technical meaning of the term, i.e. if they respond to the realization of a legitimate objective authorized by art. 13(2) of the Convention; if the interest protected by the measure proves to be more important for the promotion of democracy – in each actual case – than the unrestricted freedom of expression of an individual or organization and, lastly, if given the available alternative, the measure is the least restrictive of the freedom of expression of others. In *Herrera Ulloa* v. *Costa Rica*, the ICHR held:

> As to these requirements, the Court established that: the 'necessity' and, consequently, the lawfulness of restrictions to the freedom of expression based on article 13.2 of the American Convention will depend on their being aimed at satisfying a pressing public interest. Among several options to attain that aim, the one to be chosen should be the least restrictive of the protected right.
>
> In view of that standard, it is not sufficient to demonstrate, for example, that the law serves a useful and opportune purpose. In order to be compatible with the Convention, restrictions must be justified according to collective objectives that – on account of their importance – clearly surpass the social need to a full enjoyment of the rights guaranteed by article 13 and do not impose limits beyond the strictly necessary on the right established in that article. In other words, the restriction must be proportionate to the interest that justifies it and limited to the achievement of that legitimate objective . . . Therefore, the restriction must be proportionate to the interest that justifies it and limit itself to the achievement of that goal, with the least possible interference on the actual exercise of freedom of expression.[111] (emphasis added)

Within the context of art. 13(2) of the American Convention on Human Rights, the determination of the necessity of a measure restrictive of freedom of expression depends on which of the opposing rights is more relevant, in each case, to the realization of a democratic society. This rationale is the same used in the GATT 1994: the necessity of a measure restrictive of free trade depends on determining which of the opposing interests – e.g. trade or public health – is more relevant for society in each actual case. The interests listed in paragraph 2 of art. 13 of the American Convention and in paragraphs (a), (b) and (d) in art. XX of the GATT are merely interests that *may* justify adopting restrictive measures of freedom of expression and free trade, respectively. The final assessment of the necessity of those measures must necessarily satisfy the proportionality test.

[111] ICHR, *Herrera Ulloa* v. *Costa Rica*, paras. 121 and 123 (free translation).

2.3.3.2.1 The transformation of the necessity standard into a proportionality test Initially, the necessity standard was treated in the report of *US – Section 337* as a test on the least restrictive measure. Its function was to verify: (i) whether the measure, inconsistent with the GATT 1947, had been conceived to pursue any of the objectives authorized by paragraphs (b) or (d) in article XX; (ii) whether the measure is appropriate for the realization of the objectives that ground its adoption; and (iii) whether the measure was the least trade-restrictive alternative. As from *Korea – Beef*, the necessity standard became more complex and changed into a genuine proportionality test.[112]

Given that there are no unlimited rights and interests, and that the legislator cannot possibly devise, a priori, a solution for each and every conflict between principles or legitimate interests of equal hierarchy, the purpose of the proportionality test is to control the observance of the limits to the autonomy offered to State agencies through the weighing and balancing of opposing interests or principles.[113] The proportionality test is a method for solving conflicts between principles of identical hierarchical status.[114] In other words, it is a "meta-rule," in the sense of a norm that governs the application of other norms.[115]

The proportionality test is specifically applicable to assessing the lawfulness of concrete measures or proposals that cause collision between principles or interests, but not to solving conflicts between rules. As collision of principles happens in actual circumstances, the proportionality test is not useful to evaluate *abstract* precedence relations between potentially opposed principles.[116]

Rules are characterized for imposing definite rights or duties, and must be fully observed when applied to actual cases.[117] Conflicts between rules are solved in the field of validity, through the application of hermeneutical principles such as *lex superior derogat legi inferiori* and *lex specialis derogat generali*.[118] This type of conflict is solved by declaring that one of the conflicting rules is invalid.

Principles, according to Robert Alexy's definition, are "optimization mandates," that is, "rules that order that something be realized as far as possible within existing legal and factual possibilities."[119] As opposed to rules, principles are general and flexible norms, which are realized in different degrees. Principles set the general objectives pursued by the legal system.[120] On account of that, they are applicable in association

[112] See WTO, WT/CTE/W/203, para. 42. [113] See Andenas and Zleptnig 2007, 379.
[114] See Engle 2009, 5. [115] See Afonso da Silva 2005a, 221–222.
[116] *Ibid.*, 236. [117] See Alexy 2009, 91.
[118] See Sweet and Mathews 2008, 94. [119] See Alexy 2009, 90 (free translation).
[120] See Mitchell 2007, 797.

with rules that establish rights and duties, guiding their interpretation.[121] Principles also fulfill the important function of impelling the enactment of secondary rules, destined to actualize them.

It is possible that in the process of enactment of new rules aimed at promoting a given principle, the realization of other principles will be affected.[122] Clashes between principles are solved case by case, in the relevant field. That means that the principles comprised in a given legal system will always be valid, even if colliding. Should two principles clash as a result of the adoption of a measure aimed at realizing one of them at the cost of restricting the other, the proportionality test will indicate, *given the circumstances of the actual case*, which of the two principles has the greatest relative weight and will therefore be preferred. Once the results of the test are known, it will be possible to come to a conclusion as to the lawfulness of the controversial measure. The fact that principle P1, in a given set of circumstances, is afforded greater relative weight than principle P2 does not mean that it will always be preferred over P2. Should the circumstances where the principles were applied vary, it may happen that P2 will have greater weight than P1 and will have precedence over it. Consequently, applying the proportionality test does not result in a *general* rule of precedence among opposing principles, to be applied in any circumstance.[123]

In the domestic sphere, the main function of the proportionality test is to serve as a mechanism to review the lawfulness of pieces of legislation, administrative actions and judicial rulings, focused on promoting a given constitutional principle, at the cost of restricting one or more principles of identical normative status.[124] Still in the domestic sphere, the proportionality test is also applied by the executive and legislative powers to assess the lawfulness of legislative proposals and proposed administrative actions, which may produce tensions among constitutional principles, prior to their implementation.[125]

In the field of the multilateral trade system, the proportionality test is used by the organs of the DSB as a tool to control the lawfulness of State measures aimed at realizing one of the public objectives authorized by the WTO at the cost of restricting free trade:[126] for example, a State measure banning imports of retreaded tyres in order to protect human,

121 See Verschuuren 2003, 64. Kolb (2006, 11), contra, argues that in the field of international law, the general principles of law may also serve as a source of rules, autonomously applicable in the process of controversy-solving, regardless of support by any positive rule.

122 See Hilf and Goetz 2003, 10.

123 See Desmedt 2001, 474.

124 See Andenas and Zleptnig 2007, 375, 379.

125 See Sweet and Mathews 2008, 161.

126 Andenas and Zleptnig 2007, 385.

animal and environmental health in the domestic sphere. Free trade, as well as environmental protection, and human and animal health are objectives that share equal status within the WTO system. They are all listed in the preamble of the Marrakesh Agreement as interests of equal relevance for the members of the organization. Such interests characterize WTO fundamental principles. In cases of clashes between them caused by the implementation of a measure aimed at promoting one or more of those interests at the price of impinging on others, the proportionality test provides verification of the necessity (lawfulness) of the measure adopted. Briefly, within the sphere of the WTO, the proportionality test plays the role of setting limits on the autonomy of Member States to enact restrictions to free trade.

The proportionality test contributes in at least three ways to peace in social and international relations. Firstly, its application provides a balance between conflicting principles and interests in a given context since it does not favor any one of them, in advance and abstractly.[127] Secondly, because it ensures the maximization of all principles or interests in collision, including those that are restricted by a State measure. Finally, as the application of the proportionality test implies a rational conflict-solving method, whose premises are the weighing and balancing and comparing of *all* conflicting interests, interested parties are confident that the decision at the end of the process will be legitimate, even if contrary to their individual interests.[128]

The proportionality test comprises three sub-tests that are cumulatively applied: the suitability sub-test, the necessity sub-test and the proportionality *stricto senso* sub-test. The role played by each of these sub-tests will be discussed below.

Suitability sub-test The suitability sub-test's function is to assess whether the measure investigated (M) was devised in ways that will substantially contribute to realize the legitimate objectives that led to its adoption. The suitability sub-test assesses the existence of a causal connection between the means and ends pursued,[129] as well as the lawfulness of the objectives pursued.[130]

The suitability sub-test has the nature of a "negative criterion," apt for rejecting means that are inappropriate to realize the objectives pursued by M.[131] Its function is to prevent the adoption of measures that, in

127 Sweet and Mathews 2008, 91.
128 See, e.g., Franck 2008, 217; Kingsbury and Schill 2009, 40.
129 See Desmedt 2001, 444; Afonso da Silva 2004, 225.
130 See Kingsbury and Schill 2009, 29.
131 See Alexy 2009, 590.

addition to not promoting the objectives chosen, also harm other relevant interests.[132] The purpose of the suitability sub-test is not to enquire if the chosen measure is the most appropriate means to promote the objectives pursued, nor does it question the advantages of pursuing the objectives chosen; these tasks are the exclusive domain of the State which makes the proposal.[133] The sole function of the sub-test is to assess whether M is truly appropriate to attain such objectives.[134] Within the field of international trade, the suitability test serves to avoid the implementation of measures that, theoretically, will promote a relevant public objective but which, in reality, intend to create disguised distortions in trade.[135]

Assessing the suitability of M involves: (i) *precise* identification of the objectives pursued by M, including their level of protection, e.g. protection of human life at the highest possible level; (ii) confirmation of the legitimacy of those objectives, i.e. whether they are permitted by the legal order; and (iii) identification of the immediate effects produced by M and assessment whether such effects lead to the realization of the objectives pursued, e.g. in *Brazil – Retreaded Tyres* the WTO examined whether the measure aimed at banning imports of retreaded tyres would, in actual fact, lead to a reduction in the volume of discarded tyres and whether the reduction in the volume of discarded tyres contributed to the preservation of human, animal and environmental health.[136]

Necessity sub-test Whereas States enjoy autonomy to determine the objectives of their public policies, and the suitability sub-test does not question their convenience or the level of protection chosen for those objectives, State autonomy to choose the *means* to promote them is limited. The sub-test of necessity *stricto sensu* implies a quantitative evaluation of the measure. Its specific function is to check whether the particular measure (M) is the alternative that is less detrimental to the interests that are harmed – among those appropriate to promote the realization of the chosen objectives.

Determining the necessity of M in a strict sense involves two steps.[137] In the first place, alternative measures to M must be identified, equally appropriate to promote the same objective and *at the same level.*[138] Should it prove impossible to identify a measure able to promote the same objective pursued by M, note may be taken of two or more complementary measures that, jointly, appear as appropriate to promote the objective

[132] See Andenas and Zleptnig 2007, 378. [133] WTO, S/WPDR/W/27, para. 12.
[134] See Ortino 2005, 34. [135] See Andenas and Zleptnig 2007, 388.
[136] WTO, WT/DS332/R, para. 7.120. [137] See Kingsbury and Schill 2009, 29.
[138] See Afonso da Silva 2005, 226.

equally well. It is important to recall that only those measures reasonably available to the State proposing M are to be taken into account. Even if a measure seems appropriate in technical terms to promote the same objective as M, if its implementation requires economic, administrative and technological costs beyond the capacity of its proponent, it should not be considered among the set of alternative measures. It is easily inferred, therefore, that some measures reasonably available for an industrialized country are not necessarily available in the case of a less developed country.

Secondly, the sub-test of necessity *stricto sensu* requires evaluating whether the alternative measures identified are less restrictive of the right affected by M, while they do not impinge on the realization of any other right.[139] For example, if in order to realize principle P1 M restricts P2, a measure will be considered less restrictive than M if it is less restrictive of P2, and does not affect any other right, e.g. P3. Within the context of the multilateral trade system, the sub-test of necessity requires the search for an alternative measure able to promote certain public objectives and that is *significantly* less restrictive than M of the free trade of goods, services or IPRs.

Summing up, M will be judged necessary if it proves indispensable, because there is no other alternative that will promote the same objective as M, or if among all reasonable alternatives M proves to interfere less than any other in the realization of the rights affected.[140] That is why the sub-test of necessity is also termed the least restrictive measure test[141] or the least onerous means test.

The sub-test of necessity favors harmony between conflicting rights and interests, as it only admits a measure that, besides proving appropriate for the promotion of the objectives selected by the State, is also the least restrictive of the rights affected by M.[142] Upon selecting the least onerous means to realize the objectives pursued by M, the social harms caused by the measure are lessened[143] insofar as the affected interests are realized to the greatest possible extent, considering the actual possibilities available to the relevant State.[144]

Sub-test of proportionality stricto sensu Despite the suitability and necessity (in a strict sense) of a State measure (M), it is not necessarily lawful. It is also essential to analyze the measure in qualitative terms; that

139 See Alexy 2009, 170.
140 See, e.g., Andenas and Zleptnig 2007, 412; Franck 2008, p. 729.
141 See Sweet and Mathews 2008, 143–144.
142 See Andenas and Zleptnig 2007, 378–379. 143 *Ibid.*, 389.
144 Alexy 2009, 119.

is, whether the benefits it promotes are proportionate to the restrictions caused to the relevant principle or interest affected (P1). In other words, at this stage, assessment must check if the social benefits created by M surpass its side effects.[145]

In the hypothesis that measure M aims to realize P1 and its undesired effect is a restriction of P2, in order to evaluate if M is proportionate in a strict sense, it is necessary to weigh and balance P1 and P2. Such a process involves three steps. The first two require an analysis of empirical data in order to establish as correctly as possible the relative weight of the colliding interests.[146] At first, in view of the actual circumstances, the *real* social benefits ensuing from the realization of P1 through the enactment of M are verified.[147] The entire set of consequences caused by the promotion of P1 must be classified as of slight, medium or great social importance. Right after that, the degree to which P2 was affected and the *actual* consequences of its restriction through the enactment of M are to be established. The set of harms caused by the impingement on P2 must be equally classified in terms of slight, medium or great social importance. Lastly, the social benefits that accrue by the promotion of P1 must be compared to the harms caused by the restriction of P2. M will be judged proportional in a strict sense if the social benefits accrued through the promotion of P1 surpass the harms caused by the restriction of P2.[148]

If the proportionality test comprised only the sub-tests of suitability and necessity *stricto sensu*, it would be reasonable to enact a measure promoting a truly insignificant interest, albeit legitimate, at the price of restricting an interest of significant social weight. The purpose of the sub-test of proportionality is precisely to prevent the enactment of abusive measures that do more harm than good to society,[149] or, in the words of Afonso da Silva, its function is to "avert state measures that, though adequate and necessary, restrict basic rights beyond what the objective pursued can justify."[150] The more relevant for society the interests promoted by the measure under scrutiny, the higher the degree to which the affected principle/interest may be restricted will be. Conversely, if the measure envisages superfluous aims, it will only be able to minimally restrict the affected principle/interest.[151]

The premise of the proportionality test is the adoption by the State of a measure that generates tension between two or more principles or

145 See Sweet and Mathews 2008, 109; Xiuli 2007, 637.
146 See Alexy 2009, 174–175. 147 *Ibid.*, 601ff.
148 See Ortino 2005, 35. 149 See Sweet and Mathews 2008, 105–106.
150 See Afonso da Silva 2005a, 230. 151 See Andenas and Zleptnig 2007, 392.

interests, all sharing equal hierarchical status. Its ultimate function is to balance the colliding principles, ensuring that they can all be realized in the highest possible degree, even if one of them obtains precedence within a given context.[152] The main feature of the test is its comparative evaluation, be it between means and ends (suitability sub-test), between the measure assessed and alternative measures (sub-test of necessity) or between benefits obtained and potential harms (sub-test of proportionality *stricto sensu*).

Summing up, for a challenged measure to be considered necessary at the time when the necessity standard was treated as a least restrictive measure test, it was enough to prove its suitability in promoting one of the interests listed in paragraphs (a), (b) and (d) of art. XX in the GATT 1947, and for the challenged State, to prove that there was no less trade-restricting alternative at its disposal. In other words, the political objectives referred to in the paragraphs of art. XX mentioned above were automatically considered "overriding public policy goals"[153] relative to the trade interests that were restricted. At present, when the necessity standard is characterized as a proportionality test, there is no longer a fixed reply as to the priority of two opposing interests – e.g. trade versus protection of human health. In the light of the new approach, paragraphs (a), (b) and (d) of art. XX merely pre-indicate the objectives that *may* justify measures inconsistent with the GATT. In order to establish which of the opposing objectives enjoys priority, in an actual case, there must be an assessment of the social weight of the objective specifically pursued by the measure under scrutiny vis-à-vis the trade interests that have been harmed. It is therefore possible to find situations where a measure that aims to promote one of the objectives listed in art. XX will be considered unnecessary because, from the point of view of the interests of society, the interest it pursues has less social relevance than the trade interest it would impinge on.

If the WTO system were exclusively devoted to trade-related purposes, there would certainly be no reason why its Appellate Body should have turned the necessity standard into a proportionality test since in case of conflicts between commercial and non-commercial interests, the former would always take priority over the latter. In the context of art. XX of GATT 1994, the United States correctly argued in its defense in *US – Shrimp*, that "[i]t is legal error to jump from the observation that the GATT 1994 is a trade agreement to the conclusion that trade concerns

152 See Xiuli 2007, 644.
153 GATT, DS10/R – 37S/200 (*Thailand – Cigarettes*), Panel Report, para. 74.

must prevail over all other concerns in all situations arising under GATT rules."[154] Given the multiplicity of social and environmental objectives pursued by the WTO system, this observation should be generalized to the other agreements covered by the WTO.

In view of the fact that the WTO pursues the expansion of free trade in goods, services and intellectual property as a means to continually improve the quality of life of humanity, including its natural environment,[155] the application of the proportionality test ensures that free trade will be constrained only when useful for the promotion of pressing social interests. When restrictive measures do not pass the proportionality test (i.e. they are unnecessary) it means that free trade, in that particular case, is a more adequate means to promote public interest than the restrictive measure that was rejected. In conclusion, the transformation of the necessity standard into a proportionality test leads to the ongoing protection of the higher interests of society.

2.3.3.2.2 The necessity standard in the context of art. 8 of the TRIPS Agreement Against the argument that the meaning of the necessity standard, developed under the GATT 1994, would not be applicable in other contexts, it is important to note that the Appellate Body itself has already applied it under another agreement. In *US – Gambling*, Antigua and Barbuda demanded a panel to examine the lawfulness of US laws that forbade access to US citizens to betting and gambling services through the internet. The US defended the legitimacy of the legislation under scrutiny on the basis of paragraph (a) in art. XIV General Agreement on Trade in Services (GATS). Art. XIV GATS establishes the political space provided to WTO Members to adopt exceptional measures restrictive of trade in services. Some of the paragraphs of that provision, which indicate the objectives that might ground the exceptions to free trade in services, were drawn up in accordance with the guidelines set in paragraphs (a), (b) and (d) in art. XX GATT. The chapeau and paragraph (a) of art. XIV GATS read as follows:

> Subject to the requirement that such measures are not applied in a manner which would constitute a means of arbitrary or unjustifiable discrimination between countries where like conditions prevail, or a disguised restriction on trade in services, nothing in this Agreement shall be construed to prevent the adoption or enforcement by any Member of measures: (a) Necessary to protect public morals or to maintain public order

[154] WTO, WT/DS58/AB/R, para. 16.
[155] See the preamble to the Marrakesh Agreement.

The WTO Appellate Body held it was correct to interpret the necessity standard in art. XIV GATS in the same way as the necessity standard in art. XX GATT 1994, in accordance with the understanding established in *Korea – Beef*.[156] The Appellate Body reaffirmed the process the challenged measure has to go through in order to be deemed necessary and recommended that the respondent State prove the "necessity" of the measure challenged, through the process of "weighing and balancing" introduced by *Korea – Beef*.[157]

In view of the consolidated opinion of the DSB on the contents of the necessity standard and the full applicability of the interpretation developed under art. XX of the GATT 1994 in different contexts, the necessity standard in Art. 8 of the TRIPS Agreement constitutes a proportionality test, formed by sub-tests of suitability, necessity and proportionality *stricto sensu*. In other words, evidence of the necessity for an exceptional measure (M) which restricts the scope of a certain IPR involves, cumulatively, proof of its suitability, necessity and proportionality in the strict sense.

Proof of the suitability of the measure implies:

- identifying the political objectives pursued by the measure and the level of protection those objectives will receive;
- verifying whether the political objectives pursued are authorized by art. 8 of the TRIPS Agreement; and
- identifying the actual effects produced by the measure and assessing its capacity to promote the objectives which, formally, backed its adoption/proposal.

Proving the necessity of the measure implies:

- identification of alternative measures, capable of promoting the same objective promoted by M, but that interfere less with the exercise of the affected intellectual property right; and
- an assessment of the technical and economic costs of the alternative measures identified, in order to verify which are "reasonably available" to the State proposing M.

If there is no alternative measure that is reasonably available to the State proposing M, the policy maker should investigate whether the measure is proportionate in the strict sense by:

- identifying the social benefits promoted by M and assessing its value in terms of its social relevance (low, average or great);
- identifying any harm to trade caused by M and assessing its value, in terms of social relevance (low, average or great); and

[156] WTO, WT/DS285/AB/R, Appellate Body Report, paras. 304–308, 310 and 323.

[157] *Ibid.*, paras. 310, 323 and 326.

- comparing the benefits accrued by the adoption of M1 and the negative impact on the interests of IPR owners. Should benefits surpass harms, M will be proportionate.

If the measure goes through the three steps successfully, it will be deemed necessary, in terms of art. 8 of the TRIPS Agreement. Nevertheless, even if necessary, it will not necessarily be lawful. In order to qualify as lawful, the measure will also have to prove that it is consistent with the provisions of the TRIPS Agreement.

2.3.3.3 The consistency standard of art. 8 of the TRIPS Agreement One of the purposes of the TRIPS Agreement is to eliminate distortions in international trade through the prohibition of trade in goods that have misappropriated protected IPRs in the territory of WTO Members. With this aim in view, the TRIPS Agreement sets minimum standards for the protection of IPRs to be observed by all WTO Members.[158] In order to ensure that these minimum standards prove effective, art. 8 of the TRIPS Agreement states that the measures envisaged by the members of the organization to promote legitimate interests must be "consistent with the provisions of this Agreement."

Art. 8, by providing that measures aimed at promoting public policy interests should be necessary *and* consistent with the provisions of the TRIPS Agreement, does not denote that the exclusive rights granted by it shall not be subject to any exceptions that restrict their scope.[159] If we were to understand that those measures cannot interfere, under any hypothesis, with the exclusive rights of the holders of IPRs, the necessity standard, mentioned in art. 8, and the general exception clauses of the TRIPS Agreement *in toto* would have no effect. This interpretation is prevented by the principle of effectiveness insofar as it blocks the enactment of the objectives of the WTO and the TRIPS Agreement and deprives provisions of the TRIPS Agreement of any force. Added to that, it constitutes an abuse of rights since it prevents WTO Members from making use of their prerogative to enact measures aimed at protecting public interests.

In the light of the principle of good faith and of the objectives of the WTO and the TRIPS Agreement, the most suitable conclusion to reach is that the consistency standard establishes that proposed measures that interfere with the exercise of the exclusive rights guaranteed by the TRIPS Agreement must comply strictly with the minimum obligations established thereby, namely: (i) depending on the intellectual property right subject to the measure, the conditions imposed by the pertinent

[158] See Frankel 2005–2006, 375–376. [159] See Ruse-Khan 2008, 36.

general exception clause (i.e. arts. 9(2) BC and 13, 17, 26 (2) or 30 TRIPS); and (ii) all the other minimum relevant obligations enshrined in those provisions that do not contain the list of exclusive rights granted to the holders of copyrights, trademarks, industrial designs and patents.

The set of minimum obligations to be observed by any exception to IPRs varies depending on the nature of the affected rights (copyrights, rights conferred by patents, trademarks or industrial designs). Nevertheless, any exception to an IPR must respect two basic principles of the TRIPS Agreement: national treatment and the most-favored-nation principle.

The most-favored-nation principle, enshrined in art. 4 TRIPS, provides that, apart from expressly indicated exceptional cases, "[w]ith regard to the protection of intellectual property, any advantage, favour, privilege or immunity granted by a Member to the nationals of any other country shall be accorded immediately and unconditionally to the nationals of all other Members." This means that save in exceptional cases mentioned in the provision, WTO Members cannot create exceptions affecting the IPRs of nationals from particular countries while protecting the IPRs of the nationals of other countries. Should a WTO Member rule, for example, that the patents of nationals of one State in particular shall not be covered by the research exception prescribed in its legal order, that protection must be automatically expanded to all other members of the organization.

The principle of national treatment, in turn, provides that, except in cases expressly indicated in art. 3 TRIPS, foreigners must receive treatment no less favorable than the treatment conferred by the State to its own nationals. National treatment prevents WTO Members from setting up exceptions to IPRs affecting the intellectual property of the nationals of a given country whilst protecting the intellectual property among its own nationals. This stance would provide the nationals favored with an unfair advantage over foreign owners of IPRs. The national treatment is simply the application of the principle of equality among nationals and foreigners whereas the treatment of most favored nation represents the application of the principle of equality among foreigners.

The remaining obligations that WTO Members must observe when exercising the prerogatives guaranteed by arts. 9(2) BC, 13, 17, 26(2) and 30 TRIPS, will be addressed in the following sections.

2.3.3.3.1 Additional obligations that shall be observed by copyright exceptions Besides the principles of national and of most-favored-nation treatment (arts. 3 and 4), copyright exceptions shall observe the following obligations:

- prohibition of the adoption of exceptions that produce the effect of preventing the legal protection of the categories of literary and artistic works that, in accordance with art. 2, paragraphs (1), (3) and (5) BC and art. 10 TRIPS shall be eligible for copyright protection; and
- ensuring the minimum term of protection guaranteed by art. 12 TRIPS and art. 7 BC.

Pursuant to the principle *lex specialis derogat generali*, in respect of exceptions adopted under arts. 9(2), 10 and 10bis BC, they shall respect the area occupied by the system of compulsory licenses governed by the appendix to the BC (Paris Act), which includes special provisions for developing countries aimed at facilitating access to literary works to the satisfaction of educational interests in their territories.

Without getting into details, art. II of the appendix authorizes any developing country "which has declared that it will avail itself of the faculty provided for in this Article . . . so far as works published in printed or analogous forms of reproduction are concerned, to substitute for the exclusive right of translation provided for in Article 8 [of the Convention] a system of non-exclusive and non-transferable licenses, granted by the competent authority," in order to authorize others to translate and publish, in print or in any other similar form of reproduction, copies of such works with the purpose of meeting the local educational demands. Art. III of the appendix provides that any developing country that has declared that it will "avail itself of the faculty provided for in this Article shall be entitled to substitute for the exclusive right of reproduction provided for in Article 9 [of the Berne Convention] a system of non-exclusive and non-transferable licenses, granted by the competent authority," in order to authorize others to reproduce and publish works produced in printed form or in any other similar form of reproduction, when the works in question have not been offered for sale in the local market in sufficient quantities to meet the needs of the general public or educational demands.

In other words, the goal pursued by the compulsory licensing system established by the appendix to the BC is to allow institutions based in developing countries – e.g. publishing houses, universities – to undertake the translation *and* publication of works published in foreign languages or the reproduction *and* publication of works published in the local language, not available in the local market, with the aim of meeting local educational needs.

Therefore, it is not any act of reproduction of a literary work, for scientific and educational purposes, which depends on a compulsory license issued according to the complex procedure described in the appendix to the BC, but only the act of reproduction *and* publication or translation *and* publication of works published in printed form or in any other similar form of reproduction. It is important to note that "publish" under art. 3(3) BC means the manufacture of copies of a work and their offer to the public in quantities sufficient "to satisfy the reasonable requirements of the public, having regard to the nature of the work." As pointed out by Ricketson, a work will only be considered "published" if made available to the general public in sufficient quantities to meet, in a reasonable manner, their needs. Works that are only distributed to a limited group of individuals are not considered "published":

> The meaning of "the public": These words have appeared in each of the successive texts of the definition of "published words." Giving them their ordinary meaning, there is no warrant for interpreting them as referring to any restricted group of persons or "sub-publics," even though, as we have seen, the "public" for any particular work may be very small, or even non-existent, at the time of publication. The essential requirement is that there is no limitation placed on the persons to whom the work is made available, as is the case when an edition of a book is limited to a special class of persons, such as members of a professional organization or a closed group of subscribers, or when a film is exhibited to a limited audience, as at a film festival.[160]

2.3.3.3.2 Additional obligations that shall be observed by the exceptions to the rights conferred by trademarks Besides the principles of national and most-favored-nation treatment, the exceptions to the exclusive rights granted to trademark holders shall also respect the following obligations:

(a) Prohibition of adopting exceptions that produce the practical effect of preventing the protection of distinctive signs that, in accordance with art. 15 of the TRIPS Agreement, should be eligible to receive protection;
(b) Ensuring that the term of protection of any trademark registration will not be less than seven years (art. 18);
(c) Ensuring the right to renew indefinitely the registrations of trademarks (art. 18);
(d) Prohibition of compulsory licensing trademarks (art. 21); and
(e) Ensuring the right of trademark holders to assign their trademarks with or without the transfer of the business to which they belong (art. 21).

2.3.3.3.3 Additional obligations that shall be observed by the exceptions to the rights conferred by protected industrial designs Besides the principles of national and most-favored-nation treatment, the exceptions to the rights

[160] Ricketson 1987, 187.

conferred by protected industrial designs shall also observe the following obligations:

(a) prohibition of adopting exceptions that engender the effect of preventing the protection of industrial designs that, pursuant to art. 25(1) TRIPS, should be eligible for protection;
(b) prohibition of adopting exceptions that produce the effect of preventing the legal protection of textile designs (art. 25(2)); and
(c) ensuring that the duration of protection available to industrial designs amounts to at least 10 years (art. 26(3)).

2.3.3.3.4 Additional obligations that shall be observed by the exceptions to the exclusive rights conferred by a patent Besides having to comply with the principles of national treatment and of the most-favored-nation, the exceptions to the rights conferred by patents shall respect the following obligations: (i) the duty to protect all categories of inventions that shall be protected by all WTO Members; (ii) the minimum term of protection of patents set by the TRIPS Agreement; (iii) ensuring respect to the field covered by the compulsory licensing system; (iv) the principle of non-discrimination based on national origins, the field of technology and the manner of exploitation of the invention. The contents of these obligations will be detailed below.

2.3.3.3.4.1 Guarantee of protection to all categories of inventions that shall be protected by all WTO Members WTO Members are obliged to grant protection to inventions in all fields of technology, provided patentability conditions are met.[161] WTO Members, however, enjoy autonomy not to protect some controversial matters: plants and animals, including human genetic material, essentially biological processes for the production of plants or animals;[162] "diagnostic, therapeutic and surgical methods for the treatment of humans or animals";[163] and inventions "the prevention within their territory of the commercial exploitation of which is necessary to protect *ordre public* or morality, including to protect human, animal or plant life or health or to avoid serious prejudice to the environment."[164] In the area of biotechnology, the only matters that WTO Members are obliged to protect are microorganisms, non-biological and microbiological processes.

In the face of these obligations, WTO Members are not free to set up exceptions that may prevent the actual protection of those categories of inventions that, pursuant to art. 27 TRIPS, shall be eligible for patent

161 Art. 27(1) TRIPS. 162 Art. 27(3(b) TRIPS.
163 Art. 27(3)(a) TRIPS. 164 Art. 27(2) TRIPS.

protection. This implies that exceptions must never strip patent owners of *all* the means of exploitation of their patents, stated in art. 28(1) TRIPS. Should that not be the case, they would become instrumental to a non-onerous expropriation of private property. If the exception posited preserves at least one of the means to exploit patents provided by art. 28(1) it suffices for it not to qualify as a case of undue expropriation of the patents concerned.

2.3.3.3.4.2 Minimum term of protection of patents In terms of art. 33 of the TRIPS Agreement, "[t]he term of protection [to patents] available shall not end before the expiration of a period of twenty years counted as from the filing date." On the basis of art. 1(1) TRIPS, WTO Members may extend that term of protection, but not shorten it. Additionally, whenever they decide to lengthen it, the period beyond twenty years must be expressly stated.

2.3.3.3.4.3 Respect for the area occupied by the TRIPS compulsory licensing system By virtue of the *lex specialis derogat generali* principle, the general exception clause of patent law (art. 30) must yield to the special provisions that govern the granting of compulsory licenses (art. 31).[165] With the purpose of restricting the rights granted by patents to protect crucial public interests, WTO Members are free to grant compulsory licenses and even choose the grounds that justify their concession.[166] Art. 31 and the Decision of the WTO General Council of August 30, 2003 formulate the rules and procedures to be followed by WTO Members when granting compulsory licenses. The TRIPS Agreement and the Decision of the General Council expressly state some objectives that can only be pursued through the non-authorized use of patents if the third party obtains a compulsory license, namely:

- to correct anti-competitive practices, regardless of the field of technology where the patented innovation belongs;[167]
- in the case of patents that protect semi-conductor technologies, to respond to public non-commercial interests or correct anti-competitive practices;[168]
- to promote the exploitation of a patented invention by the State or a third party authorized by the State, in cases of national emergency or non-commercial public use;[169]

[165] See Gervais 1998, 159. [166] Art. 5(b), WTO, WT/MIN(01)/DEC/2.
[167] Art. 31(k) TRIPS. [168] Art. 31(c) TRIPS.
[169] Art. 31, chapeau combined with paragraph (b), TRIPS.

- to authorize imports of pharmaceutical products by a State that lacks the productive capacity to meet local needs and to authorize exports of pharmaceutical products to a State that lacks an adequate productive capacity in the pharmaceutical sector;[170] and
- to permit the exploitation of a dependent patent, i.e., "a patent ('the second patent') which cannot be exploited without infringing another patent ('the first patent')."[171]

Amongst the objectives listed above, one of them merits special attention in view of its relevance for technological and industrial progress: The objective that aims to permit the exploitation of dependent patents. There is increasing development of new innovations that embody technologies patented by third parties. It may happen that those complex inventions are never introduced into the market due to the obstacles faced when trying to obtain voluntary licenses for the patented inventions "absorbed" by the new one.

Art. 31(l) authorizes WTO Members to grant compulsory licenses when a patented invention finds that its commercial exploitation is barred by *one* blocking patent. It is important to emphasize that art. 31(l) merely governs the granting of compulsory licenses when the new invention is patented and the exploitation of the dependent patent is prevented by a *single* patent.[172] One of the requirements the petitioner of the compulsory license will have to comply with is to demonstrate that his patented invention (the second patent) "involves an important technical progress of considerable economic significance in relation to the invention claimed in the first patent."[173] The rationale of this requirement is to prevent unfair competitors who might "develop" innovations that derive substantially from previous patented inventions of vast socio-economic importance, from taking advantage of the market of the blocking patent.

On account of the area covered by art. 31(l), WTO Members do not have to mandate a third party to resort to the compulsory licensing system when his invention incorporates only one patented innovation if its developer chooses to keep it in the public domain or, in cases when the new invention has been patented, as long as it includes two or more patented inputs. Under the protection of art. 30 of the TRIPS

170 WTO, Decision of the General Council of 30 August 2003 (WT/L/540 and Corr.1).
171 Art. 31 (l) TRIPS.
172 Art. 31(l) TRIPS rules "Where the law of a Member allows for other use of the subject matter of a patent without the authorization of the right holder, including use by the government or third parties authorized by the government, the following provisions shall be respected: (l) where such use is authorized to permit the exploitation of a patent ("*the second patent*") which cannot be exploited without infringing another patent ("*the first patent*"), the following additional conditions shall apply" (emphasis added).
173 Art. 31(l)(i) TRIPS.

Agreement, WTO Members are free to design exceptions specifically focused on solving these problems.

2.3.3.3.4.4 Non-discrimination based on national origins, the field of technology and the manner of exploitation of the invention Art. 27(1) of the TRIPS Agreement settles that "patents shall be available and patent rights enjoyable without discrimination as to the place of innovation, the field of technology and whether products are imported or locally produced." This provision introduces the non-discrimination principle, based on national origin, the field of technology and the manner of exploitation of the patent. This means that all WTO Members shall grant patent protection and guarantee patent holders the exercise of the rights granted regardless of the territory where the subject matter of the patents was developed, the technological field where the subject matter of the patent belongs and the method of exploitation, i.e. exploitation through local production or importation. The substance of this principle merits special attention in virtue of its potential restriction of the autonomy of WTO Members in formulating specific exceptions with the purpose of overcoming technical problems caused by the expansion of the patent system to new technological fields.

In order to fully understand the contents of the principle of non-discrimination it is essential to analyze the meaning of the word "discrimination." The *Compact Oxford English Dictionary* provides the following meanings of the verb "discriminate": (1) recognize a distinction; differentiate; (2) make an unjust or prejudicial distinction in the treatment of different categories of people or things, especially on the grounds of race, sex, or age.[174] Briefly, "discrimination" may be understood as the simple action of differentiating or as an action of differentiation based on illegitimate reasons.

If the word "discrimination" is understood as the mere action of making distinctions between categories, every exception to rights granted by patents would be rejected, when devised to respond to a problem faced by specific technological sectors. Consequently, only technically neutral exceptions would be authorized, applicable to all categories of inventions, regardless of the technological field they are linked with.

On the other hand, if "discrimination" is understood as making distinctions on the basis of illegitimate justifications, legitimate exceptions would be those that have an impact exclusively on a given technological field, when grounded on objective and legitimate justifications. That interpretative option is the one that best coincides with the WTO, as it

[174] Oxford University Press 2009.

allows each WTO Member to posit specific solutions to the challenges posed by each field of technology. Furthermore, it also resembles the understanding upheld by the ECtHR in the *Belgian Linguistic Case Relating*. In that case, the ECtHR concluded that a State measure that treats categories of individuals differently is not discriminatory, provided it is justified and proportionate:

following the principles which may be extracted from the legal practice of a large number of democratic States, [the Court] holds that the principle of equality of treatment is violated if the distinction has *no objective and reasonable justification*. The existence of such a justification must be assessed in relation to the aim and effects of the measure under consideration, regard being had to the principles which normally prevail in democratic societies. A difference of treatment in the exercise of a right laid down in the Convention must not only pursue a legitimate aim: Article 14 (art. 14) is likewise violated when it is clearly established that there is no reasonable relationship of proportionality between the means employed and the aim sought to be realised.[175] (emphasis added)

If exceptions focused on overcoming a specific problem faced by a given technological sector had to be written in technically neutral terms, their application in connection with inventions from other technical sectors might harm them through an unnecessary dilution of the rights of patent holders. If we recall that the protection of intellectual property must promote technological innovation, among other things, an interpretation of art. 27(l) that requires exceptions to be technologically neutral – in whatever possible circumstances – contradicts the word and the spirit of the TRIPS Agreement. This understanding was argued by Canada in *Canada – Pharmaceutical Patents*:

Canada argued that the scope of Article 30 would be reduced to insignificance if governments were required to treat all fields of technology the same, for if all exceptions had to apply to every product it would be far more difficult to . . . target particular social problems, as are anticipated, according to Canada, by Articles 7 and 8 of the TRIPS Agreement. Conversely, Canada argued, requiring that exceptions be applied to all products would cause needless deprivation of patent rights for those products as to which full enforcement of patent rights causes no problem.[176]

Consistently with this interpretation, In *Canada – Pharmaceutical Patents* the Panel affirmed that discrimination is not to be confused with differential treatment, the latter being legally possible: differential treatment

[175] *Case Relating to Certain Aspects of the Laws on the Use of Languages in Education in Belgium* v. *Belgium*, 30–31.

[176] WTO, WT/DS114/R, Panel Report, para. 7.89.

involves imposing a disadvantageous differential treatment to the detriment of a class or category based on legitimate reasons. Discriminatory treatment, on the other hand, implies imposing differential disadvantageous treatment to the detriment of a group or category without legitimate reasons.

There are two categories of discriminatory treatment: *de jure* discrimination is an explicitly different treatment of categories or classes. *De facto* discrimination is caused by giving a neutral and egalitarian treatment to classes and categories, whose consequences harm a given class or category, with no fair reason to justify it:

> It [discrimination] is a normative term, pejorative in connotation, referring to results of the *unjustified* imposition of differentially disadvantageous treatment. Discrimination may arise from explicitly different treatment, sometimes called 'de jure discrimination', but it may also arise from ostensibly identical treatment which, due to differences in circumstances, produces differentially disadvantageous effects, sometimes called 'de facto discrimination.' The criteria to judge the justification of a differential treatment are infinitely complex . . . As noted above, de facto discrimination is a general term describing the legal conclusion that an ostensibly neutral measure transgresses a non-discrimination norm because its actual effect is to impose differentially disadvantageous consequences on certain parties, and because those differential effects are found *to be wrong or unjustifiable.* Two main issues figure in the application of that general concept in most legal systems. One is the question of de facto discriminatory effect – whether the actual effect of the measure is to impose differentially disadvantageous consequences on certain parties. The other, related to the *justification* for the disadvantageous effects, is the issue of purpose – not an inquiry into the subjective purposes of the officials responsible for the measure, but an inquiry into the objective characteristics of the measure from which one can infer the existence or non-existence of discriminatory objectives.[177] (emphasis added)

It was probably on account of the difference between discriminatory and differential treatment that the Panel held that "Article 27 does not prohibit bona fide exceptions to deal with problems that may exist only in certain product areas."[178] But, in contradiction with its own observations, the Panel held that for an exception not to be judged discriminatory it must be written in a technologically neutral style, with the purpose of expanding its application to every field of technology. It added that even when a given exception is granted on account of existing problems in a particular sector of technology, it does not mean it will be considered discriminatory, provided it is written in neutral terms.[179]

[177] *Ibid.*, paras. 7.94 and 7.101. [178] *Ibid.*, para. 7.92. [179] *Ibid.*, para. 7.104.

The conclusion of the Panel contradicts not merely its own stance, but also the objectives of the TRIPS Agreement. Delivering differential treatment to inventions stemming from diverse fields of technology may prove to be the only way to ensure that, all things considered, patent owners associated with each of the various technological sectors and their respective users will enjoy a relatively similar level of protection.[180] Furthermore, it is relevant to note that a substantial number of Patent Offices all over the world establish special rules to assess patentability criteria for specific fields of technology.[181] In recent years some of the largest industrialized countries have already altered, via judicial or legislative powers, the scope of research exceptions in order to foster the productive use of innovations from specific fields of technology[182] and, on the international scene, the Budapest Treaty on the International Recognition of the Deposit of Microorganisms for the Purposes of Patent Procedure[183] has established that Contracting States should authorize deposits of samples of microorganisms to facilitate the description of microbiological inventions. In so doing, it sanctioned a change in the traditional rules of patent regimes, which oblige anyone filing a patent application to describe his innovation in a thorough manner that would permit a person skilled in the art to reproduce it without undue burden. These examples and the fact that no State contests the non-discriminatory character of those pieces of legislation demonstrate that granting differential treatment to innovations from different technical sectors does not equate with an act of discrimination.

In summary, in terms of art. 27(1) of the TRIPS Agreement, WTO Members are authorized to implement exceptions to the rights granted by patents, in order to deal with specific problems in various sectors of technology, provided they supply legitimate reasons. Justifications qualified as legitimate are those listed in art. 8 of the TRIPS Agreement

[180] Such is the stance held by Australia and USA, as interested third parties, in *Canada – Pharmaceutical Patents* (*ibid.*, 104–106).

[181] For example, in 1997 the Japan Patent Office adopted "Implementing Guidelines for Innovations in Specific Fields." It established specific regulations for patentability examination of biological innovations and those related to computer software (www.jpo.go.jp/tetuzuki_e/t_tokkyo_e/sisine.htm). The United States Patent and Trademark Office also enacted specific rules to evaluate compliance with patentability conditions of inventions from the biotechnological sector (www.uspto.gov/web/offices/pac/mpep/documents/2400.htm; www.uspto.gov/web/offices/pac/mpep/documents/1600.htm). In 1998, the European Community approved Directive 98/44/EC on the legal protection of biotechnological innovations.

[182] It is worth noting the new legislation in Switzerland and Belgium (see Chapter 5 section 5.4).

[183] As at July 2011 the Treaty of Budapest includes seventy-five contracting parties (www.wipo.int/treaties/en/ShowResults.jsp?lang=en&treaty_id=7).

and those associated with the promotion of the objectives of the TRIPS Agreement and the WTO.

2.4 Context of the general exception clauses of the TRIPS Agreement

Art. 31(1) of the VCLT establishes that "[a] treaty shall be interpreted in good faith in accordance with the ordinary meaning to be given to the terms of the treaty *in their context*." The context of the treaties includes its text, the preamble and annexes, as well as "any agreement relating to the treaty which was made between all the parties in connection with the conclusion of the treaty"[184] and "any instrument which was made by one or more parties in connection with the conclusion of the treaty and accepted by the other parties as an instrument related to the treaty."[185]

A treaty is much more than the sum of its parts.[186] That is why in the process of interpretation of its provisions the treaty must be seen as a consistent whole, whose parts influence each other.[187] The purpose of interpreting the terms of a treaty in its context is to avoid distortions of its meaning, ensure that all the provisions of the treaty are faithfully observed and, lastly, contribute to the full realization of its objectives.[188] The function of the context is identical to that of the objectives of the treaty and the other elements included in the general rule of interpretation: to guide the interpreter in the selection of the most appropriate meaning of the terms of a treaty, among all their possible meanings.[189]

Consequently, it is not correct to limit research on the meaning of the terms of the general exception clauses of the TRIPS Agreement as if they had an autonomous existence, independent from the other provisions of the TRIPS Agreement and the WTO legal framework. The normative meaning of these provisions must surface from the wider context, including the TRIPS Agreement, the provisions of international treaties

[184] Art. 31(2) (a) CVDT. [185] Art. 31(2) (b) CVDT.

[186] See Lauterpacht 1949, 76.

[187] See, e.g., Brownlie 1998, 634; International Law Commission 1966, 221; McNair 1961, 381–382; Sinclair 1984, 127.

[188] In *US – Gasoline*, the WTO Appellate Body admitted that it is indispensable to interpret the terms in art. XX (g) GATT 1994 within its context as a way to ensure the realization of the wider objectives of the GATT: "Article XX(g) and its phrase, 'relating to the conservation of exhaustible natural resources,' need to be read in context and in such a manner as to give effect to the purposes and objects of the *General Agreement*" (emphasis added) (WTO, WT/DS2/AB/R, 16–17).

[189] Gardiner 2008, 178.

on intellectual property included in their text by way of reference (e.g. the provisions of the Conventions of Berne and Paris), the Marrakesh Agreement and, when relevant, other WTO agreements, as they all make up a single undertaking. This does not mean that all the provisions of those agreements provide relevant information for an interpretation of the general exception clauses of the TRIPS; useful rules must be distinguished from irrelevant ones.[190]

When the general exception clauses of the TRIPS are interpreted in the light of the objectives pursued by the WTO system and by the TRIPS, as well as in the light of TRIPS guiding principles, enshrined in art. 8, the interpreter's attention is already focused on the relevant context for the proper explanation of their terms. As we have already seen, art. 8 – interpreted in the light of the case law related to paragraphs (b) and (d) in art. XX of the GATT 1994 – establishes the guiding principles of the general exception clauses of the TRIPS Agreement. The necessity standard in art. 8 leads to a harmonization of the various commercial and non-commercial objectives pursued by the WTO system, promoting their realization to the highest possible degree. As to the consistency standard, it guarantees compliance with the minimum standards established by the TRIPS. The association between these two standards opens the way for the realization of objective of the TRIPS Agreement which states that "[t]he protection and enforcement of intellectual property rights should contribute . . . to a balance of rights and obligations [towards society]."[191]

In addition to the context of the treaty, art. 31(3) VCLT still demands that the interpreter of the general exception clauses of the TRIPS Agreement takes into account "any subsequent agreement between the parties regarding the interpretation of the treaty or the application of its provisions," "any subsequent practice in the application of the treaty which establishes the agreement of the parties regarding its interpretation" and "any relevant rules of international law applicable in the relations between the parties." In the following sections, these elements will be examined separately.

2.4.1 *Interpretative agreements and subsequent State practices*

In *Japan – Alcoholic Beverages*, the WTO Appellate Body defined subsequent state practice in interpreting a treaty "as a 'concordant, common and consistent' sequence of acts or pronouncements which is sufficient

[190] Bederman 2001, 315. [191] Art. 7 TRIPS.

to establish a discernible pattern implying the agreement of the parties regarding its interpretation. An isolated act is generally not sufficient to establish subsequent practice; it is a sequence of acts establishing the agreement of the parties that is relevant."[192]

The purpose of both the subsequent practice and the interpretative agreement is to ascertain the will of the parties on how to interpret a particular provision of the treaty they signed. There is a slight difference between a subsequent interpretative agreement and a subsequent practice enacted by the parties to a treaty. The difference lies in how the will of the contracting parties is formalized: in the case of the agreement, this will takes shape in a written instrument, which is not necessarily a treaty.[193]

The interpreter may only take into account later agreements and State practices supported by the same parties or agencies authorized to modify the treaty.[194] In view of the fact that a treaty is the result of a consensus reached by its contracting parties, it is only natural that an actual or tacit agreement as to how to interpret it should also reflect the consensus of those parties.[195] This means that the agreements and practices carried out by some of the parties to a treaty should be discarded since they do not reflect the collective will of all the contracting parties. Should the interpreter have permission to take into account any agreement or practice backed by some of the contracting parties to the treaty, the latter could unilaterally impose their will and opinion on the other parties to the treaty.

Given the large membership of the WTO – to date 153 – and the current cultural and socio-economic diversity, it is highly improbable that a tacit agreement will have taken shape among all of them over the past years as to how to interpret each one of the general exception clauses of the TRIPS Agreement. Whereas industrialized countries tend to interpret these provisions according to the interpretations put forward in *Canada – Pharmaceutical Patents*, *United States – Section 110(5) of US Copyright Act* and in *EC – Trademarks and Geographical Indications*, developing countries are inclined to favor a more flexible interpretation, aiming at safeguarding their discretion to adopt measures that restrict the scope of IPRs. And even among the industrialized countries, there is no consensus on the meaning of these provisions: it is sufficient to recall that in these disputes, the opposing parties and third countries concerned argued different interpretations of the terms of arts. 13, 17 and 30 TRIPS.

[192] WTO, WT/DS8, 10,11/AB/R, Appellate Body Report, p. 11 (footnotes omitted).
[193] See Gardiner 2008, 219. [194] See Sinclair 1984, 136.
[195] See Berderman 2001, 308; Aust 2000, 189.

Although, on the one hand, there is no State practice to be considered in the process of interpretation of the general exception clauses of the TRIPS Agreement, on the other hand and so far as art. 30 of the TRIPS is concerned, in the category of written interpretative agreements the Doha Ministerial Declaration on the TRIPS Agreement and Public Health of 2001 (Doha Declaration) must be included.[196] Notwithstanding that, although widely celebrated, the Doha Declaration did not provide new information that might help in the interpretation of the TRIPS Agreement. Actually, it only confirmed the tools that had already been provided by the TRIPS Agreement and WTO law to its Members. When correctly applied, these tools favor the dissemination and transfer of technologies patented in their territories, to meet public interests, particularly the right to health.[197] Among those tools, the Declaration included the international public law customary rules of treaty interpretation, i.e. the rules codified by the VCLT.[198] The much celebrated passage in the Doha Declaration that states that "the TRIPS Agreement does not and should not prevent Members from taking measures to protect public health,"[199] only indicates that if the tools provided by the TRIPS Agreement are properly exploited, "the Agreement can and should be interpreted and implemented in a manner supportive of WTO members' right to protect public health,"[200] as well as other vital interests such as those mentioned in the preamble of the Marrakesh Agreement or in art. 8 TRIPS.[201]

Although from a legal perspective, the Doha Declaration only confirms the flexibilities and tools provided by the TRIPS Agreement, it does make a contribution since it removes mistaken understandings, characterized by confusion between the history of imbalanced negotiations of the Agreement and the room it provides for implementing measures devoted to protect pressing social interests.[202]

[196] WTO, WT/MIN(01)/DEC/2.

[197] Taubman (2007, 109) calls the Doha Declaration "a tautology, asserting the existing law of TRIPS so as to validate options within that law." In a similar sense, see Ruse-Khan 2008, 43.

[198] WTO, WT/MIN(01)/DEC/2, para. 5(a). The other tools mentioned in the Declaration are: grant of compulsory licenses and freedom to determine the justification for granting them; adoption of the principle of international exhaustion of IPRs and freedom to define what constitutes "national emergency." The Declaration itself acknowledged that the list of tools provided by the TRIPS Agreement is longer and it definitely includes art. 30, when interpreted in accordance with the VCLT rules of treaty interpretation.

[199] WTO, WT/MIN(01)/DEC/2, para. 4. [200] *Ibid.* [201] See Ruse-Khan 2008, 44.

[202] See Taubman 2007, 119.

2.4.2 *Rules of international law applicable in the relations between the parties*

Art. 31(3)(c) VCLT introduced the principle of systemic integration in the general rule of interpretation of treaties,[203] according to which the interpreter of a treaty is obliged to interpret it within the larger context of the international legal system,[204] that is, in the light of "any relevant rules of international law applicable in the relations between the parties." The following passage from the Panel Report on the *EC – Biotech Products* case is helpful on this issue:

> It is important to note that Article 31(3)(c) *mandates* a treaty interpreter to take into account other rules of international law ("[t]here shall be taken into account"); *it does not merely give a treaty interpreter the option of doing so.* It is true that the obligation is to "take account" of such rules, and thus no particular outcome is prescribed. However, Article 31(1) makes clear that a treaty is to be interpreted "in good faith." Thus, where consideration of all other interpretative elements set out in Article 31 results in more than one permissible interpretation, a treaty interpreter following the instructions of Article 31(3)(c) in good faith would in our view need *to settle for that interpretation which is more in accord with other applicable rules of international law.*" (emphasis added)[205]

The expression "rules of international law" includes all the sources of public international law listed in art. 38 of the Statute of the International Court of Justice (ICJ), namely treaties, customary international law and the general principles recognized by civilized nations.

The rationale that accounts for adopting that hermeneutical principle is derived from the fact that treaties do not occur in a legal void. In view of this, the process of interpretation of the rules of a treaty must take into account all the rules of international law related to the subject of the treaty in need of interpretation and applicable to the relationships among the parties. The purpose pursued by the principle of systemic interpretation is to build a consistent international order,[206] in which all norms are in harmony with each other and mutually supportive.

Having said that, art. 31(3)(c) VCLT does not lead to the conclusion that the rules of international law will be preferred over the provisions of a treaty whenever there is any conflict. It merely establishes that the interpreter should choose, among the interpretative options available for an ambiguous provision, the one that best harmonizes with the rules of

203 See Koskenniemi 2006, para. 413.
204 See Sinclair 1984, 139; Yambrusic 1987, 182.
205 WTO, WT/DS291/R, WT/DS292/R, WT/DS293/R, Panel Report, para. 7.69.
206 See Koskenniemi 2006, para. 414.

international law in order to avoid unnecessary collisions. Along that line, in *Korea – Government Procurement* the Panel Report acknowledged that

> Customary international law applies generally to the economic relations between the WTO Members. Such international law applies to the extent that the WTO treaty agreements do not "contract out" from it. To put it another way, to the extent there is no conflict or inconsistency, or an expression in a covered WTO agreement that implies differently, we are of the view that the customary rules of international law apply to the WTO treaties and to the process of treaty formation under the WTO.[207]

Art. 31 (3)(c) does not clarify whether the rules of international law should be binding on all the parties to the treaty being interpreted or only on the parties in a dispute in order to be admitted into the process of interpretation. According to the understanding expressed in the report on *EC – Biotech Products*, for any rule of international law to be legitimately utilized in the process of interpretation of the TRIPS Agreement, it must be binding on *all* 153 WTO Members.[208] Certainly, such stance prevents the large majority of treaties from being used as legal aids in the process of interpretation. Nevertheless, and in contradiction with its own stance, the Panel did remark that the standpoint adopted in the case does not prevent – or authorize, either – the use of rules of international law that only bind the parties in litigation.[209]

The Panel decided to include only those rules that are binding on all WTO Members in order to prevent, among other things, the adoption of various interpretations of the same treaty, according to the identity of the litigating parties. Besides ignoring the actual wording of art. 31(3)(c), which does not use the expression "all parties,"[210] it also overlooks the fact that the VCLT itself allowed the contracting parties to the same treaty to have different rights and duties. As pointed out by Gardiner, the VCLT authorizes in certain circumstances: (i) parties to a treaty to express reservations (art. 19); (ii) two or more parties to a treaty to sign a valid agreement between them, which alters their rights and duties, without interfering in the rights and duties of others (art. 41); and (iii) some of the parties to temporarily suspend the execution of a treaty between them (art. 72).[211]

207 WTO, WT/DS163/R, Report of the Panel, para. 7.96. Along the same lines see Hestermeyer 2007, 220; Mitchell 2007, 829.

208 WTO, WT/DS291/R, WT/DS292/R, WT/DS293/R, Panel Report, paras. 7.71, 7.74, 7.68. The Panel, however, reaffirmed its power to resort to international instruments, binding on all WTO Members or otherwise, as data to contribute in the clarification of the technical terms used in the agreements covered by the WTO. In that case, international documents are merely used as "technical dictionaries."

209 *Ibid.*, para. 7.72.

210 See Frankel 2006, 421.

211 See Gardiner 2008, 265.

The Panel also grounded its stance on the meaning of the term "parties," used in art. 31(3)(c) VCLT, on the basis of the imperative of respect for the sovereign rights of States to assume obligations autonomously. Should any of the norms of the WTO system be interpreted in the light of a rule on international law that is not binding on all Members of the organization, the interpretation arrived at would impose an undue obligation on States that are not bound to abide by it.[212] This stance defies logic as it simultaneously respects the sovereign rights of some States and ignores the sovereign rights of others that, in good faith, took over international commitments that affect their rights and duties ensuing from WTO treaties. If in the process of interpretation of the WTO agreements, the organs of the DSB do not take into account the international commitments undertaken by WTO Members, many States may stop complying with vitally important duties, pledged before the international community. Such a stance will undoubtedly impact on the realization of the social objectives pursued by the WTO and will thus infringe the principle of good faith – more specifically, the principle of *pacta sunt servanda* and the doctrine of abuse of rights.

Given the intimate link between interpreting and applying a treaty and, consequently, between the principle of *pacta sunt servanda* and the general rule of interpretation of treaties, it is essential to identify two contexts in which international provisions may be interpreted: a general context, where the aim of the interpreter is to clarify the general rights and duties of the contracting parties, and the specific context of inter-state dispute. Within the general context, the interpretation selected in *EC – Biotech Products* is correct: it only admits the rules of international law that apply to all the parties to the treaty under interpretation. On the other hand, in the context of an inter-State dispute, the correct thing to do is to consider all the rules that are binding on *all* the parties in the *litigation*. Such is the interpretation that best harmonizes with the duties that ensue from the principle of *pact sunt servanda* (art. 26 VCLT) and with the fact that each State holds a whole set of rights and duties, which is valid whether it operates within or outside the field of the WTO.[213] This option also coincides with the principle *pacta tertiis nec nocent nec prosunt*, sanctioned by art. 34 VCLT, which prohibits any treaty to create rights or duties "for a third State without its consent."

Even if it is deemed correct that the interpreter of the TRIPS Agreement should only consider the rules of international law that are binding on all WTO Members, he will still have to take into account, inter

212 WTO, WTO, WT/DS291/R, WT/DS292/R, WT/DS293/R, Panel Report, para. 7.71.
213 See Koskenniemi 2006, para. 447.

alia, international customary norms and the general principles of right, acknowledged by civilized nations (general principles of law).[214]

Customary norms of international law emerge from the harmonious and repetitive practice of States, performed with a sense of legal obligation (customary norms).[215] *General principles of law*, in turn, encompass binding rules formulated in the same way in a wide range of jurisdictions, as well as those general norms (written or unwritten) that pervade and underpin national legal orders.[216] A typical example of a general principle of law is the one prohibiting unjust enrichment. This principle underpins criminal, civil, commercial and even international binding rules. By virtue of its massive presence in the legal systems of a multitude of states, these principles are recognized by international law, and may even be embedded in widely accepted international treaties.[217] The general principles of law, therefore, have a universal character.[218]

Among the customary norms of international law, there should be considered, when interpreting the general exception clauses of the TRIPS, those crystallized in the Universal Declaration of Human Rights (UDHR) – e.g. the rights to health, life, food, freedom of expression and to freely participate in the cultural life of the community. On this issue, Judge Cançado Trindade, from the International Court of Justice, affirmed, in a separate opinion, that the UDHR belongs to the domain of customary international law and, therefore, binds the whole international community:

> The Universal Declaration is widely recognized as having inspired, and paved the way for, the adoption of more than 70 human rights treaties, and as having served as a model for the enactment of numerous human rights norms in national constitutions and legislations, and helped to ground decisions of national and international courts. The Declaration has been incorporated into the domain of customary international law, much contributing to render human rights the common language of humankind.[219]

The customary norms enshrined in the UDHR are upheld by the TRIPS Agreement through its art. 8, which authorizes WTO Members to introduce exceptions to IPRs aimed at furthering legitimate social interests, and therefore, amongst others, those sheltered by the Universal Declaration.[220]

[214] *Ibid.*, para. 462. [215] Jalet 1962, 1053.
[216] See Friedmann 1963, 28 4–285; Jalet 1962, 1085.
[217] See Mitchell 2007, 801. [218] See Jalet 1962, 1044.
[219] Cançado Trindade 2010, para. 203. [220] See section 2.3.3.1 above.

Among the general principles of law, the principle of proportionality has special importance for determining the correct meaning of the general exception clauses of the TRIPS Agreement, as wisely noted by Kur and Ruse-Khan.[221] This is because, as a principle, the role of any exception to an IPR is to resolve or mitigate a conflict between, on the one hand, certain exclusive rights and, on the other, other rights of the same hierarchy, whose observance depends on facilitated access to proprietary intellectual goods, e.g. human and environmental rights. The principle of proportionality has exactly the function of preventing the abusive use of the prerogative to reduce the scope of IPRs through the establishment of exceptions.

2.4.2.1 Principle of proportionality The principle or rule of proportionality is deemed a German creation that was consolidated in the course of the nineteenth and twentieth centuries, particularly after it was acknowledged by the Federal Constitutional Court of Germany and was then spread all over the world.[222] The principle of proportionality rules that no right or legitimate interest of third parties must be restricted by a State measure – even with the purpose of promoting an equally legitimate interest – in a disproportionate, unnecessary manner.[223] This means that the State measure that restricts the rights or interests of others must: (i) be designed in a manner that it is suitable to promote the objective it pursues; (ii) be the least costly means amongst the possible means to fulfill the goal pursued, or in other words, the measure must be the least restrictive of the legitimate rights of others; and (iii) the measure must create social benefits that surpass the prejudice caused to the rights of others.[224] Briefly, the normative content of the principle of proportionality is the proportionality test examined above.[225]

The principle of proportionality is acknowledged universally, though not always expressly.[226] Beyond doubt, it has the status of a general principle of international law. At the domestic level, the principle of proportionality is recognized by courts of countries within the civil law system (e.g. Germany, Brazil, France) and within the common law system

221 Kur 2008; Ruse-Khan 2008.
222 See Hilf and Puth 2002, 4.
223 See Hilf and Goetz 2003, 18.
224 See, e.g., Hilf and Goetz 2003, 20; Kolb 2006, 8; ruling rendered by the Supreme Court of Israel in the case *Beit Sourik Village Council* v. *The Government of Israel*, paras. 40–41.
225 See section 2.3.3.2.1 above.
226 See, e.g., Andenas and Zleptnig 2007; Franck 2008; Hilf and Puth 2002; Sweet and Mathews 2008.

(e.g. South Africa, Canada, USA[227]),[228] as a tool, for instance, for resolving conflicts between fundamental rights and other rights of equal hierarchy and also for determining the type and the duration of criminal sanctions, depending on the severity of the crimes committed.[229]

In the international sphere, to date, it has been acknowledged by the European Court of Justice,[230] the European Court of Human Rights,[231] the Inter-American system of protection of human rights[232] and by the

[227] Besides being a contracting party to international agreements that enshrine the principle of proportionality, the US also applies it in the domestic sphere. On the application of the principle of proportionality by US courts see Cohen-Eliya and Porat 2009, 377–378, 399–405 (the authors cite, among other things, the dissenting opinion of Justice Breyer, in *District of Columbia* v. *Heller*, a ruling by the US Supreme Court in 2008). Still on the recognition of the principle of proportionality by US courts, it is interesting to note the judgment of Justice Panelli, of the California Supreme Court, in *John Moore* v. *The Regents of the University of California*. In the dispute, John Moore claimed, among other things, the recognition of his right of ownership over his biological materials and products derived therefrom, extracted by Dr. Golde of the University of California at Los Angeles (UCLA) without his express consent, to carry out scientific and commercial activities. When assessing the appropriateness of upholding Moore's claims, Justice Panelli had recourse to the proportionality test. According to his understanding, the recognition of property rights over biological materials would harm the scientific freedom so far enjoyed by the nascent biotechnology industry and, accordingly, society as a whole. The reversible benefits in favor of Moore would be unable to justify such interference. Justice Panelli concluded that holding Dr. Golde liable for failing to obtain the prior and informed consent from Moore was enough to safeguard the economic interests of the plaintiff without harming the progress of the biotechnology industry. In other words, among the measures available to safeguard Moore's economic interests, the judge chose the one which: (i) appeared capable of protecting the plaintiff's economic interests; (ii) seemed the least onerous to the interests of the business and scientific sectors and (iii) produced overall social benefits that outweighed the harms inflicted on society and the plaintiff.

[228] See, e.g., Sweet and Mathews 2008; Cohen-Eliya and Porat (2009, 380–381) cite court rulings and references that attest to the recognition of this principle by the courts of Brazil, South Korea, Ireland, South Africa, Israel, Australia and New Zealand.

[229] See Pereira 2006, 148–154.

[230] The principle of proportionality is acknowledged as a principle of European Community law. See, e.g., ECJ, *Internationale Handelsgesellschaft mbH* v. *Einfuhr- und Vorratsstelle für Getreide und Futtermittel* (Case 11–70); ECJ, *United Kingdom of Great Britain and Northern Ireland* v. *Commission of the European Communities* (Case C- 180–96).

[231] See, e.g., ECtHR, Case *Relating to Certain Aspects of the Laws on the Use of Languages in Education in Belgium* v. *Belgium*; *Case of the Sunday Times* v. *The United Kingdom*, 1979, paras. 59 and 62; ECtHR, *Affaire Orban et autres* c. *France* 2009, para. 44.

[232] The two bodies that compose the Inter-American system of human rights are the Inter-American Court of Human Rights (ICHR) and the Inter-American Commission on Human Rights. On the acknowledgement of the principle of proportionality by these two organs see, e.g., Corte Interamericana de Derechos Humanos, Opinión Consultiva OC-5/85 del 13 de noviembre de 1985, paras. 30–45; id., *Herrera Ulloa* v. *Costa Rica*, paras. 120–129; id., *Saramaka People* v. *Suriname*, para. 127; Inter-American Commission on Human Rights, Case 11.204, *Statehood Solidarity Committee* v. *United States*, para. 93; id., Case 12.553, *Jorge, José and Dante Peirano Basso* v. *Eastern Republic of Uruguay*, para. 109; id., Case 10.506, *Ms. X* v. *Argentina*, paras. 6 9–72, 92;

International Centre for the Settlement of Investment Disputes of the World Bank.[233] Additionally, the principle of proportionality is the principle that controls the legitimacy of: restrictions to the rights recognized by the ICCPR and the ICESCR;[234] the use of military forces by States in their exercise of the right to self-defense (*jus ad bellum*);[235] the use of weapons in international armed conflicts (*jus in bello*);[236] the use of non-military countermeasures applied by harmed States against States that applied illegal measures.[237]

In the WTO sphere, the principle of proportionality has been recognized explicitly and tacitly.[238] In *US – Cotton Yarn*, the Appellate Body explicitly acknowledged the principle of proportionality within the context of the application of countermeasures taken by WTO Members aggrieved by the acts/omissions of another Member of the organization that breach the terms of any one of the covered agreements of the WTO.[239]

Still in the context of the WTO, the Agreement on Technical Barriers to Trade (TBT) clearly sets the proportionality test as a tool to control the legitimacy of the measures that impose technical obstacles to international trade (art. 2(2), (3) and (5)).[240] Measures that create technical obstacles will be legitimate if: (i) they are necessary to achieve legitimate objectives, mentioned in the agreement, e.g. protection of public health, animal life or the environment; (ii) they are grounded on scientific data that justify their adoption; (iii) they are not more trade-restrictive than necessary to fulfill the objectives pursued; and (iv) they are proportionate, i.e. the proponent State must weigh and balance the potential risks of not enacting the measure and its detrimental effect on trade.

id., Case 11.625, María Eugenia Morales de Sierra *v.* Guatemala, para. 31. I thank Lilly Ching-Soto for drawing my attention to these cases.

233 ICSID numbers 144 contracting States: it includes industrialized and developing countries, countries within the civil law system and countries within the common law system. On the acknowledgement of the principle of proportionality in recent jurisprudence of ICSID, see Xiuli 2007; Kingsbury and Schill 2009 (The proportionality test is used by the ICSID in disputes involving conflicts between public interests – promoted by the policies of the contracting States – and the interests of investors to receive "a fair and equitable treatment" and not to have their property indirectly expropriated.)

234 See art. 4(1), ICCIPR and art. 4, ICESCR; Franck 2008, 758–759.

235 See Franck 2008, 720–721. 236 *Ibid.*

237 See Franck 2008, 738; Andenas and Zleptnig 2007, 399–400. On this issue, art. 51 of the "Draft articles on Responsibility of States for internationally wrongful acts" (International Law Commission 2001) states: "Countermeasures must be commensurate with the injury suffered, taking into account the gravity of the internationally wrongful act and the rights in question."

238 See, e.g., Hilf 2001; Hilf and Goetz 2003; Hilf and Puth 2002; Ruse-Khan 2008.

239 See WTO, WT/DS192/AB/R, para. 120; art. 22(4) and (7) DSU.

240 See WTO, S/WPDR/W/27.

Finally, under art. XX of GATT 1994 and art. XIV of the GATS, the WTO *tacitly* admitted the existence of the principle of proportionality, when it constructs the meaning of the necessity standard, included in these exception clauses, as a full-fledged test of proportionality.[241] The transformation of the necessity standard into a test of proportionality was the means devised by the WTO to comply with the principles of effectiveness and doctrine of abuse of rights through the highest possible realization of the various WTO objectives and the preservation of the ability offered to WTO Members to exercise their prerogative to devise exceptions to free trade with the purpose of realizing legitimate interests. Any other interpretation of the term "necessary" would automatically place one set of interests over another, and such interpretation does not comply with either the words or the spirit of the Marrakesh Agreement, nor the principle of good faith.

The principle of proportionality is an essential tool to guarantee faithful compliance with the principle of effectiveness in the interpretation of treaties, when the provision to be interpreted is an exception clause that paves the way for the realization of certain treaty objectives (e.g., health, environmental protection) while prejudicing others (commercial interests), both sets of objectives enjoying the same hierarchical rung. In the absence of the principle of proportionality, a WTO Member might adopt excessively broad exceptions, aimed at promoting social and environmental interests in ways that render the rights conferred by intellectual property completely valueless; alternatively, the scope for adopting exceptions might be understood as insignificant in order to protect the commercial interests of the holders of IPRs, even if detrimental to vital interests of society. It would then be quite difficult, if not impossible, to devise balanced exceptions that could pave the way for the realization of all the aims pursued by the WTO system, because the interpreter might arbitrarily give preference to the realization of a particular interest over all the others that the organization pursues. As a result, some of the objectives of the Marrakesh Agreement would become a dead letter.

The principle of proportionality proves equally crucial in checking whether the exercise of a given right that interferes with the exercise of another right of equal hierarchy qualifies as an abuse of rights. As opposed to the clauses concerned with national treatment and most-favored nation, the principle of proportionality stresses the relevance of the values protected by the measure. Even if a measure grants equal treatment to nationals and foreigners, it can still prove abusive.[242]

[241] See section 2.3.3.2.1 above. [242] See Xiuli 2007, 638–639.

The normal exercise of a right may cause prejudice to others insofar as it restricts the space where they can exercise their own rights. It would be acceptable if protected by the law; however, if prejudice is disproportionate, there is an abuse of rights. If application of the principle of proportionality demonstrates that a given exception protects an insignificant social interest, which causes social prejudice that supersedes its benefits, the State proposing the measure will be abusing its rights as it fails to comply with the social function of the prerogative provided by the legal order.[243] The principle of proportionality therefore serves to effectively apply the principle that forbids abuse of rights by ensuring a balance between conflicting rights, when it is not possible to avoid their clash. This function serves to indicate that the principle of proportionality is a corollary of the doctrine of abuse of rights. In this sense, Cheng notes that the function of the doctrine of abuse of rights is to draw the limits of conflicting rights, in order to strike a balance between them. That is precisely the function of the principle of proportionality:

The reasonable and bona fide exercise of a right implies an exercise which is genuinely in pursuit of those interests which the right is destined to protect and which is not calculated to cause any unfair prejudice to the legitimate interests of another State, whether these interests be secured by treaty or by general international law . . . The exact line dividing the right from the obligation, or, in other words, the line delimiting the rights of both parties is traced at a point where there is a reasonable *balance between the conflicting interests involved.* This becomes the limit between the right and obligation, and constitutes, in effect, the limit between the respective rights of the parties. The protection of the law extends as far as this limit, which is the more often undefined save by the principle of good faith. Any violation of this limit constitutes an abuse of right and a breach of the obligation – an unlawful act. In this way, the principle of good faith, by recognizing their interdependence, harmonises *the rights and obligations of every person, as well as all the rights and obligations within the legal order as a whole.*[244] (emphasis added)

[243] According to Cohen-Eliya and Porat (2009, 400–401) in the US, the proportionality test is used as a tool to verify whether the State practiced an abuse, in the form of a misuse of power, that is, it is employed to clarify whether the state adopted a measure with a purpose not authorized by law. If the application of the sub-tests of suitability and necessity indicate, respectively, that there is no rational relationship between the contested measure and the goal it should promote, and that the measure adopted is more costly to the right affected than required to achieve the goal pursued thereby, then there is an abuse of rights. There will also be an abuse of rights when the measure adopted pursues an interest of minimal social value in comparison to the interest affected thereby. This result indicates that the state measure is abusive, because it pursues, in actual fact, a purpose not authorized by law.

[244] Cheng 1953, 131–132.

The fact that the principle of proportionality has to be considered in the process of determining the meaning of the general exception clauses of TRIPS confirms the soundness of the proposed interpretation for the necessity standard enshrined in art. 8 TRIPS: even if the interpreter rejects the case law related to art. XX GATT 1994 as an aid to clarify the meaning of the necessity standard of art. 8, the principle of proportionality – in its condition as general principle of law – should be taken into account in the process of ascertaining its meaning and therefore the meaning of the terms of the general exception clauses of TRIPS.

2.5 Supplementary means of interpretation

Once the process of interpretation – done in accordance with the general rule of interpretation of the Vienna Convention – is completed, the interpreter *may* resort "to supplementary means of interpretation . . . in order to confirm the meaning resulting from the application of article 31, or to determine the meaning when the interpretation according to article 31: (a) leaves the meaning ambiguous or obscure; or (b) leads to a result which is manifestly absurd or unreasonable." This means the interpreter is not obliged to resort to supplementary means of interpretation but he can do so to confirm the accuracy of the interpretation arrived at by applying the general rule of interpretation of the VCLT or to amend the interpretation he devised, if it is ambiguous, obscure, absurd or unreasonable. If the interpretation worked out solves potential ambiguities and, additionally, is reasonable, the process of interpretation is over.[245] Although it is not mandatory, the fact is that when a court interprets a provision of a treaty, it very frequently goes through all the aspects mentioned in the general rule of interpretation (art. 31) as well as applying the supplementary means of interpretation (art. 32).

Art. 32 VCLT does not constitute an exhaustive list of the supplementary means of interpretation; it only includes the most common, namely the preparatory work of the treaty and the circumstances of its conclusion.[246] The category of preparatory work includes the successive drafts of the treaty under consideration, drawn up in the course of negotiations, the registry of the debates that led to the conclusion of negotiations and declarations by the president of the negotiating committee, not contested by the negotiating parties.[247] The fact that art. 32 VCLT authorizes the use of the preparatory work as a supplementary means of interpretation does not necessarily mean it will always prove useful. It

[245] See Gardiner 2008, 329. [246] *Ibid.*, 302.
[247] See Bederman 2001, 194; Aust 2000, 198.

must be used with care as it may fail to offer solid information to clarify the meaning of a term or of an ambiguous provision.[248] If preparatory work is to prove useful for the process of interpretation it should show unequivocally the *common* will of all negotiating parties and not merely the will of one or more parties as to the meaning of a given provision.

As far as the general exception clauses of the TRIPS Agreement are concerned, the preparatory work related to the negotiation of arts. 13, 17, 26(2) and 30, notably the minutes of the TRIPS agreement debated during the GATT Uruguay Round has not served to clarify the correct meaning of terms.[249] However, the records of the Revision Conference on the Berne Convention for the Protection of Literary and Artistic Works seem useful to confirm or clarify the meaning of the terms of art. 9(2) BC and art. 13 TRIPS, because of the similarity of the wording of these provisions.

The circumstances that surround the conclusion of a treaty denote the historical context where negotiations took place and the motives which led to its conclusion.[250] Preparatory work, other historical evidence, the objectives of the treaty consigned in its preamble can witness the historical circumstances that motivated its negotiations.[251] Depending on the treaty, there may be an overlap between the circumstances that prevailed in its negotiation and conclusion, the preparatory work and the objectives of the treaty.[252] Such is the case with the TRIPS Agreement: the circumstances that prevailed in its negotiations and the motives for its conclusion are stated in the preamble and in art. 7 – namely, to foster investment in innovation, restrict commercial distortions and strengthen free trade of protected intellectual production.

Another frequently used supplementary means of interpretation are the canons of interpretation. Among the canons of interpretation, the principle *in dubio mitius* proves of particular importance in the process of interpretation of the general exception clauses of the TRIPS Agreement. According to the WTO Appellate Body in *EC – Hormones*, the principle *in dubio mitius*

> applies in interpreting treaties, in deference to the sovereignty of States. If the meaning of a term is ambiguous, that meaning is to be preferred which is less onerous to the party assuming an obligation, or which interferes less with the territorial and personal supremacy of a party, or involves less general restrictions upon the parties.[253]

[248] See International Law Commission 1966, 220.
[249] See Gervais 1998, 88–91, 112–113, 141–144, 158–159.
[250] See Gardiner 2008, 350. [251] See Sinclair 1984, 141.
[252] See Gardiner 2008, 344.
[253] WTO, WT/DS26/AB/R, Appellate Body Report, para. 165, footnote 154.

The purpose of the principle *in dubio mitius* is to protect the sovereignty of States in the face of obligations not clearly agreed to, by choosing the least costly alternative interpretation for the party who takes on an obligation or, *a contrario sensu*, the least advantageous interpretation for the benefitted party.[254] Naturally, States are free to limit their sovereignty through treaties. Nevertheless, when the provisions of a treaty are ambiguous on the subject of the scope of the rights and duties imposed on the contracting parties, its terms must be interpreted in ways that will cause the least possible prejudice to the sovereignty of the States that undertake obligations.[255] As with any interpretative principle, however, it is limited by the text of the treaty itself; the interpreter must not contradict it. In other words, the interpreter "cannot lightly assume that sovereign states intended to impose upon themselves the more onerous, rather than the less burdensome, obligation" when the words of the treaty are not clear on the subject.[256]

[254] Lauterpacht 1949, 59. [255] *Ibid.*, 58.
[256] WTO, WT/DS26/AB/R, Appellate Body Report, para. 165.

3 Determining the normative meaning of arts. 17, 26(2) and 30 of the TRIPS Agreement

3.1 Introduction

The present chapter proposes to investigate the correct normative meaning of arts. 17, 26(2) and 30 of the TRIPS Agreement. Article 30 – the three-step test vested in the competence of assessing the legality of the exceptions to patent rights – is the first provision to have its normative meaning investigated under the rules of treaty interpretation of the VCLT. Since the terms of this provision have already been interpreted by a WTO panel in *Canada – Pharmaceutical Patents*, the interpretation proposed in that dispute will be the starting point of the investigation. Then the terms of art. 30 will be reinterpreted in light of the interpretation rules codified by the VCLT, because, in this author's view, the Panel did not correctly apply the customary rules of treaty interpretation and therefore, to a large extent, the proposed interpretation for the terms of art. 30 is not legally valid. Once one is able to clarify the correct meaning of the terms of art. 30, then, after some adjustments, one can identify the correct meaning of arts. 17 and 26(2), provided their wording is substantially similar to the text of the three-step patent law test.

3.2 Art. 30 TRIPS according to *Canada – Pharmaceutical Patents*

In *Canada – Pharmaceutical Patents*, the EC asked the WTO DSB to initiate a panel vested in the competence of investigating the lawfulness of two patent exceptions established by the Canadian Patent Act. One of the exceptions examined in connection with the TRIPS Agreement is known as the Bolar exception or regulatory review exception, that allows producers of generic drugs, during the period of validity of the patent, to make all the necessary industrial and technical arrangements in order to obtain permission for market generics. This means that pharmaceutical companies are authorized to hire third parties to produce the active principles of the drugs they plan to market and, using that material, to prepare the various formulae of the drugs; to carry out tests of bioavailability, bioequivalence and safety, in order to assess whether the generic drugs will have the same therapeutic effects as the original drug. In many jurisdictions, that dossier is a necessary condition to obtain the generics' marketing authorization. As the process to obtain a marketing authorization may take an average of two and a half years, the Canadian legal framework allows generic companies to begin the process during the period of validity of the patents that cover the drugs.

The second exception challenged by the EC is called the stockpiling exception. This exception allows companies that have obtained a marketing permission for generic drugs (i.e., those that resort to the Bolar exception) to produce and stockpile generic products during the last six months of validity of the patent that covers the product in question, provided they are not placed on the market prior to expiry of the patent.

The purpose of both exceptions is identical: to prevent the undue extension of the term of protection of patents covering pharmaceutical products beyond the 20 years established by law and to introduce competition in the pharmaceutical market immediately after the expiration of the patent.

The Panel Report embraced an interpretation that restricted the leeway available for WTO Member States to adopt exceptions to patent rights. According to the Panel, only the Bolar exception would be legal, even if canceling the stockpiling exception might cause an extension of the term of protection of patents for pharmaceutical products beyond that established by law.

In what follows the question is addressed of how the WTO has interpreted each of the three conditions laid down by Art. 30 TRIPS, which need to be met by any exception to patent rights.

3.2.1 The first step of the test of art. 30

The first step of the test of art. 30 TRIPS provides that the exceptions to patent rights must be "limited." Canada held that the term "limited exceptions" should be interpreted as meaning exceptions "confined within definite limits"; alternatively, the notion might be understood as exceptions "restricted in scope, extent, amount."[1] The EC, on the other hand, argued that the term should denote exceptions with "narrow, small, minor, insignificant or restricted" impact on the rights granted to patent owners.[2]

[1] WTO, WT/DS114/R, Panel Report, para. 7.27. [2] *Ibid.*, para. 7.28.

The Panel acknowledged that both the interpretations suggested by Canada and the European Community were possible, but chose that proposed by the latter, in the sense that "limited exceptions" should be read as exceptions that have a minimum impact on patent rights, listed in Art. 28 of the TRIPS Agreement:

> [T]he words "limited exception" express a requirement that the exception make only a narrow curtailment of the legal rights which Article 28.1 requires to be granted to patent owners, and that the measure of that curtailment was the extent to which the affected legal rights themselves had been impaired.[3]

In other words, the report held that the purpose of the first step of the test was to assess the scope of the restriction of patent rights engendered by the exception. With that end in mind, the Panel identified which of the patent rights would be affected by the exception under scrutiny. It then determined the level of impairment of the rights affected. If the exception produced more than a "small impairment" in the scope of the rights involved, it would not qualify as "limited." This means that, according to the reading of the Panel, it is not enough to identify the *number* of rights affected by the exception; it is also necessary to examine the *level* of the impairment caused to those rights. Consequently, an exception impacting on all the rights granted by a patent, as long as it impairs the scope of these rights in an insignificant manner, would qualify as "limited."[4] No doubt there must be few cases when exceptions manage to promote a socially relevant interest through insignificant restrictions on the rights of patent holders.

The report established very clearly that, in the first step of the test, there should be no assessment of the economic effects of the exception under scrutiny: the impact may only be assessed in the later steps.[5] Despite that, in actual practice, the Panel did not follow its own conclusions. When it assessed whether the stockpiling exception should be seen as a limited exception, the Panel insisted on adopting an interpretation that retained the possibility for patent owners to obtain economic profits from their innovations, in the widest possible way. For instance, in its assessment of whether the time-limit for the application of the stockpiling exception ruled by Canadian legislation would imply a limiting feature for the exception, the Panel concluded it did not, since the exception would substantially interfere with the right to exclude third parties from the use of the innovation during a commercially significant period of time (in this case, six months).[6]

[3] *Ibid.*, para. 7.44.
[4] *Ibid.*, para. 7.32.
[5] *Ibid.*, para. 7.31.
[6] *Ibid.*, para. 7.37.

Furthermore, the Panel even went to the point of defending the inclusion of the right to exploit, exclusively, the patented subject matter for a "more or less brief" period after the expiration of the patent, i.e. the patent owner enjoys a term of protection longer than that explicitly secured:

> the Panel also considered whether the market advantage gained by the patent owner in the months after expiration of the patent could also be considered a purpose of the patent owner's rights to exclude "making" and "using" during the term of the patent. In both theory and practice, the Panel concluded that such *additional market benefits* were within the purpose of these rights . . . In practical terms, it must be recognized that enforcement of the right to exclude "making" and "using" during the patent term will necessarily give all patent owners, for all products, a short period of extended market exclusivity after the patent expires. The repeated enactment of such exclusionary rights with knowledge of their universal market effects can only be understood as an affirmation of the purpose to produce those *market effects*.[7] (emphasis added)

Upon trying to work on the definition of "limited exception" proposed by the Panel, WTO Members face the difficulty caused by the lack of an "absolute quantitative limitation" to be observed by exceptions in order to qualify as "limited."[8]

As the three-step test is built on three cumulative steps, if the exception under scrutiny does not comply successfully with the first step, it is automatically rejected. The consequence of adopting such a restrictive definition of "limited exception" is that it significantly curtails the freedom of WTO Member States to adopt exceptions to the rights conferred by patents, although they were originally envisaged for the protection of relevant social interests. If the interpretation of the Panel is correct, exceptions will rarely attain the second step of the test.

3.2.2 The second step of the test of art. 30

The second step of the test of art. 30 TRIPS provides that exceptions to the exclusive rights conferred by patents shall not unreasonably conflict with the normal exploitation of patents. In the second step of the test, the Panel focused on an analysis of the expression "normal exploitation" of patents, while neglecting to clarify the notion of an "unreasonable conflict with the normal exploitation of patents." In the understanding of the Panel, the "normal exploitation" of a patent includes all the means of patent exploitation, usually employed by patent owners, for it to operate

[7] *Ibid.*, para. 7.35. [8] See Kur 2008, 24.

as an economic incentive to innovation.[9] The report of the Panel stated that the meaning of "normal exploitation" of a patent is dynamic; it changes as new markets unfold and new technologies are used that result in a feasible exploitation of innovations within unexpected contexts.[10]

Not all economic profit derived from exercising the rights granted by the patent must be seen as resulting from a "normal exploitation" of the patent. Only profits derived from the usual application of patents, customarily employed by *all* or *most* patent holders, should qualify as "normal."[11]

On the basis of that understanding, the Panel judged that the "more or less brief" period of exclusive rights in the market granted to patent owners was "normal." It follows after expiration of the patent, since competitors usually need some time to organize their production lines before they can place the – until then protected – product in the market.[12] This means that the patent will grant its owner exclusive rights for the period of time actually specified by law and also for an additional period "more or less brief." In the opinion of the Panel that additional period, not established by law or international treaties, should be granted to patent owners as it derives from the common practice of excluding third parties from the production of patented objects:[13]

> Some of the basic rights granted to all patent owners, and routinely exercised by *all patent owners*, will typically produce a certain period of market exclusivity after the expiration of a patent. For example, the separate right to prevent "making" the patented product during the term of the patent often prevents competitors from building an inventory needed to enter the market immediately upon expiration of a patent. There is nothing abnormal about that more or less brief period of market exclusivity after the patent has expired. (emphasis added)

Fortunately, the additional long period of protection granted to owners of patents on pharmaceutical products, in the absence of a Bolar exception, was judged as abnormal by the Panel. If the Bolar exception were deemed illegal, patent owners would enjoy a long additional term of protection for their inventions since their competitors would take around two and a half years to obtain a marketing permit from health authorities. The Panel stated that such extension of the period of patent protection was not normal as it ensued from the association between patent rights rules and the requirements established by the norms that govern the commercialization of pharmaceutical products:[14]

[9] WTO, WT/DS114/R, Panel Report, para. 7.55. [10] *Ibid.*, para. 7.55.
[11] *Ibid.*, para. 7.58. [12] *Ibid.*, para. 7.56. [13] *Ibid.*, para. 7.56.
[14] *Ibid.*, para. 7.57.

The Panel considered that Canada was on firmer ground, however, in arguing that the additional period of de facto market exclusivity created by using patent rights to preclude submissions for regulatory authorization should not be considered "normal." The additional period of market exclusivity in this situation is not a natural or normal consequence of enforcing patent rights. It is an *unintended consequence* of the conjunction of the patent laws with product regulatory laws, where the combination of patent rights with the time demands of the regulatory process gives a greater than normal period of market exclusivity to the enforcement of certain patent rights. It is likewise a form of exploitation that *most patent owners* do not in fact employ. (emphasis added)

In view of the fact that art. 33 of TRIPS states that "the validity of a patent shall not be shorter than a 20-year period, counted as from the date of filing," it is not permissible to hold that patent owners enjoy a twenty-year period of protection and, cumulatively, an additional "more or less brief" period of protection. This provision allows WTO Members to grant to patent holders a term of protection longer than twenty years, but in this case, the actual term of protection shall be indicated unequivocally. In terms of the Panel interpretation, it is impossible to determine with certitude the duration of patents. Consequently, it introduces an instability factor that benefits patent owners: how is "more or less brief" determined? After two decades, any increase in the term of protection of a patent may be a long period for the market and for the consumer, subject to the existing competition and the prices set by the patent holder.

3.2.3 The third step of the test of art. 30

The third and last step of the test of art. 30 of TRIPS provides that the exceptions to the rights conferred by patents shall not "unreasonably prejudice the legitimate interests of the patent owner, taking account of the legitimate interests of third parties." At this point, the Panel focused on an analysis of the terms "legitimate interests" and left aside the definition of an "unreasonable" prejudice. Both Canada and the European Community held that "legitimate interests" were those protected by law.[15] The Panel disagreed and posited that "'legitimate interests' must be defined in the way that it is often used in legal discourse – as a normative claim calling for the protection of interests that are 'justifiable' in the sense that they are supported by the relevant public policies or other social norms."[16]

[15] *Ibid.*, paras. 7.66–7.67. [16] *Ibid.*, para. 7.69.

In order to establish if an interest is "legitimate" it is also necessary to prove that it is "compelling or widely acknowledged by the international community."[17] Evidence may be submitted through documents of intergovernmental organizations, resolutions of UN bodies, scientific studies etc. Should the opinion of the international community be clearly divided as to its importance, the interest may not be legitimate.

3.2.4 *Obstacles created by* Canada – Pharmaceutical Patents

Briefly, the Panel ruled that the words in art. 30 of the TRIPS Agreement are to be interpreted in a restrictive fashion. Its aim was to maximize the opportunities of right holders to cash in the social benefits produced by the protected innovations, even to the detriment of crucial social interests, such as the right to health or free competition. The political leeway left for creating exceptions to exclusive rights is minimal: only those that impact on fields that patent holders find irrelevant in financial terms will classify as legitimate.[18] It is worth noting that even the Panel Report acknowledges that the terms in art. 30 must be interpreted under the light of the goals of the TRIPS Agreement established, inter alia, in its arts. 7 and 8.[19] Despite that, the Panel interpreted the terms of the document as if the TRIPS Agreement focused exclusively on commercial goals.

Opting for this interpretation is a mistake: the preamble of the Marrakesh Agreement that established the World Trade Organization (Marrakesh Agreement) and art. 7 of the TRIPS Agreement provide that commercial, social and environmental values share the same ranking in the hierarchy of the WTO values. Consequently, automatically setting commercial interests above social ones in the process of interpreting the TRIPS Agreement runs counter to the very goals of the WTO system. The approach chosen by the Panel would only be justifiable if the exceptions it challenged protected *purely* commercial interests, namely, interests with the same or similar value-status as those that were limited.[20]

The biased approach that favors the protection of commercial interests, posited by the Panel, prevents WTO Members from adopting more ambitious exceptions with the purpose of promoting its cultural, scientific and economic development[21] and appeasing or at least mitigating the problems created by patents for socio-economic progress and the preservation of the environment. In the absence of an alternative interpretation of the contents of art. 30, soundly based on the pillars of the

[17] *Ibid.*, para. 7.82. [18] See Kur 2008, 31. [19] WTO, WT/DS114/R, para. 7.26.
[20] See Hilf and Goetz 2003, 35–36. [21] See Kur and Ruse-Khan 2009, p. 8.

legal system of the WTO, Members of the organization can only follow the guidelines established by the Panel.

The complexities of art. 30 compounded by the unbalanced decision in *Canada – Pharmaceutical Patents* created doubts as to the exceptions that might be legitimately adopted. These doubts deepened the challenge to establish genuinely balanced and socially responsible patent protection systems. So much so that the World Intellectual Property Organization (WIPO) – spurred by the demands of developing countries – is currently in the process of tackling the issue in more concrete terms: in 2010, the Standing Committee on the Law of Patents (SCLP) published the findings of a research project, coordinated by Lionel Bently, which investigated the exclusions and exceptions to patent rights, often incorporated into national legal systems to resolve conflicts between the rights of patent holders and pressing societal interests.[22] Also in 2010, during the 14th meeting of the SCLP, Brazil voiced its concern about the difficulties faced by developing countries in the use of the leeway afforded by the TRIPS Agreement to establish exceptions to patent rights in order to promote their own socio-economic development,[23] and recommended the SCLP to establish a broad working program which should provide, amongst other products, a handbook with models of patent exceptions that Members of the organization might include in their legal frameworks.[24]

In order to have certainty about the mandatory character of the interpretations endorsed by the Panel for the terms of art. 30, it is necessary to investigate whether they were built strictly following the rules of treaty interpretation codified by the VCLT. The following sections will examine the correct normative meaning of art. 30, through the strict observance of the interpretation rules of the VCLT. Only then can one make any statement regarding the actual space available to WTO Members to establish robust exceptions to patent rights.

3.3 Reframing the meaning of art. 30 in the light of the treaty interpretation rules of the VCLT

3.3.1 The first step of the test

The first condition set by the test in art. 30 of TRIPS is that the exceptions to exclusive rights conferred by patents are "limited." The term "limited" is likely to raise doubts as to its meaning.

[22] See Bently 2010; Sherman 2010; Barbosa and Grau-Kuntz 2010; Visser 2010; Basheer et al. 2010; Gold and Joly 2010.

[23] WIPO, SCP/14/7, paras. 21–23.

[24] *Ibid.*, para. 27.

The *American Heritage Dictionary of the English Language* provides the following definition of the term: "Confined or restricted within certain limits."[25] The *Compact Oxford English Dictionary* defines the adjective as "restricted in size, amount, or extent; few, small, or short."[26] Among the common meanings attributable to "limited," "confined within certain limits" is the one that best corresponds to the objectives of the WTO, the objectives and principles of TRIPS and the principles of good faith and proportionality. The "certain limits" that constrain the exceptions are the legitimate goals that they may pursue and the minimum obligations of TRIPS that exceptions must comply with. Specifically, this means that an exception to the patent rights listed in art. 28(1) TRIPS will be "limited" if it complies with two requirements:

(1) It pursues a legitimate objective, authorized by art. 8 of the TRIPS Agreement. In order to make sure that it actually pursues an authorized objective it is crucial to assess the general "design and structure" of the exception under analysis as well as its effects.[27] The exception will only qualify as preliminarily limited if it proves to have suitable scope for the realization of the objective pursued. Should the analysis of the suitability of the exception to realize legitimate objectives not be included in the assessment of its "limited" character, a State could rhetorically adduce that a challenged exception pursues an authorized objective insofar as, in actual practice, it is structured to promote an interest that is forbidden by the WTO system.
(2) It only explores the space authorized by the TRIPS Agreement, i.e. the exception does not infringe the minimum obligations set thereby: the clauses on national and most-favored-nation treatment; the prohibition on adopting exceptions that deliver the actual effect of preventing the patenting of the categories of inventions that, pursuant to art. 27 of TRIPS, should be eligible for protection; respect for the area occupied by the compulsory licensing system; respect for the minimum term of protection of patents (20 years from filing); the principle of non-discrimination.

The other alternative of the ordinary meaning attributed to the adjective "limited" (restricted in size, amount or extent; few, small or short) embraces the understanding espoused by the Panel in *Canada – Pharmaceutical Patents*. It interpreted the term "limited exceptions" as synonymous to exceptions that produce a slight diminution of the rights conferred by patents.[28]

[25] Houghton Mifflin 2004. [26] Oxford University Press 2009.
[27] WTO, WT/DS58/AB/R (*US – Shrimp*), Appellate Body Report, para. 141.
[28] WTO, WT/DS114/R, Panel Report, para. 7.30.

Although, in abstract terms, the meaning espoused by the Panel is plausible, it openly violates the objectives pursued by the WTO system, the principle of effectiveness in treaty interpretation and the doctrine of abuse of rights. Accordingly, the Panel's construction is not tenable. Should the expression "limited exceptions" be read as exceptions that create *de minimis* restrictions on rights conferred by patents, WTO Members would not have enough leeway to pursue the various non-commercial objectives of the WTO and the TRIPS Agreement. This is specially so because the Panel did not state an "absolute quantitative limit" against which to assess the "limited" character of exceptions.[29] When in doubt on the meaning of "limited exceptions," WTO Members would avoid enacting more daring measures and that would spell the disappearance of the space to exercise the prerogative to establish exceptions to patent rights for the realization of vital social interests.

Additionally, the interpretation followed by the Panel implies that commercial interests – in this case, the rights granted to patent holders – would be hierarchically above the other interests pursued by the WTO and the TRIPS Agreement. Neither the preamble to the Marrakesh Agreement, nor the TRIPS Agreement or its articles 7 and 8 include any indication in that sense. So much so, that both the WTO and the TRIPS Agreement pursue objectives that would hardly be realized if potentially conflicting interests were not harmonized, e.g. sustainable development.[30] There can be no doubt that such interests would not be realized if commercial interests enjoyed, a priori, automatic preference over other non-commercial interests.

It is also important to underscore that the interpretation chosen by the Panel contradicts the understanding of the WTO Appellate Body itself as regards what does *not* constitute a "limited exception". In *US – Wool Shirts and Blouses*, the Appellate Body classified the exceptions stated in art. XX of the GATT 1994 as "limited exceptions":

> Articles XX and XI: (2)(c)(i) are *limited exceptions* from obligations under certain other provisions of the GATT 1994, not positive rules establishing obligations in themselves. They are in the nature of affirmative defences.[31] (emphasis added)

[29] Kur 2008, 24. [30] See Ruse-Khan 2008, 63–67.

[31] WTO, WT/DS33/AB/R, Appellate Body Report, 18. On the same issue, see the WTO Appellate Body Report in *US – Shrimp* (WTO, WT/DS58/AB/R, para. 157: "In our view, the language of the chapeau makes clear that each of the exceptions in paragraphs (a) to (j) of Article XX is a *limited and conditional* exception from the substantive obligations contained in the other provisions of the GATT 1994, that is to say, the ultimate availability of the exception is subject to the compliance by the invoking Member with the requirements of the chapeau."

It is well known that art. XX authorizes WTO Members to implement exceptions to the rules of the GATT 1994 that have a substantial effect on free trade – e.g. a measure that sets a total ban on trade in products containing asbestos, or a ban on imports of retreaded tyres – provided they comply with the conditions established in the chapeau and in the paragraphs of this provision. On this basis, neither a slight nor a substantial impact of the exception on patent rights can interfere with its being described as "limited."

The records connected to the negotiations on art. 30 of the TRIPS Agreement are inapt to clarify its content.[32] The draft of the TRIPS Agreement distributed in July 1990 and drawn up by Lars Annell, presents a different structure of art. 30 from the one we know.[33] Annell's version includes a list with examples of exceptions to patent rights that WTO Members might include in their national codes, e.g. non-commercial actions performed in the private sphere; actions for experimental purposes; preparations of medication prescribed in pharmacies; governmental use of patents. Besides the exceptions specifically mentioned, contracting parties to the agreement maintained the prerogative to adopt other "limited" exceptions, provided the legitimate interests of patent owners and third parties were taken into consideration. In view of the lack of consensus on the subject of exceptions that might be adopted by WTO Members, the negotiators finally chose the flexible approach of the three-step test, crystallized in art. 30 of the TRIPS Agreement.[34]

In view of the failure of the preparatory work in connection with negotiations on the TRIPS Agreement to be of use in establishing the normative meaning of art. 30 of the Agreement, in *Canada – Patent Pharmaceuticals* the Panel decided to review the preparatory work associated with the negotiations of art. 9(2) of the Berne Convention.[35] In the end, that documentation proved expendable as the text of art. 30 of the TRIPS Agreement differs from the wording of art. 9(2) BC.

3.3.2 The second step of the test

The second condition established by art. 30 is that exceptions to patent rights "do not unreasonably conflict with a normal exploitation of the patent." Let us examine some possible meanings of the terms "unreasonable," "conflict," "exploitation" and "normal."

32 See, e.g., Abbott 2002, 30–32; Gervais 1998, 158–159; UNCTAD–ICTSD 2005, 431–432; WTO, WT/DS114/R (*Canada – Pharmaceutical Patents*, para. 7.29.

33 See Abbott 2002, 30–32.

34 See UNCTAD–ICTSD 2005, 431–432.

35 WTO, WT/DS114/R, Panel Report, paras. 7.14 and 7.15.

According to the *Compact Oxford English Dictionary*, "unreasonable" may be understood as a synonym for irrational, absurd, excessive, immoderate, unacceptable, unfair.[36] The verb "conflict" is defined as to "be incompatible or at variance with."[37] The noun "exploitation" may be defined as the act of employing something productively.[38] Finally, the dictionary offers the following definitions for the adjective "normal": "conforming to a standard; usual, typical, or expected."[39]

From the perspective of the ordinary meaning attributable to its terms, the expression "normal exploitation of the patent" denotes the act of making productive use thereof, through the exercise of the legitimate means commonly used by patent holders for the purpose of earning economic benefits, which serve as economic incentives to carry out R&D activities. The means universally employed by patent holders to exploit their patents are listed in art. 28 of the TRIPS Agreement, namely: "where the subject matter of a patent is a product, to prevent third parties not having the owner's consent from the acts of: making, using, offering for sale, selling, or importing[40] for these purposes that product"; and "where the subject matter of a patent is a process, to prevent third parties not having the owner's consent from the act of using the process, and from the acts of: using, offering for sale, selling, or importing for these purposes at least the product obtained directly by that process."

There are implied limits to the exercise of the right to exclude unauthorized third parties from the enjoyment of patented subject matter. Not all forms of exploitation of patents, which prima facie seem to be backed by the exclusive rights guaranteed by art. 28 of TRIPS are legitimate and, therefore, "normal." In *Canada – Pharmaceutical Patents* the Panel excluded two means of exploitation of patents from the group of normal means of exploiting patents. First, a means of exploitation that is not usually used by all or most patent holders with a view to extracting economic benefits from their patents cannot be regarded as a normal means of exploitation.[41]

Second, there should only be included in the normal means of exploitation of patents those whose exercise is "essential to the achievement of the goals of patent policy,"[42] namely: promotion of innovation and scientific and technological progress; expansion of the stock of technical

[36] "Not guided by or based on good sense"; "beyond the limits of acceptability" (Oxford University Press 2009).
[37] *Ibid.* [38] *Ibid.* [39] *Ibid.*
[40] The right to control the importation of patented subject matter is not included in the list of means of normal exploitation of patents when the domestic legal system adopts the principle of international exhaustion of patent rights.
[41] WTO, WT/DS114/R, Panel Report, para. 7.55. [42] *Ibid.*, para. 7.58.

and scientific knowledge of humanity; and facilitating public disclosure and dissemination of new technical and scientific knowledge. In other words, if the exclusive control by patent holders of a particular form of use of inventions appears as a more appropriate way of furthering the basic objectives pursued by patent regimes than its release to the public (for free or not), the exclusive control of this form of exploitation shall be characterized as a normal means of exploitation of patents. In harmony with this understanding, Bently remarks that

> patents should only be granted where, and to the extent that, such monopolies are required to rectify market failure. And they should not be granted where to do so will in fact restrict further invention . . . Some limitation on a patentee's rights can be explained by the fact that extending protection to cover the permitted act would not enhance incentives significantly (or appropriately). This is a common explanation for exceptions relating to private use (or the corollary, the limitation of the patentee's rights to commercial, trade or business uses).[43]

In addition, there shall be added to the list of abnormal (and therefore illegal) means of exploitation of patents, those forms of exploitation that: (i) are affected by market failures[44]; and (ii) if exercised, interfere with the private sphere of third parties and with groups that are not part of the consumer market of patented inventions, e.g. philanthropic organizations conducting scientific research with humanitarian purposes.

Recalling the goal of the TRIPS Agreement that the protection and enforcement of IPRs should contribute to the diffusion of technology[45] as well as the commercial nature of IPRs, one may conclude that the exercise of the rights of exclusion in face of third parties who employ patented inventions in private non-commercial contexts and in non-commercial scientific or technological projects falls outside the scope of "normal exploitation" of patents, as the use of patented inventions in non-commercial contexts does not affect the ability of patent holders to recover the investment incurred in R&D activities.[46] If the patent holders were free to control any form of use of their inventions, relevant categories of users – e.g. philanthropic institutions, universities – which do not have sufficient resources to pay the fees set by the market, would find their freedom of scientific expression constrained to the detriment

[43] Bently 2010, 56.

[44] See, e.g., Bently (2010, 57); De Borja (2008, 507); Ginsburg (2001, 12–13).

[45] Art. 7, TRIPS. The noun "diffusion" is defined by the *Compact Oxford English Dictionary* (Oxford University Press 2009) as synonymous with "the spreading of something more widely."

[46] On this point, Bently (2010, 57) points out: "Private or non-commercial uses can, in general, be thought of as uses which are unlikely to add much, if anything, to the 'incentive' provided by the patent monopoly. At the same time, allowing patents to cover such activities would impose significant costs: most obviously, there would be the transactions costs of policing and licensing such uses."

of social progress and the achievement of the goals pursued by TRIPS and the WTO.

In accordance with the ordinary meaning attributable to its terms, the requirement that exceptions should not "unreasonably" conflict with the normal exploitation of patents denotes that exceptions should not interfere excessively with the legitimate means of exploitation of patents. In the light of the principle of good faith, the objectives of the WTO, the objectives and principles of TRIPS and the principle of proportionality, the determination of the reasonableness of the interference engendered by the exceptions in the normal means of exploitation of patents implies a sub-test of necessity.

In other words, a conflict with the normal exploitation of patents brought about by an exception shall be reasonable if the exception comprises a measure that is less restrictive of the means ordinarily used by patent holders to exploit them commercially. Consequently, an assessment of the reasonability of the conflict caused by the exception entails the following:

- identifying the degree of protection of the legitimate objectives pursued by the exception;
- making sure that the excepted use may legitimately be controlled by patent holders. This being the case, the degree of restriction of the exclusive rights conferred by patents caused by the exception shall be identified; and
- identifying alternative measures to the exception, able to promote the same objectives pursued by it, with an equal level of protection, but with a lower impact on patent rights. Alternative measures that are not reasonably available to the proponent of the exception in technical, administrative and economic terms shall not be taken into account.

3.3.3 The third step of the test

The final step of the test appraises whether the exceptions "unreasonably prejudice the legitimate interests of the patent owner, taking account of the legitimate interests of third parties." The most controversial terms used in the third step of the three-step test are: "prejudice," "legitimate" and "third parties."

According to the *Compact Oxford English Dictionary*, the verb "prejudice" may be understood as synonymous with harm through the commission of an act.[47] This sense seems appropriate to the context of art. 30 of TRIPS.

[47] Oxford University Press 2009.

"Third party" may be understood as an individual outside a relationship involving two parties, or as any individual or organization that does not participate in a relationship or situation.[48] In the context of art. 30, "third parties" must be understood as a group formed by users of patented technologies (innovators, scientists, industry) and society at large (potential and actual ordinary consumers). This understanding coincides with the objectives of the WTO and the TRIPS Agreement to foster, inter alia, the interests of society.

Also according to the *Compact Oxford English Dictionary*, the adjective "legitimate" may be understood as a synonym for legal ("conforming to the law or to rules"), justifiable or reasonable ("defended with logic or justification").[49] The expression "legitimate interests," according to its ordinary meaning, may denote advantages, needs, utilities (pecuniary or moral), shielded by law in favor of patent holders (legitimate interests of patent holders) and in favor of the users of inventions (legitimate interests of third parties). Alternatively, this expression may denote utilities that must be guaranteed to patent holders or users of patented inventions, as they are grounded by common sense.

The first meaning appears to be the more harmonious with the context of art. 30 TRIPS: as remarked by François Ost any right supposes at its base an interest or utility thereby harbored or promoted. The interests protected by rights are "legitimate interests."[50] But not all utilities are legitimate interests. There are illegitimate interests – the so-called illicit interests whose realization is punishable by law. And there are ordinary interests not secured by any legal right; thus, the practice of any action harmful to these interests does not guarantee to its victims a right to claim reparation. In summary, any right protects an interest (legitimate interest), but not every interest is guaranteed by a right.[51] This understanding has been upheld by the ICJ in the *Barcelona Traction, Light and Power Company* case:

> This again is merely a different way of presenting the distinction between injury in respect of a right and injury to a simple interest. But, as the Court has indicated, evidence that damage was suffered does not *ipso facto* justify a diplomatic claim. Persons suffer damage or harm in most varied circumstances. This in itself does not involve the obligation to make reparation. Not a mere interest affected, but solely a right infringed involves responsibility, so that an act directed against and infringing only the company's rights does not involve responsibility towards the shareholders, even if their interests are affected.[52]

[48] *Ibid.* [49] *Ibid.* [50] Ost 1990, 36–37. [51] *Ibid.*
[52] ICJ, *Barcelona Traction, Light and Power Company, Limited* (Belgium v. Spain), para. 46.

The legitimate interest of patent holders, which should be considered under the third step of the test, is the preservation of the economic incentives for innovation, i.e. the right to extract the maximum economic benefits from their inventions through the exercise of the normal means of exploitation of their patents with the purpose of recovering the investments incurred. In the category of legitimate interests of third parties should be included, in particular, those interests safeguarded by international human rights instruments and MEAs,[53] such as the facilitation of access to knowledge, the expansion of the freedom of scientific expression and the strengthening of free competition in order to reduce the cost of goods and services and thereby increase their availability to the impoverished sectors of society.

The adverb "unreasonably" is equivalent to "excessively" or "immoderate." The literal meaning of this term does not assist in removing doubts about its legal content. Having said that, in the light of the principle of good faith and the objectives of the TRIPS Agreement, "unreasonable" must be interpreted as disproportionate, in accordance with the meaning given by the sub-test of proportionality *stricto sensu*. This interpretation is confirmed by the fact that the third step of the test expressly requires that the assessment of "reasonability" of the prejudices impinging on the legitimate interests of patent holders be done in the light of the interests of third parties favored by the exception under scrutiny. Along the same lines, in *Canada – Pharmaceutical Patents*, the Panel seems to acknowledge, albeit subtly, that the third step of the test in art. 30 encompasses a comparative assessment between the weight of the legitimate interests of patent holders that are harmed and the weight of the legitimate interests of third parties promoted by the exception:

> One cannot demonstrate that no legitimate interest of the patent owner has been prejudiced until one knows what claims of legitimate interest can be made. Likewise, the *weight* of legitimate third party interests cannot be fully appraised until the legitimacy and *weight* of the patent owner's legitimate interests, if any, are defined.[54] (emphasis added)

The assessment of the prejudice brought about by an exception to the legitimate interests of patent holders necessarily requires three steps. In the first one, the interpreter identifies third parties' interests promoted by the exception and classifies them according to their relevance for society (low, average or great). He then identifies the prejudice caused to

[53] Max Planck Institute and Queen Mary 2008, section 6.
[54] WTO, WT/DS114/R, Panel Report, para. 7.60.

Table 3.1 *Normative meaning of art. 30 of TRIPS when interpreted in light of the customary rules of treaty interpretation*

Steps of the test in art. 30	Meaning of each step in the test
First step: Assessment of the limited character of the exception under investigation	The process of assessment includes the following steps: 1. Identify if the exception pursues any of the objectives authorized by Art. 8 of TRIPS, including the general goals of the WTO system; 2. Assess whether the exception is suitable for promoting the objectives that determined its adoption; and 3. Consider if the exception complies with the limitations established by the TRIPS Agreement, namely: • clauses on national and most-favored-nation treatment (arts. 3 and 4); • prohibition of adopting exceptions that produce the effect of preventing the protection of the categories of inventions that, pursuant to art. 27 of TRIPS, should be patentable; • respect for the area occupied by the system of compulsory licenses (art. 31 and Decision of the General Council, 2003); • minimum term of protection of patents (art. 33); and • principle of non-discrimination, based on national origin, the field of technology and the method of exploitation of the innovation (art. 27(1)). if the exception pursues a legitimate objective, is appropriate and also abides by the limits fixed by TRIPS, it will successfully pass the first step of the test.
Second step: Assessment of the reasonability of the interference caused by the exception in the normal exploitation of patents	The process of assessment involves the following steps: 1. Identification of the level of protection of the legitimate objective pursued by the exception; 2. Check if the excepted use may be legitimately controlled by patent holders. This being the case, the degree of restriction of the affected rights caused by the exception should be identified; and 3. Identification of alternative measures to the exception examined, able to promote the same objectives pursued by it, and at the same level, but with a weaker impact on patent rights. Alternative measures that are not reasonably available to the State proposing the exception under scrutiny should not be considered. It should be reasonably available in technical, administrative and economic terms. If there is no less onerous alternative measure than the one under analysis, the latter will have passed the second step of the test.

Table 3.1 (*cont.*)

Steps of the test in art. 30	Meaning of each step in the test
Third step: Assessment of the reasonability of the prejudice caused by the exception on the legitimate interests of the patent holders	The process of assessment entails the following steps: 1. Identification of the total social benefits promoted by the exception, and its qualification according to its relevance for society (low, average or great); 2. Identification of the prejudice inflicted on the interests of patent owners ensuing from the adoption of the exception and its qualification according to its relevance for society (low, average or great); and 3. Comparative assessment between benefits brought about by the exception and its negative impact on the interests of patent owners. If benefits elicited by the exception under scrutiny are more relevant than the prejudice caused, the latter will be considered reasonable and the exception will be legal.

the individual interests of patent owners, as a result of the implementation of the exception and classifies them according to their relevance for society (low, average or great). Lastly, he will compare the benefits accrued through the adoption of the exception as opposed to the negative effects on the interests of patent holders. Should the benefits exceed the prejudice, the latter will be judged "reasonable" and, consequently, the exception will be legitimate.

3.3.4 *Summary of the normative meaning of art. 30 resulting from the application of the general rule of interpretation of the VCLT*

When art. 30 of the TRIPS Agreement is interpreted in the light of the elements composing the general rule of interpretation of the VCLT it receives a new meaning: its three steps constitute a *sui generis* proportionality test insofar as it adds the standard of consistency with the TRIPS Agreement to the three sub-tests traditionally present in the proportionality test (Table 3.1). The interpretation of the three-step test as a *sui generis* test of proportionality widens the political room available to WTO Members to adopt exceptions to patent rights; it permits the effective realization of multiple non-commercial public interests and, lastly, it harmonizes the interests of patent holders with those held by society at large related to, inter alia, scientific progress and human rights.

Given that the wording of arts. 30, 17 and 26(2) resemble each other substantially, the normative meaning of art. 30, summarized in Table 3.1, serves as a platform to clarify the normative meaning of the other two provisions. In the following sections, taking as reference the normative meaning of art. 30, the normative content of arts. 17 and 26(2) of TRIPS will be investigated.

3.4 Assessment test of the legitimacy of exceptions to the rights conferred by trademarks (art. 17)

With the purpose of preventing the commission of acts of unfair competition and the dilution of the distinctive character of trademarks, protected trademarks bestow on their holders the broad "exclusive right to prevent all third parties not having the owner's consent from using in the course of trade identical or similar signs for goods or services which are identical or similar to those in respect of which the trademark is registered where such use would result in a likelihood of confusion" (art. 16(1)).

In its turn, the owners of well-known trademarks – i.e. those which have acquired wide recognition among the consumer public – enjoy more extensive rights than those provided by ordinary registered trademarks. Provided that the unregistered trademark is well-known in the jurisdiction where its owner seeks protection, he shall enjoy the same rights guaranteed by a registered trademark (art. 16(2)). In addition to that, the owner of a well-known trademark has the right to prevent the use of identical or similar signs to his in relation to goods or services which are *not* similar to those in respect of which his trademark is registered, provided that: (i) the "use of that trademark in relation to those goods or services would indicate a connection between those goods or services and the owner of the registered trademark"; and (ii) "the interests of the owner of the registered trademark are likely to be damaged by such use" (art. 16(3)).

Art. 17 of the TRIPS Agreement authorizes WTO Members to provide exceptions to the rights conferred by trademarks, provided they are "limited" and take account of the legitimate interests of the owners of trademarks and of third parties. This provision has been interpreted by a WTO Panel in the *EC – Trademarks and Geographical Indications* case. In summary, in this dispute Australia and the US challenged the legality of an EC regulation (EC Regulation 2081/92 on the protection of geographical indications and designations of origin for agricultural products and foodstuffs, and its related implementing and enforcement measures), which established a regime of coexistence between trademarks and geographical indications similar to protected pre-existing trademarks. Under the regime of coexistence, the owners of certain trademarks were not entitled to object to the registration and use of geographical indications substantially similar to their pre-existing trademarks. The EC argued that the coexistence regime puts together a legitimate exception to the exclusive rights conferred by trademarks, backed by art. 17 TRIPS.

Art. 17 of the TRIPS Agreement, unlike other general exception clauses thereof, explicitly identifies an example of lawful use – fair use of descriptive terms – and sets only two conditions that must be complied with by the exceptions to trademark rights.

Regarding the meaning of the first condition (limited nature of the exception), the Panel followed the guideline taken in *Canada – Pharmaceutical Patents*, according to which an exception is considered "limited" if it features strict limits and produces only "a small diminution" of the rights conferred on the owners of the affected trademarks.[55]

At first, the Panel seems to have been of the opinion that that plays no role in determining the limited character of an exception: the number of third parties who may benefit from the exception; the number of goods or services that may use the signs affected by the exception; and the number of trademarks that may be affected by the exception. The central factor in the evaluation process of the limited nature of the exception would be its ability to prejudice the distinctiveness of the affected trademarks:

> The limited exceptions apply "to the rights conferred by a trademark"... Accordingly, the fact that it may affect only few trademarks or few trademark owners is irrelevant to the question whether an exception is limited. The issue is whether the exception to the *rights conferred by a trademark* is narrow.[56]

> Fair use of descriptive terms is inherently limited in terms of the sign which may be used and the degree of likelihood of confusion which may result from its use, as a purely descriptive term on its own is not distinctive and is not protectable as a trademark. *Fair use of descriptive terms is not limited in terms of the number of third parties who may benefit, nor in terms of the quantity of goods or services with respect to which they use the descriptive terms*, although implicitly it only applies to those third parties who would use those terms in the course of trade and to those goods or services which those terms describe. *The number of trademarks or trademark owners affected is irrelevant*, although implicitly it would only affect those marks which can consist of, or include, signs that can be used in a descriptive manner. According to the text, this is a "limited" exception for the purposes of Article 17.[57] (emphasis added)

However, in contradiction to this approach, the Panel ended up endorsing the opinion that an exception may be deemed "limited" if it prevents a

[55] WTO, WT/DS174/R, Panel Report, para. 7.650.
[56] *Ibid.* [57] *Ibid.*, para. 7.654.

trademark owner from exercising his exclusive right with regard to:[58] (i) a limited group of third parties (potential beneficiaries of the exception);[59] and/or (ii) a limited group of identical or similar signs to his, whose use may generate, at most, a low degree of likelihood of confusion with his own;[60] and/or (iii) a limited group of goods or services in respect of which identical or similar signs to his may be used in the course of trade.[61]

As regards the second and final condition that must be complied with by exceptions (i.e. the duty to take account of the legitimate interests of the owner of the trademark and of third parties), the Panel upheld the opinion adopted in *Canada – Pharmaceutical Patents* that legitimate interests are those "supported by relevant public policies or other social norms."[62] The Panel considered as the core legitimate interest of trademark owners the preservation of the distinctiveness of their trademarks and, consequently, of their economic value:

> The function of trademarks can be understood by reference to Article 15.1 [of TRIPS] as distinguishing goods and services of undertakings in the course of trade. Every trademark owner has a legitimate interest in preserving the distinctiveness, or capacity to distinguish, of its trademark so that it can perform that function. This includes its interest in using its own trademark in connection with the relevant goods and services of its own and authorized undertakings. Taking account of that legitimate interest will also take account of the trademark owner's interest in the economic value of its mark arising from the reputation that it enjoys and the quality that it denotes.[63]

In the category of legitimate interests of third parties are included those of consumers who "have a legitimate interest in being able to distinguish the goods and services of one undertaking from those of another, and to avoid confusion,"[64] and those of *users* of distinctive signs (e.g. manufacturing companies, traders), who have a legitimate interest in identifying unequivocally their products and services in the course of trade.[65] In practice, the Panel only considered "legitimate" eminently commercial interests.

The legitimate interests of the owner of the trademark affected by an exception and those of consumers in general will be duly taken into account by the exception when it allows the goods bearing the affected trademark to be distinguished from those which use an identical or similar sign and the respective undertakings.[66] In other words, the legitimate interests of the owners of trademarks and those of consumers will be

58 *Ibid.*, para. 7.653.
59 *Ibid.*, para. 7.656.
60 *Ibid.*, paras. 7.657, 7.658 and 7.670.
61 *Ibid.*, para. 7.655.
62 *Ibid.*, para. 7.663.
63 *Ibid.*, para. 7.664.
64 *Ibid.*, para. 7.675.
65 *Ibid.*, para. 7.681.
66 *Ibid.*, para. 7.672.

duly considered when the excepted use made by the third party creates little or no likelihood of confusion.

The legitimate interests of the commercial beneficiaries of an exception (e.g. manufacturing companies, traders) will be taken into account thereby, provided they are required to honestly identify their products and services in the course of trade, i.e. where the uses made of the affected trademarks do not mislead the public as to the origin of the commercialized goods and/or services.

In summary, according to the Panel, the final step of the test in art. 17 requires that any exceptions to the exclusive rights conferred by trademarks take into account: (i) the legitimate interest of trademark owners in preserving the distinctiveness thereof; (ii) the interest of the beneficiaries of the exception in identifying fairly the origin of their products and services and (iii) the consumer's interest in not being misled.

The interpretation proposed for art. 17 of TRIPS, in *EC – Trademarks and Geographical Indications* features at least four technical issues. Firstly, to interpret the expression "limited exceptions," the Panel adopted as a parameter the interpretation developed in *Canada – Pharmaceutical Patents* for the same expression. For the reasons outlined previously in this chapter,[67] the interpretations proposed by the WTO for most of the terms of art. 30, including the expression "limited exceptions," are not legally sustainable. The limited nature of an exception should not have any relation to, for example, the number of trademarks affected thereby or the number of beneficiaries of the exception, or the degree of constraint on the exclusive rights bestowed on trademark owners. The limited nature has to do with compliance with the minimum obligations set by TRIPS (the limits within which an exception can be adopted). Accordingly, the interpretation proposed in *EC – Trademarks and Geographical Indications* for the terms of the first step of the test in art. 17 should also be disregarded.

Secondly, as regards the final condition laid down by art. 17, the Panel makes the mistake of considering "legitimate" only those interests backed by social norms and/or public policies. As already explained above, the interpreter shall exclusively take into account the interests sheltered by legal norms.[68] In the case of trademark holders, their legitimate interests are those safeguarded by the rights guaranteed by TRIPS. As for third parties, their legitimate interests are those shielded, inter alia, by international treaties on human rights and MEAs.

Thirdly, the Panel limited itself to include consumers and economic agents in the list of "third parties" whose legitimate interests should

[67] See section 3.2.4 above. [68] See section 3.3.3 above.

be taken into account by the exceptions. Considering that the WTO and the TRIPS Agreement do not pursue exclusively interests of an economic nature, it is advisable to include in the group of third parties other individuals and institutions that may have a legitimate interest in using a mark which is identical or similar to those protected, e.g. NGOs or the press.

Finally, the Panel included an excessively limited number of interests in the list of legitimate interests of third parties to be considered – and safeguarded – by the exceptions, namely the interests of consumers not to be misled as to the origin of marketed products and services and the interests of economic agents to identify, in a non-confusing manner, their goods and services. In light of the broad social, economic and environmental goals pursued by the WTO, it is more accurate to include in that list all those interests authorized by art. 8 of TRIPS, including those listed in the preamble to the Marrakesh Agreement.[69]

Due to these misconceptions, an alternative interpretation to the test set out in art. 17 of TRIPS is proposed, partially based on the normative meaning of the terms of art. 30, as previously construed (Table 3.1). "Partially," because although the wording of these provisions has similarities, there are also important differences that should not be ignored by the interpreter. Thus, Art. 30 lays down three conditions with which the exceptions to patent rights must comply, while art. 17 sets out only two conditions with which the exceptions to trademarks shall comply; and whereas the third step of the test in art. 30 states that the exceptions to the rights conferred by patents shall not "unreasonably prejudice the legitimate interests of the patent owner, taking account of the legitimate interests of third parties," the final step of the test in art. 17 provides that the exceptions to the rights conferred by trademarks shall "take account of the legitimate interests of the owner of the trademark and of third parties." These differences prevent the unrestricted use of the interpretation developed for art. 30 with a view to clarifying the meaning of art. 17.

In order to clarify the meaning of the expression "limited exceptions" used in art. 17, it is advisable to have recourse to the meaning previously developed for the same expression in the context of art. 30 of the TRIPS.[70] However, some adjustments must be made in order to prevent the first step of the test from overlapping, even partially, with its second step. Thus, in contrast to what occurs in the test of art. 30, the first step of the test in art. 17 is not suited to assess whether the goals pursued by the exception are sanctioned by art. 8 of the TRIPS Agreement. Such a

[69] See Chapter 2, section 2.3.3.1. [70] See section 3.3.1 above.

function is performed by the second step of the test as a means of ensuring that the exceptions investigated, in actual fact, take into account – and safeguard – the legitimate interests of third parties. Taking as a guideline the meaning of that expression in the context of art. 30, an exception to the rights conferred by a trademark shall be "limited" provided it observes the following obligations set out by TRIPS:

- ensuring observance of the principles on national treatment and most-favored-nation treatment (arts. 3 and 4);
- ensuring that the term of protection of any trademark registration will not be less than seven years (art. 18);
- ensuring the right to renew indefinitely the registrations of trademarks (art. 18);
- prohibition of compulsory licensing trademarks (art. 21);
- prohibition of adopting exceptions that produce the practical effect of preventing the protection of distinctive signs that, in accordance with art. 15 of the TRIPS Agreement, should be eligible to receive protection; and
- ensuring the right of trademarks holders to assign their trademarks with or without the transfer of the business to which they belong (art. 21).

Regarding the second step of the test in art. 17 of TRIPS, since its wording is different, in important aspects, from the text of the third step of the test enshrined in art. 30, the interpretation previously construed for the latter is irrelevant for determining the meaning of the former. That said, the text of the second step of the test indicates that an exception to the rights conferred by a trademark will successfully meet the test if it simultaneously shields the legitimate interests of the owners of trademarks and those of third parties.

The legitimate interests of the owners of trademarks will be duly taken into consideration by the exception if the distinctiveness of the affected trademarks is preserved, i.e. they retain their commercial magnetism and ability to identify a single providing source of certain products and services. This implies that: (i) if the affected sign is an ordinary registered trademark, the exception is not free to support the use "in the course of trade [of] identical or similar signs for goods or services which are identical or similar to those in respect of which the trademark is registered, where such use would result in a likelihood of confusion";[71] (ii) if the trademark affected by the exception is a well-known mark, the exception is not free to authorize the use in the course of trade of identical or similar

[71] Art. 16(1), TRIPS.

signs for goods or services in general, where such use would result in a likelihood of confusion about the origin of goods and services.[72]

The legitimate interests of third parties – e.g. economic agents in general, consumers, individuals in general, NGOs, press agencies – will be duly taken into consideration by the investigated exception, when the uses supported thereby foster, in actual fact, any of the legitimate interests allowed by art. 8 of TRIPS. In other words, the excepted use should be a suitable means of furthering any of the public goals authorized by TRIPS. To summarize: the exceptions, as a matter of principle, aim at promoting the legitimate interests of third parties – e.g. freedom of speech, free enterprise, free competition – but they should not overlook the fundamental interest of the owners of affected trademarks to preserve their distinctiveness, especially because this is also in the interest of consumers and necessary for the proper functioning of the market.

3.5 Assessment test of the legitimacy of exceptions to the rights conferred by protected industrial designs (art. 26.2)

Pursuant to art. 26 (1) TRIPS, "[t] he owner of a protected industrial design shall have the right to prevent third parties not having the owner's consent from making, selling or importing articles bearing or embodying a design which is a copy, or substantially a copy, of the protected design, when such acts are undertaken for commercial purposes."

The WTO Members may provide limited exceptions to the rights conferred by protected industrial designs, inasmuch as they: (1) are "limited"; (2) "do not unreasonably conflict with the normal exploitation of protected industrial designs"; and, finally, (3) "do not unreasonably prejudice the legitimate interests of the owner of the protected design, taking account of the legitimate interests of third parties." Since the wording of the test in art. 26(2) of TRIPS is remarkably similar to the wording of the test in art. 30, it is reasonable and acceptable to apply the previously proposed interpretation for the latter (Table 3.1) to determine the normative meaning of the former.

The process of assessing the limited character of an exception to the rights conferred on the holders of protected industrial designs comprises the following steps: first, checking if the exception pursues any of the goals allowed by art. 8 of the TRIPS Agreement, including any of the general objectives pursued by the WTO system, set out in the preamble to the Marrakesh Agreement; second, assessing whether the exception

[72] Art. 16(2) and (3), TRIPS.

is suitable to promote the objectives that motivated its adoption; and finally, evaluating whether the exception observes the limits set out by the TRIPS Agreement, namely:

- the duty to respect the principles of national and of the most-favored-nation treatment (arts. 3 and 4);
- the prohibition against adopting exceptions that generate the actual effect of preventing the protection of the categories of industrial designs that, pursuant to art. 25(1) of TRIPS, shall be eligible to receive legal protection;
- ensuring that the duration of the protection available to industrial designs amounts to at least 10 years (art. 26(3)); and
- the prohibition against adopting exceptions that produce the effect of preventing the legal protection of textile designs (art. 25(2)).

The second phase of the test of art. 26(2) of TRIPS requires that exceptions to the rights conferred on owners of industrial designs do not conflict unreasonably with the normal exploitation of the affected industrial designs. "Normal exploitation" is defined here as the means usually employed for all or most of the owners of protected industrial designs to extract economic benefits therefrom. Not included in this category is any unusual means of exploitation used by a limited group of holders of industrial designs.[73] There should also not be included in the list of normal means of exploitation the exercise of the exclusive rights guaranteed by art. 26(1) to the detriment of third parties making use of protected industrial designs for non-commercial purposes.[74] Nor should a "normal means of exploitation" of industrial designs include those forms of exploitation that are not essential to achieving the goals pursued by the legal regimes devoted to the protection of industrial designs,[75] namely those of adding value to functional products (e.g. cars, watches, household appliances, motorcycles) by means of product differentiation, and of fostering creativity through the recovery of the investments made in the development of industrial designs and generating new resources to fund future creative projects. The interpretation proposed here for what is "normal exploitation of industrial designs" reconciles the economic interests of the owners of industrial designs with those of the other sectors of society, preventing the former from exercising their exclusive rights in an abusive manner.

Having as parameters the interpretation previously reached for the second phase of the three-step test of patent law, in the second step of the test enshrined in art. 26(2), the interpreter is required to assess

[73] WTO, WT/DS114/R (*Canada – Pharmaceutical Patents*), para. 7.55.
[74] See Art. 26(1) *in fine*. [75] WTO, WT/DS114/R, para. 7.58.

whether the exception under investigation consists of the least restrictive means to achieve the objective pursued thereby.[76] In other words, the exception will satisfy the second step of the test provided there are no other alternative measures reasonably available to the proponent State, able to promote the same goal pursued thereby and at the same level.

The third and final step of the test in art. 26(2) provides that the exceptions to the rights bestowed on the holders of industrial designs shall "not unreasonably prejudice the legitimate interests of the owner of the protected design, taking account of the legitimate interests of third parties," in the process of gauging the reasonableness of the harms engendered. As previously anticipated, the normative meaning of the final step of the three-step test of patent law will be taken as an aid for clarifying the meaning of the final step of the test in art. 26(2).[77]

The legitimate interests of the owners of protected industrial designs are twofold and are supported by TRIPS. The first is to recover the investments incurred in the development of industrial designs and to generate resources to fund the development of new industrial designs. That is, the right holders have a legitimate interest in preserving the economic incentives for innovation. The second legitimate interest safeguarded by TRIPS is the conservation of the ability of industrial designs to play the role of aggregator of value and of the distinguishing factors of functional products.

For their part, the legitimate interests of third parties are those safeguarded by, inter alia, MEAs, human rights instruments and consumers' rights. The exception will successfully pass the final stage of the test provided that the social benefits produced thereby outweigh the individual losses inflicted on the legitimate interests of the owners of industrial designs.

[76] See section 3.3.2 above. [77] See section 3.3.3 above.

4 Determining the normative meaning of art. 13 of the TRIPS Agreement and art. 9(2) of the Berne Convention

4.1 Introduction

In the WTO framework, the three-step test of copyright law, developed during the Stockholm Revision Conference of the Berne Convention (1967), occupies the role of general controlling the lawfulness of the exceptions to copyright. It is set out in art. 9(2) BC and art. 13 TRIPS.[1] Each of these provisions plays a distinct role.

Art. 9(2) BC has the sole function of controlling the legality of the exceptions to the right of reproduction. More specifically, it is vested in the competence of regulating the space *non-occupied* by the BC provisions that govern the adoption of special exceptions to the right of reproduction – e.g. arts. 10, 10bis, 11bis(3) and 13(1).[2] Although the wording of art. 9(2) is not explicit on this point, the records of the Stockholm Revision Conference indicate that States enjoy the discretion to include in the scope of exceptions to the right of reproduction the right of the beneficiaries of such exceptions to make translations of the works affected thereby as well as the right to distribute the copies made.[3] In other words, legitimate exceptions to the right of reproduction, complying with the requirements laid down by the BC, allow their beneficiaries to make translations of works to the extent necessary to make use of these exceptions, as well as to distribute the copies extracted under the

[1] Outside the realm of the WTO, the test is enshrined in art. 10 of the WCT and in art. 16(2) WPPT.

[2] See WIPO 1971b, 1145.

[3] Lipszyc (2001, 183) and Ficsor (2003, 283) argue that the right of distribution is encompassed by the right of reproduction. During the Stockholm Conference on the revision of the Berne Convention, Austria, Italy and Morocco submitted a proposal for the legal recognition of the right of general circulation (or the right of distribution of copies of protected works).The proposal was rejected by the participating states (WIPO 1971b, 856). That means that copyright holders do not enjoy a separate right of distribution. This may be the possible justification for art. 5(4) of Directive 2001/29/EC authorizing Members of the EU to include in the scope of the exceptions to the right of reproduction the right to distribute copies, regardless of the authorization of the affected right holders.

ruling of the applicable exceptions. If art. 9(2) of the BC prevented others from translating works written in foreign languages, in order to make use of the available exceptions to the right of reproduction, this provision would create a discrimination based on the language in which the work was published. For example, Brazil, which adopted an exception that allows educational institutions to make copies for use in the classroom, the beneficiaries of the exception, in practice, will tend to make photocopies of works published in Portuguese. Consequently, the exception will harm the rights of Brazilian and Portuguese authors much more than the rights held by authors from other nations. Moreover, such a restrictive view is not consistent with the global orientation of the Berne Convention, which was designed to facilitate the international dissemination of literary and artistic works from all backgrounds, nor with the principle of national treatment, since the exceptions to the right of reproduction would be much more harmful to the economic interests of national authors. In the same spirit, if art. 9(2) BC prevented third parties from distributing copies of protected works, made under the ruling of legitimate exceptions, copyright holders would have the prerogative to deprive the exceptions to the right of reproduction of any practical effect.

Art. 13 TRIPS provides that "Members shall confine limitations or exceptions to exclusive rights to certain special cases which do not conflict with a normal exploitation of the work and do not unreasonably prejudice the legitimate interests of the right holder." At first, it could be inferred from the reading of this provision that it serves as the foundation for the establishment of copyright exceptions beyond those expressly authorized by the BC exception clauses,[4] transposed to the TRIPS Agreement through its art. 9(1). Nevertheless, the term "confine" reveals that this provision has as one of its core functions to control or limit the scope of the copyright exceptions adopted under the BC special exception clauses, e.g. the clauses set out in arts. 10, 10bis, 11bis (2) and (3), 13(1).[5] In practical terms, this implies that, in relation to the BC exception clauses which include indeterminate terms (e.g. the expression "compatible with fair practice" employed in art. 10(2)), art. 13 TRIPS plays the role of a hermeneutic tool by evidencing the normative content of these terms.[6] But where the BC exception clauses lay down clearly conditions that the beneficiaries must meet, the function of art. 13 TRIPS is to establish additional conditions to be observed by the beneficiaries.[7] This is the

4 See Gervais 1998, 88–91

5 See, e.g., WTO, WT/DS160/R (*US – Section 110(5) Copyright Act*), para. 6.94; Brennan 2002, 224.

6 See Senftleben 2004, 124; Geiger 2008b, 948.

7 See Senftleben 2004, 124.

case, for example, with the exceptions provided in arts. 10bis (1) and (2), 11bis(2) and (3), and 13(1), paragraph 1 of the Berne Convention. Consequently, in respect of the rights guaranteed by the Berne Convention, WTO Members are not entitled to use art. 13 TRIPS to justify the adoption of exceptions expressly not authorized by that convention. That is so because of art. 20 BC – a provision which is part and parcel of TRIPS – and art. 2(2) TRIPS. The former provision provides that "[t]he Governments of the countries of the Union reserve the right to enter into special agreements among themselves, in so far as such agreements grant to authors more extensive rights than those granted by the [Berne] Convention, or contain other provisions not contrary to this Convention." The latter provision, in its turn, states that "[n]othing in Parts I to IV of this Agreement [TRIPS] shall derogate from existing obligations that Members may have to each other under . . . the Berne Convention." Thus, the TRIPS Agreement should be interpreted and applied so as not to constrain the rights guaranteed by the Berne Convention beyond what is authorized by arts. 1–21 and the appendix of the latter.

The final function performed by art. 13 TRIPS is to control the legality of the exceptions to rental rights, enshrined by art. 11 TRIPS, and of the exceptions to new exclusive rights to be guaranteed by future amendments to TRIPS. The exceptions to these rights need only meet the requirements laid down in art. 13.

At first sight, the wording of art. 9(2) BC and art. 13 TRIPS seems to indicate that their sole addressees are the legislators from WTO Members. That is, these tests serve to guide national parliaments to enact only those copyright exceptions that pass the scrutiny of the three-step test of copyright law. Accordingly, courts could only use the three-step test to settle private disputes where national norms explicitly indicate that the test should govern the application of the copyright exceptions. This is the case with the exception enshrined in art. 46 (VII) of the Brazilian Copyright Act (LDA or Law no. 9609/98), which reads: "[t]he following shall not constitute violation of copyright: VIII – the reproduction in any work of short extracts from existing works, regardless of their nature, or of the whole work in the case of a work of three-dimensional art, on condition that the reproduction is not itself the main subject matter of the new work and does not jeopardize the normal exploitation of the work reproduced or unjustifiably prejudice the author's legitimate interests." This is equally the case with art. 5(5) of the EC Directive 2001/29/EC on the harmonization of certain aspects of copyright and related rights in the information society, pursuant to which "[t] he exceptions and limitations provided for in paragraphs 1, 2, 3 and 4 shall only be applied in certain special cases which do not conflict with a normal exploitation of the work or other subject-matter and do not unreasonably prejudice the legitimate interests of the rightholder." In these cases, the three-step test is employed to clarify the scope of the copyright exceptions incorporated into domestic legal systems.

In addition to that, in Brazil, the judiciary has in recent times been attributing to the three steps of the copyright law two other functions: (i) to clarify the scope of *any* exception provided in the Brazilian Copyright Act, even where the wording of the provisions does not require the application of the test for this purpose;[8] and (ii) to govern the establishment of copyright exceptions by case law, where there is no legal rule which exempts certain unauthorized uses of protected works from the control of copyright holders.[9] There is no legal impediment to transpose the understanding upheld by the Brazilian courts to other WTO Members.

On account of the important roles played by art. 9(2) BC and art. 13 TRIPS, it is urgent to elucidate their normative meaning. Dependent on the scope of these tests is the freedom enjoyed by the WTO Members to adopt, not only at the domestic but also at the international level, copyright exceptions designed to further interests of higher value. That is so, since art. 20 BC prohibits its contracting parties – as well as WTO Members, pursuant to arts. 2(2) and 9(1) TRIPS – from negotiating agreements on copyright that include provisions contrary thereto or that reduce the rights guaranteed thereby. Unless arts. 9(2) BC and art. 13 TRIPS bestow on WTO Members a wide latitude to adopt socially efficient copyright exceptions, it is hard to foresee a bright future for the recent initiatives, sponsored by developing countries at the WIPO Standing Committee on Copyright and Neighbouring Rights, aimed at negotiating international legal instruments on copyright exceptions, specially designed to meet the needs of libraries, archives and educational institutions, as well as those of visually impaired persons and other persons with print disabilities.[10]

In the following sections, firstly, there is an examination of the interpretation proposed by the WTO in *US – Section 110(5) Copyright Act* in relation to the terms of the test in art. 13 TRIPS. The correct normative meaning of this provision and of art. 9(2) of the BC, *in its condition of*

[8] See Civil Appeal no. 2002.51.01.015719-6 (Rapporteur: Justice Liliane Roriz. Applicant: Soc. Bras. de Autores Teatrais-SBAT. Respondent: Fundação Oswaldo Cruz), ruled by the Federal Regional Court of the 2nd Region on November 24, 2009.

[9] See 3rd chamber of the STJ, Special Appeal no. 964404 (Applicant: Mitra Arquidiocesana de Vitória. Respondent: Central Bureau of Collection and Distribution of Royaties – ECAD), ruled on March 15, 2011.

[10] WIPO 2010.

being part and parcel of the TRIPS Agreement is then investigated.[11] This implies that the interpretation proposed for the latter provision may not necessarily be utilized by those States that are only contracting parties to the Berne Convention.

4.2 Art. 13 of TRIPS according to *US – Section 110(5) Copyright Act*

In 2000, art. 13 TRIPS was interpreted by the WTO in the *US – Section 110(5) Copyright Act* case. In the dispute, the EC challenged the lawfulness of two copyright exceptions provided in subparagraphs (A) and (B) of Sec. 110(5) of the US Copyright Act, namely, the "business" exemption and the "homestyle" exemption. These exceptions were allegedly inconsistent with arts. 11(a)(ii) and 11bis (1)(iii) BC. Briefly, the exceptions authorized, without an authorization and the payment of fees, the amplification of music broadcasts by small restaurants, retail outlets and food service and drinking establishments which met certain conditions laid down by law. The Panel took the view that the exceptions that were challenged would only be TRIPS compliant inasmuch as they passed the test enshrined in art. 13 TRIPS.

Art. 13 authorizes WTO Members to enact copyright exceptions, provided they comply with three cumulative conditions: (1) the exceptions shall be confined to certain special cases; (2) they shall not conflict with a normal exploitation of the affected works; and (3) they shall not unreasonably prejudice the legitimate interests of the affected copyright holders. As will be seen below, these conditions were interpreted in overly conservative fashion, so as to give undue protection to the economic interests of copyright holders.

4.2.1 *First step: exceptions shall be confined to certain special cases*

The Panel construed the expression "certain special cases" as synonymous with clearly defined exceptions;[12] in other words, exceptions shall be devised in a way that allows the secure particularization of the excepted acts, affected works and of their potential beneficiaries. In addition, copyright exceptions should have limited scope in *quantitative* and *qualitative* terms.[13] This implies that the exceptions should apply only under exceptional circumstances and benefit only a small fraction of the potential consumers of the works affected thereby.[14]

[11] See art. 9(1) TRIPS. [12] WTO, WT/DS160/R, Panel Report, para. 6.108.
[13] *Ibid.*, para. 6.109. [14] *Ibid.*, para. 6.113.

Rejecting the arguments advanced by the US and the EC, the Panel considered that "certain special cases" should not be treated synonymously with "special purposes," in the sense of "legitimate public policy purposes."[15] The ultimate concern of the Panel was not to evaluate the legitimacy of the goals that motivated the adoption of the exceptions in dispute, but to assess their actual and potential negative impacts on the ability of copyright holders to reap economic benefits from the works affected thereby.

4.2.2 *Second step: exceptions shall not conflict with a normal exploitation of the affected works*

In the opinion of the Panel, means of "normal exploitation" of works are all those forms of commercial exploitation of copyrighted works capable of generating "significant or tangible commercial gains."[16] The markets capable of generating significant or tangible revenues are the only ones that should be under the control of copyright holders.[17] That implies that in order for the exempted uses to be lawful they shall "not enter into economic competition with non-exempted uses."[18]

The Panel stressed that "normal exploitation" is not "equated with full use of all exclusive rights conferred by copyrights." If that were the case, there would be no room for establishing any copyright exceptions and art. 13 would become a dead letter.[19] It is important to emphasize that the only exempted uses that threaten the normal exploitation of works are those that "enter into economic competition with the ways that right holders normally extract economic value from that right to the work (i.e., the copyright) and thereby *deprive them of significant or tangible commercial gains*."[20] It should therefore be possible to establish an exception that ensures to third parties the freedom to exercise forms of economically relevant exploitation, so long such exploitation does not cause the copyright holders concerned significant or tangible economic prejudice.[21] However, the establishment of exceptions which satisfy these criteria is a complex task, and the Panel has not set any absolute quantitative parameters capable of distinguishing the sources of "significant or tangible commercial gains" from other sources.

The notion of "normal exploitation" implies that each of the exclusive rights associated with a work should be treated as a right independent of the others (principle of independence of exploitation rights), as it is

[15] *Ibid.*, paras. 6.111–6.112, 6.157. [16] *Ibid.*, para. 6.183. [17] *Ibid.*, para. 6.198.
[18] *Ibid.*, para. 6.181. [19] *Ibid.*, para. 6.167.
[20] *Ibid.*, para. 6.183 (emphasis added). [21] *Ibid.*, para. 6.182.

legally feasible and often the case that each of the rights that make up the set of copyrights associated with a particular work belongs to a different individual.[22] Thus, an exception that dramatically prejudices the right to reproduce a particular literary work, but that does not affect in any degree the right to communicate it to the public, would be prohibited, because the holder of the right of reproduction would be stripped of the means to exploit the work while the holder of the right of communication would conserve the right to fully exploit the work.[23]

The identification of the forms of "normal exploitation" of a work, which should be exclusively guaranteed to copyright holders, involves both an *empirical* and *normative* investigation. From the empirical perspective, normal exploitation of a particular category of works comprises all spheres of the market in which copyright holders typically exploit them. This does not imply that the interpreter should only consider those forms of normal exploitation often utilized by copyright holders up to the time of the enactment of exceptions. There should also be taken into consideration those markets which are economically important but under-exploited, "due to lack of effective or affordable means of enforcement" of their rights.[24] An indication that a certain market is under-exploited due to lack of effective or affordable means of enforcement of rights can be seen in the fact that some users enjoy a license to exploit a given category of works, while other users do not have any license, when both groups of users find themselves in a similar situation.[25] *A contrario sensu*, when the right holders enjoy legal and institutional mechanisms which empower them to exploit their works in a particular market niche, and deliberately decide not to do so, this omission points to the fact that the market that is ignored has no real economic importance to the right holders concerned. Thus, the exercise of copyrights in such a market characterizes an abnormal and hence illegitimate exploitation.[26]

From the normative perspective, "normal exploitation" includes all forms of exploitation that are already capable of generating considerable economic revenues to copyright holders, as well as those that, under present technical and market conditions, may gain economic relevance in the future.[27]

[22] *Ibid.*, para. 6.173. On this subject, art. 31 of the Brazilian Copyright Act (Law no. 9.610/98) reads as follows: "The various forms of use of literary, artistic or scientific works or phonograms shall be mutually independent, and any authorization granted by the author or the producer, as the case may be, for one such use shall not constitute authorization of any other of the uses."

[23] WTO, WT/DS160/R, Panel Report, para. 6.172.

[24] *Ibid.*, para. 6.188.

[25] *Ibid.*, paras. 6.188 and 6.247.

[26] *Ibid.*, paras. 6.215–6.216 and 6.218.

[27] *Ibid.*, para. 6.189.

4.2.3 *Third step: exceptions shall not unreasonably prejudice the legitimate interests of the copyright holders concerned*

In the opinion of the Panel, the third and final stage of the test in art. 13 has the function of assessing the level of any economic loss caused by the exception arising from the inability of copyright holders to exercise their exclusive rights so as to reap economic benefits from their works. In order to assess whether the loss reached an unreasonable level, the Panel deemed it necessary to calculate the actual and potential economic losses suffered by the right holders affected by the exception.[28] The economic losses would only be reasonable if of little significance.[29] *A contrario sensu*, they would be unreasonable if they represented a source of significant or tangible revenues to the right holders.[30]

4.2.4 *Why US – Section 110(5) Copyright Act is legally irrelevant to future disputes*

Regarding the first step of the test set out in art. 13, the Panel found that the expression "certain special cases" would be synonymous with exceptions that are clearly defined, with a constrained scope of application, in quantitative and qualitative terms. The interpretation proposed for the first step of the test was motivated by the goal of preventing the enactment of any exception that could conflict with a normal exploitation of the affected works and generate significant (unjustified) losses to copyright holders, by virtue of the broad scope of the exceptions, in terms of works affected, number of beneficiaries and/or uses exempted. It is legally indefensible to uphold an interpretation for the first step of the test that somehow anticipates the analysis to be conducted under the second and third steps of the test.[31] The first step of the test must therefore mean something different from what has been proposed by the Panel.

In the opinion of the Panel, the interpreter, under the second step of the test, must determine whether the exception, whose legality is questioned, warrants to the holders of the curtailed exclusive right all forms of exploitation of works capable of generating, at present as well as in the future, significant or tangible economic benefits to them. Consequently, only those exceptions are lawful that: (i) do not impair the exploitation of any actual or potential market of the works affected, or (ii) impair the

[28] *Ibid.*, para. 6.247.
[29] *Ibid.*, paras. 6.226–6.227 and 6.231.
[30] *Ibid.*, para. 6.229.
[31] See Senftleben 2004, 152.

exploitation of markets capable of generating meager economic benefits to copyright holders.

To understand the practical effects of this opinion, it is necessary to bear in mind that today the latest technological developments have turned into reality the wish long held by copyright holders to have control that is effective, almost absolute and on a global scale over the use of their works.[32] The expansion of the technical capacity for control over literary and artistic works and the reduction of transaction costs has enabled the creation of a plethora of profitable new markets that can successfully be exploited by copyright holders. In other words, current technologies allow copyright holders to consider any form of use of a work as a normal way of exploitation thereof.[33] Therefore, in the current technological context, it would be no exaggeration to say that the view adopted by the WTO of what constitutes "normal exploitation of a work" has substantially curtailed, if not entirely done away with, the space for the adoption of copyright exceptions. On this point, Heide makes an insightful observation:

> Consider the industrious author who decides that he wishes to charge for every conceivable use made of his work. He is convinced that this is feasible and accordingly labels all hard copies of his work with a World Wide Web address where any user can contact him and arrange a particular use for a certain fee. This author has already arranged the hosting of the web site offering a menu of choices, which, among other things, enables the visitor and potential user to click on one button should the user be interested in commenting on or critiquing the work, another button if a parody is desired, and another if the user intends to incorporate the author's work as part of his own. In such an already feasible scenario, every use can be licensed and arguably falls within the realm of "normal" exploitation. If this reality is combined with current understanding of the hierarchy of Article 9 (2), where if a proposed use threatens the normal exploitation of a work the consideration of the three-step test comes to an end and any contemplated exception permitting the proposed use is therefore not authorized by the test, where does this lead us? In an environment where few, if any, practical problems prevent contracting directly with the end user for the user's desired use of a work and where on-line contracts and technological devices enable an author to monitor the use of his work, such an interpretation potentially transforms the three-step test into a one-step test, and in the process renders it, depending on the perspective taken, either totally effective or completely ineffective.[34]

If the WTO's legal understanding were correct, art. 13 TRIPS – as well as art. 9(2) BC – would fall into disuse, because very rarely would

[32] See, e.g., Jehoram 2005, 364; Ricketson and Ginsburg 2006, 772–773.
[33] See Heide 1999, 107; Ginsburg 2001, 14.
[34] Heide 1999, 106. In the same vein see Geiger 2007a, 6; Geiger 2006c, 692; Sun 2007, 297.

a copyright exception get through its sieve.[35] Accordingly, the interpretation endorsed by the Panel breaches the principle of effectiveness in treaty interpretation, according to which the interpreter must always choose the interpretation that gives meaning and function to the provision that ensures the integrity of the text of the treaty and that enables the realization of the purposes of the treaty to the maximum extent possible.

Finally, in the opinion of the Panel, the third step of the test has the function of ascertaining whether the economic prejudice caused by the exception is reasonable. For that, they would have to be at best minimal or irrelevant in economic terms. If a given exception passes successfully through the second step of the test, that implies that it does not interfere with the normal exploitation of the affected works, and therefore it does not shut down a source of tangible or significant economic revenues to the detriment of copyright holders. Consequently, the prejudice provoked by an exception which gets through the sieve of the second step should be, at worst, irrelevant and, therefore, reasonable. Thus, an exception that passes the second step of the test will necessarily pass the third step. The transformation of the three-step test into a two-step test testifies to the inadequacy and illegitimacy of the interpretation adopted by the WTO Panel, as it breaches once again the principle of effectiveness in the interpretation of treaties, which enjoins the interpreter from adopting an interpretation that renders parts of the treaty redundant or useless.[36]

The illegitimacy of the interpretation embraced in *US – Section 110 (5) Copyright Act* is confirmed by the way the Panel applied the general rule of treaty interpretation of the VCLT. The broad socio-economic objectives of the WTO and of TRIPS did not exert any explicit or tacit role in the process of construing the terms of art. 13. In addition, the Panel overlooked the need to interpret the wording of art. 13 in harmony with general principles of law, notably with the principle of proportionality.

The Panel opted to adopt a restrictive interpretation of the scope of art. 13, because in its view, art. 9(2) BC "was not intended to provide for exceptions or limitations except for those of a limited nature."[37] Although the matrix of art. 13 TRIPS is the provision found in art. 9(2) BC, it must be recalled each provision is inserted into a different legal context:

[35] See, e.g., Senftleben 2004, 181; Koelman 2006, 408.

[36] See WTO, WT/DS2/AB/R (*US – Gasoline*), Appellate Body Report, p. 27. Similarly, the WTO Appellate Body in *Korea – Dairy* reiterated the understanding that "[i]n light of the interpretive principle of effectiveness, it is the duty of any treaty interpreter to 'read all applicable provisions of a treaty in a way that gives meaning to all of them, harmoniously.' An important corollary of this principle is that a treaty should be interpreted as a whole, and, in particular, its sections and parts should be read as a whole" (footnotes omitted) (WTO, WT/DS98/AB/R, para. 81).

[37] WTO, WT/DS160/R, Panel Report, para. 6.97.

the fact that the WTO pursues broad socio-economic and environmental goals, while the preamble of the Berne Convention elects as its goal "to protect, in as effective and uniform a manner as possible, the rights of authors in their literary and artistic works,"[38] shows that the normative meaning of art. 9(2) BC may not necessarily coincide with the legal meaning of art. 13 TRIPS.

The interpretation adopted by the Panel was guided by the "hermeneutical rule named *odiosa restringenda* (hateful things should be restricted),"[39] premised on ensuring absolute priority to copyrights over other rights through the restrictive interpretation of the scope of the copyright exceptions. An interpretation that privileges, in an absolute fashion, the economic interests of copyright holders over the legitimate interests of other sectors of society breaches the principles of prohibition of abuse of rights and of proportionality.

In summary, the Panel did not interpret art. 13 TRIPS in accordance with the general rule of treaty interpretation, codified by the VCLT, because it has not sought to select an interpretation of its terms that harmonizes with: the objectives pursued by the WTO and the specific objectives of the TRIPS; the principle of good faith (doctrine of abuse of rights and the principle of effectiveness in treaty interpretation); the necessity and consistency standards, provided in art. 8 of the TRIPS Agreement; and the principle of proportionality. These are sufficient reasons for the WTO Members and the organs of the DSB to discard the interpretation endorsed by the Panel and to search for an interpretation built upon a strict application of the interpretative rules of the VCLT. Such a task will be addressed in the following sections.

4.3 Interpreting art. 13 TRIPS and art. 9(2) BC in accordance with the customary rules of treaty interpretation

4.3.1 The first step

The first step of the test in art. 13 provides that copyright exceptions are confined to "certain special cases." The *Compact Oxford English Dictionary* includes the following meanings to the noun "case": "an instance of a particular situation"; "the situation affecting or relating to a particular person or thing."[40] In the context of art. 13, the term "case" may be interpreted as a set of circumstances; a situation or a problem.

[38] Preamble to the BC. [39] Soares 2000, 873. [40] Oxford University Press 2009.

Because of the great similarity between the wording of art. 9(2) BC and art. 13 TRIPS, it is useful to refer to the preparatory work concerning the negotiation of the former. A 1964 report of the preparatory study group for the Stockholm Review Conference of the Berne Convention brought out a first proposal for what would become the test enshrined in art. 9(2), worded as follows: "However, it shall be a matter for legislation in the countries of the Union, having regard to the provisions of this Convention, to limit the recognition and the exercising of that right, for specified purposes and on the condition that these purposes should not enter into economic competition with these works." In light of the terms of the embryo of art. 9 (2), the term "cases" should be understood as synonymous with aims, purposes.[41]

The *Compact Oxford English Dictionary* attributes several meanings to "certain," but the ones that best fit the wording of the provision in question are as follows: "known for sure; established beyond doubt"; "specific but not explicitly named or stated."[42] In other words, "certain" may be interpreted as synonymous with defined; clearly laid down.

The adjective "special" is defined by the same dictionary in several ways, but the ones that make any sense vis-à-vis the wording of art. 13 TRIPS are as follows: "better, greater, or otherwise different from what is usual"; "exceptionally good or precious"; "belonging specifically to a particular person or place"; "designed or organized for a particular person, purpose, or occasion."[43] That adjective may denote something out of the ordinary, or something that has a specific/limited function, application or scope.

Bearing in mind the ordinary meanings attributable to the terms "case," "certain" and "special," and the wide range of objectives pursued by the WTO and the TRIPS Agreement[44], the expression "certain special cases" may be construed in two different ways: (1) clearly pre-set extraordinary goals; (2) a limited situation, in the sense of a situation constrained by certain pre-defined limits. The second alternative seems to be more consonant with the text and context of art. 13.

That said, the first step of the test demands that any copyright exception shall be directed to promote any of the legitimate objectives authorized by art. 8 TRIPS, including those interests furthered by the special exception clauses of the Berne Convention, e.g. education, access to information and freedom of expression.[45]

[41] See BIRPI 1967b, 48. [42] Oxford University Press 2009. [43] *Ibid.*
[44] See Chapter 2, sections 2.3.1 and 2.3.2. [45] See Senftleben 2004, 157.

For an exception to go through the first step of the test, it is also necessary to ensure the existence of a real link between means and ends, as well as the necessity of the exception, so as to prevent its utilization for the practice of an abuse of rights. If the exception is not suitable to promote any of the special objectives pursued by the WTO and TRIPS, there will be an abuse of power, as it will be clear that the actual goal pursued by the measure is different from that stated. And if the exception impinges on the exclusive rights of third parties to a greater extent than necessary to promote the goal that triggered its adoption, it will be equally clear that the stated purpose of the exception is inconsistent with the actual goal.

In addition, exceptions to copyright should also be confined within the limits set by TRIPS for the sake of safeguarding the legitimate interests of copyright holders. Those limits are:

- prohibiting the enacting of exceptions which produce the effect of impeding the legal protection of the categories of literary and artistic works which, under art. 2, paragraphs 1, 3 and 5 BC and art. 10 TRIPS, should be eligible for protection in the territory of the WTO Members;
- complying with the clauses providing national and most-favored-nation treatment (arts. 3 and 4 TRIPS);
- ensuring the minimum term of protection guaranteed by art. 12 TRIPS and art. 7 of the BC; and
- With specific regard to the exceptions brought to the reproduction right under arts. 10 and 10bis BC, respecting the area of the compulsory licensing system laid down in the appendix to the BC (Paris Act).

In summary, the first step of art. 13 TRIPS comprises the sub-tests of suitability and necessity and the test of consistency with the TRIPS provisions. The mere fact that a situation (or a "case") complies with those limits set by TRIPS makes it "special."

But how should the first step of the test in art. 9(2) BC be construed? With regard to the WTO Members, the first step of the test in art. 9(2) BC features the same normative content as the first step of the test in art. 13 TRIPS. It should be noted that the exceptions to the right of reproduction, adopted under art. 9(2) BC, shall respect the area of the compulsory licensing system, enshrined in the appendix to the BC. That is so because, by virtue of art. 9(1) TRIPS and the requirements laid down by art. 31 VCLT, art. 9(2) BC should be read in the context of the WTO legal framework and in light of the WTO objectives listed in the Marrakesh Agreement, and the objectives and principles of TRIPS.

4.3.2 The second step

The second step of the test in art. 13 TRIPS prohibits copyright exceptions from conflicting with a normal exploitation of the works affected thereby. According to the ordinary meaning attributable to the terms "exploitation"[46] and "normal,"[47] the expression "normal exploitation of the work" can be considered as the typical means to which copyright holders resort at present and those to which they most probably will resort in the future in order to reap economic benefits from their works. On this basis, all forms of exploitation capable of generating, at present or in the future, economic benefits should be controlled by copyright holders. This approach is socially and legally untenable, since it prevents, to a large extent, the enactment of valuable copyright exceptions, including exceptions tailored to support the creation of new works by widening the access to creative inputs by new authors.

At first sight, the interpretation advocated by Senftleben seems more appropriate, whereby the second step of the test prohibits the establishment of exceptions that prejudice the control by the right holders of those forms of exploitation of the affected works which represent, now or in the future, a "major source of income" or the "lion's share of royalty revenue."[48] The difficulty with this interpretation is how to objectively differentiate the main sources of income (i.e. those that should be reserved to the copyright holders) from those able to produce modest economic benefits. Once the class of copyright holders comprises individuals and organizations with heterogeneous interests, what may seem insignificant to large business conglomerates may be deemed extremely desirable to many authors, especially those who struggle to produce independently.

In order to determine the correct normative meaning of the second step of the test in art. 13, it is indispensable to bear in mind that the notion of "normal means of exploitation" of works relies on four objective premises. These premises serve to underscore that not all forms of exploitation of works, capable of producing at present or in the future fruits of significant economic weight to right holders, are "normal," and therefore, legitimate.[49]

[46] *The Compact Oxford English Dictionary* provides two distinct meanings to "exploitation": "the action of making use of and benefiting from resources"; and "the fact of making use of a situation to gain unfair advantage for oneself." In the context of an international treaty, only the first definition seems appropriate.

[47] "Normal" is defined by the *Compact Oxford English Dictionary* as follows: "conforming to a standard; usual, typical, or expected."

[48] See Senftleben 2004, 188.

[49] See Ricketson 1987, 483.

The first is the existence of an actual or potential market,[50] from which copyright holders have technological capacity and economic interest to extract significant economic benefits. Given the commercial nature of copyrights,[51] it should not be counted as a "normal means of exploitation" of a work where the exercise of copyrights occurs in the spheres made up of individuals and/or institutions devoid of economic capacity to acquire works in the market, simply because these individuals and institutions are not part of the consumer market for these works, and also because it is not credible to assume that individuals who remain living in those conditions will in the future enter the market for these works. It would be, for example, abnormal and thus legally indefensible to exercise the exclusive rights associated with textbooks in regions with very low per capita income, where people have to choose between food or books. This is the case in many parts of sub-Saharan Africa and the Northern and Northeastern regions of Brazil. Consequently, when assessing whether a particular exception affects the normal exploitation of a certain category of works in a given territory, the interpreter should include in the consumer market for the relevant works only those groups of individuals and institutions who actually are in a position to purchase them.[52]

Secondly, one should only include in the notion of "normal means of exploitation of a work" those usually employed by all or most of the holders of the exclusive right curtailed, with the purpose of reaping economic benefits from their works. Thus unusual means of exploitation of a work used by a limited group of copyright holders should not be taken into account.[53]

Thirdly, even if there is a market that copyright holders have the ability and the economic interest to exploit, its exclusive exploitation by copyright holders will be considered "normal" provided this is the most appropriate way of fostering the basic objectives pursued by copyright

[50] The *Compact Oxford English Dictionary* provides the following definitions for "market": "a regular gathering of people for the purchase and sale of provisions, livestock, and other commodities"; "an area or arena in which commercial dealings are conducted"; "a demand for a particular commodity or service."

[51] Gervais (2005, 10–11) argues that the core objective of copyright regimes is to control the commercial use and reuse of copyrighted works and prevent free-riders from performing actions which affect the normal commercial exploitation of these goods. Thus, copyright – and the other branches of intellectual property law – should not guarantee their holders an absolute right of exclusion, but a right to exclude others from the unauthorized commercial enjoyment of protected intellectual goods. In other words, "the author has a right in respect of any commercially significant use; use that would normally be the subject of a commercial transaction" (*ibid.*, 30).

[52] See Geiger 2008, 947.

[53] See WTO, WT/DS114/R (*Canada – Pharmaceutical Patents*), Panel Report, para. 7.55.

regimes.[54] This implies that when evaluating whether a particular form of use of a work should be treated as a normal means of exploitation, one must ask the question: in relation to the core goals of copyright policy – i.e. promoting the continuous creation and wider dissemination of new works, expanding society's stock of knowledge to advance its material, cultural and spiritual progress, promoting cultural diversity – what is more relevant in achieving these goals? Bestowing on copyright holders the ability to control certain uses of their works and to demand remuneration for such uses, *or* under certain circumstances excluding such uses from the sphere of control given to copyright holders? Those uses undertaken by third parties that are essential to the achievement of the goals of copyright policy neither should be under the control of copyright holders, nor should they guarantee the right to receive a remuneration.[55] This is exactly the reason why art. 10(1) BC does not allow copyright holders to prevent third parties from making quotations from their works or to make the use of quotations conditional upon the payment of an equitable remuneration, even if there is a market for this type of use and a cost-effective technical means to achieve it. To uphold a principle that copyright holders are entitled to benefit from all forms of uses of their works that may generate a tangible economic benefit would lead to a potential conflict between art. 10 BC and art. 13 TRIPS. In addition, it would undermine the realization of fundamental human rights, such as the rights to education and to freedom of creative and scientific expression.

The fourth and final premise of the notion of "normal exploitation" is the public availability of works in sufficient quantity "to satisfy the reasonable requirements of the public, having regard to the nature of the work."[56] If a copyright holder does not make his work available to the public in adequate quantities to satisfy the reasonable demands of potential consumers, this work is not being normally exploited. Copyright consists of an exchange: the copyright holders receive a wide range of exclusive rights in respect of their works. In exchange, society receives the right to enjoy these works. If copyright holders do not comply with their commitment, it is only natural that the scope of their rights will be

[54] See, e.g., Ginsburg 2001, 8; Ricketson and Ginsburg 2006, 772–773; Geiger 2006c, 692.

[55] Senftleben (2004, 230–233) develops a similar reasoning under the third step of the test in order to identify the legitimate interests of authors and of other copyright holders. In his view, certain economic (and/or moral) interests of copyright holders, safeguarded by the right constrained by a given exception, are "legitimate" if their preservation is a more suitable way of achieving any of the fundamental goals of copyright regimes than the investigated exception.

[56] Art. 3(3) BC.

constrained in order to prevent their abusive exercise. The practical effect of the fourth premise of the notion of "normal exploitation" of a work is of great importance for the users of copyrighted works, in particular those of an educational and scientific character: for instance, the holders of copyrights linked to literary works do not enjoy the right to prevent individuals domiciled in a particular country from freely taking copies thereof for educational purposes, provided their works are unavailable in that market (e.g. the work is out of print or is not being distributed locally), since they have not expressed genuine interest in exploiting them in that jurisdiction.[57] In short, if there is no exploitation of a work by its rights holder, the unauthorized use made by third parties is not able to conflict with its normal exploitation.

In the event that the exception affects any of the forms of normal exploitation of works enjoyed by the holders of the restrained exclusive right, then the interpreter shall identify the forms of interference with the normal exploitation that are authorized by the second step of the test.

Senftleben argues that the payment of an equitable remuneration to the right holders affected by the exception would not be expedient to "remedy" the interference engendered by the exception to the normal exploitation of the relevant works.[58] The payment of a fee would be merely a means of preventing the prejudice produced by the exception on the legitimate interests of copyright holders being deemed "unreasonable" under the third step of the test.

The interpretation advocated by Senftleben has a shortcoming: it makes illegal those exceptions adopted under art. 11bis (2) BC.[59] The said provision allows WTO Members to establish compulsory general licenses for the exploitation of broadcasting and related rights. A system of compulsory general licenses affects the ability of right holders to control all forms of exploitation deemed economically relevant, covered by broadcasting and related rights, as they replace them with a right to remuneration. Senftleben's interpretation does not appear appropriate.

[57] See Universidade de São Paulo 2005, 12–15.
[58] Senftleben 2004, 130–133.
[59] Senftleben (2004, 201–202) argues that "The potential incompatibility of compulsory licenses based on article 11bis(2) with the three-step test thus results from the great latitude allowed to national legislation. Article 11bis(2) fails to make it a condition that the economic core of copyright is to be left untouched, as required by the second criterion of the three-step test. There is no safeguard preventing national legislation from encroaching upon the core when determining the conditions under which the rights granted in article 11bis(1) BC may be exercised. That particularly broadcasting, subjected to the author's control by article 11bis(1)(i), constitutes a major source of income, however, can hardly be denied, for instance, in the field of cinematographic works. The fact that article 11bis(2) obliges national legislation to ensure the payment of equitable remuneration is irrelevant in the context of the prohibition of a conflict with a normal exploitation. It does not reconcile the two provisions."

According to the principle of effectiveness, the interpreter must always choose the interpretation that ensures the harmonic observance of all provisions of a treaty. As TRIPS incorporates by reference art. 11bis(2) BC, this provision shall coexist harmoniously with art. 13 TRIPS, otherwise the TRIPS negotiators would have excluded it from the text of TRIPS as they did with art. 6 bis BC.

With the purpose of harmonizing those provisions, Ricketson argues that art. 13 would not apply to the exceptions adopted under arts. 11bis(2) and 13(1) BC, as art. 13 TRIPS authorizes the adoption of non-onerous copyright exceptions, and those two provisions only allow the adoption of onerous exceptions (compulsory licenses).[60] However, the wording of art. 13 clearly indicates that it is vested in the competence of controlling the legality of all exceptions adopted under the umbrella of TRIPS and, accordingly, under the BC. If it were otherwise, art. 13 would indicate clearly the exceptions whose legality is not controlled thereby.

Because of the need to ensure a harmonious coexistence between arts. 13 TRIPS and 11bis (2) BC, and to promote the goals of TRIPS and of the WTO, notably the promotion of technological innovation, the transfer and the dissemination of technology,[61] socio-economic welfare and the balance between the rights and obligations of the holders of IPRs, it seems more appropriate to embrace the understanding that the second step of the test prohibits copyright exceptions from obstructing the generation of significant commercial gains to the benefit of right holders.

Given the meaning proposed here for the second step, an exception that authorizes third parties to exercise one or more forms of normal exploitation of a particular category of works, against the payment of an equitable remuneration for the relevant right holders, would be considered lawful.[62] The remuneration would be judged equitable if, on the one hand, it conserves sufficient incentives for the continuous creation and dissemination of new works[63] and if, on the other, it is adequate given the economic capacity of the users and the objectives pursued by the exception. This implies that when the interests of society warrant it, the remuneration may be fixed at a level below the market rate.[64] Thus,

[60] Ricketson and Ginsburg 2006, 862.
[61] As already indicated in the introduction, the facilitated access to literary and artistic works is essential for the formation of a critical mass able to master the use of new scientific and technological tools and to innovate.
[62] According to Geiger (2007a, 7–8) and Koelman (2006, 409), this is the understanding upheld by the German Federal Supreme Court.
[63] See Max Planck Institute and Queen Mary 2008.
[64] *Ibid.*

an exception conceived to promote access to educational goods by the population of an impoverished developing country may be associated with the payment of quite a low fee, when compared to that charged to students in industrialized countries.

However, to treat "normal exploitation of copyrighted works" as a synonym for "extracting from them significant commercial gains" allows the unrestricted transformation of exclusive rights into a right of remuneration. Such a transformation goes against the character of IPRs, whose main attribute is to confer on their holders the right to exclude unauthorized third parties from the enjoyment of proprietary goods. Therefore, it is more appropriate to take the view that only when expressly authorized by the BC (e.g. art. 11bis (2)) or TRIPS will an exception be lawful that takes from the control of the affected right holders *all* forms of normal exploitation of their works guaranteed by the restricted right, in exchange for the payment of an equitable remuneration. Only in these cases will the payment of a remuneration to the holders of the restricted right ensure that the exception does not conflict with a normal exploitation of the relevant works. In the remaining cases, an exception to a particular exclusive right will not conflict with a normal exploitation of the affected works if:

(i) it does not affect any of the forms of normal exploitation of the concerned works guaranteed by the restricted exclusive right, capable of generating significant commercial gains to the right holders; or

(ii) the exception affects one or more forms of normal exploitation of the relevant works, guaranteed by the restricted exclusive right, provided the affected right holders are entitled to receive an equitable remuneration for the unauthorized use of their works, and the exception leaves untouched at least one of the forms of normal exploitation of the works, capable of producing, *at present*, significant commercial gains.

It is important to note that if, in the process of assessing the impact of an exception on the normal exploitation of the works, no account is taken of the payment of an equitable remuneration to the relevant copyright holders, very rarely would any exception pass the scrutiny of that step of the test, since many exceptions produce more than minor effects on exclusive rights. Therefore, the realization of important objectives of the TRIPS and of the WTO system would be hampered. Under these conditions, there would be no legal justification for including art. 13 – and art. 9.2 of the BC – in the body of TRIPS, with the function of controlling the legality of copyright exceptions, since the uses that produce merely insignificant impacts on the normal exploitation of the relevant works are already tacitly allowed by the principle *de minimis lex non curat*, i.e. the law is not concerned with trifles.[65] As remarked by Ricketson, any exception, as a matter of principle, has the capacity to produce more than insignificant effects on the rights of affected parties.[66] The interpretation proposed for the second step of the test in art. 13 favors the dissemination of knowledge and the freedom of creative and scientific expression, safeguards the economic interests of copyright holders, promotes the objectives of TRIPS and of the WTO system and reconciles art. 11bis (2) BC and art. 13 TRIPS.

The interpretation here proposed for the second condition laid down by art. 13 TRIPS may be transposed to the context of art. 9(2) BC – in its capacity of a provision incorporated by TRIPS – with the caveat that the latter only governs the adoption of exceptions to the right of reproduction. Given that art. 9(2) BC does not authorize the granting of compulsory general licenses[67], an exception will not conflict with a normal exploitation of works: (i) where it does not encroach on any of the forms of normal exploitation of the relevant works, guaranteed by the right of reproduction; or (ii) where it encroaches on one or more forms of normal exploitation of the relevant works, guaranteed by the right of reproduction, provided that the affected right holders are entitled to receive a fair remuneration by virtue of the unauthorized reproduction of their works, and the exception leaves untouched *at least* one of the forms of normal exploitation capable of producing, *at present*, significant economic gains.

4.3.3 The third step

The final stage of the test set out in art. 13 of TRIPS requires that copyright exceptions do not *unreasonably* prejudice the legitimate interests of the affected right holders. To elucidate the correct meaning of the final step of the test it is firstly necessary to identify the legitimate interests of

[65] See Ricketson 2003, 36; Ricketson and Ginsburg 2006, 770.

[66] Ricketson 2003, 36–37.

[67] During the Stockholm Conference, the delegations of India and Romania advocated in favor of the amendment of the proposed art. 9(2) under negotiation, with the purpose of enabling the granting of compulsory general licenses for the reproduction of protected works. That is, the licenses would allow the general replacement of the exclusive right of reproduction with a right of remuneration. These proposals were rejected (WIPO 1971b, 857). However, Eugen Ulmer, Chair of Main Committee I, pointed out that art. 9(2) BC shelters the compulsory licensing of the right of reproduction in some unspecified cases: "The Chairman said that, as the principle of a compulsory general license, which had been proposed by the Delegation of India (S/86), had been rejected, the Main Committee could not reopen the discussion. The countries of the Union were, however, entitled to introduce a compulsory license in some cases, as was done by the German legislation which the Delegation of India had mentioned" (WIPO 1971b, 884).

copyright holders and, secondly, the means of assessing the unreasonable nature of the prejudice inflicted on these interests.

As regards the legitimate interests of copyright holders, art. 9(1) TRIPS provides that "Members [of the WTO] shall not have rights or obligations under this Agreement in respect of the rights conferred under Article 6bis of that Convention [BC] or of the rights derived therefrom." This means that under the third step of the test, the moral interests of an individual to safeguard their honor and reputation, which are protected by the rights of attribution and integrity, are not included in the list of legitimate interests of right holders that should be considered. Only those interests of an economic nature should be taken into account. The same observation applies to art. 9(2) BC when it is seen as a constitutive element of TRIPS.

As explained previously, the legitimate interests of copyright holders are those underpinning the exclusive rights guaranteed by the BC and TRIPS.[68] In this author's view, copyright holders possess two core legitimate interests of an economic nature. First, the interest to maximize the economic gains from their works in the markets which they may *legitimately* control during the lifetime of their rights, in order to recoup the investments incurred in the process of creating works and raise sufficient resources to finance new creative activities. That is why copyright holders are entitled to exclude third parties from the unauthorized enjoyment of their works: it is through the exercise of this prerogative that copyright holders can set the agenda of applications of their works and thus try to allocate them to the more productive uses (from an economic perspective). The second is to have facilitated access to the works of others, since these are essential inputs to the process of creating new works and products of the mind.

Copyright exceptions safeguard both the legitimate interests of copyright holders and those of the users of proprietary works. On the one hand, by allowing the continuous creation of new works from past contributions and their wide dissemination, copyright exceptions boost the moral and economic interests of the authors and also those of the companies engaged in the exploitation of goods derived therefrom.[69] On the other hand, by facilitating access to copyrighted works for socially valuable purposes, copyright exceptions strengthen competition and promote the observance of several human rights, notably the right to freedom of expression, the right to education, the right to cultural participation (i.e. the right to consume literary and artistic works and to engage in

[68] See Chapter 3, section 3.3.3. [69] See Goldstein 2001, 293.

creative activities) and the right to enjoy scientific advancements and their applications.[70]

Art. 13 TRIPS does not prohibit copyright exceptions from affecting the legitimate interests of copyright holders, since, as a general rule, any exception will cause them some sort of detriment.[71] Even when the exception ensures an equitable remuneration to the holders of the affected rights, their legitimate economic interests may be affected, as it is conceivable that the remuneration fixed by a collective management organization or by the competent state authority may be lower than that which would be fixed by the right holders themselves. What TRIPS prohibits is that the prejudice generated should reach unreasonable levels.

With the purpose of determining the reasonable character of the prejudice caused by an exception to the legitimate interests of copyright holders, it is appropriate to resort to the interpretation previously construed for the third step of the test in art. 30 of TRIPS.[72] Taking it as a reference, it can be said that the prejudice caused by a given exception will be reasonable provided it engenders social benefits that outweigh the losses suffered by the affected copyright holders.[73] In other words, the exception under investigation will pass the scrutiny of the third step if it is proportionate in the strict sense.[74] Although the wording of the third

[70] See Sun 2007, 313–319. [71] See Von Lewinski 2008, 163.

[72] See Chapter 3, section 3.3.3.

[73] According to Geiger (2008b, 948–949) such approach was adopted by the Civil Chamber of the Supreme Court of Switzerland, in a ruling handed down on June 26, 2007. Along the same lines, see Geiger 2007a, 18; Geiger 2008a, 195–196 ("the author should not be in the position to control all sorts of use of his work, but he has to tolerate certain interferences as long as they are justified by values that are superior to the copyright owner's interests.")

[74] See Chapter 2, section 2.3.3.2.1. Some authors put forward interpretations for the third step of the test which are similar to the one proposed here. Among them can be cited, for example: Ginsburg (2001, 16), who argues that the prejudices caused by the exception will be reasonable if the weight of the interests held by the beneficiaries of the exception significantly outweigh the interests of the affected right holders, or, in case there is parity between the benefits and losses brought about by the exception, if the exception ensures a remuneration for the right holders. Ficsor (2003, 60) interprets the term "unreasonable" as denoting "a balancing tool between the legal interests of the author and some other reasonable, justified interests to be taken into account." Senftleben (2004, 236–239) argues that the prejudices will be "reasonable" if the exception is cumulatively appropriate to promote the objective pursued thereby and necessary to achieve that goal, i.e. it is the least restrictive measure, among the alternatives available to the concerned State, to promote the objective referred to. According to the author, in the process of assessing the "necessity" of the exception, onerous compulsory licenses should *not* be included in the list of alternative measures available to the concerned State, because they would always be the least restrictive means of limiting the legitimate interests of copyright holders. If the exception under scrutiny is suitable, but *unnecessary* to achieve the objective pursued thereby, it will be considered lawful if it ensures the payment of an equitable remuneration to the affected right holders.

step of the test in art. 13 differs from the text of the final step of the test in art. 30, the requirement to weigh and compare the social benefits produced by the exception with the prejudice caused thereby to the legitimate interests of copyright holders is, in practice, implied in the term "unreasonably". This approach does not violate the text of art. 13 and is the option that best fits with: the wide array of commercial, social and environmental objectives pursued by the legal framework of the WTO; the fact that there is no hierarchy among the various commercial, social and environmental objectives pursued by the WTO; the necessity standard enshrined in art. 8 of TRIPS; the principle of proportionality; the requirement to identify a truly diverse meaning for each of the steps of the test in art. 13 (principle of effectiveness); and the obligation to discard interpretative options that lead to the practice of abuse of rights through the excessive protection of an interest at the expense of other interests of equal rank.

The interpretation developed here for the last step of the three-step test of art. 13 TRIPS can be fully applied in the context of art. 9(2) BC – in its capacity as a TRIPS provision – despite some differences in the wording of these provisions. Thus, while the final step of the test in art. 9(2) BC provides that copyright exceptions shall not unreasonably prejudice the legitimate interests of *authors*, the third stage of the test in art. 13 TRIPS requires that copyright exceptions do not unreasonably prejudice the legitimate interests of *right holders*.

The author and the rights holder are not necessarily the same person. An author may – and usually does – grant licenses for the exploitation of the exclusive rights associated with his work for various individuals and companies against the payment of a fee. Nevertheless, the difference in wording does not produce tangible practical effects. Often, the licensee represents, directly or indirectly, the author's own interests, especially those of an economic nature. As many authors do not control the means to directly exploit their works and products derived therefrom, they tend to choose to enter into licensing agreements with third parties whose business operations benefit themselves and the authors of the exploited works, either because they diffuse the works, making them known, or because their activities generate royalties to authors.[75] There is therefore a large convergence between the economic interests of copyright holders and those of authors, although this convergence is not absolute.[76] In line with this understanding, both under the final step of the test in art. 9(2) BC and of the test in art. 13 TRIPS, note should be taken of the prejudice caused by the exception to the legitimate interests of authors

[75] See Senftleben 2004, 218. [76] See Geiger 2008b, 12.

and also to the economic interests of those responsible for the commercial exploitation of the affected works.[77]

It is contended that the interpretation advanced here as to the terms of the tests set out in art. 9(2) BC and art. 13 TRIPS is reasonable, in particular because it does not conflict with the wording of these provisions and it is balanced enough to realize the many disparate goals of the WTO and TRIPS. For this reason, there is no obligation to have recourse to supplementary means of interpretation in order to confirm the interpretation reached or clarify the terms of the provisions referred to. Even so, in the next section, I turn to the records of the Stockholm Revision Conference on the Berne Convention, held in 1967, in search of aids that serve to confirm or modify the interpretation proposed here. It is worth clarifying that the records of the negotiations related to art. 13 of TRIPS will not be utilized, since they do not provide information that could be useful in elucidating the meaning of its terms.[78] However, by virtue of the fact that art. 13 TRIPS is substantially similar to the text of art. 9(2) BC, the records of the Stockholm Revision Conference, at first sight, *may* be useful to clarify the terms of both provisions.

4.3.4 Aids offered by the records of the Stockholm Revision Conference

In 1964, the preparatory Study Group for the Stockholm Revision Conference of the Berne Convention (Study Group), made up by representatives of the Government of Sweden and BIRPI, deemed it highly desirable to incorporate into the Berne Convention a provision that recognized the general right of reproduction of copyrighted works. However, in order to consider this proposal palatable, it was considered indispensable to bestow on the BC contracting parties the right to establish exceptions to the reproduction right, especially because at that time the legislation of several parties already included different exceptions to the right of reproduction, backed by cultural and public purposes. In this context, it was unlikely that these States would agree to take out, to a large extent, the exceptions already incorporated.[79] The Study Group proposed the following wording for the embryo of art. 9(2) BC:

[77] See, e.g., Nordemann *et al.* 1983, 109; Geiger 2008b, 947 and Senftleben 2004, 218. In line with the same understanding, the second sentence of art. 2(6) BC provides: "This protection [afforded by copyright] shall operate for the benefit of the author and his successors in title."

[78] See Gervais 1998, 88–91.

[79] See BIRPI 1967b, 46.

However, it shall be a matter for legislation in the countries of the Union, having regard to the provisions of this Convention, to limit the recognition and the exercising of that right, for specified purposes and on the condition that these purposes should not enter into economic competition with these works.[80]

The Study Group's report makes clear that the proposed formula merely authorizes the exemption of those forms of reproduction of works that: (i) pursue clearly identifiable goals; and (ii) do not enter into economic competition with "the forms of exploiting a work which have, or are likely to acquire, considerable economic or practical importance."[81] These observations taken from the 1964 report seem to support the view widely endorsed by the WTO and several authors that: (i) the second step of the test does not authorize the establishment of exceptions that may affect the rights of copyright holders to control all forms of exploitation of a work which are capable of generating, at present or in future, significant economic gains; and (ii) the payment of an equitable remuneration to the concerned copyright holders is not able to remedy the interference provoked by the exception in the normal exploitation of the affected works.[82]

Nevertheless, the Study Group notes that the formula proposed for the embryo of art. 9(2) provides a variable space for the adoption of exceptions to the right of reproduction: the payment of a fee to the concerned authors expands the space available for the establishment of exceptions to the right of reproduction.[83] The report clarifies unequivocally that the payment of a remuneration to the prejudiced authors supports the establishment of exceptions that, to some extent, interfere with their ability to control "all the forms of exploiting a work which have, or are likely to acquire, considerable economic or practical importance." Despite the difference in wording, the second step of the test proposed by the Study Group seems to perform the same function as the second step of the test enshrined in art. 9(2) BC.[84] If this is the case, it would be erroneous to state that an exception that affects a form of exploitation of works that have or may acquire considerable economic importance, provided it guarantees to the concerned authors an equitable remuneration, does not satisfy the second step of the test in art. 9(2) of the BC. Thus, the

[80] *Ibid.*, 48. [81] *Ibid.*, 48–49.

[82] See, e.g., Senftleben 2004, 133: "the payment of equitable remuneration has no influence on the decision whether or not a limitation conflicts with a normal exploitation."

[83] BIRPI 1967b, 49: "The formula proposed expresses, among other things, the thought that it is advisable to take special precautions before countenancing exceptions that may be applied without giving authors the right to claim remuneration. *If this right is granted, the scope for the power to make exceptions widens to some extent*" (emphasis added).

[84] See Ficsor 2003, 58.

notion of "normal exploitation of works" is not absolute. If it were so, the determination of the legality of an exception which affects a form of exploitation of a work that bears economic importance, would not be influenced by the payment of a remuneration to the affected right holders.

However, as observed earlier, the preparatory work should only be considered as a supplementary means of interpretation when it is able to clarify, unequivocally, the common understanding of the negotiating parties regarding the normative meaning of a controversial provision.[85] The Study Group was composed solely of representatives of the Government of Sweden and BIRPI. The other contracting States of the Berne Convention did not take part in their discussions and in preparing its report. Upon completion, the report prepared by the Study Group was referred to a Committee of Governmental Experts – this one open to participation by all contracting parties to the BC[86] – for evaluation. As we shall see, the formula proposed by the 1964 report for art. 9(2) BC was substantially amended by the Governmental Committee. Accordingly, many of the remarks made by the 1964 Study Group regarding the scope of this provision are not necessarily acceptable to clarify the meaning of the terms of the final version of the three-step test set out in art. 9(2).

When, in 1965, the formula proposed by the Study Group for the embryo of art. 9(2) was submitted to the Committee of Governmental Experts, the committee, recognizing the difficulty of finding a formula capable of supporting the exceptions to the the right of reproduction already comprised by the legal orders of the contracting parties to the BC, decided to establish a working group, whose mission was to find a new text for the proposed exception clause.[87] The working group put forth a new wording for the exception clause, which, after heated discussions, was approved by the Committee of Governmental Experts with the following text:

> (2) It shall be a matter for legislation in the countries of the Union to permit the reproduction of such works (a) for private use; (b) for judicial or administrative purposes; (c) in certain particular cases where the reproduction is not contrary to the legitimate interests of the author and does not conflict with a normal exploitation of the work.[88]

The approved proposal was incorporated into the program of amendments of the BC, discussed in Main Committee I of the Stockholm

[85] See Chapter 2, section 2.5.
[86] See BIRPI 1967b, 2.
[87] See WIPO 1971a, 112–113.
[88] *Ibid.*, 113.

Revision Conference.[89] That proposal did not please all negotiating parties, in particular the delegation of the United Kingdom, which advocated a simplified wording for the proposed art. 9(2). The Main Committee welcomed the suggestion presented by the British delegation, and decided to replace the proposal incorporated in the program of the Stockholm Conference with a general formula,[90] conceived to back, inter alia, the special cases covered by the original proposal.[91] The Main Committee established a working group vested with the mission of suggesting an enhanced and simplified wording for the proposed provision. Inspired by a British proposal (proposal S/42),[92] the working group designed a general exception clause for governing the establishment of exceptions to the right of reproduction.[93] After an alteration in the order of the factors of the test proposed by the working group, the Main Committee approved the text enshrined in the present art. 9(2).

Even though the records of the discussions held in Main Committee I are not very enlightening about the meaning of the terms of art. 9(2) BC,[94] there are some observations that can be made in the light of the following passage from the records of the Main Committee I:

> If it is considered that reproduction does not conflict with the normal exploitation of the work, the next step would be to consider whether it does not unreasonably prejudice the legitimate interests of the author. Only if such is not the case would it be possible in certain special cases to introduce a compulsory license, or to provide for use without payment. A practical example may be photocopying for various purposes. If it consists of producing a very large number of copies, it may not be permitted, as it conflicts with a normal exploitation of the work. If it implies a rather large number of copies for use in industrial undertakings, it may not unreasonably prejudice the legitimate interests of the author, provided that, according to national legislation, an equitable remuneration is paid. If a small

[89] The mission of Main Committee I of the 1967 Stockholm Conference was "to revise the substantive copyright provisions (Articles 1 to 20) of the Berne Convention" (WIPO 1971b, 837).

[90] *Ibid.*, 859. [91] *Ibid.*, 884.

[92] The British proposal reads: "(2) It shall be a matter for legislation in the countries of the Union to permit the reproduction of such works or substantial parts thereof in certain special cases where the reproduction does not unreasonably prejudice the legitimate interests of the author and does not conflict with a normal exploitation of the work" (WIPO 1971b, 687).

[93] The Working Group proposal reads as follows: "Article 9(2) should read: It shall be a matter for legislation in the countries of the Union to permit the reproduction of such works in certain special cases, provided that such reproduction does not unreasonably prejudice the legitimate interests of the author and does not conflict with a normal exploitation of the work" (WIPO 1971b, 883).

[94] See, for example, the interventions of the delegates of Sweden (WIPO 1971b, 858), the Netherlands (*ibid.*), France (*ibid.*), Israel (*ibid.*, 884) and Belgium (*ibid.*, 885). See also the commentary on the Berne Convention published by WIPO (1978, 64–65).

number of copies is made, photocopying may be permitted without payment, particularly for individual or scientific use.[95]

When the report points out that it is forbidden to produce a "very large number of copies" of a work, it denotes that in the absence of an indication of the conditions under which copies can be taken, third parties could distribute them in the market in order to compete directly with the affected copyright holders. That is, an exception that generally supports the unauthorized reproduction of protected works allows the depletion of the economic value of the right of reproduction. That is why art. 9(2) BC only allows the reproduction of copyrighted works for the promotion of special purposes.

The passage from the report that indicates that the production of a "rather large number of copies" of a copyrighted work for use in industrial undertakings does not unreasonably prejudice the legitimate interests of authors affected, provided the addressees of the copies pay an equitable remuneration to the right holders concerned is often employed to support the view that the payment of an equitable remuneration is a suitable means to prevent prejudice to the legitimate economic interests of authors being deemed unreasonable. However, this passage is not usually utilized to support the view that the payment of a remuneration to the relevant right holders is adequate to prevent the emergence of a conflict with the normal exploitation of the affected works.[96]

What does follow from the passage is that the production of a "rather large number of copies" for use in business organizations does not conflict with a normal exploitation of the works reproduced without authorization. Given the economic capacity of business organizations and industrial undertakings to purchase the works they need to carry out their institutional activities – e.g. R&D activities – it is indisputable that this group of users is part of the consumer market for, inter alia, technical and scientific works. Therefore, the production of multiple copies of, for example, a chapter in a book for use by the innovation department of a company undoubtedly prejudices the normal exploitation of the right to reproduce this work by its right holder, as the copies taken are substitutes for the copies introduced into the market by the rights holder.

Having said that, the passage from the report indicates that the payment of an equitable remuneration to copyright holders, by virtue of the unauthorized reproduction of their works, is *also* a suitable means of

95 Quoted in WTO, WT/DS160/R (*US – Section 110(5) Copyright Act*), Panel Report, para. 6.73.

96 See, e.g., Senftleben 2004, 128–133; Ricketson 1987, 484; Ricketson and Ginsburg 2006, 777.

remedying the potential conflict with a normal exploitation of the works, arising from an exception, provided the exception guarantees to the holders of the right of reproduction the prerogative of controlling one or more forms of exploitation of their works, which are capable of generating significant economic gains. This interpretation can be inferred from the expression "rather large number of copies" (which should not be confused with "very large number of copies") associated with the indication of the destination of the copies taken (for use in industrial undertakings). Such limiting components imply that, even if a certain exception prejudices the exercise of the right of reproduction in a particular market sector, the exempted use will not be able to meet all the existing demand for the affected works. The remaining demand may only be satisfied by the copies made available in the market by the holders of the right of reproduction.

In summary, the payment of an equitable remuneration can render "reasonable" the prejudices to the legitimate economic interests of authors provoked by an exception, as the remuneration paid dramatically reduces the level of the prejudice suffered by them.[97] In addition, it can also prevent the exception from conflicting with the normal exploitation of the affected works. This conclusion seems to be confirmed by an example used by the WIPO's interpretation guide to the Berne Convention, authored by Claude Masouyé, Secretary of Main Committee I of the 1967 Stockholm Conference, to illustrate the scope of art. 9(2) BC:

> Another example is that of a lecturer who, aiming at supporting his argument, instead of using a quote prefers to photocopy fully a brief article featured in a magazine and read it in his speech: It is obvious that such an act does not impair the spread of the magazine. Another thing would be if the speaker had made a very large number of copies and distributed to his audience, thereby impairing the spread of the publication in question in this particular environment. In the event that the concerned author suffered a lack of income, the law should confer on him a compensation.[98]

Finally, from the third example included in the passage reproduced above – the one that considers permissible, vis-à-vis art. 9(2) BC, an exception that allows the free production of a small number of copies for private or scientific purposes – can be inferred that the production of a limited number of copies of a work for private or scientific purposes is not capable of conflicting with its normal exploitation, nor of generating

[97] See WIPO 1971b, 882: "Since any exception to the right of reproduction must inevitably prejudice the author's interests, the Working Group had attempted to limit that prejudice by introducing the term 'inéquitable' to translate the English term 'unreasonable'."

[98] Masouyé 1978, 63 (free translation).

unreasonable economic prejudice to the legitimate economic interests of authors. This example conflicts with the current understanding that the second step of the test in art. 9(2) confers on the holders of the right of reproduction the control of all forms of exploitation of their works, guaranteed by this exclusive right, which have or may acquire considerable economic or practical importance. It is natural to assume that the copies taken from literary works by students and researchers will affect, to some extent, their commercialization: the student who meets his needs through recourse to photocopying will possibly not purchase an original copy of the photocopied work. When it is recalled that, back in 1967, industrialized countries had a significant number of researchers and students enrolled in their educational institutions and that developing countries were already struggling to democratize access to education in their territories, it is obvious that the application of the hypothetical exception is capable of causing significant economic impacts on the market for educational and scientific works, due to its cumulative effect: the production of a small number of copies of copyrighted works by a large number of students potentially interferes with the commercial exploitation of the affected works. Yet this form of exploitation of works was deemed exempted by the conference records.

From the three examples included in the final report of Main Committee I a general rule can be drawn that the space available for the adoption of exceptions to the right of reproduction varies depending on the objectives pursued by the exception. If the exception has no stated goal, it is illegal, because third parties may use it to compete directly with the holders of the affected works in all available markets. Secondly, if the exception has a clear goal, but interferes with the ability of copyright holders to extract significant commercial gains from a certain form of exploitation of their works, the legality of the exception will depend on the payment of an equitable remuneration to the affected right holders. In addition, the legality of the exception will depend on the guarantee that the exception leaves untouched at least one form of exploitation of the relevant works, which are capable of generating significant commercial gains at present.[99]

As regards the third step of the test in art. 9(2) of the BC, there is one particular passage from the records of Main Committee I which

[99] This is a result of non-approval of the proposals put forward by India and Romania, addressed to authorize the compulsory general licensing of the right of reproduction of works. Thus, as the right of reproduction shall not be fully replaced by a right of remuneration, exceptions to this right must always ensure that right holders exclusively control some form of exploitation, covered by this right, capable of generating significant economic benefits.

can perhaps serve to clarify its meaning. During negotiations, the Main Committee had difficulties in translating into French the expression "unreasonably prejudice." Initially, the French version used the term "inéquitable" for the English term "unreasonable," but this translation was not deemed appropriate. The French delegation proposed to replace the term "inéquitable" used to describe the prejudice caused to the legitimate interests of authors with "appréciable." The delegation of Portugal opposed the French proposal, as it considered that such replacement would introduce a "quantitative concept" into the third step of the test. A change in this direction would be in conflict with the will of the States which participated in the drafting of art. 9(2).[100] Since none of the delegations participating in the discussions opposed the declaration voiced by Portugal, it is that view which mirrors the common understanding of the negotiators of art. 9(2). The intervention made by the Portuguese delegation confirms the inadequacy of the interpretation endorsed by the WTO panel in *US – Section 110 (5) Copyright Act*, according to which the third step of the test in art. 13 TRIPS would have the function of assessing whether a copyright exception generates a significant loss of revenues to the detriment of right holders.[101] Furthermore, based on the Portuguese intervention, it can be stated that the final step of the test in art. 9(2) of the BC has the role of assessing the unreasonable character of the prejudice engendered in *qualitative terms*. And for achieving this goal, the interpreter shall evaluate the prejudice produced by the exception, together with the social benefits created thereby.

It is possible that some interpreters of TRIPS – notably policy makers in industrialized countries, panels and the Appellate Body of the WTO – do not agree with the observations advanced here, based upon the records of the negotiations of art. 9(2) of the BC. They will argue that there is no assurance that these views reflect the common will of the negotiating States. However, it is also important to stress that nothing in the final report of Main Committee I suggests that art. 9(2) of the BC should be interpreted with the *sole* purpose of furthering the economic interests of copyright holders, through the curtailment of the room available for the adoption of exceptions to the right of reproduction. Even the States participating in the negotiations were uncertain about the scope of the new provision.

Even if the report of Main Committee I comprises elements that indicate that the terms of art. 9(2) of the BC must be understood so as to restrict substantially the room available to the adoption of exceptions to

[100] See WIPO 1971b, 884–885.
[101] WTO, WT/DS160/R, Panel Report, para. 6.229.

the right of reproduction, they shall not necessarily be used to interpret the terms of art. 9(2) BC, in its capacity as a constituent element of TRIPS, and of art. 13 TRIPS. As previously mentioned, pursuant to art. 31(1) VCLT, the provisions of a treaty must be interpreted "in good faith in accordance with the ordinary meaning to be given to the terms of the treaty in their context and in the light of its object and purpose."Although the wording of art. 9(2) BC has not been altered by its incorporation into the text of TRIPS, and the text of art. 13 TRIPS is very similar to the text of the former provision, the broad social, economic and environmental objectives of TRIPS and of the WTO[102] should not be confused with the limited objective of the BC "to protect, in as effective and uniform a manner as possible, the rights of authors in their literary and artistic works."

In addition, the context in which art. 9(2) BC – in its capacity as a constituent element of TRIPS – and art. 13 TRIPS should be construed is much broader and complex than the context within which art. 9(2) BC should be interpreted. Therefore, the records of the 1967 Stockholm Conference are not necessarily reliable sources of aids for the clarification of the meaning of art. 9(2) of the BC – seen as a component of TRIPS – and art. 13 TRIPS. For this reason, the meaning attributed to the terms of these provisions, summarized in Table 4.1 below, remains valid.

Concluding remarks on Part I

I saw all the nations of the world together, and learned not to be ashamed of mine. By measuring closely the large and strong ones, I found them smaller and weaker than justice and law. Ruy Barbosa

As I sought to demonstrate in the first part of this work, the general exception clauses of TRIPS should be interpreted as *sui generis* tests of proportionality, in the sense of a proportionality test associated with a consistency test. This result stems from the fact that art. 8 TRIPS allows WTO members to adopt exceptions to IPRs intended to further any socio-environmental interest – notably those falling under human rights treaties and MEAs – and also from the fact that the general exception clauses incorporate ambiguous terms, which, by virtue of art. 31 of the VCLT, should be interpreted, inter alia, in the light of: the multiple social, environmental and economic objectives of the WTO and TRIPS, the relevant WTO case law on art. XX of GATT 1994 and the principle of proportionality.

[102] See Chapter 2, sections 2.3.1 and 2.3.2.

Table 4.1 *Function and normative meaning of art. 9 (2) BC and art. 13 TRIPS, when interpreted in light of the customary rules of treaty interpretation*

	Art. 13 TRIPS	Art. 9(2) BC
Function of the test	Control the legality of the exceptions to the exclusive rights guaranteed by TRIPS and therefore by the BC.	Control the legality of exceptions to the right of reproduction, not backed by arts. 10, 10bis, 11bis (3) and 13(1) BC
1st step: Assessment of the special character of the exceptions	The exception shall: * be addressed to promote any of the goals allowed by art. 8 TRIPS; * be a suitable means for promoting the goal that triggered its adoption; * be the least restrictive means of the curtailed exclusive right, amongst the measures reasonably available to the proponent state; and * observe the following limits: (i) prohibit the enacting of exceptions which prevent the legal protection of the categories of works which, under art. 2(1), (3) and (5) BC and art. 10 TRIPS, should be eligible for protection; (ii) comply with the clauses of national and of most-favored-nation treatment; (iii) ensure the minimum term of protection guaranteed by art. 12 TRIPS and art. 7 BC; (iv) in respect of the exceptions to the right of reproduction, adopted under arts. 10 and 10bis BC, respect the area of the compulsory licensing system laid down in the appendix to the BC.	The same meaning attributed to the first step of the test set out in art. 13 TRIPS applies to the first step of the test in art. 9(2).
2nd step: Assess whether the exception conflicts with the normal exploitation of the works affected thereby	The exception will satisfy the second step of the test if: (a) it interferes with an abnormal form of exploitation of the relevant works, and therefore not subject to the control of copyright holders; or (b) it does not affect any of the forms of normal exploitation of the relevant works guaranteed by the curtailed exclusive right, which are capable of generating significant commercial gains to the concerned right holders; or	The same meaning attributed to the second step of the test in art. 13 applies to the second step of the test in art. 9(2), with the proviso that the latter only controls the lawfulness of exceptions to the right of reproduction and does not allow the granting of compulsory general licenses.

(cont.)

Table 4.1 (*cont.*)

	Art. 13 TRIPS	Art. 9(2) BC
	(c) it affects one or more forms of normal exploitation of the relevant works guaranteed by the curtailed exclusive right, capable of generating significant economic gains, provided: (i) the affected right holders are entitled to receive an equitable remuneration for the unauthorized use of their works; and (ii) the exception leaves untouched at least one of the forms of exploitation of the relevant works capable of generating, at present, important commercial gains; or (d) it takes from the control of the right holders all forms of normal exploitation of their works guaranteed by the curtailed exclusive right, in return for an equitable remuneration, provided the full replacement of the exclusive right by a right of remuneration is authorized by the BC (e.g. art. 11bis (2)) or TRIPS.	
3rd step: Assessment of the reasonableness of the prejudice produced by the exception	The exception will satisfy the final step of the test if the social benefits produced thereby outweigh the prejudice caused to the legitimate interests of the right holders concerned.	The same meaning attributed to the third step of the test set out in art. 13 TRIPS applies to the third step of the test in art. 9(2).

The fact that the objectives of the WTO and TRIPS overlap with a variety of human values, protected by the main international treaties on human rights and with the core values promoted by MEAs, produces the practical effect of forcing the interpreters to construe the terms of the general exception clauses of TRIPS so as to harmonize with such values and objectives. For example, the goal of the WTO system of protecting and preserving the environment and enhancing the means for doing so has the practical effect of forcing the interpreter to choose the interpretation for the terms of the provisions of TRIPS that best realizes the right to a healthy environment, provided in art. 11 of the Additional Protocol to the American Convention on Human Rights in the Area of Economic,

Social and Cultural Rights (Protocol of San Salvador) and in art. 24 of the African Charter on Human and Peoples' Rights, although so far this right has not been guaranteed by the legal framework of the WTO. The goal of "raising standards of living" of individuals covertly refers to art. 11(1) of the ICESCR. Therefore, the terms of TRIPS should be interpreted so as to promote "the right of everyone to an adequate standard of living for himself and his family, including adequate food, clothing and housing, and to the continuous improvement of living conditions." The goal of TRIPS of promoting the transfer and dissemination of technology to the mutual benefit of producers and users of technological knowledge (art. 8) remits to the international community the duty of adopting measures "necessary for the conservation, the development and the diffusion of science and culture," with a view to securing the human right to "participate in the cultural life of the community, to enjoy the arts and to share in scientific advancement and its benefits," guaranteed both by the UDHR (art. 27(1)) and the ICESCR (art. 15(1)(a)). The WTO's goal of optimizing the use of world resources in line with the objective of sustainable development requires the interpreter of TRIPS to construe its terms with the aim of promoting, *simultaneously*, innovation and creativity, the various human rights recognized by the International Bill of Human Rights and the preservation/restoration of the environment.

Finally, on the one hand, the principle of proportionality – which should be considered in the interpretation process by virtue of the necessity standard enshrined in art. 8 TRIPS and by reason of its status as a general principle of law – has the effect of preventing the interpreter of the general exception clauses from automatically conferring a higher status on the commercial interests of the holders of IPRs in relation to the social and environmental objectives pursued by the WTO system. On the other hand, it requires the interpreter to seek the interpretive option that best reconciles the economic interests of the holders of IPRs with the social and environmental interests pursued by the WTO and TRIPS.

In summary, as noted by Ruse-Khan (2008), the TRIPS Agreement, subtly, both permits and *requires* WTO Members to interpret its terms in order to safeguard the interests not only of an economic nature, but also overriding public interests, such as the environment and human dignity, despite the fact that human rights treaties and MEAs are not part of the WTO legal framework. The TRIPS Agreement is capable of promoting in a balanced manner, the set of social, economic and environmental goals pursued by the WTO system, when the interpreter understands that, despite it being the result of a strategy pursued by the business sectors of industrialized countries to promote their private interests,[103] the agreement is not confused with the will of the forces that drove its adoption.

Art. 3(2) of the DSU requires that reports and decisions rendered by the organs of the DSB do not increase or diminish the rights and obligations provided to WTO Members by virtue of the covered agreements. One could argue that interpreting the TRIPS Agreement under the customary rules of treaty interpretation codified by the VCLT has the effect of breaching this rule. However, it must be made clear that, when the VCLT rules are correctly applied, the interpreter does not add or diminish the rights and obligations conferred by the WTO agreements to its members, since the application of these rules is mandatory.[104] The sole role played by the rules of the VCLT is in *clarifying* the scope of the rights and obligations of the WTO Members.[105]

If the general exception clauses of the TRIPS Agreement had to be interpreted in accordance with the guidelines set out in *Canada – Pharmaceutical Patents, US – Section 110 (5) Copyright Act* and in *EC – Trademarks and Geographical Indications*, these provisions would always be interpreted restrictively with the aim of maximizing the protection afforded to the economic interests of the holders of IPRs. That is, the commercial interests of the holders of copyrights, industrial designs, trademarks and patents would *always* have precedence over the non-commercial interests held by society. Obviously such an approach prevents the achievement of many of the social, technological and environmental goals pursued by the WTO, since it prevents the adoption of socially efficient exceptions to IPRs. In this way, the general approach endorsed by the WTO Panels contravenes the rules of interpretation of the VCLT insofar as it unjustifiably favors the interests of one group to the detriment of other interests protected by the WTO. Underscoring the misconception of this approach, the WTO Appellate Body rightly stated in *EC – Computer Equipment* that "[t]he purpose of treaty interpretation under Article 31 of the *Vienna Convention* is to ascertain the *common* intentions of the parties. These *common* intentions can not be ascertained on the basis of the subjective and unilaterally determined 'expectations' of *one* of the parties to the treaty."[106]

The fact that the interpretations presented here for the general exception clauses of TRIPS differ substantially from those in the three cases ruled on by the WTO attests to the existence of two lines of jurisprudence to the TRIPS Agreement: the oral and the legal. The "oral

[103] See Taubman 2007, 110. [104] See Koskenniemi 2006, para. 447.
[105] See Mitchell 2007, 809.
[106] WTO, /DS62/AB/R, WT/DS67/AB/R, WT/DS68/AB/R, Appellate Body Report, para. 84.

jurisprudence," echoed by the dominating powers that participated in the negotiations and drafting of the agreement in the GATT Uruguay Round,[107] is intended to perpetuate the prominent position of the industrialized countries in the information economy, through the dissociation between the multilateral trading system and the international rules conceived to safeguard human rights and the environment. On the other hand, the legal line is based on the full observance of the customary rules of treaty interpretation and, therefore, should be observed by the organs of the DSB (panels and the Appellate Body), in all disputes brought to their attention. The legal line of jurisprudence has the advantage of not being premised on the view that the leeway offered to WTO members to establish exceptions to IPRs should, as a matter of principle, be narrow in scope. In accordance with this line of jurisprudence, the WTO Appellate Body held in *EC – Hormones* that "merely characterizing a treaty provision as an 'exception' does not by itself justify a 'stricter' or 'narrower' interpretation of that provision than would be warranted by examination of the ordinary meaning of the actual treaty words, viewed in context and in the light of the treaty's object and purpose, or, in other words, by applying the normal rules of treaty interpretation."[108]

Nevertheless, in actual practice, the oral line of jurisprudence has a strong impact on the views backed by the organs of the DSB in the disputes involving the general exception clauses of TRIPS. Therefore, the approach adopted by the organs of the WTO in such cases does not reflect the requirements set by the WTO legal framework, but a serious technical miscomprehension.[109] What remains to be clarified is whether the balanced interpretations proposed for the general exception clauses of the TRIPS Agreement are also applicable to the WTO Members that are also parties to bilateral or regional free trade agreements which entail TRIPS-plus rules.

Art. 1(1) of the TRIPS Agreement authorizes, but does not mandate, WTO Members to "implement in their law more extensive protection than is required by this [TRIPS] Agreement, provided that such protection does not contravene the provisions of the TRIPS Agreement. This means that although the TRIPS Agreement authorizes the ongoing strengthening of the protection granted to IPRs,[110] there are absolute limits that must be respected, which have been called "ceilings" by Kur and Ruse-Khan.[111] By way of illustration, one could take: art. 9(2) of TRIPS,

107 Taubman 2007, 111.
108 WTO, WT/DS26/AB/R, Appellate Body Report, para. 104.
109 Frankel (2005, 369) argues that although the organs of the DSB recognize that the rules enshrined in arts. 31 and 32 VCLT represent the customary rules of treaty interpretation, they tend to misapply them in IPRs disputes.
110 See Dinwoodie and Dreyfuss 2007, 449.
111 Kur and Ruse-Khan 2009, 5.

which prohibits the copyright protection of "ideas, procedures, methods of operation or mathematical concepts as such";[112] the clauses providing national and most-favored-nation treatment; and the provisions that make explicit some of the goals and principles of the Agreement (arts. 7 and 8). And what about the general exception clauses of the TRIPS Agreement? Do those provisions also represent mandatory "ceilings" to be observed? In other words: if WTO Members wish to grant to IPRs more extensive protection than is required by the TRIPS Agreement, are they authorized to negotiate bilateral, regional or multilateral agreements that forbid the exercise of the prerogatives offered by the general exception clauses of TRIPS, or that set additional requirements for the exercise of those prerogatives, so as to narrow their scope?

In view of the whole set of objectives and principles of the TRIPS Agreement and of the WTO system, the answer to that question is negative. There is no doubt that the general exception clauses of TRIPS provide prerogatives to WTO Members, which may be exercised or not according to each member's needs. On the other hand, banning or restricting the exercise of those prerogatives would go against the objectives and principles of the TRIPS Agreement and of the WTO, as it would curtail the future adoption of measures aimed at protecting multiple commercial and non-commercial goals pursued by the WTO system. On account of the prohibition or restriction of the exercise of the prerogatives conferred by the general exception clauses, whenever there are cases of imbalance, States would lack the means to realize many of the objectives pursued by the TRIPS Agreement and the WTO through the adoption of exceptions, capable of mitigating the negative impact caused by IPRs.

Whereas the WTO Members may only provide more extensive protection to IPRs than that required under TRIPS, "provided that such protection does not contravene the provisions of this Agreement," the more extensive protection conferred will be lawful if it is aimed at furthering the objectives of TRIPS, indicated in art. 7, and if it observes the general principles of the agreement referred to in art. 8. Undoubtedly, many of the objectives of TRIPS will be unattainable if the space provided by TRIPS for the establishment of exceptions to IPRs diminishes. For this reason, strengthening the protection afforded to IPRs cannot be accomplished by removing or restricting the scope of the general exception clauses of TRIPS. Any new bilateral, regional or multilateral treaty which imposes on a WTO Member the obligation to adopt a restrictive

112 Kur and Ruse-Khan (2009) also mention as examples of explicit "ceilings" arts. 2(8), 10(1) of the BC, art. 10(2) TRIPS and arts. 5ter, 6bis of the Paris Convention.

interpretation for the terms of the general exception clauses of TRIPS, or imposes additional conditions to the exercise of the prerogatives ensured by these provisions, or prohibits the exercise of these prerogatives, will therefore be invalid. The general exception clauses, despite their designation, shall not be seen by WTO Members as aberrations to be curtailed or cut off from the realm of TRIPS. They are actually essential tools for creating a balance between public and private interests. Moreover, when well designed, they also promote innovation and creativity, by strengthening the intellectual public domain.

Summing up, the exercise of the privilege offered by art. 1(1) of the TRIPS Agreement cannot be used merely and simply to strengthen IPRs. It should be employed to carry out the whole set of objectives pursued by the TRIPS Agreement and the WTO system, and to ensure compliance with TRIPS principles, encapsulated in art. 8. The exercise of the privilege in ways that will promote the realization of some of the objectives of the TRIPS Agreement – e.g. commercial interests of some groups – and hinder or prevent the realization of others – e.g. non-commercial interests – represents an abuse of power *(détournement de pouvoir)* as well as a breach of the principle of effectiveness in treaty interpretation, as it renders useless arts. 7 and 8 TRIPS. On this ground, the strengthening of IPRs cannot be achieved through the inception of new obstacles to the establishment of exceptions to IPRs.

Before closing Part I, an important comment is appropriate. Annette Kur holds that the principle of proportionality is an unwritten principle of the WTO system and, as such, might be applied autonomously, even within the scope of the TRIPS Agreement.[113] In her opinion, the constitutive elements of the general exception clauses of the TRIPS Agreement would serve merely to specify the aspects to be used in the process of applying the proportionality test. This means that control of the legitimacy of exceptions to IPRs corresponds to the proportionality test, and not to the general exception clauses. In more precise terms: for example, guided by the elements of art. 30, in the process of assessing the legitimacy of an exception to the rights conferred by patents, the interpreter would first identify the situations that are covered by the exception and its scope. Secondly, he would assess the economic impact brought about by the exception and check if the latter still preserved economic incentives for third parties to keep investing in innovation. Thirdly, the interpreter would have to identify both the interests promoted and those prejudiced by the exception.[114] On the basis of these data gathered, the interpreter then applies the test of proportionality in order to verify the legitimacy

[113] See Kur 2008, 39. [114] *Ibid.*, 41.

of the exception. The exception is lawful if it satisfies the proportionality test.

Although in some points the interpretation posited by Kur resembles that proposed in this work, they are different in at least two aspects. Even though we both agree that the principle of proportionality permeates the agreements covered by the WTO, it should not be applied autonomously, without strictly following the words of the provision to be interpreted. The principle of proportionality – seen either as an integral part of art. 8 of the TRIPS Agreement or as a general principle of law – may only be applied in the process of clarification of the terms of the general exception clauses of TRIPS. Thus, an interpretation that the principle of proportionality may be applied autonomously, with the aim of controlling the lawfulness of the exceptions to IPRs, breaches the customary rules of treaty interpretation codified by the VCLT.

Secondly, whereas I hold that the general exception clauses of TRIPS comprise sub-tests that shall be applied sequentially and cumulatively, and through which all exceptions must necessarily pass in order to be deemed legitimate, Kur posits that the each of the general exception clauses is an indivisible whole,[115] whose elements are to be seen as one in the course of a general assessment. This implies that, for instance, if a patent exception does not pass the filter of one of the steps of art. 30, it may still be pronounced legitimate.[116] The interpretation proposed conflicts with the words of the general exception clauses themselves. If these provisions indicate that the conditions listed therein must be cumulatively observed, they should not be contradicted. In fact, the interpretation proposed by Kur seems to transform the general exception clauses into fair use-type defenses.

115 On this point, Kur (2008, 41) states: "instead of constituting three separate units, the three steps are nothing but individual elements informing one overall assessment."

116 Kur notes (*ibid.*, 42): "Considering that the philosophy underlying TRIPS as a trade-related instrument is in favour of free competition rather than its restriction, it seems logical that the proponents of a limitation should be given the benefit of doubt, if the assessment undertaken on the basis of the three steps should lead to inconclusive results."

Part II

Putting to the test the capacity of the general exception clauses of the TRIPS Agreement to promote the pillars of sustainable development

5 Patents and the R&D and genetic diagnostic test exceptions

> As we enjoy great advantages from the inventions of others, we should be glad to serve others by any invention of ours.
>
> Benjamin Franklin[1]

5.1 Introduction

Advances in molecular biology and new information technologies have provided humanity with a more precise understanding of genes and their various roles in the working of living beings. They have permitted a rapid sequencing of the genomes of different living organisms and the identification of the potential function of genes; they have opened up ways for humans to interfere in the functioning of genes and to manipulate them for socially useful purposes.[2]

Until fairly recently, the patent system simply granted legal protection to innovations described as consumer end-products. It excluded natural phenomena and resources already present in nature from the list of materials eligible for protection. Consequently, the only products subject to protection were tangible products, developed through an innovative use of technical information and the forces of nature. Techniques for the extraction of biochemical molecules from their natural environment could also receive protection insofar as the natural forces and resources were maintained within the public domain.[3] This meant that the technical information permeating the patented innovations was freely accessible. Such were the means employed by patent law to ensure ample leeway for the business sector to develop alternative products to those under protection. This justified adopting research exceptions that were limited in scope, since patents did not limit freedom of innovation.[4]

From the 1980s onward, the rapid and astounding scientific development of biological sciences prompted the courts and administrations of

[1] Walljasper 2010, 61. [2] See Walsh *et al.*, 289. [3] Dreyfuss 2004, 466.
[4] *Ibid.*, 462.

developed and developing countries to update their patent laws in order to permit the protection of innovations that, up to that moment, were not eligible for protection.[5] As a result, many States currently grant protection, inter alia, to microorganisms, recombinant proteins, transgenic plants and animals and DNA sequences and fragments, including those of human origin.[6]

Many of the innovations developed by emerging sectors in the economy, especially the pharmaceutical and biotechnology sectors, exhibit special features: they can serve both as end-products, ready for use by the ordinary consumer and as raw material, aimed at the scientific community. Consequently, the dividing line between consumer end-products and foundational developments became blurred.[7]

One of the main consequences of granting patents for foundational developments is that it may set potential hurdles for the scientific and technological development of society. They do not only grant patent holders the right to control the product that has been effectively developed (product markets); they can also control the freedom of third parties to innovate on the basis of the inventions whose patents they hold (innovation markets).[8]

In view of substantial scientific progress in the last decades, developing new innovations – in biotechnology as in other fields – has become a simpler and less creative task.[9] In response to the lower level of inventiveness involved in the process of innovation and to the demand of R&D institutions, patent legislation around the globe has facilitated compliance with the substantive criteria of patentability and has enlarged the definition of the notion of invention.[10] The combination of laxer patentability criteria and wider technical knowledge has fostered the rapid increase in the number of patents granted worldwide.

Within this new context, marked by the salient role played by science in economic development, university institutions have been seen as drivers of industrial development. Thus, the US Congress passed the Bayh–Dole Act in 1980, which authorized universities and public research institutions to patent innovations financed with US public funds. By virtue of

[5] The driving force of the international trend towards legal reform was the decision in 1980 of the US Supreme Court in *Diamond* v. *Chakrabarty*, 447 US 303 (1980). It authorized granting patents to all categories of inventions, including those that comprise living beings, insofar as they are the result of human activity.

[6] See Hoffman 2003, 1018–1019. [7] See Dreyfuss 2004, 463. [8] *Ibid.*

[9] The Royal Society 2003, para. 3.29, remarks that the stock of technical knowledge of mankind has been expanding at high speed. The result is that the "qualitative leap" introduced by new patented inventions results from the application of technologies that make the process of technological development routine.

[10] See Hoffman 2003, 1012.

this law between 1991 and 2000, a group of 84 American universities found a 238% increase in the volume of patent applications filed, a 161% increase in the number of licensing agreements concluded and a 520% increase in the volume of royalties received.[11] In the belief that if they followed the US model of over-valued private property their countries would achieve economic success, legislators in the other countries in the Organisation for Economic Co-operation and Development (OECD) as well as developing countries adopted policies similar to the US model.[12]

Originally, the purpose of those policies was to facilitate the passage from scientific knowledge produced in universities to products and processes useful for society. It was presumed that patents would induce industry to invest in using inventions in new technologies and products.[13] Within that context, innovations, information and research tools that until then had been confined to the public domain were protected by IPRs or, worse still, kept secret.[14] In actual practice, the public bias of the policies modeled upon the Bayh–Dole Act is in obvious decline, mainly because it allows the patenting of foundational, upstream innovations which are crucial for the progress of science and technology.[15]

Even though universities and public research institutions depend on liberal access to knowledge and technology produced by third parties in order to comply with their educational mission, currently they tend to opt for licensing policies that restrict access to the knowledge produced within their premises. Instead of setting the dissemination and updating of knowledge as a top priority, many universities adopt a "gold rush mentality."[16] They choose policies aimed at maximizing profits, even if it runs counter to the very purpose of their existence: the welfare of society.[17] And, with such goals in mind, universities do not hesitate to apply harsh and antisocial legal strategies: a growing number of universities in the USA and elsewhere are suing for the non-authorized use of their innovations.[18] Judicial settlements between the academic and the private sector can reach colossal figures.[19]

The international dissemination of university policies of patenting as much as possible has undermined the social norms of science that ruled the practice and conduct of the scientific community over the centuries.

11 See Thursby and Thursby 2003, 1031.
12 See, e.g., Clift 2007, 80 and Conceição *et al.* 2004, 558.
13 See SACGHS 2009, 43.
14 See Walsh *et al.* 2003, 296.
15 See Eisenberg and Rai 2001, 158.
16 See, e.g., Dreyfuss 2004, 464; National Research Council 2006, 45; The Royal Society 2003, para. 2.13.
17 See National Institutes of Health 1998, 3.
18 See Eisenberg 2003, 1018–1019.
19 *Ibid.*

Briefly put, the norms of science are based on the paradigm of collaboration and promotion of the wide dissemination and sharing of the fruits of scientific research. According to the so-called norm of "communism" and on the basis of the belief that the point of departure of any research is the knowledge that makes up the common heritage of humanity, members of the scientific community had the moral duty to offer the results of their research to society.[20] Their sole reward was public esteem in view of their scientific contribution.[21] However, as the role of science in economic progress grew ever more relevant, competition for the use of scientific knowledge for purposes of production triggered the erosion of the social norms of open science[22] and gave birth to entrepreneurial science. In this new scenario, the social norms of science are deemed obsolete and are being replaced by the norms of intellectual property.[23] In other words, scientific institutions, including those financed with public funds that should therefore be committed to the promotion of free access to knowledge and scientific progress, have drawn up norms that limit its access and use. They justify this new stance saying that it encourages the development of humanity.[24] The reward of scientists and universities for their contribution to scientific knowledge is no longer social prestige. Patents and contracts of benefit sharing have become the new currency for professional advancement.[25]

The problem of substantially widening the list of inventions eligible for protection, simplifying the procedure to secure patents and encouraging universities and public research institutions to act as private businesses, lies in the broad freedom granted to patent holders to set the agenda for the application of their inventions.[26] In no way can we presume that patent holders will automatically promote the public interest, when they are actually defending their own individual interests.[27] Essentially, the aim of patent holders is to maximize their profits and maintain the status quo for the longest possible time. With that end in mind, they can adopt strategies aimed at a restriction of competition and the pace of scientific and technological development, by not exploring their invention, refusing to grant licenses to third parties or charging abusive royalty fees. These practices clash with the legitimate interest of society in being able to

[20] In Merton's view (1977, 365), innovations do not belong to the scientist who brings them to light since any progress in science is based on the collaboration between the past and current generations.
[21] *Ibid.*, 363. [22] See Stiglitz 1995, 8. [23] See Merton 1988, 623.
[24] See Eisenberg 1989, 1047–1048. [25] See Baca 2006, 5.
[26] See Gitter 2001, 1680. [27] See SACGHS 2009, 39–40.

gain access to patented technologies in order to better understand and improve them, and benefit from them.[28]

Recalling that scientific-technological development is a cumulative process, dependent on ongoing access to a vast wealth of information, knowledge and technical tools, the widening of the reach of private dominion over foundational scientific and technological progress – in the absence of limiting rules (e.g. exceptions to patent rights) – places the welfare of substantial sectors of humanity at risk, particularly those with lower purchasing power.

In the course of this chapter, the main current obstacles set by biotech patents to the progress of science, technology and society will be specifically identified. Also addressed is the importance of exceptions to patent rights – specifically, the so-called research use exceptions – for the promotion of social, scientific and technological progress, and this chapter will investigate the failure of the exceptions to patent rights, incorporated into the legal system of a few dozen countries to overcome the problems previously identified, generally produced by biotechnology patents.[29] Given the inadequacy of the existing exceptions in force in a substantial number of jurisdictions, two patent exceptions are proposed: a R&D exception, designed to promote scientific, technological and commercial progress, and a genetic diagnostic test exception, conceived to foster the development of genetic diagnostic tests and their widespread access by all sectors of society. Finally, the legality of these hypothetical exceptions will be evaluated in light of art. 30 of the TRIPS Agreement.

5.2 Potential obstacles set by biotech patents to the progress of science and technology

5.2.1 Challenges created by gene patents

Patent law permits the claim of protection for products, processes and uses/applications that comply with the three conditions for patentability.

[28] See De Larena 2005, 787–788.

[29] As noted in the introduction to this work, the present study does not aim at identifying exhaustively all the challenges posed by the current intellectual property regimes. For a more comprehensive view about the potential problems created in various sectors by IPRs (such as software, agriculture, public health) see, for example, the report by the Commission on Intellectual Property Rights (2002). For a more complete overview in respect of the exceptions and exclusions commonly adopted by States to overcome or mitigate the problems posed by current patent regimes, see, for example, Barbosa and Grau-Kuntz (2010); Basheer *et al.* (2010); Gold and Joly (2010); Sherman (2010); Visser (2010).

In the field of genetic innovation,[30] there is a tendency to claim protection for the following categories of inventions:[31]

- Recombinant biotechnological products with industrial appeal – e.g. therapeutic proteins such as erythropoietin and insulin and the growth hormone – and genes and DNA sequences responsible for their production. Patents extend their protection to genes and natural proteins when isolated from their natural context and applied in commercial or industrial activities.[32]
- Vectors used when transferring genetic material from one organism to another, to form transgenic organisms.
- Processes to produce genetically modified organisms, as well as the product derived from those processes, i.e. cells, transgenic plants and animals.
- Genes and DNA sequences associated with diseases, the proteins produced by them, as well as their industrial application. These genes and proteins allow an understanding of the etiology and the development process of diseases and serve also as drug targets. The biopharmaceutical industry develops therapies that act on genetic mutations or on the product of mutant genes with the purpose of suppressing the production of proteins that trigger illnesses, for example.
- Genes associated with disease in order to use them in diagnostic tests. That patent category claims, among other elements, the healthy gene, genetic mutations associated with the presence of a disease, a molecular description of genes and their genetic mutations.[33]

When product patents are conferred on biotechnological innovations they tend to confer disproportionate privileges on patent holders, in the name of small contributions to the state of the art.[34] Product patents that cover new genes (and other genetic innovations) and their products (proteins, enzymes) extend the protection to that material and its molecular description, regardless of where they are incorporated and the purposes of their application, even if the patent holder has not divulged the entire array of possible applications of the matter claimed.[35] An

[30] The OECD 2006 report points out that the category of genetic inventions encompasses "nucleic acids, nucleotide sequences and their expression products, transformed cell lines, vectors, as well as methods, technologies and materials for making, using or analyzing such nucleic acids, nucleotide sequences, cell lines or vectors" (p. 4).

[31] See Crespi 2001, 6–8; OECD 2002, 28.

[32] See Danish Council of Ethics 2004, 45.

[33] This matter is further developed in section 5.2.2 below.

[34] See Dinwoodie and Dreyfuss 2007, 455.

[35] Along this line, art. 9 of the European Directive 98/44/EC reads: "The protection conferred by a patent on a product containing or consisting of genetic information shall extend to all material, save as provided in Article 5(1), in which the product

individual may obtain a patent for a particular gene, sequence it and identify a plausible function for it, albeit not proved.[36] The patent holder will have the right to control all the numerous applications of the gene, including those he did not anticipate.[37] Should third parties discover a new function for the patented gene, they will be entitled to demand protection for the new use identified. However, employing a use patent will hinge on the permission of the owner of the product patent.[38]

Genetic innovations are not valued exclusively for the technical effects produced by tangible biochemical molecules, but for their informational content as well.[39] In the case of patents that protect genetic tests, for example, the aspect of interest is the molecular description of the healthy gene and the genetic mutations, which signal the presence of a disease. With proteins, what matters to the industrial sector is the information connected to their three-dimensional structure. The identification of the shape of proteins proves useful in the discovery of their function. In the case of proteins involved in diseases, their three-dimensional structure operates as a parameter in developing new drugs, thus blocking their action on the body, with no relevant side effects.[40] Consequently, the protection of genetic innovations covers biochemical materials as well as the information permeating such materials, e.g. the molecular description of DNA sequences (polynucleotide sequences) that permeate a gene and the molecular description of the proteins produced by them (polypeptide sequences).[41]

The peculiar features of genetic inventions spell potential hurdles for innovation. In the first stages of the biotechnology industry, patents for genetic innovations behaved very much like patents for pharma-chemical products: organizations claimed protection for genetic sequences that produced proteins of therapeutic worth, for the recombinant vector that transferred the relevant genetic sequence to the host organism, and for the host cell modified by the vector.[42] In other words, the purpose of those patents was to ensure protection to the "biological factories" and tangible therapeutic products aimed at the consumer. At present, there is a tendency to target also the control of genetic and proteomic *information* that may serve as inputs in the development of a wide range of

is incorporated and in which the genetic information is contained and performs its function."

[36] It is possible to claim the protection of genes, genetic sequences and proteins, whose function is merely presumed by the "inventor," insofar as they are structurally *similar* to other molecules previously studied by science (Eisenberg *et al.* 2002, 197).

[37] See OECD 2006, 30. [38] See SACGHS 2009, 36.

[39] See Dreyfuss 2004, 466. [40] See Eisenberg *et al.* 2002, 205.

[41] See Danish Council of Ethics 2004, 43; Paradise and Janson 2006, 148.

[42] Eisenberg *et al.* 2002, 191–192.

new products. It is fairly usual to claim protection for genetic sequences and proteins, described respectively in terms of nitrogen bases (A,C,T and G[43]) and amino acids, when fixed in a computer-readable format, e.g. included in databases.[44] The implications of this kind of patent claim are serious as it is through computers that organizations identify the potential function of a genetic sequence.[45] If the freedom to use genetic information becomes controlled, it blocks the door to the discovery of the function of unknown genes until the relevant patents have expired.

With patents granted for both tangible products and the informational content of genetic and proteomic materials, the balance in the patent system was broken. Until not long ago, a patent owner would receive an exclusive right for a limited period of time in exchange for disclosing and authorizing the use of information on his innovation and the concepts that permeated it. At present, the owner of a genetic innovation is allowed to claim rights on tangible products (biochemical molecules) and their informational content.[46]

Upon considering the importance of genetics for the information economy over the last decades, we witness a dramatic increase in the number of patents for genetic innovations.[47] This dramatic growth proves that the field of research is equally undermined. Some recent studies will serve as an appropriate illustration. In 2001, a survey launched by the American Society of Human Genetics showed that 49% of the scientists interviewed had experienced obstacles in some of their research as a result of patents that had been granted for genetic inventions.[48] In 2002, the OECD published a study on the impact of genetic patents on the speed of scientific and technological development in Germany and the US. Two of their observations are of particular importance to this study. Firstly, although the OECD study did not identify cases of systematic abuse, it received confirmation of the fact that because of the rise in the number of gene patents, the costly and sluggish task of identifying and licensing patents required by research projects had become a compulsory phase of the R&D process.[49] Secondly, the German and US organizations

43 A, C, T and G stand, respectively, for: adenine, cytosine, thiamine and guanine.
44 Eisenberg *et al.* 2002, 200.
45 As previously noted, researchers compare the molecular description of unknown genetic sequences with the molecular description of well-known genetic consequences, present in other living beings, in order to identify similar sequences. This allows them to deduce their function.
46 See Eisenberg *et al.* 2002, 201.
47 See, e.g., OECD 2002, 8 and Freeburg 2005, 411.
48 See Paradise and Janson 2006, 149.
49 See OECD 2002, 50–51.

surveyed tended to abandon projects associated with sectors affected by an excessive number of patents.[50] That is an unspoken acknowledgement that patents cause high transaction costs and are an obstacle to innovation. The Swiss Federal Institute of Intellectual Property published a study based on empirical research carried out in 2003 jointly with the local private innovation sector. It indicates that the growing numbers of gene patents slow the rhythm of innovation.[51] In 2009, an inquiry of the European Commission identified a significant number of cases in which patents were liable to affect marketing of new innovations and R&D projects.[52] In addition, the report indicates that in 20% of the 99 cases identified, third parties had not received a license from the holders of the patents in question.[53]

Advocates of the patent system underrate this and other evidence of the detrimental character of patents because they judge that the number of cases when patents brought about the failure of research projects is irrelevant. Notwithstanding that, it is important to emphasize that, in *qualitative* terms one interrupted project may cause huge and unknown damage to humanity. Failure to launch one particular project may curtail the chances of finding the cure for a serious disease or a technology able to contribute to the recovery of our ailing planet. Briefly, lack of evidence that patents have become a hurdle for the progress of science and technology is no proof that the problem does not exist.

Patent-related obstacles to innovation that have an impact on genetic inventions are so real that, together with an increase in interest and the practice of patenting this category of inventions, there is also a growing tendency in industry to encourage and support initiatives focused on introducing information and knowledge on the human genome and proteome into the public domain.[54] Therefore, even the most enthusiastic advocates of the patent system tacitly acknowledge that the proliferation of genetic patents may slacken the pace of the development of science and technology.

[50] *Ibid.*, 51. [51] See Thumm 2003, 69.

[52] The European study noted: "In total, the inquiry reveals at least 1,100 instances where the patents held by an originator company potentially overlap with the medicines, R&D programmes and/or patents held by another originator company for their medicine. In these cases originator companies might find their research activities blocked, with detrimental effects on the innovation process" (European Commission 2009, 16).

[53] *Ibid.*

[54] See Eisenberg *et al.* 2002, 193. On this point, the article points out the following successful initiatives: the International HapMap Project, the Protein Data Bank, the Protein Structure Initiative and the Merck Gene Index Project.

5.2.2 Patents on genes associated with disease and genetic tests

The life span of a human being and the quality of his life depend, inter alia, on his access to efficient health treatments. That is why it is crucially important that every individual should have access to diagnostic and predictive tests able to accurately identify current diseases and predisposition to others. Once the international scientific community ended the sequencing of the human genome in 2003, the process of identification of genes associated with diseases was speeded up. This involved a similar acceleration in the development of new genetic tests,[55] which are applicable both to diagnosis and prognosis of diseases.[56]

By July 2011, the international market offered diagnostic tests for over 2,300 genetics-based diseases.[57] This figure continues to increase and so does patenting of genes associated with diseases.[58] Normally, patents claimed for genetic tests encompass the following items: (i) molecular description of the healthy version of a gene which, when altered or absent, triggers the onset of or indicates predisposition to a particular disease;[59] (ii) the molecular description of the proteins produced by the gene; (iii) a molecular description of one or more mutations of the gene, that indicate the presence of the disease or predisposition to it, as well as the location of these mutations within the chromosomes; (iv) methods to perform comparative analyses between the gene used as reference (healthy material) and the gene of the patient; (v) the use of the gene and/or the proteins produced by it, in its role as "target" for the development of new therapeutic products.[60]

Patents on genes and proteins associated with diseases create bottlenecks in the progress of biomedical science. In the case of diseases

[55] Genetic tests are characterized as "an analysis of human chromosomes, deoxyribonucleic acid (DNA), ribonucleic acid (RNA), genes, and/or gene products (e.g., enzymes and other types of proteins), which is predominately used to detect heritable or somatic mutations, genotypes, or phenotypes related to disease and health. Genetic or genomic tests detect inherited and somatic variations in the genome, transcriptome, and proteome. The tests can be used to analyze one or a few genes, many genes, or the entire genome" (SACGHS 2009, 9).

[56] *Ibid.*

[57] See www.ncbi.nlm.nih.gov/sites/GeneTests/?db=GeneTests. Accessed on July 24, 2011.

[58] In 2006, 4,382 of the 23,688 human genes were under patent protection in the US (Stix 2006).

[59] In general terms, genes are responsible for the production of a variety of proteins which are indispensable for the good functioning of living organisms. The mutation of a gene, associated to a disease, can begin to produce proteins that cause diseases. When the gene is not there, it will stop producing a protein required by the organism for its correct functioning.

[60] See, e.g., Bostyn 2004, 74; HUGO Intellectual Property Committee 2003, 2; OECD 2002, 6, 25.

caused by mutations in one gene (monogenic diseases) patenting this gene hinders the development of competing diagnostic tests as all potential competitors are forced to adopt the healthy version of the patented gene as a reference.[61] Since there are no competing diagnoses, patients cannot be sure about the quality of the test available in the market nor do they have the means to obtain a confirmation of the results.[62] In the absence of competitors, the patent holder, apart from having the right to fix too high a price for it, has no incentive to continually improve the quality of his product.[63]

In diseases based on mutations of various genes (polygenic diseases),[64] patents on those genes obstruct the development of diagnostic tests, especially when each gene belongs to a different patent owner.[65]

In addition, patents affect the quality of diagnostic tests. The quality of these products is proportional to their ability to identify the largest possible number of mutations of genes that indicate the presence of a disease or susceptibility to develop it. Patents on the various mutations of a gene implied in a given disease hinder the development of highly sensitive tests.[66] Let us say, for example, that current scientific knowledge has identified ten mutations for one particular gene: they all denote the presence of or predisposition to disease X. If each mutation corresponds to a different patent, developing a diagnostic test focused on that disease will require ten different licenses. A laboratory committed to developing a high quality diagnostic test may not obtain the necessary licenses or, even if it does, the cost of the new test may be high, which means that the poorest groups will be unable to have it.

Briefly, as far as genetic tests are concerned, granting patents for genes, their mutations and proteins *may* cause the following side effects: (i) developing low-quality (low sensitivity) tests with the consequent inability to identify the existence of some of the possible mutations of the gene, associated with the presence/predisposition to a disease; (ii) developing good sensitivity tests that are, however, more costly and thus inaccessible for the marginalized groups of society; and (iii) halting the development of diagnostic tests in view of the impossibility of obtaining all the relevant licenses for the various genes and genetic mutations required. In any case, lives will be cost for lack of early or appropriate diagnosis.[67]

Problems do not end there. There are at least three other issues that merit attention. As they wish to claim protection for their

[61] SACGHS 2009, 2. [62] *Ibid.*, p. 3. [63] *Ibid.*, p. 105.

[64] Diseases caused by mutations of only one gene are rare. Most diseases are associated with mutations of several genes, e.g., hypertension, diabetes, Alzheimer's disease (Paradise and Janson 2006, 149).

[65] See SACGHS 2009, 106. [66] See Bostyn 2004, 74. [67] Aymé *et al.* 2008, 4.

discovery, those who have discovered genes associated with diseases tend to postpone publication of their finding.[68] The identification of unknown genetic mutations linked to the development of diseases depends on a large number of genetic tests; if there is no freedom to use the patented invention, crucial mutations will remain veiled. Lastly, despite the usual statement that patents that protect genes do not control their natural version, in view of the fact that there is an identity between the molecular description of the natural gene and its synthetic version, the patent eventually controls the natural gene.[69]

The positive or negative effects that may ensue from granting patents for genetic tests depend on the individual stance taken by each patent owner. As stated above, a patent owner may use it in ways that coincide with the interests of society, choosing a licensing policy that facilitates the wider dissemination of his invention. On the other hand, he can also make an abusive use of his privilege and restrict access to his invention, in ways that are detrimental to the health of patients and the progress of biomedical science and industry.[70]

The freedom enjoyed by patent holders accounts for the lack of conclusive data on the nature of the impact of genetic patents on the development of new genetic tests. Notwithstanding that, there is growing evidence that indicates that patents for genetic innovations are often employed with the purpose of interfering with the realization of superior social interests, such as the right to health, life, scientific freedom and free enterprise.[71] On the basis of such evidence, national authorities in developed countries such as Italy, the United Kingdom and Sweden,[72] and scientific organizations such as the European Society of Human Genetics,[73] the Danish Council of Ethics[74] and the Nuffield Council of Bioethics[75] oppose the indiscriminate grant of patents for genes associated with diseases and genetic tests. There is no point in discovering

[68] See Merz *et al.* 2002 (in the case of genes associated with hemochromatose, the authors of the finding only published an article on the subject one year after filing for a US patent).

[69] See Danish Council of Ethics 2004, 97.

[70] See, e.g., SACGHS 2009, 104–106 and O'Rourke 2000, 1178–1180.

[71] See, e.g., OECD 2002, 70 (although the OECD report takes a neutral stance, it identifies cases in which owners of patents for diagnostic tests made an inappropriate use of their rights); Gold and Carbone 2008 (they examine the allegedly unsuitable behavior of Myriad Genetics when it exercised its property rights impacting genes associated with breast cancer – BRCA 1 and BRCA 2. Myriad's stance caused indignation among academics, scientists and government agencies in several countries); Merz *et al.* 2002 (empirical research carried out in the US shows that 30% of the clinical laboratories interviewed stopped offering genetic tests for hemochromatose on account of the patents granted for the two genetic mutations most commonly associated with this disease).

[72] *Ibid.* [73] See Aymé *et al.* 2008. [74] See Danish Council of Ethics 2004.

[75] See Nuffield Council on Bioethics 2002.

the function of genes if the medical community has no solid grounds to diagnose or to recommend therapies, and if only the wealthiest sector of the population can benefit from the progress of science and if diagnostic tests cannot be introduced into the market.

5.2.3 Genes and unique resources

Organizations devoted to science and technology face challenges when they work on projects that require multiple patented inputs, as well as when they depend on access to only one invention. Genes, genetic sequences, RNA molecules and encoded proteins may be frequently characterized as unique and finite resources, meaning that there are no substitutes and there is no technical possibility to create them.[76]

Although patent authorities admit the presumption that homologous biochemical structures fulfill similar functions, such presumption may be wrong as small structural alterations may result in different functions.[77] Only a deeper knowledge of the functions fulfilled by the various genetic molecules and proteins will make it possible to establish precisely which of them have substitutes. An unavoidable precondition for attaining such deeper knowledge is unhindered access to research on and use of these inputs.

Owners of IPRs over unique resources enjoy extraordinary economic profits. The holder of a patent corresponding to a consumer end-product only has the right to control its production, use and marketing. In the case of unique inventions, their owners control an untold number of innovation opportunities where their innovation can play a positive role.[78] In other words, one innovation can be the source of several products.

Unique genetic resources can be protected by only a single patent or by several patents belonging to different institutions. Some genetic molecules of human origin, because of their scientific and commercial importance, are under the protection of various patents; for example, the osteogenic factor BMP7 and the gene CDKN2A, responsible for the suppression of tumors, are covered by twenty different patents, and the gene BRCA 1 associated with breast cancer is under the protection of fourteen patents.[79] Accessing these materials may not be an easy task.

As no patent holder has the economic, technical and human resources necessary to explore all the productive potential of unique inventions,[80]

[76] See Aymé *et al.* 2008, 4; Dreyfuss 2005, 1–2, 6. [77] See Hiraki 2000, 18.
[78] See Dreyfuss 2005, 14–16. [79] See Jensen and Murray 2005, 239–240.
[80] See Dreyfuss 2005, 4.

should the owners of those inventions decide to maximize their individual well-being by granting an exclusive license or refusing to grant any licenses to third parties, a wide array of processes and products will not be developed during the duration of the patent. Worse still, new fields of work will fail to be opened or strengthened.[81] Consequently, patents that protect unique resources have an impact on free competition as they guarantee an economic monopoly to their owners. This means they are entitled to fix a markedly high price for their inventions and to exclude potential competitors from the market and, to make matters worse, non-competitors too.[82]

5.2.4 *Research tools*

5.2.4.1 Definition One of the reasons that accounts for the multiplication of patents is the development of research tools aimed at spurring the development of new pharmaceutical and biotechnological products. Information, products and methods constitute tools for research projects. They are used in scientific research and in the development of new technology, particularly in the process of discovery and development of new drugs, therapeutic products, methods for diagnosis, agricultural products and inputs, and biotech products in general.[83] Research tools are frequently employed in the process of developing new products and processes, without incorporating them in the final product of the research. There are, however, some research inputs that act as building blocks in the construction of new inventions, e.g. a DNA sequence that produces a protein with pharmaceutical properties, incorporated in a host cell. Consequently, those inputs are absorbed by the new inventions. In this author's view it is appropriate that the following inputs should be included among research tools: DNA sequences; DNA libraries; genomic and proteomic libraries; clones, cell lines, transgenic mice, enzymes, receptors and ligands involved in the process of development of illnesses; laboratory methods (e.g. PCR and recombinant DNA technique); laboratory equipment; equipment for DNA sequencing; human embryonic cells.[84]

The feature that characterizes an invention as a research tool is its practical value to its consumers:[85] in cases when an invention may be used by scientists to carry out projects of scientific and technological

[81] See Walsh *et al.* 2003, 291. [82] See O'Rourke 2000, 1227.
[83] See Mueller 2001, 4; Federal Trade Commission 2003, ch. 3, 18–19.
[84] See, e.g., NIH 1999, 28205; NIH 1998, 2–5; Bauer 2005, 126–127; OECD 2006, p. 19, para. 33; Walsh *et al.* 2003, 287.
[85] See Eisenberg 1989, 1078.

research, it should be characterized as a pure research tool or as a dual-nature invention.[86] Not all research tools are "pure,"[87] in the sense that they are only used as research tools, with "no immediate therapeutic or diagnostic value."[88] There are *dual nature* inventions as well, which may be used for two different and independent purposes: as a product aimed at the ordinary consumer sector and as a research tool.[89] An example of dual nature innovation is a gene associated with a particular disease, which may be included in a diagnostic test (consumer end-product) and can also act as a new drugs target.

5.2.4.2 Problems caused by granting patents on research tools Patents connected to research tools give their holders the possibility to control the pace of scientific and technological progress. Not only does the patent grant its holder the right to exclude third parties from producing, marketing, importing and exporting the patented object; it also accords him the right to prohibit the *use* of the patented invention.[90] This means that whenever a patented research tool is employed without a valid license, it infringes the patent.

Having said that, the fact that a research tool is patented does not necessarily mean that innovation will face hurdles. When a patented research tool has substitutes, the patent owner is concerned about defeating his competitors. He will therefore establish *neutral* or simplified licensing conditions that apply to every interested user, regardless of the nature of the user's research project or economic capacity.[91]

Problems arise when the object of the patent is a unique research tool, i.e. one that lacks substitutes. This is especially relevant when it is a foundational upstream invention, crucial to develop new fields in technology. Foundational upstream inventions in biotechnology include Polymerase Chain Reaction (PCR) and Taq polymerase, the Cre-Lox system and the recombinant DNA method developed by Cohen and Boyer.[92] In the field of nanotechnology, foundational upstream inventions are scanning probe microscopy, an essential technology for handling atoms, and carbon nanotubes, fundamental structures in the creation of new materials.[93]

If the research tool is unique, the patent owner can maximize his economic profits through the establishment of abusive licensing conditions,[94] or customized licensing conditions.[95] In the latter case, in

[86] See NIH 1998, 4; Derzko 2003, 355. [87] See Waldeck und Pyrmont 2008, 381.
[88] See Bostyn 2004, 67.
[89] See Dreyfuss 2004, 468; Waldeck und Pyrmont 2008, 381.
[90] See Mueller 2001, 4–5. [91] See Strandburg 2004, 124.
[92] See OECD 2006, p. 19, para. 33; Walsh *et al.* 2003, 296. [93] See Zovko 2006, 156.
[94] See Strandburg 2004, 124–125. [95] See Mueller 2001, 15.

the course of negotiations, the patent owner will require the prospective user to specify information about the research project where the tool will be applied. He will then either determine specific licensing conditions or refuse to grant the license if he wishes to develop a similar or identical project to that described by the prospective user.

In view of the fact that research tools are indispensable for the development of a wide array of new products and processes and for opening and strengthening new fields in technology, they should be open to access by the largest possible number of institutions and individuals.[96] That is not necessarily the case at present. For instance, the private sector tends to avoid granting licenses for receptors that are present in the origins of commercially relevant diseases because they fear their competitors may develop new drugs to fight those diseases,[97] since after a drug that will impact a given receptor has been developed, it may not be possible to develop competing drugs to impact the same molecule.[98] In the case of pharmaceutical molecules, owners often refuse to grant licenses in order to prevent the discovery of new uses that will be eligible for protection. On the other hand, they wish to avoid the discovery and dissemination of information on side effects of drugs, which may hinder the owners' request to health authorities for the necessary authorization to place them in the market.[99]

A further problem linked to the privatization of research tools is connected to the strategy adopted by patent owners: they claim rights on products which have been developed thanks to the use of their tools. This may be done either by filing reach-through claims when demanding patents, or through licensing agreements that grant the owner of the licensed patent a share in the profits obtained by marketing the product created through the use of the tool or marketing rights on the new invention.[100] That kind of practice does not contribute to providing economic incentives for third parties to use the research tools at stake.[101] Let us suppose, for example, that two providers of research tools can demand exclusive licenses to exploit the end product of a given project. If they do not find a solution to the conflict, the prospective user will be unable to carry out his project. Even if the providers of technology claim non-exclusive and non-onerous licenses, economic encouragement for a third party to carry out the project will be negligible. Should many free licensees exploit the same product, competition would be so extensive that the genuine inventor will have no incentives to place his product on

[96] See Walsh *et al.* 2003, 332–333. [97] See NIH 1998, 18.
[98] See Walsh *et al.* 2003, 332–333. [99] See NIH 1998, 17–18.
[100] See Walsh *et al.* 2003, 297. [101] See NIH 1998, 9.

the market. On the other hand, someone who funds a R&D project may withdraw his support if ownership of the final product of the project is shared by other prospective competitors.

The problems ensuing from patents on research tools are compounded by legislators or national courts that suppress research use exceptions[102] or substantively curtail their scope with the purpose of allowing patent holders to recover their investment. In this context, institutions devoted to innovation are confronted with at least three major issues. Firstly, those institutions become the hostages of patent owners, since they hold rights of life and death over projects based on their research tools. Secondly, should the owners of patents demand excessively high licensing fees, only institutions that are economically strong have the means necessary to embark on research projects in science and technology. Small firms or institutions with scarce funds will be forced either to give up more ambitious projects, which require the use of multiple patented inputs, or confine their research projects to fields of lower economic and social relevance, which are less constrained by patents.[103] Lastly, institutions of science and technology waste a large portion of their time and resources on commercial dealings, striving to reach reasonable agreements. Time and resources that should be invested in the production of science and technology are used up in bureaucratic and costly negotiations.[104]

The relevant literature suggests that the obstacles created by the massive granting of patents on research tools are not so severe,[105] as users of this technology often manage to dodge the hurdles through a set of strategies:

- Obtaining licenses from the owners of the relevant patents. This is not always viable be it because they demand excessively high royalties, or because patent owners choose to grant exclusive licenses that benefit only one user, or because the licensing process is sluggish.
- Developing alternative inventions. The negative side of this strategy is its cost and the time required to develop alternatives.
- Implementing research projects in jurisdictions where the legal framework is more flexible, or in countries that do not grant protection for the relevant inventions. In view of the speedy process of harmonization of intellectual property rights through free trade agreements, this strategy is ever less relevant.
- Challenging the patents that concern the research at stake. The negative side of this strategy is the cost involved in administrative or judicial

[102] This subject is further discussed in section 5.3 below. [103] See Clift 2007, 82.
[104] See Bauer 2005, 133; Hoffman 2003, 1024. [105] See, e.g, Kang *et al.* 2009.

proceedings, the time consumed to obtain a final decision and the lack of guarantees as to the outcome of the proceedings launched.

- Use of de facto research exceptions, especially on the part of universities and public institutions of research. These "exceptions" are the consequence of the technical hurdles that patent owners meet when they try to identify breaches within non-commercial projects, as well as of the fact that patent owners do not wish to risk their good reputation if they apply an aggressive stance by prosecuting universities and, lastly, because the private sector depends on human resources and technicians provided by the universities.[106] The problem with de facto research exceptions is that their validity depends on the stance of each patent owner. Whereas some institutions are more tolerant than others and do not oppose the use of their technology by the academic and non-commercial sector, there are others that treat universities as if they were business enterprises. Having said that, it is also convenient to stress that the fact that the owner of a valuable innovation behaves reasonably in a given situation is no guarantee that he will always act in the same way. Neither is it realistic to presume that patent holders will display a friendly attitude towards the claims of universities.[107]
- Use of alternative research tools already within the public domain. The problem is that the public domain does not always have alternatives to patented inventions.
- Moving investment plans to other fields that are less crowded by IPRs. The main cost of this strategy is the cancellation of projects that would produce valuable results for society at large.

To sum up, all the strategies identified involve social costs, and none guarantees success.[108]

5.2.5 *Tragedy of the anti-commons*

There is a different problem from that created by patents associated with unique innovations, ensuing from the capacity of one innovation to trigger the development of multiple others. It concerns the effect called the tragedy of the anti-commons and it occurs whenever the development of one innovation depends on the use of a variety of proprietary inputs and its access is blocked by the transaction costs involved in procuring the

[106] See Weschler 2004, 1561–1562.
[107] Paradise and Janson (2006, 150) remark that biotechnology firms are ever more frequently visiting the courts to press universities and research institutions to pay for the protected input that they use in their research projects.
[108] See Walsh *et al.* 2003, 311, 331 ff.

necessary licenses.[109] Lacking only one authorization, within the many that are necessary to carry out a R&D project, it cannot prosper.

Since the development of new products – especially in the fields of genetic engineering,[110] information technology and nanotechnology – often requires several patented inputs and research tools, there are higher chances of facing tragedies of the anti-commons.

In order to secure some freedom to operate, organizations devoted to R&D activities no longer seek protection just for the outputs of research projects with commercial appeal. They often adopt a strategy of defensive patenting, characterized by claiming patents for the largest possible number of innovations, even if in excess and without great commercial value.[111] The owners of substantial portfolios presume that sooner or later their competitor will infringe some of their patents. In that case and in exchange for not initiating a legal process, the holder of the infringed patent may claim and obtain from the offender a non-exclusive license for the desired patent. On the other hand, when the owners of thick patent portfolios infringe the patent of a third party they benefit from greater negotiating power and can avoid court proceedings by granting licenses on some of their innovations. Lastly, in view of the fact that every agent in the innovation sector is a potential offender against the rights of third parties, the greater his patent portfolio, the more at ease he will be in his affairs.[112] In fact, the downpour of patents increases the chances of facing the tragedy of the anti-commons.[113]

5.2.6 *Royalty stacking*

Even when patent owners do not refuse to license their inventions, innovators may face obstacles; by demanding payment of extremely high fees they actually block their use, particularly by small- and medium-sized firms and public institutions of research, with tight budgets.[114] Even if the owners of patents do not charge high fees, when the scientific or technological project depends on the use of numerous technologies, there will be a royalty stacking problem, that is, the accumulation of the individual royalties required becomes excessively costly.[115]

The royalty stacking issue can occur in any field. Currently, however, the problem is more common in the pharmaceutical, agricultural and biotechnology sectors because the development of new technologies in

[109] See Basheer 2005, 59–63; Heller and Eisenberg 1998.
[110] See Federal Trade Commission 2003, ch. 3, 24–29.
[111] See Walsh *et al.* 2003, 295. [112] See Eisenberg *et al.* 2001, 212–213.
[113] See Walsh *et al.* 2003, 296. [114] See OECD 2006, p. 15, para. 13.
[115] See Gitter 2001, 1681; Adhikari 2005, 25.

these fields involves a substantial number of patented inputs.[116] With new research inputs claiming patents there are greater chances that products that require several technologies for their development will not be viable from a commercial perspective.

According to a study carried out by Walsh, Arora and Cohen, based on empirical data collected from US institutions, there are no signs that royalty stacking poses a threat to the progress of industry and science.[117] The problem does not arise because usually the total sum paid by those who develop innovations requiring multiple innovations is not high and when the total fees paid is unreasonable, patent holders are normally open to renegotiate the fees charged. Besides, industry and universities usually assess the possibility of facing this issue before initiating a research project.[118] In view of these facts, the problem is successfully avoided.

A study carried out by the OECD in association with organizations based in Germany had established that royalty stacking, taken in isolation, was not a frequent reason for the failure of innovation projects. However, it acknowledged that this situation does cause economic difficulties that can only be solved by agreements with the owners of patents,[119] which may actually fail when those owners are not willing to accept lower fees.

Summing up, it is important to insist that, even if we acknowledge that there are no conclusive data pointing to the detrimental effects of patents on the progress of science and technology, we must keep in mind that humanity is witnessing the dawn of revolutions in biotechnology and nanotechnology. With the increase of patents granted for inventions and discoveries connected to those sectors and others, the obstacles that now seem theoretical may become real and insurmountable in the future.[120] It is not wise, therefore, to ignore catastrophic predictions; they will become the reality if nothing is done to guarantee freedom in the fields of science and technology. Adopting powerful and balanced exceptions to the rights granted by patents is essential if these predictions are not to become real.

5.3 Research use exception and freedom in science and technology

Patents encourage innovation insofar as they offer R&D investors the right to exclude third parties from using, producing, marketing and

[116] See OECD 2002, 63. [117] Walsh *et al.* 2003, 299. [118] *Ibid.*, 300.
[119] OECD 2002, 48, 62. [120] See Clift 2007, 82.

importing the patented subject matter. That set of rights creates artificial, temporary scarcity and therefore offers incentives for investments in R&D and/or in turning innovations carried out in universities and public institutions into products that may be introduced in the market.[121]

Patent rights also promote innovation through public dissemination of the technical knowledge introduced by patents: filing for a patent requires a detailed description of the best way to use the protected innovations and their applications. On the basis of those descriptions and knowledge, third parties may build further knowledge and inventions, thereby ensuring the ongoing expansion of the foundations of science and technology in society. Finally, patent law contributes to scientific progress by authorizing the free utilization of the patented subject matter upon expiry of the patents as well as before, when legal regulations provide exceptions to patent rights.

Exceptions set limits to the rights granted;[122] their purpose is to protect public interests by restricting the scope of the rights of exclusion granted and, consequently, by widening the range of the rights of use by non-authorized third parties.[123] The need to establish exceptions to patent rights is justified by the range of those rights and by the fact that patent holders are not obliged to make a socially responsible use of their rights.

Exceptions are mechanisms of ex post adjustment of the scope of patents.[124] They run counter to mechanisms of ex ante adjustment, characterized by turning the process to obtain new rights into a more complex procedure, e.g. excluding some subject matter from the list of those eligible for protection. As to mechanisms of ex ante adjustments, exceptions are seen as a more appropriate way to strike a balance between the economic interests of patent holders on one side, and those of users and society on the other, as they are not significantly detrimental to incentives for investment in R&D activities.[125] In this respect, it is worth reproducing some remarks by Bently:

> It is easy to see that an exclusion, if effective, operates like an "on/off" switch, whereas exceptions are more like "dimmer switches," that can be turned down (to reduce costs), without necessarily turning off the light. The prior use defence, the experimental use defence, the private use defence, exhaustion of rights reduce incentives, they do not remove them altogether. Exceptions can be conditioned, for example by requiring some remuneration, and this highlights the much more nuanced way in which they might operate to reconcile conflicting interests.[126]

In addition to that, it is difficult to monitor the effectiveness of ex ante mechanisms of adjustment, since Patents and Trademarks Offices tend to

[121] See, e.g., SACGHS 2009, 18–19; Dreyfuss 2003, 7. [122] See Kur 2008, 7.
[123] See Dreyfuss 2005, 8. [124] *Ibid.*, 8–9. [125] *Ibid.* [126] Bently 2010, 65.

have a wide discretion to interpret and apply the standards of protection of inventions. So, although certain matters may be, in principle, excluded from the list of subject matter eligible for protection, it is always possible that the patent authorities will interpret ambiguous terms of patent law with the purpose of increasing the list of patentable subject matters.

Among the exceptions normally adopted by the international community, one of the most popular is the research use exception. Although their scope varies in each jurisdiction, they usually allow third parties to carry out scientific experiments with the protected invention, without prior permission of the patent owner. The presence of research use exceptions in a great number of legal orders demonstrates that the development of science and technology must not rest in the hands of patent holders.[127]

Leaving aside the particular features of individual domestic legislation, the purpose of research use exceptions is to provide a space where society can generate new knowledge of patented technologies and embark on an ongoing development of new products and technologies based on the contributions of the patented subject matter.[128] Since all scientific and technological innovation and progress are built upon past contributions, current inventors owe a debt to society. Offering a research use exception is one way to repay society for its contribution to the process of development of science and technology.[129]

In more specific terms, research exceptions *may* promote at least three different – albeit interrelated – interests: permitting a review and analysis of patented innovations, creating new knowledge connected to protected innovations and paving the way for the development of follow-on innovations.

Organizations that wish to protect their innovations try to avoid revealing, so far as this is possible, important details about how the innovations work to make sure third parties cannot replicate them successfully. If the purpose of the patent is to exchange public access to the technical knowledge protected by the patent for a set of temporary exclusive rights, the only way to make sure that the agreement is being complied with by the patent holders is to allow third parties to reproduce the protected innovation during the period of patent protection.[130] In this respect, it is worth reproducing a passage from the Panel Report in the *Canada – Pharmaceutical Patents case*, which indicates the importance of research use exceptions in the promotion of the legitimate interests of patent holders:

[127] See Gitter 2001, 1686. [128] See Strandburg 2004, 99–100.
[129] See Eisenberg 1989, 1057. [130] *Ibid.*, 1022.

It is often argued that this exception [research use exception] is based on the notion that a key public policy purpose underlying patent laws is to facilitate the dissemination and advancement of technical knowledge and that allowing the patent owner to prevent experimental use during the term of the patent would frustrate part of the purpose of the requirement that the nature of the invention be disclosed to the public. To the contrary, the argument concludes, under the policy of the patent laws, both society and the scientist have a "legitimate interest" in using the patent disclosure to support the advance of science and technology.[131]

It often happens that a proper understanding of the way an innovation works requires more than the perusal of the description in the patent files; replication proves imperative.[132] In the process of replicating an innovation in order to understand how it works, third parties may arrive at new ideas about its use in solving technical problems, ideas that were not perceived by the patent owner. The discovery of new features and applications of the innovations comprised in the state of the art may lead to a reallocation of investments for more productive ends.[133]

Should patents grant their owners an unlimited right to exclude third parties from using the innovation patented, there would be no point in an open disclosure of the technical knowledge under protection before the patent expires.[134] The unspoken idea underlying a research use exception is that society is free to carry out research in science and technology, using patented technical knowledge, independently from the will of patent holders and, consequently, is under no obligation to share confidential information on future projects with potential competitors.[135] Disseminating such information would pave the way for activities constituting unfair competition and would destroy any incentives to carry out R&D.

Despite the strategic role of research exceptions, it will be seen in the next section that a substantial number of States offer a relatively limited range of research exceptions, apparently ignoring the fact that the balance aimed at by patent rights cannot be struck with weak and non-functional research exceptions.[136] When patent owners are granted too many rights (unlimited or almost unlimited), no third party is authorized to use the objects patented until the patents expire. In that case, the sole beneficiary is the inventor; society must wait until the patents expire before it can apply the new knowledge and add it to the state of the art.

131 WTO, WT/DS114/R, Panel Report, para. 7.69. 132 See Hagelin 2006, 556.
133 See Strandburg 2004, 112. 134 See Eisenberg 1989, 1022.
135 *Ibid.*, 1061–1063. 136 See Freeburg 2005, 399.

5.4 Research use exceptions adopted by some members of the international community[137]

Three groups of research use exceptions have been identified. The first group includes the laws of Antigua and Barbuda,[138] Belize,[139] Botswana,[140] Cambodia,[141] China,[142] the Andean Community (Bolivia, Colombia, Ecuador and Peru),[143] Denmark,[144] Dominican Republic,[145] Estonia,[146] Finland,[147] France,[148] Germany,[149] Granada,[150] Hong Kong,[151] Hungary,[152] Ireland,[153] Iceland,[154] Luxembourg,[155] Mauritius,[156] Morocco,[157] the Netherlands and the Dutch Antilles,[158] Norway,[159] Papua New Guinea,[160] Philippines,[161] Poland,[162] United Kingdom,[163] Saint Lucia,[164] Singapore,[165] Spain,[166] Swaziland,[167]

[137] For an in-depth view in respect of the scope of many of the research use exceptions mentioned in this section see, e.g., Cook (2006) and Gold and Joly (2010).
[138] Art. 11(4)(1)(c), Patents Act 2003.
[139] Art. 33 (4)(c), Patents Act (Ch. 253), 06/21/2000.
[140] Art. 24(3)(a)(iii), Industrial Property Act, 08/21/1996.
[141] Art. 44(iii), Law on Patents, Utility Model Certificates and Industrial Designs.
[142] Art. 63(4), Patent Law of China, 2000.
[143] Art. 53(b), Decisión 486 (Régimen Común sobre Propiedad Industrial).
[144] Sec. 3(3)(iii), Act (Consolidation), 06/09/1998 (05/31/2000), No. 366 (No. 412).
[145] Art. 30(b), Ley No. 20–00 sobre Propiedad Industrial.
[146] Art. 16(3), Patents Act (Consolidation), 03/16/1994 (10/27/1999).
[147] Sec.3(3), Patents Act (Consolidation), 12/15/1967 (03/21/1997), No. 550 (No. 243).
[148] L. 61 3–5(b), Law No. 92–597 of July 1, 1992, on the Intellectual Property Code (Legislative Part) as last amended by Law No. 94–102 of February 5, 1994.
[149] § 11, Patentgesetz in der Fassung der Bekanntmachung vom 16. Dezember 1980 (BGBl. 1981 I S. 1), das zuletzt durch Artikel 1 des Gesetzes vom 31. Juli 2009 (BGBl. I S. 2521) geändert worden ist.
[150] Sec. 12 (4)(a)(iii), Industrial Property Act 2002.
[151] Sec. 75(b), Patents (Registration), Ordinance (Cap. 514 Consolidation), 1997 (1998), No. 52 (No. 341).
[152] Art. 19(6)(b), Law No. XXXIII of 1995 on the Protection of Inventions by Patents.
[153] Sec. 42(b), Patents Act, 1992.
[154] Section 3(3.3), Patent Act no. 17/1991 with amendments no. 67/1993.
[155] Art. 47(b), Loi du 20 juillet 1992 portant modification du régime des brevets d'invention.
[156] Art. 21(4)(d), Act No. 25 of 2002.
[157] Art. 55(b), Dahir n° 1–00–91 du 9 Kaada 1420 (15 février 2000) portant promulgation de la loi n° 17–97 relative à la protection de la propriété industrielle.
[158] Art. 53(3), Patents Act of the Kingdom 1995.
[159] Sec. 3(3)(3), Patents Act (as last amended by Act No. 20 of May 2004).
[160] Art. 29(4)(c), Patents and Industrial Designs Act 2000.
[161] Art. 72(3), Republic Act No. 8293.
[162] Art. 69(1)(iii), Act of June 30, 2000 on Industrial Property Law.
[163] Art. 60(5)(b), Patents Act of 1977 (as amended).
[164] Art. 2(b), Patents Act No. 16 2001 Repealing the Patents, Designs and Trademarks Act.
[165] Art. 66(2)(b), Patents Act (No. 21 of 1994) Revised Edition 1995 (No. 40).
[166] Art. 52(b), Ley 11/1986 de 20 de marzo de 1986.
[167] Art. 4(c), Patents, Designs and Trade Marks Act No. 72 of 1936, as amended by L. 5/1969.

Sweden,[168] Trinidad and Tobago,[169] Tunisia[170] and the contracting parties to the Bangui Agreement[171] (Benin, Burkina Faso, Cameroon, Central African Republic, Chad, Congo, Ivory Coast, Gabon, Guinea, Guinea-Bissau, Equatorial Guinea, Mali, Mauritania, Niger, Senegal and Togo). The laws of these countries enshrine research use exceptions which have been strongly influenced by the research exception model included in the proposal to create the European Community patent, which establishes: "Art. 9 – The rights conferred by the Community patent shall not extend to: . . . (b) acts done for experimental purposes relating to the subject-matter of the patented invention."[172]

Albania,[173] Italy,[174] Latvia,[175] Lithuania,[176] Macau,[177] Mongolia,[178] Panama,[179] Portugal,[180] Romania,[181] Slovakia,[182] Turkey[183] and Ukraine[184] adopt research use exceptions whose wording differs from the European model but still seems to agree on the same essentials.

The second group comprises the laws enacted by Saudi Arabia,[185] Bahrain,[186] Barbados,[187] Canada,[188] Cuba,[189] Cyprus,[190]

[168] Sec. 3(3), The Swedish Patents Act (Act No. 837 of 1967, as amended by Acts Nos. 149 of 1978, 433 of 1983, 937 of 1984, 233, 1156 of 1986, 1330 of 1987, 296 of 1991, 1688 of 1992 and 1406 of 1993).

[169] Art. 42(b), Patents Act, 1996 (No. 21 of 1996, as amended by Act No. 18 of 2000).

[170] Art. 47(b), Law No. 2000–84 of August 2000, on Patents.

[171] Art. 8(c), annex I, Agreement Revising the Bangui Agreement of March 2, 1977, on the Creation of an African Intellectual Property Organization.

[172] Art. 9(b), Council of the European Union 2009.

[173] Art. 27(3)(c), Law on Industrial Property No. 7819 of April 27, 1994.

[174] Art. 1(a), Law on Patents for Inventions, Royal Decree No. 1127 of June 29, 1939 (as last amended by Legislative Decree No. 198 of March 19, 1996).

[175] Art. 32(2), Republic of Latvia Patent Law 1995.

[176] Art. 26(2), Patent Law January 18, 1994 No. I-372 (as amended by December 21, 2000 No. IX-118).

[177] Art. 105(b), Industrial Property Code Decree-Law No 97/99/M of December 13, 1999.

[178] Art. 18(2) Patent Law of Mongolia 06/25/1993.

[179] Art. 19(2), Ley N° 35 de 10 de mayo de 1995.

[180] Art. 102(c), Decreto-Lei no. 36/2003 de 5 de Março.

[181] Art. 37(c), Patent Law (No. 64 of October 11, 1991).

[182] Art. 18(1), Act No. 435/2001 Coll. on Patents, Supplementary Protection Certificates, amended by Act No. 402/2002.

[183] Art. 75(b), Decree-Law No. 551 on the Protection of Patent Rights in Force as from June 27, 1995.

[184] Art. 31(2), Law No. 3687-XII of December 15, 1993 on the Protection of Rights to Inventions and Utility Models.

[185] Art. 47, Law of Patents, Layout Designs of Integrated Circuits, Plant Varieties and Industrial Designs.

[186] Art. 13(a), Law No. (14) for the year 2006 amending some provisions of Law no. (1) of the year 2004.

[187] Art. 6(1)(a), Patents Act No. 18, 07/26/2001.

[188] Sec. 55(2)(6), Canadian Patent Act R.S.C. 1985; *Micro Chemicals Ltd v. Smith Kline & French Inter-American Corporation* (1971) 25 DLR (3d) 79, 89.

[189] Art. 54(3), Decreto-Ley No. 68 (14 de mayo de 1983).

[190] Art. 27(3)(iii), Patents Law, 01/04/1998, N° 16(1).

El Salvador,[191] Arab Emirates,[192] Ghana,[193] Greece,[194] India,[195] Malaysia,[196] Malta,[197] Mozambique,[198] Namibia,[199] Nigeria,[201] New Zealand,[201] Kenya,[202] Kyrgyz Republic,[203] Sri Lanka,[204] Thailand[205] and Tanzania.[206] They adopt research exceptions that reproduce or are substantially similar to the model introduced by art. 136(1) of the WIPO Model Law for Developing Countries on Innovations, which reads as follows: "Rights under the patent shall extend to acts done for industrial or commercial purposes and in particular not to acts done only for scientific research." In the view of this auhor, such legislation forbids the use of patented innovations in projects of technological research and development, i.e. in projects that aim to develop products and processes with immediate industrial or commercial value.

The third group is formed by States that have adopted through legal and/or judicial lines research use exceptions that differ from the more usual models. Argentina,[207] Costa Rica,[208] Dominican

[191] Art. 61(c), Decreto Legislativo No. 912, del 14 de diciembre de 2005.

[192] Art. 17, Federal Law No. 44 of 1992 for Organizing and Protection of Industrial Property for Patents, Designs and Industrial Models.

[193] Art. 30(a), Patents Law, 30/12/1992, No. 305A.

[194] Art. 10(2)(a), Law No. 1733/1987.

[195] Section 47, Patents Act, 1970.

[196] Art. 37(1), Patents Act 1983 (Act 291, as last amended by the Patents (Amendment) Act 1993).

[197] Art. 27(3)(c), Patents Act, 2000.

[198] Art. 68(a), Industrial Property Code of Mozambique (Approved by Decree No. 18/99 of May 4).

[199] Art. 17(3)(c), Unified Bill on Intellectual Property Rights, 1999.

[200] Art. 6(3)(a), Industrial Property, Act (Ch. 344), 1970, No. 60.

[201] The New Zealand Patent Law (1953) does not envisage any research exception. Local case law is established, however, in the sense of permitting the use of protected innovations in non-commercial research projects (Office of the Associate Minister of Commerce 2006). In 2006, the government of New Zealand published a proposal for a research exception that will probably be adopted in the near future. If passed, the proposal will allow third parties to use patented innovations in research on the functioning of inventions; to determine the scope of the innovation; to establish the validity of the claims contained in the patent; to update the protected innovation (e.g. to discover new applications for the innovation), provided the research activities do not conflict with the normal exploitation of the innovation.

[202] Art. 58(1), Industrial Property Act No. 3 of 2001.

[203] Art. 13(ii), Patent Law of December 16, 1997.

[204] Art. 82(1), Code of Intellectual Property Act No. 52 of 1979 (as amended by Act No. 30 of 1980, No. 2 of 1983, No. 17 of 1990, No. 13 of 1997 and No. 40 of 2000).

[205] Art. 36(16)(1), Patent Act B.E. 2522 (1979) as amended by the Patent Act (No. 2) B.E. 2535 (1992) and the Patent Act (No. 3) B.E. 2542 (1999).

[206] Art. 37(1), Patents Act No. 1 of 1987.

[207] Art. 36(a), Ley de Patentes de Invención y Modelos de Utilidad (Ley 24.481 modificada por la Ley 24.572).

[208] Art. 16(2), Reformas de la Ley de Derechos de Autor y Derechos Conexos, Ley de Patentes, Modelos de Utilidad y Código Procesal Civil.

Republic,[209] Guatemala,[210] Honduras,[211] Indonesia,[212] Mexico,[213] Nicaragua,[214] Paraguay,[215] Poland[216] and Uruguay[217] allow the use of patented inventions for purposes of teaching or scientific and academic research (i.e. non-commercial purposes).

Belgium amended its patent law in 2005. One new feature introduced is a more robust research use exception than the previous one, which basically reproduced the European model previously indicated. The new exception authorizes research *on* and research *with* patented inventions.[218] In other words, the exception admits both scientific studies aimed at generating further knowledge on the features and applications of patented inventions and also scientific studies which employ the patented invention itself in its capacity as a research tool. The exception only authorizes the *use* of patented inventions in *primarily* scientific projects (non-commercial purposes). Consequently, patented innovations may be used in projects that are focused simultaneously on scientific and technological purposes. Commercial organizations cannot benefit from the exception as their aims are purely commercial.[219] The text of the exception does not clearly specify whether basic research carried out by commercial firms and research done by the commercial sector of universities fall within its scope.[220]

The United States adopts at least two research use exceptions. The ruling handed down by the Court of Appeals of the Federal Circuit in *Madey* v. *Duke University* confirmed the opinion that the US legal order allows a research exception that covers non-profit scientific activities. The exception only authorizes the use of patented scientific inventions in activities aimed at "amusement, to satisfy idle curiosity, or for strictly philosophical inquiry."[221] In other words, the use of any patented innovation is forbidden in activities promoting, directly or indirectly, the users' "legitimate business objectives." A university is not authorized, for example, to use a protected innovation for purposes of education, training or

[209] Art. 30(c), Ley No. 20–00 sobre Propiedad Industrial.
[210] Art. 130(b), Ley de Propiedad Industrial (Decreto No. 57–2000).
[211] Art. 18, Decreto No. 12–99-E. [212] Art. 16(3), Law No. 14, 2001.
[213] Art. 22(1), Ley de Propiedad Industrial 25/06/1991 (17/05/1999).
[214] Art. 46(b), Industrial Property Law, 19/09/2000, No. 354.
[215] Art. 34, Ley No. 1630 de Patentes de Invenciones.
[216] Art. 69(1)(iii), Act of June 30, 2000 on Industrial Property Law.
[217] Art 39(d), (e), Ley No. 17.164 Patentes de Invención, Modelos de Utilidad y Diseños Industriales.
[218] See Van Overwalle 2006, 906–907. [219] *Ibid.*, 907. [220] *Ibid.*, 908.
[221] United States Court of Appeals for the Federal Circuit, *Madey* v. *Duke University* 307 F.3d 1351 (2002).

academic research, even if they are not concerned with developing commercial products or processes, as they all promote, in one way or another, its institutional mission. The second exception offered by the US legal order is envisaged in 35 USC §271(e)(1).[222] In the understanding of the US Supreme Court, put forward in *Merck* v. *Integra*, the provision referred to consents to: (i) the use of patented inventions in the creation of the information necessary to file marketing approval for generic drugs; (ii) third parties to carry out experiments on patented innovations with the purpose of developing new commercial products, whose marketing depends on some government registry, provided it is made conditional on the submission of technical information based on the use of the invention covered by the patent.[223] It is worth mentioning that this second research exception protects research activities as well as technological development that do not deliver the success envisaged.

Brazil and Rwanda seem to allow the use of patented innovations in scientific research with no commercial purposes and technological innovation of a commercial nature.[224] Bulgaria permits the use of patented innovations in scientific research (for non-profit purposes) and in research and development projects (with commercial purposes) only if aimed at producing wider information on the patented innovations.[225] Slovenia[226] and Japan[227] allow research linked to the generation of further information on patented innovations, regardless of the type of final product ensuing from the project (commercial or purely scientific). Israel permits scientific or technological research based on the patented innovation, including the development of updated versions of the inventions protected or new innovations in general.[228] Jordan[229] agrees to the use of patented innovations for any type of research in science or technology. Vietnam permits non-commercial activities, technological experiments

[222] This provision states: "It shall not be an act of infringement to make, use, offer to sell, or sell within the United States or import into the United States a patented invention (other than a new animal drug or veterinary biological product . . .) solely for uses reasonably related to the development and submission of information under a Federal law which regulates the manufacture, use, or sale of drugs . . ."

[223] Supreme Court of the United States of America, *Merck KGAA, Petitioner* v. *Integra Lifesciences I, Ltd et al.* 545 US 193 (2005).

[224] Art. 43(II), Lei No. 9.279/96 (Brazil); art. 41(2), Law No. 31/2009 of 10/26/2009 (Rwanda).

[225] Arts. 20(2) and 20(4), Patents Act (Consolidation), 18/03/1993 (1999).

[226] Art. 19(b), Industrial Property Act of May 23, 2001.

[227] See Johnson 2003, 515 ff. [228] Art. 1, Patents Law 5727 (1967).

[229] Art. 21(c), Patents of Invention Law, Law No. 32 for the Year 1999 (and its amendment by Temporary Law No. 71 for the Year 2001).

for commercial purposes and teaching activities involving a patented innovation.[230]

Switzerland amended its patent legislation in 2009. It now has quite a broad research exception which allows the use of: patented inventions with the purpose of obtaining further knowledge on the subject matter of the patent, including new applications; patented innovations in education; protected biological material in activities of selection and discovery as in the development of new vegetable varieties.[231] In order to facilitate access to research tools, Swiss legislation establishes that local courts should grant non-exclusive licenses to third parties who fail in their attempts to obtain a license on reasonable terms from the patent owner or his licensee.[232]

The wording of most of the provisions indicated is ambiguous; it is impossible to identify with certainty which activities are in fact protected. Thus there is a likelihood that the scope of these research use exceptions is narrower than expected. In the absence of legal security, potential users may decide to demand licenses from right holders, which is not always possible; or they may run the risk of a dispute or, worse still, they may choose to cut their research activities to a minimum. Not even the least ambiguous legislative provisions on the scope of research exception are problem-free: they tend to obstruct research for commercial purposes, making it conditional on the authorization of the patent owners. Currently, when a growing number of universities and public institutions of research worldwide are channeling their resources towards projects with commercial purposes, this kind of exception makes no sense and curtails the development of socially relevant commercial innovations.

The overwhelming majority of the research exceptions examined allow activities focused on producing further information on the protected invention. Research that involves the *use* of the invention in the process of developing new technologies tends not to be permitted. In other words, research exceptions seem to forbid – as a general rule – research that applies patented research tools, even in non-commercial projects. In view of the fact that the main use of research tools is to contribute to scientific and commercial research, the widespread opinion is that there is no objection to allowing third parties to carry out research activities aimed at

[230] Art 125(2)(a), Law on Intellectual Property No. 50/2005/QH11 of November 29, 2005.

[231] Art. 9 (G)(I), Loi fédérale sur les brevets d'invention du 25 juin 1954.

[232] Art. 40(b)(F), Loi fédérale sur les brevets d'invention du 25 juin 1954.

exploring the features of these tools. It would be socially and economically inappropriate, however, to allow third parties to use them for the purpose for which they were created.[233] Although the view is arguable, there is no doubt that granting absolute property rights for these tools could be extremely detrimental to society.

Lastly, some States seem to have adopted research use exceptions that allow a broad use of patented inventions, including research tools, in scientific (non-commercial) and technological (commercial) activities, regardless of any payments to patent owners. That seems to be the case of exceptions conceded by the US,[234] Israel and Vietnam. If, on the one hand, this kind of exception frees scientists from the cobwebs of bureaucracy, it may on the other hand, particularly when research tools are used in commercial projects, undermine the economic incentives offered by patents to their holders.

Even if there may be doubts as to the scope of the research exceptions briefly considered above, there is one undisputed fact: the scientific and industrial communities demand clearer and more balanced exceptions, able to promote uninterruptedly the progress of science, technology, the economy and society.

The biomedical and agro-biotechnological sectors were able to develop due to regulations that favored access to new knowledge. At present, however, those rules are giving way to others that protect industrial property,[235] drawn up with the purpose of maximizing the protection of the economic interests of patent holders. Legal systems that grant over-protection to the interests of patent owners are driven by the wish to increase incentives for R&D investment. That notwithstanding, history shows that the development of science and technology does not turn solely upon systems of property rights protection; it is also built upon massive investment in science and technology[236] and the conservation of a robust public domain.

[233] On this point see, e.g., Eisenberg 1989, 1035; Cook 2006, 156–157; Federal Trade Commission 2003, ch. 4, 34 (adopting research exceptions for that category of innovations would not be convenient as it would take away all economic incentives for investing in developing new research tools); Waldeck und Pyrmont 2008, 427 (judges that research exceptions that consent to the use of research tools for their normal purpose to be a type of expropriation of private property).

[234] See 35 USC § 271(e)(1). [235] See Rai and Eisenberg 2001, 157.

[236] The US, the great champion of policies promoting the privatization of knowledge, was able to successfully adopt a strategy to foster the use of patents as a tool for innovation incentives because throughout the twentieth century its government strongly financed science and technology activities. It was only at the end of the 1990s that private investments were higher than those of public agencies, but public investments are still very high (Conceição *et al.* 2004, 568–569).

While patents are acknowledged as undisputable instruments in the promotion of investments in innovation – particularly in the biomedical and agricultural sectors[237] – these very instruments may become an obstacle to innovation on account of an unbalanced widening of the rights granted to patent owners and of the list of subject matters eligible for protection, compounded by restrictions in the exceptions to the rights granted.[238] As a consequence, the scientific public domain has been dramatically impoverished, and this has had an impact on the capacity for innovation of society in general.

A review of the research use exceptions adopted by a significant number of States shows that there is an urgent need to adopt new exceptions, drawn up in a way that will take into account, on one side, the individual interests of patent holders to recover their investments in R&D[239] and, on the other, the interests of third parties and of society to enjoy greater freedom to develop new scientific knowledge, products and commercial processes based on the contributions offered by protected innovations,[240] considering that progress in science and technology occurs through a number of small steps rather than one large step.[241]

The urgency of their demands is testified by the fact that in recent years three industrialized countries – Australia,[242] New Zealand[243] and the United Kingdom[244] – have been discussing the need to reform their legislation in order to introduce broad and unequivocal research exceptions that can pave the way for innovation,[245] also by the fact that Belgium and Switzerland have recently introduced strong research exceptions, as opposed to regularly adopted models, and by the massive number of scientific articles devoted to this matter that have been published in recent years, mostly in industrialized countries, stressing the risks involved in limiting the scope of research use exceptions.

A central objective of this chapter is to identify model exceptions to patent rights that WTO members can adopt in order to advance their scientific, technological and social progress. With these goals in mind, in the final section of the present chapter two proposals for patent exceptions will be presented, designed to overcome the problems identified in the first part of this chapter, resulting from the proliferation of patents in the

237 See Walsh *et al.* 2003, 352. 238 See Royal Society 2003, para. 6.10.
239 See Mueller 2001, 41.
240 See, e.g., Royal Society 2003, para. 1.3; Derzko 2003, 388–389.
241 O'Rourke 2000, 1183.
242 Australian legislation does not yet have a research exception (IP Australia 2009).
243 Office of the Associate Minister of Commerce 2006.
244 United Kingdom Intellectual Property Office 2009, para. 23.
245 Patent legislation in the United Kingdom already has a research exception; its ambiguous wording causes juridical uncertainty among users, however.

biotechnology sector: an R&D exception and a genetic diagnostic test exception. There is then an examination of the legality of the proposed exceptions vis-à-vis art. 30 of the TRIPS Agreement.

5.5 The R&D and genetic diagnostic test exceptions

The first exception, the R&D exception, consists of four interrelated elements. It is so called because its aim is not only to open up ways for scientists to continue to pursue projects in pure science; it also fosters the realization of projects in applied science, as well as the introduction of new products into the market. The second exception, the genetic diagnostic test exception, only affects patents concerned with human genetic materials.

Taken together, they create a truly favorable atmosphere for scientific, technological and social progress, since they preserve the economic incentives offered by patents, while offering ample space for encouraging the ongoing enrichment of the scientific and technological heritage of humanity. They also challenge the conservative stance that holds that it is impracticable to create incentives for research and promote the wide use of protected innovations.

The exceptions proposed are devised with the purpose of fostering the widest possible use of patented matters, including genetic innovations, for purely scientific, humanitarian and commercial purposes. They intend to put into practice the recommendations of best practice for licensing genetic innovations proposed by relevant organizations in the international economic and scientific fields such as: the US National Institutes of Health (NIH),[246] the OECD,[247] the European

[246] The National Institutes of Health (NIH 2005) recommends to the institutions it funds to adopt the practice of granting non-exclusive licenses, especially for genomic innovations, enacting licensing policies that will maximize the use of patented innovations, even in projects with commercial purposes, and adopting policies that facilitate the use of research tools.

[247] In 2006, the OECD admitted that despite the fact that the patents system aims to promote innovation and social well-being, there are cases when patent holders misuse their privileges and prejudice society (OECD 2006, 13). Consequently, the OECD recommended its Members to adopt certain guidelines to license genetic innovations. The OECD guidelines were devised to foster innovation through recouping of investment in R&D and widening the scope of access to patented innovations (*ibid.*, para. 10). Among the recommended principles, the following are highlighted insofar as they have had a substantial impact on the patent exceptions proposed in this book: licensing practices must promote the swift dissemination of technical information associated to genetic innovations (principle 1.B); patented innovations must be offered quickly and on reasonable terms (principle 1.A); patented innovations must be widely used to promote well-being among the peoples of industrialized and developing countries (principle 2.D); patent holders must enact licensing policies that favor freedom of research in

Society of Human Genetics,[248] the Danish Council of Ethics,[249] the Human Genome Organization,[250] the American College of Medical Genetics[251] and the Association of University Technology Managers (AUTM),[252] as well as the recommendations put forward by the UK Royal Society with the purpose of setting up an appropriate environment that will encourage progress in education, science and technology.[253] In more specific terms, the exceptions proposed prevent anti-commons tragedies, remove obstacles to follow-on innovation which might be promoted by royalty stacking and diminish the effects of anti-competitive practices that might ensue from granting patents for unique research tools.

The proposed exceptions coincide with the contemporary innovation scenario, characterized by synergy-building between university institutions and businesses. In actual practice, this means that they not only promote non-commercial scientific research but commercial projects too. Should exceptions only authorize the non-commercial use of patented items, their benefits would probably be limited. With the intention of promoting the development of entrepreneurial science, the exceptions proposed open the way to the exploitation, both commercial and non-commercial, of the inventions developed upon the basis of protected ones. Traditionally, research exceptions are devised with the purpose of opening up opportunity for research but they ignore the hurdles that developers will face when they try to introduce their research outputs

scientific institutions, even if they pursue commercial objectives (principles 3.A, 3.B and 3.D); upstream innovations (research tools) must be widely accessible (principle 4.A); patent owners must refrain from demanding excessive fees for the use of their innovations or include reach-through clauses in their licensing agreements (principle 4.C); licensing practices must promote innovation and competition (principle 5).

248 See Aymé *et al.* 2008, 8 (society demands that owners of patents related to human genetic material adopt the practice of granting non-exclusive licenses, establish reasonable fees and adopt other practices that will diminish transaction costs in order to widen the use of these innovations).

249 See Danish Council of Ethics 2004, 99 ff.

250 See HUGO Intellectual Property Committee 2003.

251 See American College of Medical Genetics 2009.

252 AUTM (Association of University Technology Managers 2007) submitted nine recommendations to be observed by technology transfer offices in universities with the purpose of expanding the use of innovations developed within these organizations. Four of them merit highlighting: (1) "universities should reserve the right to practice licensed innovations, and to allow other non-profit and governmental organizations to do so"; (2) "exclusive licenses should be structured in a manner that encourages technology development and use"; (3) "ensure broad access to research tools"; (4) "consider including provisions that address unmet needs, such as those of neglected patient populations or geographic areas, giving particular attention to improved therapeutics, diagnostics, and agricultural technologies for the developing world."

253 See Royal Society 2003, paras. 1.1, 2.1, 2.9, 3.19, 3.23 and 3.35.

in the market. Given this context, it may happen that after considerable investment has been made useful inventions never reach the market because it proves impossible to obtain the corresponding licenses from the relevant patent owners or – worse still – there is no investment in useful projects. Put more simply, traditional research exceptions merely postpone the moment when patents will create obstacles to science and technology.

Together, the two exceptions allow: (i) the carrying out of research on the patented subject matters with the purpose of confirming their functionality and *modus operandi*, thus guaranteeing that patent owners will faithfully comply with their commitment to adequately disclose the object of the patents;[254] (ii) the generation of further knowledge on the subject matter of patents; (iii) the development of alternative inventions to or improved versions of previous ones; (iv) transformative uses of patented inventions, i.e. development of new inventions, including new genetic tests.

5.5.1 General rules applicable to both exceptions

The proper functioning of the R&D and diagnostic test exceptions depends on the adoption of some mandatory rules, the existence of a patent clearing house and the use of the opportunities offered by the compulsory licensing system of the TRIPS Agreement to ensure that the process of obtaining compulsory licenses is faster and less hazardous. These issues will be examined in detail below.

5.5.1.1 Rule I: Mandatory character of the exceptions Under the influence of the amendment of the Swiss Patent Act, passed in July 2009, the legal text that institutes the proposed exceptions should render void any contract agreement affecting the exercise of exceptions to patent rights.[255] This implies that exceptions enjoy the status of rights, guaranteed to third parties and valid when opposing right holders. This is an effective means of asserting that the rights of users and those of patent holders enjoy the same degree of importance, and that exceptions to exclusive rights do not imply an "aberration" that must be strictly controlled.[256]

254 See Eisenberg 1989, 1075.

255 Art. 9(G)(I): "Patent Exceptions: The agreements that limit or nullify the exception referred to in paragraph 1 are null and void" (free translation) (Loi fédérale sur les brevets d'invention du 25 juin 1954).

256 Story *et al.* 2006, 136.

5.5.1.2 Rule II: Duty to inform In order to assist in the negotiation of voluntary licenses, in granting compulsory licenses and in the exercise of exceptions to patent rights, all patent owners should bear the duty to disclose, either on their internet sites and/or the packaging of their products, the numbers of the patents of their protected inventions.[257]

5.5.1.3 Rule III: Guarantee of access to biological materials In the case of biotechnological inventions, carrying out the excepted activities may be restricted if, for example, the biological material used as raw materials is not freely accessible to the public. On account of that, filing patent applications that involve biotechnological inventions depends on the simultaneous deposit with the relevant authorities of the invention and the biological material it is based on. Third parties should have a right of access to the samples of the biological material immediately after filing the patent application with the patent office. Third parties will take over the operational expenses linked to the multiplication and delivery of the material of interest.[258] The material received can only be reproduced to carry out the activities covered by the exceptions.

5.5.1.4 Rule IV: Prohibition of reach-through patent claims and contractual clauses The aim of all patent holders is the maximization of their economic profits. That is why whenever possible, they include reach-through claims in the patent applications they file, which, upon approval by the patent office, grant a property right that covers all products and processes that ensue from the application of their innovation.[259] This type of claim is basically included in applications that cover research tools, as it guarantees right holders a share in the work of third parties. Given the fact that research tools very often play a crucial role in the development of a vast array of products and processes but are not subsequently incorporated in the final output of researches, the absence of reach-through claims means that the owners of research tools are not entitled to any special profit, in addition to that derived from the use of the tool.

Many owners of patents on research tools, whose patents do not include reach-through claims, include reach-through clauses in their licensing contracts. These grant them co-property rights on the results of

[257] SACGHS 2009, 115.
[258] Based on art. 13, Directive 98/44/EC of the European Parliament and of the Council of July 6, 1998 on the legal protection of biotechnological innovations.
[259] Hindle 2005.

research carried out by applying the patented tool, or a share in the profits ensuing from marketing the technologies developed, or a non-onerous license – exclusive or otherwise – to exploit the new inventions.[260]

Seen by themselves, these reach-through patent claims and contractual clauses appear acceptable and they even seem to provide an incentive for patent holders to facilitate the licensing of their inventions since they will benefit from the success of others.[261] Things look different, however, when analyzed within the actual context of the innovation sector. At present, research institutions usually employ a wide variety of research tools to execute one particular project.[262] If the inputs used were subject to reach-through claims or clauses, the final product of the research would probably never reach the market either because it would belong to several individuals and institutions, who do not necessarily share the same interests, or because a lion's share of the profits would belong to the owners of the tools used, and the surplus would not be enough to justify the production and marketing of the product.[263]

A fundamental principle of patent law requires that patent applications disclose their subject matter in a manner sufficiently detailed for a person skilled in the art to be able to carry it out at no undue cost.[264] If reach-through claims are protected, the patent holder will enjoy protection for something that was not disclosed in the patent – i.e. for someone else's innovation – which may well fail to comply with the three substantive patentability conditions. Permission to widen the scope of rights granted to owners of research tools means granting them a differential treatment lacking any legitimate justification, since a research tool by itself does not specify what inventions may derive from its application, nor how to actually arrive at an invention.

Regardless of the relevance of a research tool for research in science and technology, the outputs of those projects depend on other inputs and, more importantly, on the great efforts and skills of the researchers involved. Allowing owners of research tools to claim rights on the fruits

260 See NIH 1998, 9–19. 261 See Dreyfuss 2005, 17.

262 See Eisenberg *et al.* 2002, 206. 263 See Derzko 2003, 399; NIH 1998, 9–21.

264 Along the same line, Justice Arbour, Supreme Court of Canada, in *Monsanto Canada Inc.* v. *Schmeiser* [2004] 1 SCR 902 held: "The scope of the patent protection should be both 'fair' and 'reasonably predictable' . . . The inventor may not get exclusive rights to an invention that was not part of the public disclosure of the invention. The public must be able to predict the activities that will infringe on the exclusive rights granted to the patentee . . . So long as the claims are interpreted fairly and knowledgeably, if the patentee has limited the claims, then the public is entitled to rely on that limitation: . . . An inventor cannot enlarge the scope of the grant of exclusive rights beyond that which has been specified: . . . The claims are invalid if they are broader than the disclosure" (paras. 123–124).

of the labor of others can lead to an abuse of rights: the undue expansion of the scope of patents permits its owners to enrich themselves unjustly at the expense of the genuine developers of new inventions,[265] compounded by the fact that the practice interferes with the pace of development and the introduction of new products into the market.

In view of this fact, it is only legitimate to claim protection for the invention actually developed and characterized in the patent application.[266] Otherwise, the patent holder would receive more rights than justified by his contribution to society.[267] If it is illegal to claim rights on inventions ensuing from the application of a research tool, it is equally illegal to claim a share in the profits obtained from its marketing. In view of this and in accordance with art. 29(1) of the TRIPS Agreement, WTO Members have the duty to prevent the grant of those claims, as a way to ensure proportionality between patent rights and contributions to the state of the art. Additionally and on account of its anti-competitive effects, art. 40(2) TRIPS allows WTO Members to forbid patent owners from including reach-through clauses in their licensing contracts.

5.5.1.5 Rule V: Establishment of a patent clearing house[268] A patent clearing house (PCH, or management organization) is an independent agency whose institutional mission is to reduce as much as possible the transaction costs involved in the process of transfer of patented technologies.[269] Its ultimate aim is to catalyze transfers of new technologies for scientific and productive purposes, without affecting the economic incentives offered to individuals and institutions to engage in R&D activities.[270] In the specific case of the proposals made here, the establishment of a PCH by law and the mandatory participation of all patent holders is recommended. Lacking the full participation of all patent holders, a PCH would prove unsustainable.[271]

The PCH proposed would, among other things, be vested with the competence to:[272]

- inform on valid patents in the territory under the agency's jurisdiction, contributing to the dissemination and transfer of protected inventions;
- draw up and sign standard licensing agreements with prospective users of protected inventions. Once the clauses of those agreements are

[265] See Federal Trade Commission 2003, ch. 3, p. 27.
[266] See Bostyn 2004, 68. [267] See Royal Society 2003, para. 3.35.
[268] Component based on the suggestions presented by the OECD (2002, 82; 2006, 20), the Human Genome Organization (HUGO Intellectual Property Committee 2003, 3) and the European Society of Human Genetics (Aymé *et al.* 2008, 8).
[269] See OECD 2002, 73–74. [270] See Sheremeta and Gold 2003, 18–19.
[271] See Van Overwalle *et al.* 2006, 146. [272] *Ibid.*, 145–146.

standardized, users of protected technologies will not endure any type of discrimination by patent owners and access to patented technologies will be smooth;

- collect royalty fees paid by users of patented technology and transfer the funds to patent owners or whoever is entitled to them;
- monitor breaches of signed contracts and rights granted to patent owners by the clauses that introduce exceptions to patent rights. In case of a breach, the PCH will refer to its administrative court, which is entitled to issue executive titles when there is proof that the fee owed by the user of the protected technology has not been paid. This prevents courts from being overloaded with new claims, whilst turning the process of cashing in the fees due into a more efficient procedure;
- receive and examine applications for compulsory licenses and grant them, provided all legal requirements are complied with;
- receive and judge appeals lodged by patent owners whose patents have been compulsorily licensed with the purpose of invalidating the licenses granted or the fees set by the PCH;
- receive and disclose to the public any information received from owners of patents associated with human genetic material, as well as from users of these inventions, on discoveries of new genetic mutations linked to predisposition to disease. These data shall be included in a public database. In their daily routine, institutions involved in diagnostic and predictive genetic tests usually discover new information on genes and other biochemical molecules present in the human body, which may signal connections to illnesses thus contributing to more precise diagnoses. Such information is undoubtedly vital for human health. Consequently, patent holders and users should be obliged to make public disclosure of all these discoveries. The PCH, on its side, should widely disseminate the information received;
- pre-set the fees, in a neutral manner, for each category of invention under administration. The PCH should determine different royalties according to: the special features of the invention; the industrial sector where the innovation will be applied; the role of the invention in the development of a new technology; and the objectives pursued by the R&D project where the patented input will be applied.[273] In order to

[273] Different techniques can be used to calculate the royalty fees to be paid to the owners of innovations used when developing new products and processes. The assessment of those techniques falls beyond the scope of this study. On the various techniques that may be applied, see Razgaitis 2007; on the "25% rule" see Goldscheider 1995 (that rule, based on licensing practices employed by industries in industrialized countries, establishes that the licensee must pay the licensor of technology 25% of the profits before taxation, obtained from marketing the patented innovation).

fulfill this task correctly, the PCH will have a collective body, formed by specialists on the evaluation of intellectual assets, representing the various industrial sectors;

- establish a top limit to the combined royalty fees, in order to prevent royalty stacking from making complex products commercially unfeasible – i.e. technologies whose development involves multiple patented inventions. If the composition of a complex product includes ten patented innovations, for example, and the combined royalty fees surpass a specified top limit, royalty fees would be proportionally lowered until the top limit is reached.[274] The limit would vary with each type of technology. In the pharmaceutical sector, for instance, Phillip Grubb, from Novartis International, drawing from his experience in the area, states that the maximum percentage that combined royalty fees could represent in the total profits of a pharmaceutical product is 20%; above that benchmark the technology would become economically unfeasible;[275] and
- determine also a bottom line for royalty fees, i.e. a line that cannot be crossed when lowering royalty fees.[276] That bottom limit would be specifically established for each type of technology; thus, in view of their vital importance for the development of innumerable products, unique innovations without substitutes in the market would be subject to a higher bottom line than an ordinary innovation for which there are substitutes in the market. The more important the innovation for developing a new product, the higher the fees to be paid to its owner. Adopting a mechanism for lowering the royalty fees to be paid to owners of innovations included in complex technologies benefits all concerned, including society. In the absence of such a mechanism, probably neither the developer of the new technology, nor the owners of the technologies used would obtain any benefits. Simply put, it is wiser to earn less than to earn nothing.

5.5.1.6 Rule VI: De-bureaucratization of the procedures for granting compulsory licenses WTO Members tend to include the words in art. 31 of the TRIPS Agreement in their legal frameworks without any changes. This causes huge problems to whoever wishes to obtain a compulsory license. Without going into the specific features of the rules of the TRIPS Agreement, a third party wishing to obtain a compulsory license will have to proceed as follows.[277] In the first place, he must try to obtain a voluntary

[274] See Jones *et al.* 2007, 1125. [275] Grubb 2002, 3. [276] Jones *et al.* 2007, 1125.

[277] The standard compulsory licensing procedure admits exceptions in cases of emergencies (art. 31 (b)) and in cases when the petitioner lacks industrial capacity within the

license from the owner of the patent or of the patent application filed he is interested in. If "within a reasonable period of time" he has not obtained a license "on reasonable commercial terms and conditions," the third party may require the relevant authorities to grant him a compulsory license. If there is evidence justifying a compulsory license – for instance, anti-competitive practices through exercise of patent rights, or the existence of a patent that cannot be exploited without infringing another patent – the State authorities shall grant a non-exclusive license and set the fee to be paid to the patent owner, the scope of the license and its duration. The owner of the patent for which a compulsory license has been granted is entitled to challenge the validity of the license – e.g. because the legal requirements have not been complied with – or the royalty fees to be paid.

It is commonly understood that, historically, the rules of the Paris Convention for the protection of Industrial Property (art. 5) and of the TRIPS Agreement on granting compulsory licenses (art. 31) were devised to ensure that obtaining compulsory licenses would be as difficult as possible. Obtaining them may, in fact, prove impossible if WTO Members do not clearly establish in their domestic legislation: when compulsory licenses may be claimed; what qualifies as a "reasonable period of time" to obtain a voluntary license; which commercial conditions are abusive; what guidelines must be followed by the relevant authority in the process of establishing the fees to be paid to the owner of a licensed patent; the period of time within which the relevant authorities must hand down the decision regarding the claim for a license; and the effects produced by the appeal lodged by the patent owner.

The decision of the General Council of the WTO of 2003, for example, that allows resort to the system of compulsory licensing to facilitate imports of patented drugs by a State with no productive capacity was used by Rwanda only once over a six-year period. At present, developing countries are trying to join forces at the WTO to reform the solution reached in 2003 so that it will be less bureaucratic and more efficient.[278] In the domestic sphere, it is worth noting the Nortox S.A. case. In October 2003, Nortox asked the Brazilian National Institute of Industrial Property (INPI) for a compulsory license of a patent owned by Ishihara Sangyo Kaisha, based on the fact that it was not being exploited in the country. In January 2007, more than three years after the beginning of

pharmaceutical sector and he needs to contact industry in another county in order to meet the demands of local markets. See WTO, Decision of the General Council of 30 August 2003 – WT/L/540 and Corr. 1.

278 See Mara 2010.

the proceedings, the INPI declined to grant the compulsory license. It accepted as proof of exploitation of the patent a licensing contract signed between the patent holder and Hokko do Brasil Indústria Química e Agropecuária.[279] The INPI took too long to examine the Nortox request and adopted a broad interpretation of the notion of exploitation of a patent.

WTO Members are advised to follow all the procedures specified below when granting compulsory licenses for unique research tools and blocking patents in order to minimize the obstacles involved in the granting of compulsory licenses. It is important to emphasize that these procedures come within the flexibilities offered by the TRIPS Agreement.[280]

5.5.1.6.1 Compulsory licensing for unique research tools As we shall see, the terms of the exception that is proposed state that the owners of patents related to unique research tools are obliged to offer them in the market, though they still retain the right to determine the fee to be paid.[281] Should the fee set too high a benchmark, the third party may try to negotiate a discount. In order to avoid endless negotiations leading nowhere, the patent owner or his licensee will have to reply within a 30-day period. Once the period is over, the interested party can require a compulsory license from the PCH. Since the period of protection of a patent begins on the date when the application is filed, third parties can demand a compulsory license as from that moment, that is, before the patent is granted.[282]

After the request has been filed, it will be the task of the PCH to compare the fee established by the patent owner for the commercial use of his research tool with regular fees, applied in analogous circumstances for similar innovations. Besides that, and in order to assess the excessive cost suggested, the PCH will have to consider the institutional standing of the person/institution who requested the compulsory license, i.e. (i) small or medium-sized business; (ii) university; (iii) governmental agency; or (iv) large enterprise. Fixing the appropriate fee is always a challenge for any institution. Nevertheless, since one of the main tasks of the PCH is to determine the fees to be paid according to the various categories of innovations, the assessment of the excessive character of the fees set by the patent owner should be carried out easily and within a reasonable period of time.

279 See Advocacia Geral da União 2007.

280 See Chapter 2, section 2.3.3.3.4.3.

281 See section 5.5.5 below.

282 Within the WTO legal framework, art. 5(A)(4) of the Paris Convention is the only provision that sets a time limit for filing requests for compulsory licenses on the ground of failure or insufficient exploitation of a patent by its owner or licensee.

If the disproportionate cost of the fee demanded by the patent owner is effectively proved, the PCH will be obliged to grant the compulsory license to the petitioner. Besides the fee to be paid, it will also indicate the scope of the license and its duration. In other words, the organization is not entitled to inquire into the convenience of granting the compulsory license required. Once the overstated cost of the fee has been proved, the third party will be entitled to receive a license.[283] The PCH will have to conclude the procedure within 60 days, as from receipt of the application.

In accordance with the rules of the TRIPS Agreement,[284] the owner of the patent that is compulsorily licensed has the right to challenge its granting and/or the remuneration established. He can only lodge the appeal before a high ranking agency of the PCH, which must reply within 180 days. The appeal lodged by the patent owner will not interrupt the license, i.e., it will continue to be valid during the process.

5.5.1.6.2 Compulsory licensing of blocking patents As already seen, in terms of art. 31(1) of the TRIPS Agreement, if a patented invention cannot be exploited without infringing a previous one, the owner of the patent which covers the new invention will endeavor to obtain a voluntary license from the owner of the blocking patent; should it prove impossible, he will request a compulsory license.[285] In order to avoid an undue bureaucratization of the process to obtain compulsory licenses for blocking patents, the process to apply and obtain one should be very similar to the one that regulates the grant of compulsory licenses for patents that cover research tools. In other words, the third party who develops a new patented invention must strive to negotiate a voluntary license with the owner of the blocking patent or with the holder of the patent application. Should the owner of the patent or of the patent application fail to reply within a 30-day period, or should he refuse to grant the license required, or impose unreasonable commercial conditions, the owner of the subservient patent may apply to the PCH for a compulsory license.

The PCH will have to establish whether the new invention involves "an important technical advance of considerable economic significance." If, for example, the new invention meets a demand or problem faced by society and/or industry, or allows for a more efficient use of natural

[283] The idea of granting compulsory licenses to third parties to use research tools was inspired by art. 40b of the Swiss Patent Act, amended in 2009 (Loi fédérale sur les brevets d'invention du 25 juin 1954). The TRIPS Agreement grants to WTO Members the freedom to determine the grounds for granting compulsory licenses (Doha Declaration, para. 5b). Consequently, they are free to grant compulsory licenses for patents that cover research tools.

[284] Art. 31, (i) and (j), TRIPS.

[285] See Chapter 2, section 2.3.3.3.4.3.

resources as well as resources in the fields of energy and information, it will signify important technical progress that merits protection. PCH will therefore fix the amount to be paid by the licensee, on the basis of the fees paid in similar situations. The whole process will be concluded within a 60-day period, as from the date when the request was lodged. The earlier comments on the right of the patent owner against whom a compulsory license has been obtained to challenge the PCH decision are of equal application in this situation.

The establishment of strict deadlines for the patent holder to respond to the requests of third parties and for the assessment of applications for compulsory licenses by the PCH, the delegation of the task of setting the royalty fees to a team formed by licensing experts and specialists in assessment of intellectual assets and the creation of a form of arbitration court exclusively focused on hearing the appeals lodged by patent owners – all these factors make the system of compulsory licenses created by the TRIPS Agreement into a more manageable procedure. Having said that, one must add that in actual fact, even with the introduction of deadlines and less room for the relevant authority to refrain from granting the licenses required, the workload, the technical complexity of the issue and the possible political interference of patent holders in the evaluation process of the applications may create obstacles to the granting of compulsory licenses. That is the reason why the exceptions proposed in this study seek to avoid the use of a compulsory licensing system as much as possible.

The following sections will go through the proposed R&D exception, which is subdivided into four parts to facilitate analysis of its characteristics. Then its legality will be investigated in the light of art. 30 of TRIPS.

5.5.2 *R&D exception – first component: uses focused on generating knowledge on the subject matter of the patent and developing new innovations*

The first part of the exception covers all categories of inventions – for example, research tools and dual character inventions (i.e. those that serve as end-user products and as research tools) – belonging to any field of technology. Given its technological neutrality, the first part of the exception does not create any type of discrimination. The first part of the exception benefits commercial, non-profit and scientific organizations that carry out commercial, scientific or not-for-profit projects.

The exception exempts activities focused on generating knowledge about the patented subject matter, but not its use for its original purpose. The activities excepted are difficult to control by patent owners and are therefore usually carried out in the laboratories of public or private institutions.[286] Besides being difficult, if not impossible, to control, guaranteeing the right to research on the subject matter of patents is a corollary to the duty of patent owners to disclose detailed information on the way their inventions work and how they can be applied. Unless others are allowed to experiment on the patented invention, the patent holder might disclose information of secondary relevance. Consequently, by the end of the period of patent protection, society will be harmed because the information provided was not sufficient to reproduce the protected subject matter successfully.[287] In short, the recognition of the rights of third parties to investigate the objects of patents favors the creation of balanced patent regimes. The activities exempted by the first part of the exception are as follows:[288]

(1) examining the functioning of protected inventions, including within educational institutions in the course of teaching activities;[289]
(2) developing alternative inventions, even for commercial purposes, in cases when the new invention does *not* absorb the patented invention that is the object of the research; that is, the object of the patent is examined to make sure that the new invention does not impinge on another patent;
(3) making sure that the invention works as described in the patent. This proviso benefits potential licensees of a patent, who will only decide to negotiate a license when they are reassured about the real benefits to be derived from the object of the patent. It is also useful to confirm that the invention was described in a sufficiently complete manner in the patent. The importance of excepting this use can be inferred from the problems Brazil had to face after it granted a compulsory license for the drug called Efavirenz. The industry benefitted by the compulsory license took around two years to produce the drug

286 See Caruso 2003, 240. 287 See Strandburg 2004, 94, 102.

288 The scope of the first component of the R&D exception draws on: a US bill titled Patent Competitiveness and Technological Act (quoted in Johnson 2003, 529); the patent exception proposed by the American Intellectual Property Association (2004, 25); the research use exception proposed by the Canadian Biotechnology Advisory Committee (Advisory Council of Intellectual Property 2005, 25) and the bill presented for public consultation by the Australian government in 2009 (IP Australia 2009).

289 This component draws on art. 9(I)(d) of the Swiss Patent Act (Loi fédérale sur les brevets d'invention du 25 juin 1954), which provides: "The effects of patents shall not extend to the use of the invention for purposes of instruction at educational institutions" (free translation).

because the subject matter of the patent had not been disclosed in a sufficiently complete way;[290]

(4) confirming the validity of the patent claims and assessing its scope. The proposed exception is useful to clearly establish the scope of complex inventions – when the scope cannot be inferred from the written claims included in the patent – as well as to prove the lack of validity of patent claims in case of administrative or judicial proceedings;

(5) examining the technical features of the invention, including new applications unknown by science and not disclosed in the patent, e.g. identification of a new use for a pharmaceutical product.[291] Should a new application of the protected invention be discovered, its commercial exploitation will depend on a voluntary license granted by the owner of the patent under research or on a compulsory license. This item in the exception was inspired by the practice adopted in Germany, Italy and France and a recommendation of the European Parliament addressed to the European Patent Office. These countries restrict the scope of patents of products that use human genetic resources to the functions disclosed in the patent, in order to pave the way for research on new functions and applications of these resources and prevent protection for speculative claims;[292]

(6) developing an updated version of a previous invention. The third party may produce and use the patented subject matter to be enhanced, as far as it proves necessary to carry out the project. This type of project may pursue either commercial or non-commercial aims. Both are free, even if there is a chance that the final product of the project will embody the invention under research. In the latter case, the commercial exploitation of the improved version of the patented invention will depend on its compliance with the same requirements listed in section 5.5.4 below.

Carrying out the activities included in the exception is independent of payment of any fee to patent owners, as it does not affect the capacity of the latter to carry out the commercial exploitation of their innovations. Should the activities protected by the exception be linked to the payment

290 See WIPO, SCP/14/7, para. 16.

291 The inclusion of this activity in the scope of the R&D exception was spurred by the results of the empirical research carried out by the United Kingdom Intellectual Property Office in 2008. According to the results released, the biomedical sector demands freedom to investigate whether pharmaceutical and biotechnology innovations developed by their competitors can be applied for ends different from those aimed at by the original developers (United Kingdom Intellectual Property Office 2009, paras. 13 and 15).

292 See Aymé *et al.* 2008, 6; European Parliament 2005, para. 5.

of a fee, social interests of uncontested relevance would be at risk. The same rationale applies when a third party aims to develop an updated version of a patented innovation, since the mere project of improving a patented innovation does not constitute a commercial exploitation.

5.5.3 *R&D exception – second component: scientific and humanitarian uses*

All categories of inventions, coming from any sector of technology, are subject to the second component of the R&D exception. In view of its technological neutrality, this limb of the exception undoubtedly does not create discrimination of any kind.

Those benefitted by the exception are non-profit organizations, commercial organizations and scientific institutions that carry out non-commercial scientific projects and humanitarian projects, that is, projects focused on developing new products and processes, aimed at meeting the needs of marginalized groups in developing countries and in least developed countries.

Patent owners shall not be able to prevent non-authorized third parties from performing the following activities, which involve the use of their inventions for their original purposes:

(1) research activities with direct use of patented inventions, provided the user is a *non-profit* organization and is committed not to restrict disclosure and dissemination of research results, be it through IPR claims, or by including the research outputs in databases not accessible to the public, or by making the transfer of research results conditional upon licensing agreements;[293] and
(2) regardless of whether the institution is a commercial, scientific or philanthropic organization, it may develop and distribute products or processes for *humanitarian ends*, with the purpose of meeting the needs of poor countries, provided the products are offered free of charge to the peoples of those countries. Developers must also commit themselves to refrain from claiming IPRs on the results of their research. The activities carried out by philanthropic institutions such as the Bill and Melinda Gates Foundation, devoted to the development of new therapies, vaccines and plant varieties to meet the basic needs of peoples in developing countries, as well as philanthropic

[293] Based on Dreyfuss 2003 and Dreyfuss 2004 (see section 5.6.2.3.2). The obligation to introduce in the public domain the result of their research is a guarantee that universities will not misuse their status as scientific institutions to obtain unfair advantages by acting as commercial institutions.

projects led by pharmaceutical companies and public research institutions would also be covered by the exception.

Carrying out the activities included in the exception is independent of payment of any fee to patent owners, as the exploitation of patented innovations in non-commercial scientific projects and in humanitarian projects does not interfere with the commercial exploitation of patents. If patent owners received royalties for the use of their inventions in the field of purely scientific or philanthropic projects, the institutions concerned would probably refrain from using them in view of budgetary constraints.

5.5.4 R&D exception – third component: dual inventions, when used as research tools

Dual nature inventions,[294] from every field of technology, are affected by the third part of the R&D exception. The third part is non-discriminatory as it bears upon the patents of all fields of technology whose object is a dual invention.

Commercial and scientific organizations that carry out commercial projects focused on developing new products and processes may benefit from the exception. Third parties may use dual-character patented inventions as a research tool in the process of the development of new commercial innovations. Use of these inventions is subject to payment of a fee established by the patent clearing house (PCH). The exception proposed does not interfere with the exclusive rights granted to the concerned patent owner whenever its subject matter is exploited as a *consumer end-product*. Consequently, the patent holder may: exploit his invention directly; grant licenses; and prevent third parties from using, producing, marketing and importing it as a consumer end-product. Abuses by the patent owner in exploiting the patent as a consumer end-product may be countered or lessened through the system of compulsory licenses, e.g. granting compulsory licenses to meet market needs or in cases of anti-competitive use of the patent.

Prior to clarifying the functioning of the exception, when a new invention is developed, it is essential to highlight the fact that the third component of the R&D exception occupies the space left free by the compulsory licensing regime of the TRIPS Agreement.[295] It should be recalled that according to TRIPS, the Member States of the WTO are only obliged to govern the access to patented inventions by a non-authorized third party through the compulsory licensing regime, insofar as the exploitation of the new patented invention is blocked by a previous patent; that

294 See section 5.2.4.1 above. 295 See Chapter 2, section 2.3.3.3.4.3.

is, if the new invention is patented and its composition incorporates only one patented input. Under different circumstances, the Members will be entitled to govern the access to the patented inventions embodied in the composition of the new invention – be it patented or not – by different mechanisms, for instance, by a liability rule.

Should the user of a protected dual invention manage to develop a new one, including an improved version of a previous invention, compliance with the following obligations arises:

(1) if the new invention is *not* patented and *incorporates one or more* patented inputs – regardless of the technical category to which the inventions belong – its launching will be subject to payment to patent holders of royalties to be determined neutrally by the PCH and levied on the profits from the new product;
(2) if the new invention *is patented* and *incorporates two or more* patented inputs, it may be marketed, provided its owner pays the holders of the relevant patents the royalty fees established neutrally by the PCH;
3) if the new product is patented and it *incorporates only one* patented input, the user of the invention must try to obtain a voluntary license from the patent holder. Should he fail, he may apply for a compulsory license for the blocking patent from the PCH;
(4) if the new invention was developed through the use of a dual-character invention, but does not absorb it, the patent owner will not be entitled to receive a new remuneration, besides that already paid when the input was accessed.

Summing up, the use of dual inventions for R&D ends and the commercial exploitation of new inventions ensuing from the R&D project are governed by a liability rule in cases 1, 2 and 4.[296] In other words, beneficiaries of the exception are entitled to an *automatic* license to use the inventions concerned by the exception, provided they pay the fee neutrally determined by an organization (PCH) that has no links with the patent holders. The exercise of an automatic license, as opposed to a compulsory license, is guaranteed by a liability rule which does not depend on any governmental intervention.

An example may help understand how the posited exception works: the subject matter of a given patent is a protein X that is marketed as a pharmaceutical product. That protein can also be used as a research tool, opening the way for the development of new pharmaceutical products that do not incorporate it, or for developing new products that do incorporate it. According to the terms of the exception proposed, no

[296] This proposal is largely based on the "compensatory liability rule" developed by Reichman (2000).

individual or organization is authorized to use, produce, market or import protein X in its capacity as a consumer end-product. Whenever protein X is used as a research tool, the patent owner cannot oppose its use in R&D projects, provided the user pays the fee indicated by the PCH. Should the R&D project meet success, and the user manages to develop and patent a new product that incorporates protein X, he will have to resort to the compulsory license system if he cannot obtain a voluntary license from the patent owner. If the new innovation *incorporates two or more* patented innovations, once it is patented the owner of the new innovation will be entitled to introduce it in the market, regardless of the will of the relevant patent holders, subject to payment of the royalties set by the patent clearing house. In cases when the new invention is not patented, regardless of the number of patents incorporated in its composition, the developer of the new invention will be able to exploit it, provided he pays the royalty fees determined by the patent clearing house. Lastly, if the final invention does not embody any patented invention, the user will not have to pay any other fees to the owner of the patents used, apart from those paid prior to launching the project.

The curtailment of the exclusion rights of holders of dual-character inventions, when used as research tools, goes back in some ways to the patent policy that existed in the period preceding the emergence of the biotechnology industry, since the R&D exception allows the free – but remunerated – use of pre-market inventions in order to encourage the continuous progress of industry and science.

5.5.4.1 Differential treatment and graduated rates The remuneration scheme of the PCH governing the third and fourth components of the exception is designed to allow the owners of the inventions used to recoup their investments, while simultaneously fostering a wide use of the protected inventions for productive purposes. That is why third parties wishing to use a dual invention, *qua* research tool, in commercial projects will make an advance payment established neutrally by the PCH. For the purpose of promoting competition and the commercial development of small organizations and universities, the PCH has the duty to establish different fees according to the category each user belongs to: (i) small and medium-sized companies; (ii) universities; (iii) large companies; (iv) governmental agencies.

The policy of differential fees democratizes science and technology, since it allows various actors in the innovation sector to access the inputs necessary for their activities.[297] Widening access promotes social welfare,

[297] See Walsh *et al.* 2003, 333.

since the inventions that a given group may not be interested in developing may come to be developed by another group. Charging different fees to small business, universities and governmental institutions also benefits patent owners since it discourages the non-authorized reproduction of research tools in laboratories.[298]

If a user succeeds in developing a new product whose composition embodies patented inventions belonging to third parties, the PCH shall determine the royalty fees due in a neutral and graduated manner. The fees will vary according to the type of product developed, i.e. consumer end-product, bulk products, research tools and technical updates of previous inventions, and the market where the new innovations will be exploited, i.e. industrialized countries, developing countries or least developed countries.

The remuneration system suggested is inspired by the remuneration scheme applied by the University of Stanford to govern the licensing of Cohen and Boyer's recombinant DNA technique without which there would probably be no biotechnology industry. The licensing policy adopted aimed to combine the need to derive economic profits, useful to fund its research activities, with the needs of small, medium and large corporations and research centers to use the new technique for commercial and scientific purposes. In order to harmonize both purposes, Stanford offered a non-onerous license to non-profit organizations devoted to scientific research and, acknowledging the importance of the technique of recombinant DNA for the progress of biotechnology and the development of countless new products and biotechnological processes, it decided to grant only non-exclusive licenses.[299]

In a joint decision with the representatives of various industrial sectors, the university established non-discriminatory fees that aimed to be reasonable and mindful of the reality of the productive sector. In the terms of the Stanford policy, all users of the Cohen and Boyer technique were to pay a fee prior to its use. The purpose of the fee was to allow the university to recoup its investments insofar as it was not related to the success of the projects which would apply the technique. Whenever there was a development of a new product, licensees had to pay a royalty fee that would impact the sale of the products developed through application of the technique. In order to further the use of the technique, the university sanctioned gradual fees: the sum to be paid upon access to the invention was variable, according to the size of the business. The royalty percentage on the profits of the products developed with the technique also varied according to the category where the product belonged.[300]

[298] *Ibid.*, 302. [299] See Feldman *et al.* 2007, 1799. [300] *Ibid.*, 1800–1803.

Due to the success of the licensing policy applied, the technique was widely used; the resources obtained led to the creation of a fund that was used to finance litigation against breaches of patents owned by Stanford University.[301] That fund contributed to further the university's patent rights. As third parties realized that the university had the funds necessary to go to court, they were more inclined to sign licensing agreements.

5.5.5 R&D exception – fourth component: unique research tools The fourth part of the R&D exception affects patents on unique research tools, i.e. inventions proceeding from all fields of technology, which *only* serve as research tools and have no available substitutes in the market, such as the recombinant DNA technique of Boyer and Cohen and the polymerase chain reaction (PCR). The exception concerns all patents whose subject matter is a research tool, regardless of the field of technology it is connected to. Commercial and scientific organizations and universities that carry out R&D projects for commercial purposes may benefit from the exception.

Exclusive rights bestowed on patent holders are fully preserved by the fourth limb of the R&D exception, albeit with some constraints. In order to guarantee the ongoing development of new technologies and avert anti-competitive effects associated with the refusal to license unique research tools, owners of this category of research tools shall be obliged to introduce them into the market under non-discriminatory conditions to anyone wishing to use them in commercial projects. In other words, patent holders will be obliged to grant non-exclusive licenses on unique research tools and will be unable to determine the licensing conditions individually according to the economic power of the interested parties and the objectives pursued by the projects where the tools are to be applied. Should patent owners choose to exploit them through their licensees, the above mentioned obligation will be part and parcel of the licenses and will bind the licensees.

The patent holder will only be entitled to charge a fee prior to the use of the research tool. Although the patent owner is free to determine the amount to be paid in accordance with his own interests, he will be obliged to determine different fees depending on the category of the prospective user: (i) small and medium-sized business; (ii) universities; (iii) governmental institutions; and (iv) large business.

If the R&D project results in a new invention, which can even be an enhanced version of a previous innovation, the person responsible must observe the following obligations:

[301] *Ibid.*, 1799.

(1) if he decides to patent the new invention, and it *incorporates at least two* patented inputs – regardless of their technical category – the new product can be introduced in the market, whatever the wishes of the patent owner, but the produce of its marketing will be subject to a royalty fee, determined by the PCH. The fee will bear upon the profits ensuing from marketing the new invention and will be payable until expiry of the patents used;
(2) if he decides *not* to patent the new invention, and it *incorporates one or more* patented innovations, the developer may exploit it commercially provided he agrees to pay a royalty fee neutrally established by the PCH. The fee will bear upon the profits ensuing from marketing the invention and will be payable during the period of patent protection corresponding to the inventions employed;
(3) if he chooses to patent the new invention and it *incorporates only one* patented innovation, its marketing will rest on a voluntary license granted by the owner of the relevant patent or, lacking that, on a compulsory license;
(4) finally, if the composition of the new invention does not include any patented input, the owner of the research tool applied in the course of its development will only be entitled to the fee paid prior to the access to the research tool.[302]

For the sake of avoiding prolonged, costly and unproductive juridical discussions, the patent clearing house will draw up a list of unique research tools through a committee formed by representatives of the scientific and industrial communities. The list will be revisited every six months; industry and research institutions will be able to suggest inventions to be included in the list.

Briefly, access to and use of a unique research tool is subject to the authorization of the patent owner. He will keep the right to exclude third parties from using, producing, marketing and importing the invention, as he will be the only one entitled to establish the fees to be paid – though he will have to deal differently with the various categories of users. Neither the State nor any institution will be entitled to determine the fee to be required for each category of users. If the prospective user disagrees with the fee established, he shall have no access to the invention. In cases when third parties manage to develop a new invention in cases (1) and (2) mentioned above, its marketing will be conditioned to the payment of a royalty fee previously established from a neutral standpoint by the PCH. The fee will bear upon the profits ensuing from marketing the new

[302] In all cases, the fees to be paid will be determined by the management organization in a graduated way, in accordance with the terms laid down in section 5.5.4.1.

invention. In case (3), the exploitation of the invention will turn upon the procurement of a voluntary license or, lacking that, a compulsory one. In case (4), the user can freely exploit his invention.

5.6 Assessment of the lawfulness of the R&D exception

5.6.1 First step: assessment of the limited character of the exception

The purpose of the R&D exception is to: (i) make sure that the scope of patents will be proportionate to their contribution to the state of the art; (ii) meet the neglected needs of peoples in developing countries, to the greatest possible extent; (iii) speed up the process of follow-on innovation, in all fields of technology, even through the direct use of patented inventions; (iv) promote scientific and technological freedom to the greatest degree; (v) stimulate the development of industrial activities in the field of innovation and strengthen competition, both to the greatest degree; and (vi) safeguard educational and scientific activities from any interference by patent owners.

The proposed exception promotes those aims through: (i) the establishment of a patent clearing house; (ii) preventing anti-commons tragedies and neutralizing the obstacles set up by royalty stacking, when the inventions developed embody multiple proprietary inputs; (iii) speeding up access to unique inventions; (iv) offering R&D institutions wide freedom to market the fruits of their research, even if they include inventions of others; (v) forbidding reach-through patent claims and contract clauses; (vi) maximizing the use of patented inventions for educational, scientific and commercial purposes; and (vii) reducing the bureaucracy associated with grants of compulsory licenses.

In short, the R&D exception complies with its objectives through guaranteeing the right of facilitated access to and use of patented inventions for educational, scientific and technological ends. The right of access to patented inventions permits the training of future scientists and teachers, as well as the generation of new scientific knowledge and new technologies – e.g. therapies, cultivars, chemical supplies, machinery and processes – able to meet the needs of all sectors of humanity, including the most neglected. The ongoing growth and enrichment of the technical stock of humanity drives the progress of science and technology, strengthening its capacity to meet challenges in different fields. The development and introduction of new technologies in the market remedies human needs in the fields of medicine, nutrition and the environment as well as the demands of industry. On the other hand, the rapid development of new products and technology strengthens competition and makes them more accessible even for marginalized sectors of society.

The objectives pursued by the R&D exception are legitimate and the means used to achieve them – guaranteed facilitated access to and use of patented inventions – are appropriate. In support of the assessment made here one can point to one of the recommendations included in the Development Agenda of the World Intellectual Property Organization (WIPO), approved in its 2007 General Assembly, which focuses on studying the appropriate means to simplify access to information and technology for developing and least developed countries in ways that "foster creativity and innovation."[303] Along the same lines, the international community has emphasized on various occasions the crucial role of free access to knowledge in the development process in science and technology.[304]

At the same time, the R&D exception is compatible with the limits established by the minimum standards of the TRIPS Agreement insofar as: it is designed to affect patents owned both by locals and by foreigners (arts. 3 and 4); it applies to patents that cover inventions from all fields of technology and does not prevent the protection of any of the categories of inventions that, pursuant to art. 27 of TRIPS, should be eligible to receive protection; it strictly respects the area occupied by the TRIPS compulsory licensing regime; and it does not shorten the minimum term of protection that WTO Members must guarantee to patents (art. 33). Accordingly, the R&D exception shall be deemed "limited."

5.6.2 *Second step: assessment of the reasonableness of the interference caused by the exception*

The first component of the R&D exception allows the performance of activities focused on generating knowledge on the patented matters, but not their actual use for the purposes for which they were designed. The exemption of these forms of exploitation of the patented inventions is more "essential to the achievement of the goals of patent policy"[305] – i.e. promotion of innovation and advancement of science and technology,

[303] OMPI 2007, para. 19.

[304] See, e.g., art. 27(1), UDHR; art. 15(3) ICESCR; UNGA, Resolution 62/201, paras. 1(b), 2 and 8; UNGA, Resolution A/RES/60/209, para. 22; UNGA, Resolution A/RES/35/56, paras. 117, 118 and 121; UNGA, Resolution 62/194, para. 4; UNGA, Resolution A/RES/44/14; Resolution 62/98, para. 7, (k) and (o); WIPO 2007, recommendation nos. 23, 25, 28 and 45.

[305] WTO, WT/DS114/R (*Canada – Pharmaceutical Patents*), Panel Report, para. 7.58.

expanding the stock of scientific and technical knowledge and wide dissemination of the new knowledge generated – than their exclusive control by patent holders.

The second component of the R&D exception authorizes third parties to apply patented inventions for the purposes for which they were conceived for the sole purpose of carrying out non-profit research or developing new products and processes for humanitarian purposes, geared to meet the pressing needs of marginalized people in developing countries. On the one hand, the forms of exploitation of patents exempted by the second part of the exception do not interfere with the ability of patent holders to recoup their expenditures on R&D activities, since, as a rule, the beneficiary institutions do not have sufficient economic resources to license them, as their projects were not designed to generate any profits. On the other hand, they promote scientific and technological advancements in areas usually neglected by the business sector and widen the dissemination of knowledge. Thus, the exemption of these forms of exploitation of patented inventions appears to be more "essential to the achievement of the goals of patent policy" than their exclusive control by patent holders; at the same time, it does not prejudice any legitimate economic interest of the patent holders concerned. Therefore, the first and second components of the R&D exception pass the scrutiny of the second step of the test, since they affect abnormal forms of exploitation of patents and, accordingly, lie outside the sphere of control granted to patent holders by art. 28(1) TRIPS.

The third and fourth components of the exception authorize, respectively, the employment of dual inventions as research tools, and the use of unique research tools in the process of developing new technologies with commercial purposes. The forms of exploitation covered thereby fall within the control of patent holders. The open question is whether these two components of the R&D exception, taken together, conflict unreasonably with a normal exploitation of the patents affected thereby.

The assessment of the reasonability of the interference fostered by the third and fourth components of the R&D exception in the normal exploitation of patents involves researching alternative measures, able to realize the same set of objectives pursued by the proposed components of the exception – to speed up the process of follow-on innovation, in all fields of technology, to promote scientific and technological freedom to the greatest degree, to stimulate the development of industrial activities in the field of innovation and strengthen competition, both to the greatest degree – albeit involving a smaller impact on patent rights.

Based on a review of the literature, three categories of potential alternative measures to the third and fourth parts of the R&D exception can be identified. The first category comprises proposals resting on the compulsory licensing mechanism governed by art. 31 TRIPS. The second category comprises proposals which draw on the "fair use" test enshrined in the US Copyright Act. The last category comprises *sui generis* proposals, which do not fall within the other two categories. Before we can prove that any of these measures, individually or in association, qualifies as an alternative to the third and fourth components of the R&D exception, we must assess their capacity to comply with the objectives fostered by these components of the exception whilst causing less prejudice to patent rights.

5.6.2.1 Proposals of exceptions governed by the TRIPS compulsory licensing system In recent years, several proposals of research use exceptions, which rest on the mechanism of compulsory licensing in art. 31 TRIPS, have been presented.[306] The scope of these proposals vary: they may aim to facilitate access to research tools in general, or to biotechnology research tools, or to any category of invention. Regardless of their differences, they are all conceived to harmonize the economic interests of patent holders in maximizing their revenues with those of society in having ready access to patented inputs. Irrespective of the differences between the proposals, any exception that has as its gravitational axis the system of compulsory licensing of TRIPS will create obstacles to the advancement of science, technology, the economy and free competition.

Obtaining a compulsory license depends on setting an administrative or judicial process in motion, whose core governing rules are enshrined in art. 31 TRIPS. That is costly and slow, and it may not come to the expected favorable end.[307] As a rule, government agencies in charge of issuing compulsory licenses can take an indefinite period of time to decide on the requests submitted, and may even decide not to grant them. Even if the petitioner submits solid evidence in favor of the license grant, he may not receive it since the relevant authorities usually enjoy wide discretionary power to assess the circumstances of the case. This is also compounded by the fact that trivial political discourse – often echoed by patent holders and their defenders – describing compulsory licenses as a case of expropriation of private property and a direct attack on incentives for innovation, can prove very enticing.[308] Even if the relevant

306 See, e.g., Derzko 2003; Freeburg 2005; Gitter 2001; Hoffman 2003; Schmieder 2004; Strandburg 2004.

307 See Kratiger 2007, 1324.

308 In 2007, the government of Brazil issued a compulsory license that allowed government-owned laboratories to produce an antiretroviral drug called Efavirenz.

agency is persuaded of the need to grant the license claimed, it will find it very difficult, if it is not knowledgeable about current licensing market practices, to determine an appropriate fee, which will mean a greater delay in granting the license.[309] These difficulties increase the delay in the granting of compulsory licenses and the chances that the remuneration will be set at an excessive level, which will prevent many institutions from accessing the licensed inventions.

Granting a compulsory license does not mean the end of obstacles encountered by prospective users, since the TRIPS Agreement rules that WTO Members should offer the holders of licensed patents the right to challenge their validity and the fee that has been set. If a court has the competence to rule on any challenges, many years may elapse until the final, irrevocable decision to grant the compulsory license is reached. The total amount of time spent on the process of obtaining a compulsory license is incompatible with the demands of the innovation sector. Once the decision is finally confirmed, it may be far too late. Moreover, an exception whose exercise depends on the establishment of bureaucratic and expensive proceedings has a discriminatory character, because only wealthy institutions have the means to make use of it.

Although some argue that a compulsory licensing scheme is an incentive for patent owners to grant voluntary licenses in reasonable terms,[310] this is not necessarily true. The legal orders of a large majority of WTO Members, including highly industrialized countries, include provisions to grant compulsory licenses, but that does not prevent agents of the innovation sector from facing problems when trying to access patented inputs. On this subject, the case of CellPro is an illuminating example. In the United States, the Bayh–Dole Act authorizes US government agencies to grant, in special circumstances, compulsory licenses on patents connected to inventions developed with government funds. On the basis of this legislation, CellPro applied for a compulsory license at the US National Institutes of Health (NIH) to exploit four patents owned by Johns Hopkins University, whose subject matter had been developed with public resources. Unfortunately, the petition was denied and CellPro was forced to leave the market.[311]

In response, Brazil became the target of an international campaign set on presenting the country as ignoring international rules of intellectual property (WIPO, SCP/14/7, para. 15). This kind of campaign discourages developing and least developed countries from employing that mechanism in order to avoid trade retaliations. On this point, it is worth mentioning that in 2007 Brazil was included in the Watch List of the United States Trade Representative on account of its interest in granting compulsory licenses (USTR 2007, 2).

[309] See Hagelin 2006, 544. [310] See Schmieder 2004, 230.
[311] See Freeburg 2005, 409.

To sum up, exceptions to patent rights, whose central mechanism is that of compulsory licensing, involve bureaucratic, expensive and unsafe regimes for governing access to socially valuable inventions, mainly because there is no certainty that the compulsory license will be granted. The decision to grant a compulsory license is always preceded by an analysis of the circumstances of the case, and the time for the competent body to reach a conclusion regarding the fulfillment of the legal conditions can be protracted. An exception with such characteristics would be unable to comply to a sufficient extent with the objectives in the third and fourth components of the R&D exception, since they are unsuitable to facilitate the development and commercialization, without delay, of inventions whose development depends on the application of research tools, or whose composition incorporates a patented input. In view of the difficulties associated with securing a compulsory license, the R&D exception resorts to this tool only in circumstances where there is no available alternative to overcome the hurdles set by patents. Scientific, technological and social progress cannot be held hostage to luck. Consequently, exceptions based on compulsory licensing schemes do not qualify as alternatives to the third and fourth components of the R&D exception.

5.6.2.2 Proposals based on the "fair use" defense The "fair use" test, included in the US Copyright Act (1976 Copyright Act Revisions, 17 U.S.C. § 107) controls the legitimacy of non-authorized uses of copyrighted works. The US legal framework does not adopt an exhaustive list of the various uses of copyrighted works that may be employed by non-authorized third parties. Excepted uses are determined case by case by the courts, within the context of actual lawsuits filed by the holder of copyright whose rights have been infringed.

In the process of establishing the legitimacy of a contested use, the judge will consider four factors. Under *the first factor* the court identifies the goal pursued by the unauthorized user of the copyrighted work. This factor weighs in favor of the user if the use aims at realizing a public interest, instead of a commercial interest. Under *the second factor* of the fair use test, the court looks at the nature of the copyrighted work. The more creative the work or the more resource-intensive was the process of creation of the copyrighted work, the stronger the protection granted by the court to the copyright will be. Accordingly, the court will be less prone to consider this factor in favor of a party whose use interferes substantially with the means of recouping the investments incurred by the copyright holder. Under the *third factor* the court looks at the nature and extent of the unauthorized use. So the more transformative the utilization of the copyrighted work, the greater are the chances that the third factor will weigh in favor of the user. Under the *fourth factor* the court examines the circumstances of the actual use and assesses the social benefits promoted by the non-authorized use and the individual detriments endured by the owner of the affected copyright. If the non-authorized use creates benefits that surpass individual detriments, there is a greater chance that the court will decide that this factor weighs in favor of the user.

Every single factor of the fair use test makes up an indivisible test, whose parts are not detachable from each other. This means that not all four factors have to weigh in favor of the use in order to characterize it as fair. If *most* of the factors favor the legitimacy of the use under scrutiny, the court will regard it as fair and legitimate. Thus the fair use test may, in some cases, be not conclusive, where two of the factors weigh in favor of the user and the other two weigh in favor of the copyright holder.

O'Rourke proposed a patent exception inspired by the fair use test in the US Copyright Act.[312] The fair use test proposed by O'Rourke includes five factors, none of them being determining. The final balance between all factors will establish whether a particular non-authorized use of a patented invention is legitimate or otherwise.[313]

Under the first factor of the test the court examines whether the non-authorized use of the invention is more or less transformative. The greater the progress in science and technology spurred by the use, the higher the chances that the factor will contribute to the use being acknowledged as legitimate.[314] Under the second factor of the assessment, the court inquires whether the use pursues commercial, non-commercial or indirectly commercial purposes. If the test shows the use to be commercial, this will go against the use being acknowledged as legitimate.[315] Under the third factor, the court goes into the reasons that led the user to refrain from obtaining a voluntary license from the owner of the patent infringed, e.g. high transaction costs, refusal to license the patent or overstated licensing conditions.[316] The setting of abusive licensing conditions or the refusal to license weigh in favor of the legality of the challenged use. The fourth step of the evaluation includes a subtest of proportionality in a strict sense: the total social benefits promoted by the non-authorized use are assessed and compared to the detriment caused, including the loss of incentives to foster innovation.[317] If such benefit outweighs prejudice, that factor will favor acknowledgment of the legitimacy of the use

312 Similarly, De Larena (2005) also proposed a patent exception based on the fair use test, which is complemented by a compulsory licensing mechanism.

313 O'Rourke 2000, 1191. 314 *Ibid.*, 1206. 315 *Ibid.*, 1206.

316 *Ibid.*, 1206–1207. 317 *Ibid.*, 1207–1208.

under scrutiny. Under the final step of the assessment, the court goes into the nature of the subject matter of the patent infringed: patents covering more innovative inventions are granted greater protection. Consequently, if the subject matter of the patent that was infringed represents a technological breakthrough, the non-authorized use will have less chance of being considered legitimate.[318]

In contrast to the fair use test in the copyright regime, O'Rourke's proposal grants the courts discretion to impose on the user the duty to pay a fee to the owner of the affected patent, in cases where monetary compensation strikes a balance between the interests of the patent owner and those of the user.[319] In order to encourage patent owners to establish reasonable licensing conditions, the court would be obliged to set the royalty fees according to standards that are below those in use in the market.[320]

The most interesting aspect of the proposals of patent exceptions inspired by the fair use test is that they do not forbid, a priori, the use of patented innovations in commercial projects or projects of follow-on innovation. Having said that, these proposals have several flaws. The main one is that there is not much clarity on the activities favored by the exception. Consequently, it is impossible for non-authorized third parties to know exactly which actions are legitimate.[321] It is for this reason that, in the area of copyright, the fair use exception is known by the ironic designation "the right to consult a lawyer."[322] Until there is clear jurisprudence on the application of the fair use test of patent law – and this may take decades – users of patented inputs will be hesitant about where the boundaries and limitations to patent rights lie. And so long as there are doubts, actors from the innovation sector will probably refrain from launching projects that may involve patents belonging to others.

Increasingly, in jurisdictions whose courts are overloaded with work, the time needed to obtain a favorable judgment to carry out scientific, humanitarian and commercial activities, in the absence of permission by patent owners, can become excessively drawn out. In jurisdictions with a conservative judiciary, the test will very possibly be interpreted in ways that grant disproportionate protection to the interests of patent owners. Lastly, and due to its flexibility, the terms of the fair use test may be interpreted in ways that impinge on international duties undertaken by

[318] *Ibid.*, 1208. [319] *Ibid.*, 1210–1211. [320] *Ibid.*, 1235.
[321] See Advisory Council of Intellectual Property 2005, 48–55.
[322] Consumers International 2010, 5. Along the same lines, Okediji (2000, 118) remarks that "[t]he historical development and application of the fair use doctrine demonstrates that the only certainty involved in construing fair use is uncertainty in how a court will ultimately rule."

the State, making it liable to economic countermeasures.[323] Be that as it may, in the long run it is freedom in science and technology and the welfare of society that are harmed.

In view of the bureaucracy and legal insecurity associated with judicial proceedings aimed at determining the legitimacy of a non-authorized use of a patented invention, it is actually possible to state with considerable certainty that the following objectives, whose realization depends on the guarantee of facilitated access to patented inputs in order to fuel the process of innovation, would probably be unmet by a patent exception inspired by the fair use test: speeding up the process of follow-on innovation in every field of technology, even on the basis of the direct use of patented inputs; promoting the highest degree of scientific and technological freedom; fostering the highest degree of development of industrial activities in the innovation sector and strengthening competition as much as possible. On these grounds, patent exceptions based on the fair use model cannot be seen as an alternative to the third and fourth components of the R&D exception.

5.6.2.3 Proposals of sui generis *patent exceptions* The *sui generis* category comprises three proposals of patent exceptions: those put forward by Janice Mueller, Rochelle Dreyfuss and Rebecca Eisenberg. Below, we summarize these proposals and investigate whether any of them represent a real alternative to the third and fourth components of the R&D exception, through an ability to foster the realization, to the same degree, of the objectives contained in that exception. A caveat is in order here: certainly, there are other interesting proposals for research use exceptions that could be included in the *sui generis* category, but due to space constraints the focus here is on three proposals.

5.6.2.3.1 Janice Mueller's proposal Mueller recommends adopting an exception that regulates the use of research tools whose access is subject to a previous negotiation with patent owners; in other words, research

[323] See Advisory Council of Intellectual Property 2005, 55. In 2005, the Australian government published a paper with several proposals of research exceptions that might be adopted at the domestic level. One of them is based on the fair use test, but it specifically lists some activities that would be protected by the exception (scientific activities connected to generation of new knowledge on the subject matter of patents). Although this approach provides users with higher legal security, the problems caused by an exception structured on the basis of a fair use test do not vanish because, as in unforeseen cases, its exercise will depend on case by case intervention by the judiciary (*ibid.*, 57).

tools whose licensing conditions are established on an individual basis.[324] Given that no rational user would choose a research tool whose access rests on a prior negotiation with the rights holder when the market offers substitutes of the relevant tool, Mueller's proposal probably focuses on unique research tools.

A third party can access any research tool that complies with the condition mentioned above, provided he informs the holder of the relevant tool, in writing, of his intention to apply it in a commercial project as well as about the inventions developed through its application.[325] The owner of the research tool used will only be entitled to receive remuneration when the user develops and markets the new product.

In order to guarantee sufficient profits to cover the expenses incurred in developing the research tool, the patent holder will be entitled to a share in the profits derived from marketing the products created through its application.[326] Consequently, when the user pursues purely scientific or humanitarian goals or if the commercial project does not attain its aim, the owner of the research tool shall not be entitled to any payment. The right to remuneration will end with the expiry of the patent that protects the research tool. The amount to be paid should be established by a neutral agency, which is not linked to the holders of the patents affected by the exception.[327]

The proposal under scrutiny, though balanced insofar as it harmonizes the interests of users with those of innovators to recoup their investment, has a serious flaw. It is based on canceling *all* the exclusion rights granted by patents and replacing them with a right to receive some remuneration. The main feature of patents is to guarantee property rights to their holders, that is, the right to prevent non-authorized third parties from producing, using, marketing and importing the subject matter of patents, in given contexts. By canceling all exclusion rights granted by the relevant patents, the exception under review alters their very nature since they come to be disciplined by a liability rule whose main feature is to guarantee patent owners the right to receive remuneration. Mueller's proposal is unacceptable because it violates art. 27(1) of the TRIPS Agreement: adopting it would mean banning the possibility of patenting

[324] See Mueller 2001, 14, 54. Donna Gitter (2001, 1679–1683) posits an exception with two elements; one of which is substantially similar to Mueller's proposal. The exception put forward by Gitter, as Mueller's, is disciplined by a liability rule (i.e. it guarantees the patent owner the right to receive remuneration, instead of a right of exclusion). The only difference between them is the scope. Gitter's only covers patents that protect human DNA sequences. In view of the similarity, Gitter's proposal exhibits the same problems as Mueller's, compounded by the fact that it would cover a smaller number of inventions.

[325] Mueller 2001, 58–59. [326] *Ibid.*, 61. [327] *Ibid.*, 66–65.

research tools that are not offered in the market in neutral terms by their owners or licensees. In view of the above, there is no reason to go on to assess whether Mueller's proposal complies with the goals promoted by the R&D exception.

5.6.2.3.2 Rochelle Dreyfuss's proposal Dreyfuss proposes that universities and other non-profit organizations should be free to use patented inventions to carry out projects of research in science and technology when the owners of the relevant innovations refuse to license them in *reasonable* commercial terms. In such circumstances, those who benefit from the exception should be obliged to sign a waiver whereby they relinquish any right to claim patents on the outputs of their research and accept the duty to publish all the results of research carried out with the patented invention.[328] Should the beneficiaries of the exception develop an invention with commercial appeal, they will be able to cancel the waiver whereby they relinquished their rights and proceed to claim patents, subject to payment of royalties to the owners of the relevant patents. They must also commit themselves to grant non-exclusive licenses.[329] In other words, beneficiaries of the exception will enjoy something similar to a "retroactive compulsory license."[330]

The "retroactive compulsory license" is not identical to a compulsory license in the sense used in the TRIPS Agreement. It is automatically granted to beneficiaries of the exception from the moment they express their wish to patent the results of their research. Consequently, granting it does not require compliance with the strict conditions established in art. 31 of TRIPS. When the exception is exercised by an institution willing to patent the results of its research, the exception is disciplined by a liability rule since it guarantees patent users an automatic license upon payment of a fee to the owners of the patents involved.

The exception described above implies indisputable advantages for the scientific sector, as it authorizes the use of any category of inventions; it simplifies the use of patented research tools; it expands the scientific public domain, either through widening the group of inputs that might be used in processes of scientific research or because the results of research done under the safeguard of the exception will be introduced into the public domain.[331]

Having said that, Dreyfuss's proposal also exhibits some shortcomings. The first one is the need to determine who is to judge the reasonableness of the terms of the license offered by the patent owner to a university.

[328] Dreyfuss 2004, 471. [329] *Ibid.*, 471–472. [330] *Ibid.*, 472.
[331] *Ibid.*, 471–472.

There being no absolute benchmarks to define the notion of "reasonable terms," the requirement in the proposed exception paves the way for frequent interventions by the courts and this is undesirable, for the reasons already mentioned.[332] As exercising the exception is subject to a judicial stamp, it ends up resembling a non-onerous compulsory licensing scheme, administered by the courts.

The proposal appears to overlook that, in terms of art. 31(l) of the TRIPS Agreement, if the exploitation of a patent that protects the new invention (A) infringes patent (B), the exploitation of A can only occur after the owner of B has granted a voluntary license or, failing that, when the owner of A has obtained a compulsory license. As compliance with this scheme is mandatory for all WTO Members, it is impossible to adopt an exception which aims to solve the problem of blocking patents, within the framework of a liability rule.[333]

The proposal grants a discriminatory treatment to the business sector: when universities and non-profit institutions find a product with a market potential, they keep the prerogative to patent it for profit. If benefitted institutions can pursue commercial purposes, it would be right to offer an exception to the business sector in order to further the use of protected inventions. Research and university institutions would otherwise have an unfair advantage over other actors in the commercial sector.

Lastly, the proposal does not specify who would be responsible for establishing the fee due to owners of the relevant patent whenever the benefitted institutions choose to patent the results of their research projects. If royalty fees are not standardized, the process of fixing them will be sluggish and the fees might prove excessively high, especially if opportunities are given to patent owners to influence the price-fixing process.

Dreyfuss's proposal does not promote, to the same degree, the goals pursued by the third and fourth components of the R&D exception and should therefore not be considered a viable alternative. With respect to the goals of *speeding up the process of follow-on innovation, in every field of technology*, and *promoting the highest degree of scientific and technological freedom*, her proposal does not benefit the private sector. In addition to that, it does not deal with the challenge of expediting the granting of compulsory licenses for blocking patents. Finally, the proposal does not specify what institution would be in charge of establishing the fees due from the benefitted institutions to the owners of the relevant patents. It may happen that, according to the structure of the institution chosen, the process of fixing the royalty fees to be paid may prove sluggish and

332 See section 5.6.2.2 above.

333 See Chapter 2, section 2.3.3.3.4.3.

vulnerable to the influence of patent holders. As a result, marketing of the new innovations is stopped until their developers were reassured of their commercial viability. After having invested, often large sums of money, to develop an invention, its owner is hostage to the judgment of the agent in charge of determining the fee to be paid. If the fee is too high, all expenses will be lost and, undoubtedly, other institutions will not be encouraged to embark on projects able to result in new technologies with a commercial potential.

In respect of the goals of *fostering the development of industrial activities in the innovation sector*, and *strengthening competition, both to the greatest possible degree*, Dreyfuss's proposal realizes these objectives only marginally since fostering projects with commercial aims is not its goal. It merely guarantees freedom to market the patented innovations in cases when non-profit institutions manage to develop, unintentionally, an innovation with market potential.

5.6.2.3.3 Rebecca Eisenberg's proposal Eisenberg recommended the adoption of a research use exception that includes three components.[334] In the first place, the exception authorizes the use of the patented inventions to confirm if the technical specifications of the patent have been clearly and fully disclosed and to prove that the invention works as stated in the patent.[335] Secondly, the exception bans the use of research tools for their original purposes.[336] Lacking a license, third parties would have to refrain from using the relevant tool. Lastly, the exception permits follow-on innovation activities, including the development of improved versions of previous inventions and new substitutes. If the research project develops a new invention and its commercial exploitation proves impossible without infringing a previous patent, its commercial exploitation will be made conditional on a voluntary license granted by the owner of the relevant patent.[337] On this issue, the exception merely postpones the moment when patents will cause trouble: they will not obstruct the pursuit of projects that depend on the use of a patented input, but they will certainly affect the marketing process of their fruits. In the case of businesses, this possibility may suffice to discourage investment in R&D.

If a third party develops an enhanced version of a prior technology or a substitute – that is, an innovation corresponding to *the same technical field* as the previous invention – and it does *not* infringe the patent of the prior invention, the owner of the new invention will be obliged to

[334] Caruso (2003) put forward a research exception substantially similar to Eisenberg's. The comments we make here also apply to Caruso's proposal.
[335] Eisenberg 1989, 1078. [336] *Ibid.* [337] *Ibid.*, 1076.

pay a fee to the owner of the invention employed as reference in his technological research process. In other words, the new invention can be marketed freely, provided the corresponding fee has been paid. The remuneration to be paid will be set by a court that should make sure that the patent holder who provided the inventive idea employed receives an appropriate fee.

Eisenberg's aim is to guarantee an equitable remuneration to patent holders whose subject matter served as intellectual aid to the development of substitutes or better technologies since, once the latter have been introduced in the market, the previous inventions will probably lose their market share. From the author's perspective, the problem does not lie in losing competitors in the market; the trouble lies in not receiving adequate reward for the contribution to the state of the art. If innovators do not receive a fair reward for their contribution, they will refrain from engaging in R&D activities.[338]

The major difficulty associated with Eisenberg's proposal is proving that a better or an alternative invention to that of a competitor, whose exploitation does *not* infringe the competitor's patent, was developed upon the basis of the technical contribution provided by a patent that was not infringed. The difficulty is even greater if the new invention competes against a wide array of similar technologies. In that case, the invention was probably developed against the parameters of all the inventions with which it competes. If that is so, who is to receive the fee guaranteed by the exception? Automatically granting to the owner of an invention (X) the right to receive remuneration from the owners of any alternative or superior version of X is tantamount to granting him the right to indirectly control the marketing of products that compete with X. There is no doubt that such privilege may potentially restrict competition. Briefly, Eisenberg's proposal guarantees the patent owner a reach-through claim that he can wield against developers of inventions that are alternative or superior to the subject matter of his patent.

Bearing in mind the scope of the third and fourth components of the R&D exception, the third component comprised in Eisenberg's proposal is the only one that is of interest. However, this component does not qualify as a viable alternative to those components for the following reasons. With respect to the goal of speeding up the process of follow-on innovation, in every field of technology, Eisenberg's proposal does not rule out the emergence of problems such as the tragedy of the anti-commons and royalty stacking. In addition, it creates problems for market inventions that, while not infringing any patent, were inspired by

338 *Ibid.*, 1075.

protected innovations. With respect to the goals of promoting scientific and technological freedom, fostering the development of industrial activities in the innovation sector and strengthening competition, all of them to the greatest possible degree, the proposal furthers the use of patented inventions that are not research tools in R&D projects, but it is not concerned with the introduction of the results of those projects in the market.

5.6.2.4 Conclusions on the proposals examined None of the proposals assessed, even if assessed jointly, can promote the objectives contained in the third and fourth components of the R&D exception; at least, not to the same degree. For these proposals to qualify, in conjunction, as an alternative measure to the third and fourth components of the R&D exception, each one of them should be able to promote, to the same degree, one or more of the objectives in those components. That would mean that, taken together, they would attain all the objectives. This is not the case, essentially because the proposals examined tend to facilitate the production of new knowledge on the subject matter of patents, but few of them are concerned about furthering the use of research tools for their original purposes and lessening the bureaucracy that hinders the development and market distribution of new products and technologies.

In terms of legal security and dynamism, none of the proposals can produce the advantages provided by the components of the R&D exception, as they are based on a patent clearing house, whose structure responds to the need to determine responsibly and without delay the remuneration to be made to the owners of the relevant patents. They are also based on a liability rule that guarantees an automatic license to the beneficiaries of the exception, regardless of the will of the owners of the relevant patents and of any case-by-case intervention from the State. The dynamic way in which the third and fourth components of the R&D exception work together spells advantages for the progress of science, technology and society. None of the exceptions examined, by themselves or linked to others, can provide the same advantages. Guaranteeing innovators swift and non-discriminatory access to all the research tools and inputs required by their projects will contribute to a faster development of new technologies in every field. Less bureaucratization in the R&D process means a saving of resources, both natural and human.

Given that we have not been able to identify any measure able to attain, to the same degree, all the goals promoted by the third and fourth components of the R&D exception, there is no need to assess whether the proposals examined have less impact on patent rights. We come, therefore, to the last stage of the evaluation.

5.6.3 *Third step: assessment of the reasonableness of the degree of harm caused by the R&D exception*

The main purpose of the R&D exception is to further the access to and productive use – scientific, educational, industrial and humanitarian – of patented inventions from all technology fields and to speed up the introduction into the market, without delay, of new technologies, final products for the ordinary end-consumer and research tools. Lastly, the R&D exception intends to maximize the productive use of patented inventions that will contribute to the well-being of all sectors of society.

Guaranteeing – on fair terms – rapid access to knowledge and protected technology promotes, inter alia: ideal conditions for the creation and/or expansion of business and scientific institutions, which, in their turn, mean new direct or indirect jobs; the democratization of science and technology, provided small institutions can also apply patented technology to further their institutional mission; the generation of new scientific and technological knowledge that helps humans to solve sooner and more efficiently the problems that affect its progress and welfare, including environmental challenges created by over-exploitation of natural resources, global warming, desertification and soil erosion, pollution of the atmosphere and water, intensive use of fossil fuels and rapid loss of biodiversity. Less bureaucratization in the introduction of new technology and products into the market enhances competition, which lowers prices of products and technology and this, in turn, opens access to them by less wealthy consumers and the production sectors. Promoting the development of technology and products that aim to meet the neglected needs of materially poor peoples improves their living conditions and provides the prospects of a dignified future. Summing up, the R&D exception fosters freedom of expression in science and technology, guarantees freedom in commercial initiative and furthers the creation of jobs and environmental protection, all of which are of crucial interest to any society.

On the other hand, and from the point of view of the patent holder, the patent allows him to receive profits, obtained through the right to exclude third parties from using, producing, marketing and importing the subject matter of the patent over a limited period of time. This enables him to recover the funds invested in the development and commercialization of the subject matter of the patent. In general, exceptions to patent rights deprive the patent owner – in limited terms – of the right to exclude non-authorized third parties from enjoying the protected subject matter. Consequently, in some respects, it interferes with his capacity to recoup the resources invested. The R&D exception, however, is designed to foster the optimal use of patented knowledge and technology, without interfering with the possibility of the owners of the affected patents to recover their investment. In this sense, many of the activities covered by the exception can only be carried on by non-authorized third parties after paying a fee determined by the patent clearing house according to current market practice. The use of protected inventions by non-authorized third parties is not conditional upon payment of a fee only in those cases when: (i) it aims to generate new information on the subject matter of the patent, thus, research on the way the invention operates, development of a substitute to the protected invention, confirmation of its functioning, confirmation of the validity of patent claims or investigation of new features of the invention; (ii) it is for humanitarian or purely scientific purposes; or (iii) it aims to develop a new invention, whose composition may incorporate one or more protected inputs. In the latter case, if it includes patented material, the commercial exploitation of the new invention will be conditional upon payment of remuneration to the patent holder.

As the affected patents continue to fulfill their mission, the interests of patent holders affected by the R&D exception are of minimal importance for society, if the social harms caused carry any weight, in particular because the exception favors the interests of patent holders by guaranteeing their freedom to use the inputs required by their day-to-day innovative activities. In the absence of an R&D exception, the objectives pursued by TRIPS to promote scientific and technological progress and its wide dissemination for the benefit of the well-being of society would be empty words.

The R&D exception, seen as an indivisible whole, is accordingly legitimate when judged against the WTO legal framework, since it produces social benefits that go well beyond any prejudices caused to the interests of patent owners.

5.7 The genetic diagnostic test exception and its functioning

The most appropriate means to promote the wide application of genetic and proteomic material of human origin in the development of predictive and diagnostic genetic tests (genetic tests)[339] is to exclude them from the list of patentable subject matter. This policy is possible on the basis of

[339] In this work, genetic test is understood as "any test, designed to detect disease, to predict the potential for a medical disorder, or to predict the effectiveness of therapeutics, which uses either an ordered listing of nucleotides comprising a portion of a human or human pathogen genetic code or the proteins encoded by such nucleotides" (Rivers 2002).

art. 27(3)(b) of the TRIPS Agreement that authorizes WTO members to exclude animal material (including of human origin) from patentability.

However, a pure and simple exclusion of that material from the list of patentable materials may discourage private business and university institutions from investing in research in the genetic field. In order to avoid this pitfall, and given that not every State wishes or is able – in view of the duties imposed by TRIPS-plus-type agreements – to leave out human genetic and proteomic materials from the list of patentable material, an exception for genetic diagnostic testing is proposed. It will authorize third parties in general (commercial and non-profit organizations) to research and employ genetic and proteomic materials of human origin (e.g. DNA sequences, proteins encoded thereby) as well as human genetic and proteomic data,[340] which are under patent protection, in the development of diagnostic tests. Once a diagnostic test is developed, if it incorporates any proprietary objects (genetic and/or proteomic material and/or its molecular description), the developer will be liable to pay a remuneration to the patent owners whose objects have been used. The trigger for the payment of a fee is the marketing of the test or its commercial application in the laboratory. Consequently, if the test is offered for free for the benefit of marginalized individuals by, for example, a philanthropic organization, no fee will be due, since the non-commercial use of patented inventions lies outside the sphere under the control of patent holders.[341] The remuneration payable shall be determined on a non-discriminatory basis by the PCH, which will vary depending on the degree of importance of the material/information utilized in the development of the new product. In more objective terms, the use of proteomic and genetic material and their molecular description will be governed by a liability rule.

The practical effect of the proposed exception is to ban the patenting of diagnostic tests that incorporate genetic and proteomic resources of human origin, isolated without modification from their natural environment, as well as their molecular descriptions. As a result of the freedom granted to WTO Members to define what is an invention and to determine the content of the substantive conditions of patentability – i.e. novelty, inventive step and industrial application – there is no legal obstacle

[340] Art 2 of the International Declaration of Human Genetic Data defines human genetic data as "[i]nformation about heritable characteristics of individuals obtained by analysis of nucleic acids or by other scientific analysis" and human proteomic data as "information pertaining to an individual's proteins including their expression, modification and interaction)."

[341] See section 3.3.2.

to rule out the adoption of the measure that is proposed for the following reasons.

Firstly, according to the new position advocated by the US Department of Justice,[342] the following do not constitute an invention: genomic and proteomic materials technically isolated from their natural environment, their molecular description, and the determination of the correlation between, on the one hand, a particular DNA sequence or protein, and, on the other, the presence or predisposition to a given disease. Patenting the correlation between a genetic sequence or a protein and the presence of a predisposition to an illness is tantamount to protecting a law of nature, a matter not subject to private appropriation. A summary of the position recently upheld by the US government is given in the following excerpts, taken from the amicus curiae brief filed by the US Department of Justice with the Court of Appeals for the Federal Circuit, to support the settlement in *The Association for Molecular Pathology et al.* v. *USPTO and Myriad Genetics*, which involves the challenging of patents covering genes associated with breast and ovarian cancer (BRCA 1 and BRCA 2), granted by the US Patent and Trademark Office:

> Such compositions – e.g., cDNAs, vectors, recombinant plasmids, and chimeric proteins, as well as countless industrial products, such as vaccines and genetically modified crops, created with the aid of such molecules – are in every meaningful sense the fruits of human ingenuity and thus qualify as "human-made inventions" eligible for patent protection under section 101 [35 U.S.C. § 101]. The district court correctly held, however, that genomic DNA that has merely been isolated from the human body, without further alteration or manipulation, is not patent-eligible. Unlike the genetically engineered microorganism in Chakrabarty, the unique chain of chemical base pairs that induces a human cell to express a BRCA protein is not a "human-made invention." Nor is the fact that particular natural mutations in that unique chain increase a woman's chance of contracting breast or ovarian cancer. Indeed, the relationship between a naturally occurring nucleotide sequence and the molecule it expresses in a human cell – that is, the relationship between genotype and phenotype – is simply a law of nature. The chemical structure of phenotype is simply a law of nature. The chemical structure of native human genes is a product of nature, and it is no less a product of nature when that structure is "isolated" from its natural environment than are cotton fibers that have been separated from cotton seeds or coal that has been extracted from the earth. The scope of Section 101 is purposefully wide and its threshold is not difficult to cross. See Bilski, 130 S.Ct. at 3225. New and useful methods of identifying, isolating, extracting, or using genes and genetic information may be patented (subject to the prohibition against patenting abstract ideas), as may nearly any man-made transformation or manipulation of the raw materials of the genome, such as cDNAs. Thus, the patent laws embrace gene replacement

342 See US Department of Justice 2010.

therapies, engineered biologic drugs, methods of modifying the properties of plants or generating biofuels, and similar advanced applications of biotechnology. Crossing the threshold of section 101, however, requires something more than identifying and isolating what has always existed in nature, no matter how difficult or useful that discovery may be.[343]

The fact that a particular segment of the human genome codes for the BRCA1 protein in a human cell, for example, rather than for adrenaline or insulin or nothing at all, is not within the power of science to alter. Such basic natural relationships may not be the subject of a patent.[344] (emphasis added)

Secondly, even if those materials and information are considered inventions eligible for patent protection, it must be borne in mind that developing a diagnostic test is a simple task once certain issues have been clarified, namely the meaning of the presence of a given genetic sequence and/or protein in the human organism, in terms of presence or absence of illnesses, as well as the molecular description of this material. The test involves collecting biological material from the patient, and the molecular description of the relevant gene or protein, which represents the genetic or proteomic profile of a healthy patient or a sick individual or someone who shows a disposition to the development of a given illness.[345] It is thus possible to oppose patents on genetic tests because their development does not involve inventive skills.

Under the proposed exception developers of diagnostic tests and all their users are under a duty to publish all the relevant information on links between genetic mutations and predisposition to illnesses obtained in the process of laboratory tests. That information will be accessible through a central database, public and accessible over the entire country, managed by the PCH.[346] This obligation contributes to enact the political commitment made by the international community that took shape in the International Declaration of Human Genetic Data to further the international dissemination of scientific information on human genetic and proteomic material.[347]

A possible argument against adopting an exception for diagnostic tests is the lack of economic incentives for institutions to invest funds in the development of genetic tests. Recent empirical data, however, suggest that patents are not a condition *sine qua non* for the development of new genetic tests. Members of the scientific community are spurred

343 *Ibid.*, 9–10. 344 *Ibid.*, 18–19.

345 See Advisory Council on Intellectual Property 2005, 53.

346 Based on the OECD's recommendation (2006, para. 25).

347 See art. 18(b) and (c) and art. 19, International Declaration of Human Genetic Data; art. 12(a) and (b) and art. 18, Universal Declaration on the Human Genome and Human Rights.

by values such as prestige and commitment to the public interest and not exclusively by the desire to receive royalties. The proof is that non-patented diagnostic tests are routinely introduced into the US market.[348]

5.8 Assessment of the lawfulness of the genetic diagnostic test exception in the light of art. 30 TRIPS

5.8.1 First step: assessment of the limited character of the exception

The exception under scrutiny removes the barriers that prevent the freer development and distribution of new diagnostic tests. It is devised in order to: encourage the production of scientific and technological knowledge in the area of genetics; foster the rapid development and introduction of new tests on the market, including tests developed by public research institutions for free distribution; strengthen free competition in the industry of genetic testing and enhance the quality of the tests offered; promote the technical training of an unlimited number of professionals in the fields of innovation and health; reduce the price of genetic tests, thus increasing their accessibility and increase the chances of individuals having an early diagnosis for serious illnesses, leading to better prospects of cure and treatment. These interests are protected by the TRIPS Agreement insofar as they are public interests "in sectors of vital importance" for the "socio-economic and technological development" of any society.

Those goals are promoted through guaranteeing the right of facilitated access and use of genetic and proteomic material and the molecular descriptions of this material in the development of diagnostic tests and through the duty imposed on the beneficiaries of the exception to disclose the knowledge obtained about the links between genetic mutations and predisposition to illnesses. The means used to carry out the objectives pursued by the exception under scrutiny are appropriate.[349]

In addition, the exception complies with the limits set by the TRIPS Agreement.[350] Firstly, because it affects both the patents of domestic and foreign owners (arts. 3 and 4). Secondly, it does not prevent the protection of any of the categories of inventions that, pursuant to art. 27, should be eligible for patent protection. Thirdly, it does not shorten the minimum term of protection that WTO Members must guarantee to patents (art. 33). Fourthly, it strictly observes the area occupied by the system of compulsory licensing (art. 31): given that the proposed exception leads

348 See SACGHS 2009, 99–100, 111.
349 See American College of Medical Genetics 1999.
350 See Chapter 2, sections 2.3.3.3.4.1–4.

to the effect of banning the patenting of diagnostic tests comprising proteomic and genetic material of human origin, as well as their molecular description, the limits established by art. 31(1) do not apply. There is therefore no impediment to the adoption of an exception resting on a liability rule, even though the test developed merely incorporates a single patented invention.[351] Finally, the proposed exception observes the principle of non-discrimination (art. 27(1)), although it affects only patents related to genetic and proteomic material/information of human origin. Enacting an exception involving only those patents is not discriminatory, since those inputs enjoy a special status.[352]

The special status of the human genome and proteome is due, inter alia, to the fact that "they can be predictive of genetic predispositions concerning individuals"; "they may contain information the significance of which is not necessarily known at the time of the collection of biological samples";[353] human genes and proteins are limited in number;[354] they are naturally occurring substances, not produced by humans;[355] and, most importantly, "[t]he human genome underlies the fundamental unity of all members of the human family, as well as the recognition of their inherent dignity and diversity." Consequently, they constitute a common heritage of humanity.[356] An apparently special feature that is present in the genome of a given individual will be shared by an untold number of individuals. Therefore, no institution or individual enjoys a legitimate right to claim exclusive rights on a resource and/or information shared by the human family, without prior authorization by each co-holder of rights;[357] this stance would constitute a misappropriation of the resources of third parties and unjust enrichment.

Furthermore, although patent holders frequently argue that patents on human genes and proteins do not extend protection to material preserved by individuals, a simple example illustrates the weakness of this argument. Let us consider a scenario in which a patent was issued in Brazil for a prostate cancer gene X. In such a circumstance, if a patient were to donate a sample of his genetic material to a local research institution to be used in research projects focused on the development of diagnostic breakthrough tests or new therapies for treating prostate cancer, and the sample included the prostate cancer gene X, the prospective user would require the authorization of the patent holder to donate the sample

[351] See Chapter 2, section 2.3.3.3.4.3. [352] See Chapter 2, section 2.3.3.3.4.4.
[353] Art. 4 (a) (i) and (iii), International Declaration on Human Genetic Data.
[354] See OECD 2002, 11. [355] See American College of Medical Genetics 1999.
[356] See art. 1, Universal Declaration on the Human Genome and Human Rights.
[357] See Danish Council of Ethics 2004, 63–78.

because the patent holder would own rights controlling any use of the gene.[358] There can be no doubt that patents have a bearing on privacy and the rights of individuals over their own genetic material.

Despite arguments against their privatization, a significant number of States do not oppose patenting human genetic and proteomic material and molecular information. They hold that they are an ordinary "invention," produced by the combination of the human intellect and natural raw materials. With that reality as backdrop, the purpose of the proposed exception is to mitigate the socially detrimental effects produced *specifically* by patents concerned with human genes and proteins and their molecular description. This is done by providing ample room for the development of genetic diagnostic tests. In other words, the proposed exception is premised on the understanding that the patents conferred on genetic and proteomic material/information will be even more objectionable if the objects protected do not widely benefit all sectors of humanity. In view of the special status of this material and this information and the vital goals pursued by the exception – e.g. promoting the right to health and life of innumerable individuals – it cannot be judged discriminatory.

5.8.2 Second step: assessment of the reasonableness of the interference caused by the exception

The reasonableness of the interference caused by the exception for diagnostic tests in the normal exploitation of the patents concerned is contingent on the non-existence of an alternative measure that would promote the same goals, to the same degree, as the exception proposed here, but with fewer restrictions on the rights guaranteed to patent holders. We will examine the potential of three measures to qualify as alternatives to the exception.

5.8.2.1 Proposal of Lynn Rivers In 2002, Lynn Rivers, who was a member of the US Congress at the time, noted that patent holders who work with genetic material from various sources often act in an abusive manner. Based on that, she put forward a bill called the Genomic Research and Diagnostic Accessibility Act. If sanctioned, it would have introduced two exceptions in the USA legal order: a research exception and an exception to be used in diagnostics. We are only concerned with the latter one here. The exception for diagnostic use put forward by Rivers authorizes

[358] See Paradise and Jason 2006, 152; Rivers 2002.

laboratories, universities and private institutions to use patented genetic and proteomic material to develop and carry out diagnostic and predictive tests,[359] independently from any fees to be paid to the owners of the patents involved.

Rivers's bill can promote exactly the same interests protected by the exception for diagnostic tests proposed in this work, even to the same extent of protection. However, from the perspective of the owners of the patents involved, her proposal is more burdensome than the one forwarded here, since it does not guarantee patent holders the right to a fair remuneration when third parties develop and sell genetic tests.

5.8.2.2 Proposals based on a compulsory licensing scheme Under the Swiss Patent Act, amended in July 2009, the local public authority can grant a compulsory license for the exploitation of a patent whose subject matter is a diagnostic test whenever a judicial or administrative process has proved that the patent owner used it to promote anticompetitive practices.[360] The Swiss law is unable to promote the same objectives as the proposed exception for diagnostic tests and not merely because obtaining a compulsory license is conditional upon the complex task of showing that the owner of the relevant patent performed anticompetitive actions. The main reason why it cannot further those objectives is that it does not permit the development of new tests, nor does it bind the owners of diagnostic tests to publicly disclose their discoveries connected to causal links between genetic mutations and illnesses. The only objective that the Swiss law is able to further, albeit at a much lower level than the exception for diagnostic tests, is the right to health, and that is so because granting a compulsory license would possibly lower the cost of the test that is the subject matter of the licensed patent.

At first it seems a superior alternative to the Swiss model – that is, authorizing the granting of compulsory licenses not only to remedy anticompetitive practices, but also allowing third parties to use proteomic and genetic material/information of human origin for the development of diagnostic tests, whenever patent holders refuse to grant non-exclusive voluntary licenses on commercially reasonable terms.[361] Yet a measure with such a profile does not seem suitable to promote the same interests safeguarded by the diagnostic test exception, at least not to the same extent. As we have seen, the grant of a compulsory license is an expensive

[359] Rivers 2002, E354.
[360] See art. 40c (G), Loi fédérale sur les brevets d'invention du 25 juin 1954.
[361] Along the same lines, see Cook 2006, 163–164, 168.

lottery, and even if the applicants successfully obtain the licenses pursued, the time required for this may be excessive.[362] The delay comes at a price that no civilized society should be prepared to pay, namely the loss of human lives.

Since there is no alternative measure genuinely capable of promoting the same interests protected by the exception for diagnostic tests and imposing fewer restrictions on the rights of the owners of the relevant patents, it can be said that the exception for diagnostic tests successfully satisfies the second step of the test set out in art. 30 TRIPS.

5.8.3 Third step: assessment of the reasonableness of the prejudice caused by the exception

The reasonability of the prejudice caused by the exception for diagnostic tests on the legitimate interests of patent holders is assessed by balancing the social benefit promoted against the prejudice caused to the interests of patent owners. The exception for diagnostic tests furthers interests that are of vital importance for any society: it protects the rights of human beings to health and life; drives the progress of science and technology in the field of diagnosis and encourages the creation of jobs in the academic world, in the innovation industry and in clinical laboratories, on the basis of a larger variety of genetic tests available in the market.

On the other hand, the exception interferes in the exercise of the rights of patent holders to enjoin third parties from producing, using and marketing the patented inventions affected by the exception, whenever third parties aim to develop genetic tests. This does not imply, however, that the legitimate economic interests of patent owners are unprotected. The exception guarantees that they will receive a fee whenever new genetic tests are marketed. Since the exception examined maintains the economic incentives offered by patents to individuals and institutions to invest in R&D, the owners of the relevant patents are basically deprived of the right to hinder socially relevant applications of their inventions. In view of the fact that patents should work as a spring to promote innovation, the prejudice suffered by the owners of the relevant patents is of no social relevance, particularly when it is recalled that the exception for diagnostic tests is equally beneficial for the innovation sector, since it grants its members ample freedom to develop and distribute genetic tests, for a profit or free of charge.

[362] See section 5.6.2.1 above.

Given that the social benefit brought about by the exception is of crucial importance and the prejudice to the legitimate interests of patent holders is almost irrelevant, there can be no doubt that the exception put forward here passes the final step of the test in art. 30 of the TRIPS Agreement. Consequently, it is legitimate.

6 Trademarks and the parody and criticism exception

6.1 Introduction

The holders of protected trademarks enjoy the broad "exclusive right to prevent all third parties not having the owner's consent from using in *the course of trade* identical or similar signs for goods or services which are identical or similar to those in respect of which the trademark is registered where such use would result in a likelihood of confusion" (art. 16(1) TRIPS). The exclusive right granted to a holder of a trademark has the function of safeguarding its distinctiveness, that is, its ability to identify the origin of identical and similar products or services bearing it and differentiate them from other products and services provided by other competitors. In this context, the Court of Justice of the European Union (CJEU) in *Gillette Company, Gillette Group Finland Oy* v. *LA-Laboratories* held that:

> the essential function of a trade mark is to guarantee the identity of origin of the marked goods or services to the consumer or end user by enabling him, without any possibility of confusion, to distinguish the goods or services from others which have another origin. For the trade mark to be able to fulfil its essential role in the system of undistorted competition . . . it must offer a guarantee that all the goods or services bearing it have been manufactured or supplied under the control of a single undertaking which is responsible for their quality.[1]

In short, through the individualization of products and services, trademarks promote free and fair trade and safeguard consumer interests.[2]

[1] CJEU, *The Gillette Company, Gillette Group Finland Oy* c. *LA-Laboratories Ltd Ou* (C-228/03), March 17, 2005, para. 26. Along the same lines, the CJEU held in *Google France SARL, Google Inc.* c. *Louis Vuitton Malletier SA et al.* (C-236/08 – C-238/08, para. 82): "The essential function of a trade mark is to guarantee the identity of the origin of the marked goods or service to the consumer or end user by enabling him to distinguish the goods or service from others which have another origin." According to the same court, trademarks also perform other functions, "in particular that of guaranteeing the quality of the goods or services in question and those of communication, investment or advertising" (para. 77).

[2] See Ghidini 2006, 79–80.

Lately, well-known trademarks have been used by NGOs in actions that adopt the tactic called "naming and shaming."[3] In their campaigns, NGOs use the trademarks owned by large companies as raw material for public awareness campaigns regarding the socially detrimental actions undertaken by companies that own these trademarks. Many of these campaigns, particularly those sponsored by environmental organizations, are designed to ensure the ultimate effectiveness of two principles of the Rio Declaration: principle 8 which states: "To achieve sustainable development and a higher quality of life for all people, States should reduce and eliminate unsustainable patterns of production and consumption and promote appropriate demographic policies"; and principle 10, which imposes on States the obligation to "facilitate and encourage public awareness and participation by making information widely available." The public awareness campaigns promoted by NGOs – which involve, among other things, the elaboration of parodies of trademarks owned by large conglomerates – are effective ways of informing and leading consumers to purchase products and services provided by companies committed to the sustainability of the environment.

By way of illustration, it is worth mentioning the recent campaign titled "Tar Sands,"[4] launched in 2009 by Greenpeace against British Petroleum (BP).[5] In 2000, BP embraced the slogan "Beyond Petroleum" and a new logo comprising a flower in shades of green and yellow, which greatly resembles a lily pad. The campaign aimed at renewing the image of BP intended to express the commitment of this company to explore clean energy sources, more appropriate to a context of global warming. However, at present, BP plans to explore, in Alberta, Canada, tar sand deposits through an aggressive extraction technique, which involves the production of large amounts of greenhouse gases and consumes huge amounts of water. The deposits of tar sands are located under a boreal forest. To extract it, the oil companies operating in the region have to cut down the forest and open large craters to enable the removal of the tar sand deposits.[6] This entire process is highly damaging to the environment, being responsible for: the recent wave of forest destruction in Canada; the production of toxic wastes that are poisoning and destroying the water sources and fragile ecosystems of Alberta; the increase in the production of greenhouse gases; and for the weakening of indigenous communities based in the region. Due to BP's plans, Greenpeace

[3] See Abramovay 2010, 100.

[4] "Tar sands" is a mixture consisting of water, sands and bitumen.

[5] All information about the Greenpeace campaign is taken from the following website: www.greenpeace.org.uk/files/tarsands/index.html. Acessed on June 24, 2011.

[6] See Greenpeace UK 2010.

launched an international campaign, which ironically called BP by the names "British Polluters" and "Bad People." In addition to criticizing the BP, the environmental organization launched an international competition, which called for people around the world to redesign the logo of the British company, because, in their view, the current logo of BP was inconsistent with its environmentally harmful policy. Greenpeace received numerous proposals of logos for BP, all posted on their international website on the internet. The overwhelming majority of the posted creations were parodies[7] of the figurative trademark owned by BP (the flower referred to above), which associated BP with the destruction of the environment and its resources.[8] Concerned that BP's reputation could be permanently damaged, its shareholders asked the company's management committee to review the environmental and image costs associated with the "Tar Sands" project.[9]

Although the exclusive rights conferred by trademarks may only be exercised in the sphere of trade, their owners, especially the wealthy conglomerates, may use their exclusive rights, in particular through the courts, in order to try to silence voices capable of publicizing information about their actions.

The first part of this chapter examines some cases from Brazil, India, France[10] and South Africa, marked by a conflict between the right to free speech and trademark law. In most reported cases, the owners of well-known trademarks sought to exercise their exclusive rights to narrow the right of freedom of expression enjoyed by individuals and organizations responsible for disseminating messages that could affect their commercial interests. Then, a "parody and criticism exception" is proposed, designed to prevent the exclusive right conferred by trademarks from prejudicing the right of freedom of expression of others. Finally, the legality of the

[7] A parody associates the appropriation of well-known trademarks with new elements, in order to convey critical, witty or funny messages. Thus, a parody necessarily refers to the satirized and/or criticized trademark and communicates to the public that it is not the parodied trademark. This is the sense of the ruling handed down by the United States Court of Appeals for the 4th Circuit in the *Louis Vuitton* case: "But that is the essence of a parody – the invocation of a famous mark in the consumer's mind, so long as the distinction between the marks is also readily recognized. While a trademark parody necessarily copies enough of the original design to bring it to mind as a target, a successful parody also distinguishes itself and, because of the implicit message communicated by the parody, allows the consumer to appreciate it."

[8] All logos submitted are available at: www.flickr.com/photos/greenpeaceuk/sets/72157623796911855/. Accessed on July 15, 2011.

[9] See Pals 2010.

[10] The selection of the French cases examined in this chapter was inspired by Geiger (2004; 2007b).

proposed exception is evaluated by applying the test set out in art. 17 of the TRIPS Agreement.

6.2 Some cases involving conflicts between the exclusive right conferred by trademarks and freedom of expression

6.2.1 Laugh It Off *case*

Laugh It Off Promotions (Laugh It Off) is a small South African company dedicated to manufacturing and marketing T-shirts that display parodies of well-known trademarks as a way of communicating to the public, among other things, criticism of the practices of companies that own the parodied trademarks. The strategy used by Laugh It Off has been called "ideological jujitsu," characterized by using the weight and strength of well-known trademarks against themselves, as the trademarks utilized as "raw materials" for the parodies are easily recognizable to most people. One of the targets of Laugh It Off was the beer trademark "Carling Black Label."

South African Breweries International owns three trademarks in South Africa: (a) the word trademark "Carling Black Label"; (b) the semi-figurative trademark containing the following inscription: "Carling – Enjoyed by Men Around the World"; and (c) the semi-figurative trademark containing the inscription "Carling Beer Black Label: America's lusty, lively beer. Brewed in South Africa." Those trademarks are used in South Africa by the licensee South African Breweries (SAB) for the marketing of its beers.

At the end of 2001, it came to the attention of SAB that Laugh It Off was commercializing T-shirts that displayed a parody of the trademarks referred to above. In the semi-figurative trademark "Carling Black Label," the words "Black Label" were replaced with "Black Labour" and "Carling Beer" with "White Guilt." The inscriptions "America's lusty lively beer" and "enjoyed by men around the world" were replaced respectively with "Africa's lusty lively exploitation since 1652" and "no regard given worldwide."

SAB filed a lawsuit in South Africa, which requested a ban on the marketing of these shirts, based on art. 34(1)(c) of the Trade Marks Act 194 of 1993, which bestows on the holder of a well-known trademark the right to enjoin third parties from performing any acts capable of harming its distinctiveness, either by blurring or tarnishment.

Laugh It Off centered its defense on art. 16(1) of the South African Constitution, which guarantees the right to freedom of expression. The court of first instance (Cape High Court) ruled in favor of SAB and considered that Laugh It Off's activities did not fall within the sphere protected by the right to freedom of expression, since the defendant's actions were commercial. In addition, the court noted that the parody echoed a racist message, and this is prohibited by the South African Constitution (art. 16(2)(c)).[11]

The court ruling was upheld by the Supreme Court of Appeal, which held that the clothing company had abused its freedom of expression. According to the court, the parody conveyed the message that SAB had been exploiting black labor from time immemorial and that they should therefore feel guilt for this. In addition, the parody allegedly conveyed the message that SAB internationally did not care about the exploitation of human beings.[12] The court ruled that such messages bear the *ability* to tarnish the reputation of the trademark "Carling Black Label," as it created in the mind of consumers a degrading association. The fact that Laugh It Off's business revolved around the sale of shirts bearing parodies of well-known trademarks was indicative of the predatory intent of the clothing company.[13] The court, however, clarified that the law of South Africa did not prevent the parodying of protected trademarks if the parodies were not used in the course of trade. Thus, these parodies could not be affixed on commercially distributed products and services.[14]

Laugh It Off appealed to the Constitutional Court of South Africa. On May 27, 2005, the Constitutional Court reversed the ruling rendered by the Court of Appeals and authorized the marketing of the controversial shirts. The opinion of Justice Moseneke, which was followed by the nine judges of the Constitutional Court, assessed whether the parody of the well-known beer trademark had the capacity to dilute its distinctiveness, either through its blurring or its tarnishment.[15]

Justice Moseneke stressed the necessity to interpret the terms of section 34(1)(c) of the Trade Marks Act in harmony with the constitutional right to freedom of expression. In his view, when interpreting the anti-dilution clause of the Act, the courts should always opt for the interpretation that is the least restrictive of the freedom of expression, among the alternatives capable of preventing the dilution of the distinctiveness of well-known trademarks:

> A finding of unfair use or likelihood of detriment to the repute of the marks hinges on whether the offending expression is protected under section 16(1) of the Constitution or not. If the expression is constitutionally protected, what is unfair or detrimental, or not, in the context of section 34(1)(c) must then be

[11] Constitutional Court of South Africa, *Laugh It Off Promotions CC* v. *South African Breweries International* (Finance), para. 15.

[12] *Ibid.*, para. 20. [13] *Ibid.*, para. 24. [14] *Ibid.*, para. 23. [15] *Ibid.*, para. 41.

mediated against the competing claim for free expression... The injunction to construe statutes consistent with the Constitution means that, where reasonably possible, the court is obliged to promote the rights entrenched by it... That in turn impels us to a construction of section 34(1)(c) most compatible with the right to free expression. The anti-dilution provision must bear a meaning which is the least destructive of other entrenched rights and in this case free expression rights. The reach of the statutory prohibition must be curtailed to the least intrusive means necessary to achieve the purpose of the section. Courts must be astute not to convert the anti-dilution safeguard of renowned trade marks usually controlled by powerful financial interests into a monopoly adverse to other claims of expressive conduct of at least equal cogency and worth in our broader society.[16]

From this premise, Justice Moseneke construed the understanding that, under section 34(1)(c) of the Trade Marks Act, the owner of a well-known trademark is entitled only to prevent the propagation of a parody if the parody features a real likelihood of generating *substantial* economic prejudice to his business.[17] The judge concluded that there was no evidence that the shirts sold by Laugh It Off would be capable of causing substantial economic damage to the mark. The fact that the parody conveyed unpleasant messages about the "dignity" of the trademark "Carling Black Label" was not enough to prevent the sale of the shirts.[18]

Justice Sachs agreed with Justice Moseneke's opinion, and added some remarks in support of the opinion. He stressed that a good parody appropriates, to a large extent, the work of others. For this reason, the mere unauthorized appropriation of a trademark is not a sufficient reason to prevent the dissemination of a parody.[19] In order to evaluate the legitimacy of a parody, Sachs proposed a sort of "fair use" test, composed of a non-exhaustive list of factors that must be weighed by the court.

First, Sachs emphasized that in the balancing process, the commercial nature of the activities performed by the author of the parody was not enough to characterize it as abusive. Nevertheless, the court will investigate whether those activities are primarily communicative or commercial.[20] Second, to assess the alleged abusive nature of the parody, Sachs deemed immaterial whether the message conveyed by the parody can also be transmitted by a more direct means that does not involve the misrepresentation of the trademark. If the lack of alternative means was decisive in the process of reviewing the legality of parodies, parodies of trademarks would be banned altogether.[21] Third, Sachs noted that the medium used to divulge the parody and the context of its use are factors that will be considered in the assessment of the legitimacy of a parody. In the instant case, the judge found that the reproduction of the challenged

[16] *Ibid.*, paras. 44 and 49. [17] *Ibid.*, para. 50. [18] *Ibid.*, paras. 55–56.
[19] *Ibid.*, para. 77. [20] *Ibid.*, paras. 85–86. [21] *Ibid.*, para. 87.

parody on T-shirts, whose consumer audience consisted of young and critical people, was suggestive of the appropriateness of the means used to disseminate it.[22] Finally, Sachs explained that the fact that the parody lacked good taste did not weigh against its legitimacy. If only parodies in "good taste" were legitimate, society would only hear one voice, possibly the one belonging to influential organizations. All in all, who would be given the right to evaluate whether a parody displayed "good taste"?[23]

Sachs considered the challenged parody to be legitimate, because in the present social context, where trademarks attain the status of cultural icons, parodies are unique means of transmitting social criticism. Sachs emphasized that the parody elaborated by Laugh It Off did not criticize the quality of the products marketed under the trademark "Carling Black Label," nor was it used for the promotion of a competing product. The sale of the T-shirts was just a way to make sustainable the "political" activities performed by Laugh It Off. The parody served to instigate public debate on controversial issues.[24] The challenged parody would be, therefore, unable to destroy or weaken the distinctiveness of the affected trademark.[25] Sachs rightly pointed out that the role of intellectual property law is to prevent the misappropriation of intangible assets. It did not fall within its function to prevent the dissemination of critical messages against trademarks owners, though these messages may be deemed unfair.[26]

6.2.2 Areva *case*

The *Société des Participations du Commissariat à l'Energie Atomique* (SPCEA), better known by its trade name Areva, is the world's leading producer of equipment and provider of services aimed at generating nuclear energy. The Areva Group holds two semi-figurative trademarks: one consists of a stylized "A"; the other one is constituted by the same stylized vowel underlined by the word "Areva." Both trademarks were registered for various classes of goods and services, including the class related to telecommunications services, communications services via the internet and the transmission of information in the fields of nuclear energy, electronic distribution and transmission of messages and information via extranets, internet or intranet in the fields of nuclear energy.

In April 2002, Greenpeace launched a campaign against the nuclear industry, accessible through the websites belonging to Greenpeace France and Greenpeace New Zealand. The campaign was intended to

[22] *Ibid.*, para. 89. [23] *Ibid.* [24] *Ibid.*, para. 102.
[25] *Ibid.*, para. 109. [26] *Ibid.*, para. 102.

alert the French and New Zealand public to the dangers to human health and the environment posed by nuclear power, to inform the public about the alarming levels of radioactive pollution generated by the activities of the Areva Group and to encourage the public to sign a petition against the release of nuclear waste into the environment. On the internet, Greenpeace promoted the campaign by posting three parodies of Areva's trademarks. One of them associates the "Areva" trademark with a skull, the radioactive symbol and a slogan against nuclear energy. The other displays a dead fish, whose body bears the "Areva" trademark written in letters of blood. The third one includes a boat, whose sail bears the trademark "Areva," skulls and an atomic bomb.

In the same year, Areva filed a lawsuit in France against Greenpeace France, Greenpeace New Zealand and FR Société Internet, for the alleged infringement of the exclusive rights conferred by the trademarks referred to above and the alleged tarnishing of the reputation of Areva. Areva requested the court to order, inter alia: (i) the immediate withdrawal of all reproductions and imitations of trademarks owned by Areva and any illicit, implicit or explicit references to those trademarks from the Greenpeace websites, (ii) the withdrawal of access to the websites of Greenpeace which made explicit or implicit references to the trademarks owned by Areva and (iii) the payment by Greenpeace of a fine of 4,500 euros.[27]

In July 2004 the High Court of Paris (TGI) ruled partially in favor of Areva.[28] In the TGI's view, Greenpeace did not infringe any exclusive right conferred by the trademarks owned by the Areva group. Nevertheless, the actions of the environmental organization conveyed the message that Areva was a source of fatality. The association of Areva's operations with death would be able to produce deleterious effects on the company's reputation. Those effects were not supported by the right to freedom of expression, as Greenpeace would have recourse to other means to spread the same message, without harming the reputation of Areva. The TGI ordered Greenpeace, among other things, to suspend any form of use of the trademarks held by Areva, including the use of the parodies referred to above, and to pay compensation amounting to 10,000 euros.

[27] High Court of Paris, *SA Société des Participations du CEA* c. *Association Greenpeace France, SA Internet Fr.* Paris, August 2, 2002, upheld by the 14th Chamber of the Court of Appeals of Paris, *SA Société des participations du Commissariat à l'Energie Atomique* c. *Association Greenpeace, SA Internet Fr.* Judgment of February 26, 2003.

[28] 3rd Chamber of the High Court of Paris, *SPCEA* c. *Greenpeace France, Greenpeace New Zealand, SA Internet Fr.* Judgment of July 9, 2004.

Both parties appealed the case to the Court of Appeals of Paris. In November 2006, the 4th Chamber of the Court of Appeals of Paris confirmed the decision of the High Court.[29] The only point reversed was the amount of the compensation due by Greenpeace; the organization was ordered to pay a symbolic compensation amounting to one euro. The Court of Appeals upheld the view that Greenpeace had abused its right to freedom of expression by generally associating the products and services provided by the Areva Group with death, since the Group provided products and services non-related to the nuclear industry. Therefore, these products and services were not necessarily hazardous to human health and to the environment.

Greenpeace appealed to the Court of Cassation. In April 2008, the Court of Cassation, relying on the right to freedom of expression recognized by art. 10 of the European Convention on Human Rights, reversed the ruling rendered by the Court of Appeals. It ruled that the actions performed by Greenpeace, notably the publication of parodies involving the trademarks owned by the Areva Group, with the aim of promoting a campaign against radioactive waste, constituted a regular means of exercising the right to freedom of expression.[30]

6.2.3 Esso *case*

In France, Société Esso SA Française (Esso) is the owner of the name trademark ESSO and of a semi-figurative trademark consisting of an oval character with white background, blue border and the inscription ESSO in red. In the spring of 2002, the Association Greenpeace France (Greenpeace) launched on its website a campaign against Esso titled "Stop Esso," arising from the actions allegedly sponsored by the American oil company that aimed to frustrate international efforts to cope with climate change, notably the 1997 Kyoto Protocol. As part of that campaign, Greenpeace released a parody of the Esso trademark, characterized by the replacement of the SS of ESSO with $$, in order to highlight the supposed financial interests underpinning the actions of the company. The phrase "Stop Esso" and the parody were reproduced on posters that read: "Their stocks go up, and the thermometer too"; "Climate enemy number one"; "Our planet, their profits."

[29] 4th Chamber of the Court of Appeals of Paris, *Greenpeace France, Greenpeace New Zealand* c. *SPCEA*. Judgment of November 17, 2006.

[30] 1st Chamber of Civil Affairs of the Court of Cassation, *Greenpeace France et New-Zealand* c. *SPCEA*. Judgment of April 8, 2008.

In 2002, Esso applied for an injunction before the TGI against Greenpeace and Société Internet FR. The oil company claimed, among other things: (i) the exclusion of any unauthorized copying of its trademarks, including parodies of its trademarks, from the websites of Greenpeace; (ii) the deletion of the word trademark ESSO from the source code of the websites belonging to Greenpeace; (iii) the prohibition of any form of use of their trademarks by Greenpeace and Internet FR.[31] From Esso's point of view, the parodies of its trademarks had the potential to mislead consumers as to the origin of the messages conveyed, and at worst, could somehow wrongly associate Esso with the Waffen Schutzstaffel of the Nazi regime (SS).

In January 2004 the TGI ruled in favor of Greenpeace.[32] In the opinion of the court, there was no basis for holding Greenpeace liable for any infringement of the exclusive rights associated with the ESSO trademark, since the environmental organization used parodies of Esso's trademark with the purpose of informing the public about the climate change policy allegedly endorsed by Esso, but not to promote similar products capable of competing with those produced and marketed by the oil company. In addition, the campaign sponsored by Greenpeace was not intended to criticize or denigrate the products and services provided by Esso. Thus, the activities of Greenpeace, according to the Court, were fully safeguarded by the right to freedom of expression.

In April, 2004, Esso appealed to the Court of Appeal of Paris, trying, in vain, to reverse the ruling. In November 2005, the Court of Appeal upheld the TGI's ruling rendered in favor of Greenpeace.[33] Esso then lodged an appeal to the Court of Cassation, which, on April 8, 2008, partially reversed the appealed ruling. The aspect of interest is the fact that it confirmed the understanding that the parodies of the ESSO trademark elaborated by Greenpeace are a proportionate and, therefore, legitimate means of promoting the institutional mission of the environmental organization.[34]

[31] High Court of Paris, *SA Société Esso* c. *Association Greenpeace France, Société Internet FR*. Interlocutory injunction of July 8, 2002, reversed by the 14th Chamber of the Court of Appeal of Paris, *Association Greenpeace France* c. *SA Société Esso*. Judgment of February 25, 2003.

[32] 3rd Chamber of the High Court of Paris, *Esso* c. *Greenpeace, Internet Fr*. Judgment of January 30, 2004.

[33] 4th Chamber of the Court of Appeal of Paris, *Esso* c. *Greenpeace France*. Judgment of November 16, 2005.

[34] Chamber of Commercial, Financial and Economic Affairs of the Court of Cassation, *La société ESSO Société Anonyme Française* c. *Association Greenpeace France*. Public hearing of April 8, 2008.

6.2.4 Danone *case*

In 2001, the Société Compagnie Gervais Danone (Danone) decided to restructure its biscuit sector by the closure of two manufacturing plants and the dismissal of its employees. The company's decision prompted employees, politicians and representatives of trade unions to call on French consumers to boycott products from Danone, as a way to persuade the company to reconsider its decision. In this same vein, in April 2001, *Société Le Réseau Voltaire pour la Liberté d'Expression* (Réseau Voltaire) launched on the internet, a campaign against Danone's social policy. The campaign included the launch of websites whose domain names were jeboycottedanone.net and jeboycottedanone.com. On these sites, the Réseau Voltaire urged French consumers to boycott Danone products while the dismissal of employees persisted. The websites also served as a forum for discussions between consumers and trade unions. In addition, the campaign involved the release of a parody of the famous semi-figurative Danone trademark, consisting of a blue polygon, which contained the word DANONE written in white letters, highlighted by a tilted red bar. In the parodied version of the trademark, the blue polygon included the inscription "je boycotte Danone," and the red bar was replaced with a black one.

In 2001, Danone filed a lawsuit before a French court, requesting an injunction against Réseau Voltaire and Société Gandi, a web hosting company. Danone sought orders: (a) banning the use of its trademarks, in any form and in any medium, by Réseau Voltaire; and (b) prohibiting Société Gandi from hosting and providing access to the website jeboycottedanone.net as well as to any other website that infringed its trademarks.

In May 2001, on an interim basis, the TGI found that the registration of the domain name jeboycottedanone.net did not constitute an infringement of the exclusive rights conferred upon Danone by its trademark, as Réseau Voltaire did not promote competing products, and also because the association of the trademark with the words "jeboycotte" made clear to consumers that Danone was not the source of the website nor of the posted messages thereon. In addition, the inclusion of the trademark "Danone" in that domain name was essential to the success of the campaign. On the other hand, the French court stressed that "to any freedom corresponds a responsibility" and that there were limits to Réseau Voltaire's freedom of expression. In the view of the TGI, the Réseau Voltaire abused its freedom of expression, because the reproduction of Danone's semi-figurative trademark on the mentioned website did not constitute a necessary measure to promote a campaign against the social policy followed by Danone. The High Court of Paris concluded that "reproduction with no necessity and no authorization constitutes counterfeit." Based on these reasons, the TGI prohibited Réseau Voltaire from continuing to use Danone's semi-figurative trademark, in any form or in any medium.[35]

In July 2001, the 3rd Chamber of the TGI delivered the first instance ruling, once again in favor of Danone. The TGI held that: the domain names registered by Réseau Voltaire did not infringe the exclusive rights stemming from Danone's trademark; the parody of Danone's semi-figurative trademark "Danone," elaborated by Réseau Voltaire, infringed the exclusive rights conferred by Danone's trademark; the French Intellectual Property Code lacked a parody exception, a typical feature of copyright regimes; and the right to freedom of expression did not shelter the actions performed by Réseau Voltaire, in particular because it was not necessary to use graphic parodies in order to convey critical messages against Danone's policies.[36]

Réseau Voltaire appealed the court ruling. In April 2003, the Paris Court of Appeal handed down a ruling favorable to the appellant, noting that: Réseau Voltaire exercised within the legal limits its right to freedom of expression; the association of Danone's trademark with the phrase "je boycotte" was enough to indicate that the Danone Group was not responsible for the websites, nor the author of the messages posted there; the parodies of Danone's trademark were not used to foster the marketing of products competing with those produced thereby; and finally, the campaign launched by Réseau Voltaire was not intended to denigrate Danone's products, but only to alert the public to the policy followed by this company. For the reasons stated, the Court of Appeal reversed the earlier decision and concluded that Réseau Voltaire did not infringe any of the exclusive rights associated with Danone's trademark.[37]

6.2.5 "Guaraná Power" case

In 2003, at the invitation of the Nordic Institute for Contemporary Art (NIFCA), the Brazilian foundation Extra Arte, the state government of Amazonas and the Danish art group Superflex, formed by three artists

[35] High Court of Paris, *Société Compagnie Gervais Danone* c. *Société Le Réseau Voltaire, Société Gandi, Valentin L.* Interlocutory injunction of May 14, 2001.

[36] 3rd Chamber of the High Court of Paris, *Sté Compagnie Gervais Danone et Sté Groupe Danone* c. *Olivier M., SA 7 Ways, Sté ELB Multimédia, Association "Le Réseau Voltaire Pour la Liberté d'expression," Sté Gandi et Valentin L.*

[37] 4th Chamber of the Court of Appeals of Paris, *Olivier M., Réseau Voltaire* c. *Compagnie Gervais Danone.*

from the visual arts field, organized a workshop in the city of Maués, Amazonas, whose goal was to identify, together with small local farmers represented by the cooperative COIAMA, strategies for the sustainable commercial exploitation of local natural resources, so as to improve their livelihoods.[38]

Maués is an important production center for seeds of the guaraná plant (Paullinia cupana). Much of the local production is purchased by multinational manufacturers of soft drinks, notably by AmBev, a conglomerate which manufactures the "Guaraná Antarctica." Workshop participants allegedly reported that in a period of four years, the price of guaraná seeds decreased from R$ 25.00/kg to R$ 4.00/kg, as a result of a purchasing cartel organized by multinational companies.[39]

During the workshop, Superflex and the members of COIAMA identified products that could be manufactured with raw materials typical of the Amazon rainforest, which could be potential competitors of similar products distributed by multinational corporations: for example, development of a cupulate bar (a chocolate bar made of cupuaçu seeds), to be named "Maués Barsin," was considered, a potential competitor of "Mars bars." Also contemplated was the launch of "Mauéscafé," an instant coffee enriched with guaraná powder, which had the potential to compete with Nestlé's "Nescafé."[40]

In 2004, after a maturation period which involved market research and identification of industrial partners abroad, Superflex identified a product that could reduce the economic dependence of local farmers on the purchases made by multinationals: a soft drink called "Guaraná Power" whose formulation includes guaraná powder, apple and lemon juice. At present, "Guaraná Power" is manufactured by the Danish company NaturFrisk A/S – Bryggeri Brewery.[41] NaturFrisk purchases seeds of Guaraná Maués from small farmers at preferential rates.[42] The negotiation of the price of the seeds is mediated by Power Foundation, a foundation established in Denmark, with the specific aim of improving the quality of life of the small farmers based in Maués. A significant part of the profits arising from the sale of "Guaraná Power" in Denmark is returned to the Brazilian small farmers.

For the visual identity of "Guaraná Power," Superflex proposed a logo consisting of a green belt, which reproduced images of Amazonian small farmers. On this green belt had been added the well-known

[38] Bradley 2003. [39] *Ibid.* On August 5, 2011, the exchange rate was US$ 1 = R$ 1.58.
[40] *Ibid.* [41] See http://thepowerfoundation.org/. Acessed on July 10, 2011.
[42] In 2006, while multinationals alleged paid around R$7/kilo of seeds of Guaraná, the Danish company paid R$15 for the same amount of raw material (Creative Commons Brazil 2006).

semi-figurative trademark "Guaraná Antarctica," partially covered by a black stripe placed diagonally. While the black band covered much of the "Guaraná Antarctica" trademark, an average consumer, who knows the well-known Brazilian trademark, would be able to identify, with ease, the logo behind the band. It seems that the logo designed by Superflex was both meant to identify the new soft drink and to convey a message of protest against the practices allegedly carried out by multinationals to the detriment of the economic sustainability of the small farming communities based in the city of Maués.

The Danish group exhibited, in various foreign art galleries, the logo designed for the "Guaraná Power" project. In 2006, in vain, Superflex tried to display its work in the São Paulo Biennale. The curators of the Biennale selected Superflex's work for public display in its 27th show. On the eve of the opening of the exhibition, the president of the Biennale decided to prevent the display of Superflex's artwork, because, according to the Biennale's lawyers, the logo of "Guaraná Power" infringed the exclusive rights bestowed by the Brazilian Industrial Property Act on the owner of the "Guaraná Antarctica" trademark.[43] In order to publicize their work and the events that spurred the development of "Guaraná Power," Superflex distributed free samples of the new soft drink in São Paulo and Rio de Janeiro.

Possibly with the aim of preventing the filing of a lawsuit by AmBev, based on the dilution of the "Guaraná Antarctica" trademark, Superflex changed the logo of "Guaraná Power": the current logo consists of two black bars placed on what appears to be the "Guaraná Antarctica" trademark. With the addition of the second stripe it is no longer possible to identify the hidden label. Only someone who knows the history of the controversies that have permeated the release of "Guaraná Power" can imagine what is covered by the stripe. In addition to changing the label, on its website devoted to recounting the genesis of the "Guaraná Power" project, Superflex had chosen to exercise self-censorship, by covering with black stripes the names of multinationals producing Guaraná soft drinks.[44]

6.2.6 Brazilian Olympic Committee case

In 2009, Kátia Rubio, professor at the School of Physical Education and Sport at the University of São Paulo (USP), published in Brazil a book entitled *Sport, Education and Olympic Values*, whose cover depicts

[43] See Cipriano 2006; Creative Commons Brasil 2006.
[44] See www.superflex.net/tools/supercopy/guarana.shtml. Accessed on July 30, 2011.

a stylized version of the well-known Olympic symbol, consisting of five interlaced rings. Within the rings were included images that refer to the Olympic games.

On January 15, 2010, the Brazilian Olympic Committee (BOC) sent a notice to Professor Rubio complaining of the alleged "misuse of the Olympic symbol consisting of five (5) interlaced rings; the term 'OLYMPIC' in the plural form; and of the unauthorized reproduction of photographs."[45] In the notice, the BOC argued that the Pelé Act (art. 15 (2), Law no. 9.615/98) conferred on itself the exclusive right to use "flags, slogans, hymns, the Olympic and Paralympic symbols, as well as the words 'Olympic Games', 'Olympics', 'Paralympics Games' and 'Paralympics'." The Committee also argued that under Law. 9279/96 (Brazilian Industrial Property Act or LPI) it had the exclusive right to use any expressions derived from the word "Olympics," by virtue of the manifold trademark registrations filed with the Brazilian Institute of Industrial Property (INPI). According to the BOC, the use of the Olympic symbol and of the word "Olympics" by Rubio went beyond the scope of the exception governed by art. 132, IV of the LPI, which prohibits the holder of a trademark from "preventing the mention of the mark in speeches, scientific or literary works or in any other type of publication, provided that it is without any commercial connotation and without prejudice to its distinctive character." Because the adaptation of the Olympic symbol was made without the prior consent of the BOC, Rubio would be subject to a penalty of up to one year imprisonment or to the payment of a fine (art. 189, II, LPI). On these grounds the BOC called for the immediate cessation of the use of the term "Olympic" and of the stylized Olympic symbol, through the seizure of all copies of Rubio's books offered for sale.

In order to obtain the support of the academic community and of the general public for the safeguarding of freedom of creative and scientific expression, Rubio published, on January 29, 2010, an open letter addressed to the BOC, where she expressed her indignation and described the request made by the BOC as an "inquisitorial" act of censorship that prevented her from writing and publishing in Brazil works on Olympic themes.[46] Rubio emphasized that for many years she had been writing on Olympic themes, having published more than a dozen books on the subject. In her view, the selection of Rio de Janeiro to host the 2016

[45] See Richer 2010.

[46] In her open letter, Rubio (2010) asks with outrage: "Have we gone back to the time of the Inquisition when only the initiated have access to the mysteries and banned publications and books have to be purged . . . ?" (free translation)

Olympic Games was a good reason to encourage the wide dissemination of the Olympic ideals in Brazil.

On February 2, 2010, Rubio's lawyers sent to the BOC an extrajudicial counter-notice, where they argued that the use made of the Olympic symbol and the word "Olympic" did not infringe any exclusive right held by the BOC, as it had exclusively educational purposes. In addition, they stated that the challenged uses were backed by the right to freedom of expression, guaranteed by art. 5, (IV) and (IX) of the Brazilian Constitution, and by the right to freedom of teaching, learning and researching, guaranteed by art. 206 (II) and (III) of the Constitution.[47]

At the time of writing, the BOC has not sent any further communication to Rubio or filed any lawsuit. A possible sign that the dispute has ended without further damage to freedom of expression is that the then President of Brazil, Luiz Inácio Lula da Silva, granted to Rubio, on June 4, 2010, the Medal of the Order of Sporting Merit, which is considered the highest sports award that can be granted by the Brazilian government.

6.2.7 Tata Sons *case*

In May 2010, Greenpeace India (Greenpeace), a branch of Greenpeace International, launched on the internet, the video game "Turtle v. Tata," a game inspired by the famous Pac-Man of the 1980s. In that game, a turtle has the mission to eat as many white dots as possible, seeking to escape from its enemies, the "Tata demons," whose outward appearance incorporates a stylized "T," a well-known figurative trademark under protection in several jurisdictions and belonging to India's largest business conglomerate, the Tata Group or the House of Tata.

The game's goal is to alert the public to the alleged environmentally deleterious effects that will result from the construction of a port, located north of the mouth of the Dhamra river on the eastern coast of India, by the Dhamra Port Company Limited (DPCL), a joint venture formed by the construction firm Larsen & Toubro Limited and Tata Steel Limited. The environmental NGO alleges that the operation of that port could endanger Indian natural sanctuaries, in particular the Gahirmatha beach, natural habitat of the Olive Ridley sea turtles. This species is protected by the Indian Wildlife Act 1972, the Migratory Species Convention and the Convention on the International Trade in Endangered Species of Wild Flora and Fauna (CITES). Although DPCL obtained the environmental permits required for the construction of the port,

[47] See Murray Neto *et al.* 2010.

Greenpeace claimed that the project violates several Indian environmental standards and should not therefore be carried out in the proposed region.[48] Their website pointed out the objective pursued by the campaign based on the videogame "Turtle v. Tata":

TATA's Dhamra port could be the beginning of the end for Gahirmatha's turtles. Your objective is simple – get the turtles to eat as many of the white dots – jellyfish and other sea creatures – while dodging the TATA demons! If you eat a power pill, you will be gifted with super-turtle powers to vanquish the demons of development that are threatening your coastal home! Of course, real life isn't quite so rosy for the turtles, and they need your help to keep fighting for a safer future.[49]

In response to Greenpeace's campaign, still in 2010, the Tata Group (Tata Sons Limited) applied for a temporary and a permanent injunction before the Delhi High Court. In particular, Tata sought the permanent banning of the use of its trademarks by Greenpeace and the payment of damages by virtue of the defamation of Tata Group's companies. Of the two requests put forward it is the first request that is relevant to the present chapter. Briefly, it is premised on art. 29(4) of the Indian Trade Marks Act 1999, which provides:

(4) A registered trade mark is infringed by a person who, not being a registered proprietor or a person using by way of permitted use, uses in the course of trade, a mark which:

(a) is identical with or similar to the registered trade mark; and

(a) is used in relation to goods or services which are not similar to those for which the trade mark is registered; and

(c) the registered trade mark has a reputation in India and the use of the mark *without due cause* takes unfair advantage of or *is detrimental to*, the distinctive character or *repute of the registered trade mark*. (emphasis added)

Tata pleaded that the defamatory use of the Tata Group's trademarks undertaken by Greenpeace (the stylized "T" and the name "Tata," employed to refer to the "enemies" of the turtles of the videogame), represented an act of infringement of such marks through their tarnishment.[50] In Tata's view, there was no legitimate justification for the unauthorized

[48] High Court of Delhi, *Tata Sons Limited* v. *Greenpeace International and Greenpeace India* (judgment pronounced on January 28, 2011 by Justice S. Ravindra Bhat), para. 17.
[49] See www.greenpeace.org/india/en/Get-Involved/Turtle-vs-TATA/. Accessed on July 13, 2011.
[50] High Court of Delhi, *Tata Sons Limited* v. *Greenpeace International & Greenpeace India*, para 15.

use of such trademarks by Greenpeace, since the port project was subject to all the environmental permits required by Indian legislation. Such environmental licenses, Tata alleged, operated to prevent Greenpeace from disseminating the idea that the realization of the project would affect the future of a certain species of sea turtles.[51] Tata also argued that the defamatory nature of Greenpeace's campaign could be seen from the fact that Tata Steel would hold only 50 percent of the projected port, yet the other partner in the project (Larsen & Toubro) was not even mentioned in the video game.

The Delhi High Court rejected the claims put forward by the Tata Group. Basing his decision on the judgments in the *Laugh it Off* and *Esso* cases, previously discussed in this chapter, and aware of the importance of freedom of expression for the preservation of democracy, Justice Ravindra Bhat found that the use of a trademark as an object of a critical comment or even of an attack does not necessarily constitute an infringement of the exclusive rights conferred on the affected trademark owner. Its use is legitimate, provided it serves to draw public attention to some of the activities performed by the owner of the trademark object of criticism or parody:

> The above analysis would show that the use of a trademark, as the object of a critical comment, or even attack, does not necessarily result in infringement. Sometimes the same mark may be used, as in *Esso*; sometimes it may be a parody (like in *Laugh it Off* and *Louis Vuitton*). If the user's intention is to focus on some activity of the trademark owners, and is 'denominative', drawing attention of the reader or viewer to the activity, such use can *prima facie* constitute 'due cause' under Section 29 (4), which would disentitle the plaintiff to a temporary injunction, as in this case. The use of TATA, and the 'T' device or logo, is clearly denominative. Similarly, describing the Tatas as having demonic attributes is hyperbolic and parodic. Through the medium of the game, the defendants seek to convey their concern and criticism of the project and its perceived impact on the turtles' habitat. The Court cannot appoint itself as a literary critic, to judge the efficacy of use of such medium, nor can it don the robes of a censor. It merely patrols the boundaries of free speech, and in exceptional cases, issues injunctions by applying the *Bonnard* principle. So far as the argument by the plaintiff that it is being 'targeted' is concerned the Court notes that the defendants submit that the major gains through the port accrue to the Tatas.[52]

It is worth clarifying that this ruling is not final and could be reversed at the appellate level.

[51] *Ibid.*, para 12. [52] *Ibid.*, para. 42.

6.2.8 *Lessons to be drawn from the cases*

In the cases examined, influential organizations relied on the exclusive rights conferred by trademarks, with the purpose of trying to silence other voices that could harm their business interests. The courts of France, India and South Africa endeavored to use – explicitly or implicitly – the right to freedom of expression as a substitute for a "parody and criticism exception," not provided by the legal orders of these countries. Although the Brazilian Industrial Property Act does not include a "parody and criticism exception," it does at least authorize others to mention protected trademarks "in speeches, scientific or literary works or in any other type of publication, provided that it is without any commercial connotation and without prejudice to its distinctive character" (art. 132, IV). In practice, however, the scope of this exception was not broad enough to support the free dissemination of the Superflex's artwork at the Biennale of São Paulo.

The judicial precedents discussed above are valuable as they confirm that human rights may play, in actual fact, the valuable role of serving as extrinsic limits to IPRs. However, one cannot ignore that the lack of a parody and criticism exception explicitly enshrined in the statutes that govern the protection of trademarks, creates social uncertainty.

The *Hertel* case, a ruling by the ECtHR, although not involving a conflict between trademark law and freedom of expression, but a conflict between freedom of expression and the norms governing the repression of unfair competition, confirms the importance of enacting an explicit parody and criticism exception at the domestic level. The Swiss scientist Hans Ulrich Hertel (Hertel) published in early 1992, in a popular newspaper in Switzerland (*Journal Franz Weber*), an article about the deleterious effects on human health produced by the consumption of food cooked in microwave ovens. Based on private investigations, the article suggested that consumption of food cooked in microwave ovens can lead to anemia, slacken the immune system and trigger the onset of serious diseases such as cancer. The newspaper responsible for publishing the article made use of graphic tools, which linked the use of microwave ovens to death. In addition, it employed a tough and incisive text, which turned Hertel's suggestive findings into categorical truths, not subject to review.

Afraid of a drop in sales of microwave ovens as a result of the article, the Swiss Association of Producers and Suppliers of Household Electrical Appliances (the Association) filed a lawsuit against the newspaper company, based on the Swiss Unfair Competition Act 1986. The

Association requested that the newspaper be prohibited from: (i) using the image of a human skeleton or any other image suggestive of death in association with the graphical representation of a microwave oven; (ii) urging the banning of microwave ovens; and (iii) making statements that emphasized that science has proven that the consumption of food cooked in microwave ovens is harmful to health. In April 1992, the district court of Vevey prohibited Franz Weber from using the image of a skeleton, of a cross or of a grave in association with the graphic representation of a microwave oven.[53]

In August 1992, the Association filed a lawsuit against Hertel, before the Commercial Court of Berne. Relying once again on the Swiss Unfair Competition Act, it demanded that Hertel be prohibited from publicly stating that the consumption of food cooked in microwave ovens represent a hazard to health, and from associating, in publications and public events, images that link the use of microwave ovens to death.[54] In March 1993, the Court upheld all the requests made by the Association, but left untouched Hertel's right to continue to carry out scientific research on the effects produced by the use of microwave ovens, and to publish the research outputs exclusively in academic publications.[55] In the opinion of the Court, the Swiss Unfair Competition Act restrains any action that may affect adversely the proper functioning of competition, prejudicing competitors by unfairly reducing their market presence. The Court ruled that Hertel, by publishing an article that drew conclusions that are controversial and not accepted by mainstream science, performed an act of unfair competition, although it neither derived commercial gains from the publication, nor promoted any competing product, nor there was evidence that the article affected the sales of microwave ovens in Switzerland.[56] The publication was characterized as an act of unfair competition, since Hertel omitted the existence of other scientific positions on the risks associated with the consumption of food cooked in microwave ovens and did not acknowledge the lack of scientific certainty about the results suggested by its investigations. Another factor that supported the finding that Hertel performed an act of unfair competition was the publication of its article in a popular newspaper, widely accessible by lay people and, therefore, susceptible to being misled.[57]

Hertel appealed the court decision. In February 1994, the Federal Court upheld the earlier ruling. In the court's view, the fact that Hertel's article, based on disputed scientific data, could encourage consumers

[53] ECtHR, case of *Hertel* v. *Switzerland*, 14–15. [54] *Ibid.*, p. 16.
[55] *Ibid.*, p. 31. [56] *Ibid.*, p. 19. [57] *Ibid.*, p. 20.

to stop purchasing microwave ovens, was sufficient to characterize the publication as an act of unfair competition.[58]

In September 1994, Hertel petitioned the European Commission of Human Rights, where he argued that the rulings rendered by the Swiss courts had infringed arts. 6, 8 and 10 of the European Convention on Human Rights (ECHR). The petition was accepted based on the alleged curtailment of Hertel's right to freedom of expression (art. 10). The case was finally ruled on by the ECtHR on 25 August 1998.

The ECtHR assessed whether the restriction on Hertel's freedom of expression, imposed by the Swiss courts, was consistent with the requirements imposed by Art. 10 (2) of the European Convention on Human Rights, namely: whether (i) the restriction was prescribed by law, (ii) its imposition was motivated by any of the legitimate goals allowed by the Convention ("national security, territorial integrity or public safety, for the prevention of disorder or crime, for the protection of health or morals, for the protection of the reputation or the rights of others, for preventing the disclosure of information received in confidence, or for maintaining the authority and impartiality of the judiciary"); (iii) the restriction was "necessary in a democratic society," that is, the restriction would be legitimate if it were directed at protecting a pressing social interest.

The ECtHR concluded that the restriction met the first two conditions: it is prescribed by law (the Swiss Unfair Competition Act) and it was designed to protect the rights of manufacturers of microwave ovens and of appliance stores ("the rights of others").[59] However, the ECtHR held that the restriction imposed did not satisfy the third condition. The Court emphasized that the discretion available to States to decide whether there is a pressing social interest that justifies the restrictions set on the freedom of expression of others, is greatly reduced when the expression pursues objectives of a public nature. Therefore the challenged measures were more subject to the ECtHR's scrutiny. In the opinion of the Court, the legal measures adopted by the Swiss courts were disproportionate, in the sense that the interests promoted thereby had less importance in the preservation of democracy than the freedom of individuals to disseminate minority views, in particular when there was no scientific certainty about the real risks posed by the use of microwave ovens to human health.[60]

Although Hertel's publication did not pursue commercial purposes, it can be inferred from the reasoning adopted by the ECtHR that the rulings delivered by the Swiss courts were considered wrong, because Hertel's

[58] *Ibid.*, p. 24. [59] *Ibid.*, 28–30. [60] *Ibid.*, 35.

work was not to be regarded as containing elements and messages actually capable of affecting the sales of microwave ovens:[61] The question that remains is, if Hertel's article had made categorical statements against the use of microwave ovens, would the ECtHR have upheld the restrictions set by the Swiss courts?

It is possible that in future disputes brought before the ECtHR or other courts, parodies and criticisms involving trademarks will not be considered to be protected by the right to freedom of expression, in cases where there is evidence that they have the potential to prejudice the businesses of the owners of the trademarks that are subject to criticism and parody, even if the messages conveyed thereby are relevant to promoting pressing social interests, e.g. protection of public health, those in the labor market and the environment.

In conclusion, the cases examined in this chapter show the difficulties faced by individuals and NGOs to defend their freedom of expression in and out of court, in the absence of a parody and criticism exception. On the one hand, it is correct to say that the right to freedom of expression has been preserved in the vast majority of the cases analyzed; on the other hand, there is no certainty that the result will be the same in future disputes, in the absence of an explicit parody and criticism exception.

6.3 Proposal of a parody and criticism exception

From a technical viewpoint, an exception for parody and criticism may seem at first unnecessary, since the exclusive rights conferred by a trademark may only be relied upon against third parties who use identical or similar signs to the protected trademark in commercial contexts, provided the use is capable of leading to confusion on the origin of the products or services which bear the identical or similar sign (art.16(1) TRIPS).[62] But doubts persist about how to define "in the course of trade" and "confusion": does the dissemination of a parody of a trademark, that may interfere with the marketing of products and services provided by the holder of the parodied trademark, constitute a commercial use of the affected trademark?[63] Is it lawful to use a parody as an identifying sign of origin of products and services?

The adoption of an exception for parody and criticism serves to prevent applications of the law that may undermine the right to freedom of expression and to prevent individuals and NGOs from conducting self-censorship. The mere possibility that trademark law could be used

[61] *Ibid.*, 33–34. [62] See Geiger 2007b, 323–324. [63] *Ibid.*

to silence voices contrary to the interests held by trademark owners, produces an overall chilling effect. In this respect, Justice Sachs makes an interesting remark in *Laugh It Off Promotions* v. *South African Breweries International*:

> Yet when applied against non-competitor parody artists, the tarnishment theory of trademark dilution may in protecting the reputation of a mark's owner, effectively act as a defamation statute. As such it could serve as an over-deterrent. It could chill public discourse because trademark law could be used to encourage prospective speakers to engage in undue self-censorship to avoid the negative consequence of speaking – namely, being involved in a ruinous lawsuit. The cost could be inordinately high for an individual faced with a lawsuit aimed at silencing a critic, not only in terms of general litigation expenses, but also through the disruption of families and emotional upheaval. Such protracted vexation can have the effect of discouraging even the hardiest of souls from exercising their free speech rights.[64]

In the absence of an exception for parody and criticism, individuals and civil society organizations, in particular those with meager resources to invest in legal and media battles, may opt to exercise self-censorship, by choosing to transmit neutral – often inefficient – messages about controversial socio-environmental issues. This seems to be the case in the "Guaraná Power" dispute: Superflex chose to delete any explicit reference to AmBev and to Guaraná Antarctica from its press releases and Guaraná Power's logo. Due to this, the original critical message conveyed was substantially depleted. So much so that, in Brazil, the existence of Guaraná Power and the alleged difficulties faced by the Amazonian small farmers in respect of the commercialization of guaraná seeds remain largely ignored.

Given the risk that the right to freedom of expression may be eroded by the exercise of the rights conferred by trademarks, it seems fully justified to propose a parody and criticism exception as follows:

> The holder of a mark may not:
> (i) prevent the mention of the mark in speeches, scientific or literary works or in any other publication, in order to comment on or criticize the organization that uses it in the course of trade, or the products and services that use or display it in commerce;
> (ii) prevent the elaboration of parodies of the mark, the public dissemination of parodies and in its affixation on commercial products or services, provided that:

[64] Constitutional Court of South Africa, *Laugh It Off Promotions CC* v. *South African Breweries International*, para. 106.

a. the parody is not confused with the mark that is the object of the parody;
b. the parody, when affixed to products, is used with the primary goal of disseminating critical messages;
c. the parody does not convey false information about the company using the mark that is the object of the parody or about the products and services marketed under the mark that is the object of the parody; and
d. the parody is not employed to inciting hatred, violence, or to make war propaganda;

(iii) prevent the use of parodies of his mark as a trademark, provided that:
a. the parody is not confused with the mark that is the object of parody;
b. the packaging of the products bearing the parody are not confused with the packaging of the products bearing the mark that is the object of the parody;
c. the parody does not convey false information about the company using the mark that is the object of the parody or about the products and services marketed under the mark that is the object of the parody; and
d. the parody is not used to instigate hatred, inciting violence or to make war propaganda.

The first component of the exception was designed having as its models art. 132, IV, of the Brazilian Industrial Property Act and §1125(c)(3)(A)(ii) of the United States Code.[65] The proposed exception sets no condition for the parody or criticism to be considered legitimate, whereas the Brazilian law requires that it should not have any commercial connotation, and that it should not interfere with the distinctiveness of the mark that is referred to. If protected trademarks could not be included in speeches and works which bear commercial bias, comparative advertising would be banned. And if trademarks were not subject to critical messages that might affect their prestige, individuals, news agencies and NGOs could no longer criticize the alleged unfair practices followed by the holders and licensees of trademarks. If the proposed exception did not offer a broad freedom in using trademarks in speeches and in any medium of communication, the right to freedom of expression – which includes the right "to seek, receive and impart information and ideas of all kinds . . . either orally, in writing or in print, in the form of art, or

[65] This US provision reads as follows: "The following shall not be actionable as dilution by blurring or dilution by tarnishment under this subsection: (A) Any fair use, including a nominative or descriptive fair use, or facilitation of such fair use, of a famous mark by another person other than as a designation of source for the person's own goods or services, including use in connection with . . . (ii) identifying and parodying, criticizing, or commenting upon the famous mark owner or the goods or services of the famous mark owner."

through any other media of his choice"[66] – would be flatly disregarded. This does not mean that the proposed exception exposes the trademark owners to unfounded accusations: if an individual or institution misuses his freedom of expression, through the dissemination of defamatory messages against the holder of a reputable trademark, the aggrieved party always has recourse to the courts in order to punish the author of the libel.

The second and third components of the proposed exception were designed having as their models the fair use-type test proposed by Justice Sachs in the ruling by the Constitutional Court of South Africa in the *Laugh It Off case*, and the proposed amendment to art. 17 of TRIPS, put forward by the research project "IP in Transition Research Programme," headed by Annette Kur and Marianne Levin.[67] The goal of both components of the proposed exception is to prevent the dilution of the distinctiveness of the parodied trademark, or through the establishment of confusion between the parody and the parodied trademark, or through the tarnishment of the parodied trademark, as a result of the disclosure of *false* information about the company that utilizes the parodied trademark in the course of trade or about the products and services bearing it.

The proposed exception does not prevent the use of parodies in the course of trade. A parody may be affixed to products that serve essentially as a means of disseminating critical messages conveyed by the parody. In concrete terms, this implies that parodies of trademarks may be affixed, for example, to garments, bags, pens, mugs, caps, posters or stickers.

A parody of a trademark may also be used in the course of trade as an identifying sign of origin of the products and services that bear it. In short, parodies may be used as trademarks. The organization that uses a parody as a trademark must observe two requirements, which aim to prevent its use as a tool of unfair competition.[68] First, the parody may not be confused with the trademark that is the object of parody, so as to prevent consumers being misled. Second, the packaging of the products that bear the parody should not be confused with the packaging of the products that bear the parodied trademark. It is natural that a parody establishes an association with the parodied trademark. However, the parody will only be legitimate if it is able to communicate to the public that it is not the parodied trademark. In this context, the Court of Appeals

[66] Art. 19(2) ICCPR. [67] See Kur and Levin 2006.

[68] These two requirements are inferred from the ruling of the Court of Appeals of the 4th Circuit in the *Louis Vuitton case*.

of the 4th US Circuit in *Louis Vuitton Malletier SA* v. *Haute Diggity Dog, LLC*, held:

> While a parody intentionally creates an association with the famous mark in order to be a parody, it also intentionally communicates, if it is successful, that it is *not* the famous mark, but rather a satire of the famous mark... It is important to note, however, that this might not be true if the parody is so similar to the famous mark that it likely could be construed as actual use of the famous mark itself.

To conclude, it is essential to clarify the apparent contradiction of proposing an exception designed to safeguard the right to freedom of expression, that prohibits the use of parodies that convey particular messages. In fact, this limitation on the exercise of the right to freedom of expression is not random or abusive; it simply reflects a requirement set by the ICCPR, which states that the right to freedom of expression should be restricted to the extent necessary "for respect of the rights or reputations of others" and "for the protection of national security or of public order (*ordre public*), or of public health or morals"(art. 19(3)).

6.3.1 *Assessment of the legality of the parody and criticism exception*

The parody and criticism exception is lawful, provided it has a "limited" character and takes into account the legitimate interests of the affected trademark owners and of third parties (art. 17 TRIPS).

As previously mentioned,[69] an exception to the exclusive rights conferred by trademarks shall be considered limited, provided it observes the limits set by the TRIPS Agreement enshrined in arts. 3, 4, 18 and 21. The exception under review fully observes the clauses on national treatment and most-favored nation (arts. 3 and 4), as it affects the trademarks owned both by nationals and foreigners. The parody and criticism exception complies with the obligations set by arts. 18 and 21 TRIPS, since it does not curtail the term of protection of a registered trademark, neither does it prejudice the right of trademark holders to license them, nor does it establish a surreptitious scheme of compulsory licensing of trademarks. Finally, the proposed exception is incapable of preventing the protection of distinctive signs that, in accordance with art. 15 of TRIPS, should be eligible to receive protection. The exception under review should be considered "limited."

The parody and criticism exception passes the scrutiny of the last step of the test set out in art. 17 TRIPS, in that it safeguards both the

[69] See Chapter 3, section 3.4.

legitimate interests of the owner of the affected trademark to preserve the distinctiveness of their trademarks and the legitimate interests of third parties, namely, the interests of a social, economic and environmental nature provided by art. 8 of the TRIPS Agreement.[70]

The exception under review actually safeguards the distinctiveness of affected trademarks for the following reasons. Firstly, the mention of trademarks in speeches and in any sort of writing is an activity that trademark owners should not control, as these activities fall outside the purely commercial sphere. Secondly, the exception only authorizes the dissemination and commercial use of parodies which are unfit to be confused with the parodied trademarks. Thirdly, the exception prohibits the dissemination of parodies conveying false information about the owners of the parodied trademark, as well as about their products and services. Consequently, the exception does not affect unfairly the reputation of the parodied trademark. Finally, the proposed exception prevents the release of parodies conveying scurrilous messages, capable of damaging the reputation of the parodied trademark. Finally, the exception is structured so as to prevent the practice of acts of unfair competition, the unjust destruction of the reputation of brands, products and services and the use of distinctive signals that can mislead the consumer about the source of the products, services and messages disseminated.

The parody and criticism exception aims to prevent trademark owners from exercising their exclusive rights for the purpose of silencing voices potentially harmful to their individual interests. In other words, the proposed exception aims to preserve the right of others to freedom of expression, which comprises the right to freely receive and impart opinions and criticism about the conduct of the private sector. Besides being universally recognized,[71] the right to freedom of expression is treated by the United Nations,[72] UNESCO,[73] the ECtHR[74] and by the ICHR[75] as one of the cornerstones of democracy. The undisputed value of freedom of expression to democracy is well summarized by the following excerpt,

70 See Chapter 3, section 3.4.

71 See art. 19, UDHR; art. 19(1), ICCPR; art. 13, American Convention on Human Rights; art. 9, African Charter on Human and People's Rights.

72 See, e.g., UNGA, Resolution 59(1), December 14, 1946.

73 See UNESCO, C/Resolution 4/9.3/2 of 1978 (Declaration on Fundamental Principles concerning the Contribution of the Mass Media to Strengthening Peace and International Understanding, to the Promotion of Human Rights and to Countering Racialism, Apartheid, and Incitement to War).

74 See, e.g., ECtHR, *Barthold* v. *Germany* (Application no. 8734/79), March 25, 1985, para. 58.

75 See, e.g., ICHR, *Perozo y otros* v. *Venezuela*, January 28, 2009, para. 116.

taken from the 2009 report of the Special Rapporteur on freedom of expression of the Inter-American Commission on Human Rights:

> the Inter-American Commission and Court have underlined in their case law that the importance of freedom of expression within the catalogue of human rights also stems from its structural relationship to democracy. This relationship, which has been characterized by the bodies of the Inter-American human rights system as "close," "indissoluble," "essential," and "fundamental" – inter alia – explains in large part the interpretive developments on the issue of freedom of expression in the various pertinent decisions of the Commission and the Court. The link between freedom of expression and democracy is so important that, according to the Inter-American Commission, the very purpose of Article 13 of the American Convention is to strengthen the operation of deliberative and pluralistic democratic systems through the protection and promotion of the free circulation of information, ideas and expression of all kinds. Likewise, Article 4 of the Inter-American Democratic Charter characterizes freedom of expression and freedom of the press as "essential components of the exercise of democracy." Similarly, the freedom of expression rapporteurs of the UN, the OSCE and the OAS recalled in their first Joint Declaration of 1999 that "freedom of expression is a fundamental international human right and a basic component of civil society based on democratic principles." Indeed, the full exercise of the right to express one's own ideas and opinions, and to circulate all available information, as well as the possibility of deliberating in an open and uninhibited manner about the matters that concern us all, is an indispensable condition for the consolidation, functioning and preservation of democratic regimes. The formation of an informed public opinion that is aware of its rights, citizen control over the conduct of public affairs and the accountability of public officials, would not be possible if this right was not guaranteed. In this same sense, the case law has emphasized that the democratic function of freedom of expression deems it a necessary condition to prevent the consolidation of authoritarian systems and to facilitate personal and collective self-determination, as well as to insure that 'the mechanism of citizen control and complaints' functions.[76]

The goal pursued by the exception under review is authorized by art. 8(1) TRIPS, as freedom of expression is a public interest of vital relevance to the progress of any democratic country. It is also authorized by art. 8(2) of the same treaty, since it allows WTO Members to adopt measures designed to prevent the abuse of IPRs by right holders.

The exception is a suitable means to achieve the goal that inspired its proposition, as it authorizes others: to make comments about the activities of the holders of trademarks and about the products and services that bear their trademarks; to disseminate critical messages through parodies;

[76] See Botero 2009, 213–215, para. 8.

and to use parodies in the course of trade, regardless of any authorization. Considering that the exception safeguards both the legitimate interests of the affected trademark owners as well as the interests of third parties, it should be considered lawful.

7 Industrial designs and the repair exception

7.1 Introduction

WTO Members "shall provide for the protection of independently created industrial designs that are new or original" (art. 25(1) TRIPS). A good definition of industrial design is the one adopted by the Brazilian Industrial Property Act (art. 95, LPI), which provides: "An industrial design is considered to be any ornamental plastic form of an object or any ornamental arrangement of lines and colors that may be applied to a product, that provides a new and original visual result in its external configuration, and that may serve as a type for industrial manufacture."

The role of the registration of an industrial design is to confer on its holder a monopoly on the outer appearance of a product, but not monopoly on the product that bears it.[1] Design protection functions as a stimulus for innovation for two basic reasons. First, by adding value to functional products, industrial designs help to differentiate them from other competitors and place the goods bearing the most valuable designs in a better competitive position. The owners of the industrial designs which occupy the best market position have a better *chance* of recouping their investments and raising funds for future creative projects.[2] Second, design protection encourages economic actors to continuously advance new designs in order to make their products more attractive to consumers and therefore more competitive.

A central objective pursued by design protection is to safeguard free competition between products. That is the reason why, for example, the holder of a protected industrial design applied to a watch has the right to prevent others from producing and selling watches that incorporate its design,[3] but not the right to enjoin third parties from developing watches that incorporate other designs.[4] Protection of the functional product behind the design is a concern of patent law, not of industrial

[1] See ECAR 2006, 7. [2] *Ibid.*, 10. [3] See art. 26(1) TRIPS.
[4] Sigmund 2005, para. 1.6.1.2.

design law.[5] In short, design protection is a tool for promoting innovation through competition. When this branch of intellectual property law works properly, a product that embodies a protected industrial design represents only a portion of the relevant market.

There are two categories of products whose plastic outward appearance is subject to legal protection: the one-unit product and complex products. To the first category belong those products that in case of damage cannot be repaired, as well as those products whose market prices do not justify their repair. In case of damage to a one-unit product, the feasible alternative available to the consumer concerned is purchasing a new one identical or similar to the damaged good. A vase is a good example of a one-unit product. To the category of complex products belong those products whose external plastic form is made up of several components. In case of damage, the broken parts of a complex good can be easily replaced with identical spare parts in order to recover its original appearance. Cars, motorcycles, watches and home appliances are examples of complex products.[6]

Design protection becomes a source of competition and a consumerist issue in those countries whose legal framework bestows on the owners of industrial designs applicable to complex products the right to control the primary market of these goods – i.e. the market for new products that incorporate protected designs – as well as their secondary market – i.e. the market of spare parts. Must-match spare parts are visually identical to those parts that make up the external configuration of complex products, e.g., fenders, bumpers, rearview mirrors and hoods. For example, in the event of a car accident, in order to recover its external appearance, the owner of the damaged car will have to purchase spare parts identical to those affected, since they are the only ones able to replace them due to the need for a perfect fit and also because they are the only ones able to restore the original appearance of the vehicle. Thus, must-match spare parts do not have market substitutes.

In some jurisdictions, where the owners of protected industrial designs applicable to complex products are entitled to control the primary and secondary markets for these goods, they are the sole providing source of spare parts for the products incorporating their designs. Under these circumstances, they can take advantage of their monopolistic position and set abusive prices. So far, these problems primarily affect the car industry, but it is possible that other sectors, where there is a strong demand for spare parts, will be affected in the future.

[5] See ECAR 2006, 6. [6] See Commission of the European Communities 2004b, 5.

Extending legal protection to spare parts injures the function of industrial design law, as it establishes "a product monopoly on the secondary market, contrary to the fundamental nature of legal protection of designs":[7] the registration of industrial designs, when it extends legal protection to spare parts, is incapable of fostering the development of new industrial designs and of ensuring free competition, given that consumers of spare parts do not seek diversity. They just seek spare parts identical to those that make up the damaged complex product. As there is no room for competitors to develop substitute products, the holder of the protected industrial design becomes a true monopolist in the secondary market.[8] In this case, the holder of the design receives more commercial benefits than his title is able to justify; instead of receiving a just reward for the design, he receives an excessive reward, by virtue of his monopoly.[9]

In those countries whose laws do not indicate unequivocally whether the holders of industrial designs have the right to control the secondary market for spare parts, right holders, in particular in the car industry, tend to make use of this omission to sponsor a maximalist interpretation of the scope of their rights, which is detrimental to the companies operating in the spare parts sector and to consumers. Under these circumstances, competition law is one of the branches of law which may be employed to prevent legal abuses. In actual practice, does competition law make unnecessary the enactment of exceptions to the rights granted to the holders of protected industrial designs?

The present chapter attempts to answer this question by analyzing the ANFAPE case, which puts three global giants of the car industry up against hundreds of small and medium-sized Brazilian manufacturers of spare parts. The chosen case suggests that competition law may not be able to prevent, *with the necessary speed and efficiency*, the performance of abuses by the holders of protected industrial designs. Based on this finding, the second part of the chapter examines a proposal for a repair exception, discussed in the context of the European Union, which appears to be able to harmonize the interests of the owners of industrial designs with the interests of consumers and of other market agents. Its legality is then examined vis-à-vis art. 26(2) TRIPS.

7.2 ANFAPE case

In April 2007, the Brazilian Association of Automotive Parts Manufacturers (ANFAPE or Association), a Brazilian non-profit association,

[7] See Sigmund 2005, para. 5.3. [8] See ECAR 2006, 7–8. [9] *Ibid.*, 10.

representing a growing number of independent manufacturers of automotive spare parts (IMASPs), filed before the Secretariat of Economic Law of the Ministry of Justice of Brazil (SDE),[10] a complaint against Volkswagen Car Industry of Brazil Ltda. (Volkswagen), FIAT Cars (Fiat) and Ford Motor Company of Brazil (Ford), by virtue of actions in the automotive spare parts market that were alleged to infringe the Brazilian economic order.

According to data submitted by ANFAPE to the SDE, the three automakers, on the basis of the exclusive rights conferred by their industrial designs registered with the Brazilian Institute of Industrial Property (INPI), had recently been filing lawsuits against IMASPs and retailers of automotive spare parts. The automakers requested the immediate cessation of the manufacture and marketing of automotive spare parts which infringed their industrial designs, as well as the cessation of the use of their registered trademarks and industrial designs in promotional flyers and packaging.[11] In simpler words, these automakers had been exercising their exclusive rights both in the primary market (new vehicles market, where automakers compete) and in the secondary market (spare parts market, "where automakers provide 'original' spare parts, and independent manufacturers provide 'parallel' spare parts").[12]

ANFAPE argued that the exercise of the exclusive rights conferred by registered industrial designs in the secondary market constituted an abuse of rights, since the registered designs had the sole function of preventing competing automakers from producing cars bearing designs which were identical or substantially similar to those under protection.[13]

ANFAPE stressed in its complaint that, for decades, manufacturers and retailers operating in the secondary market and automakers had coexisted in harmony. The former only started to become the target of judicial and extrajudicial threats from 2006/2007 onwards.[14] These facts were an indication that the exercise of the rights conferred by the protected industrial designs on the secondary market should not be treated as a normal means of exploitation of the industrial designs. This view is confirmed by the fact that only three automakers – amongst the many which operate in the Brazilian market – had been undertaking legal actions against IMASPs and retailers of spare parts.

The Association argued that the exercise of the rights conferred by industrial designs in the secondary market prejudiced free competition and consumers, as the owners of motor vehicles are only allowed to

[10] The Secretariat of Economic Law of the Ministry of Justice of Brazil (SDE), the Brazilian Administrative Council for Economic Defense (CADE) and the Secretariat for Economic Monitoring make up the Brazilian System of Competition Defense.

[11] See Farina and Tormin 2007, 4–5.

[12] See SDE 2008, 3.

[13] See Farina and Tormin 2007, 12.

[14] *Ibid.*, 6.

purchase the spare parts provided by automakers.[15] Whereas on the secondary market automakers may "exercise their monopoly power in an unrestricted way," they enjoy the prerogative of setting excessive prices for spare parts.[16]

The Association pointed out that if automakers enjoyed the right to control both the primary market for new cars and the secondary market for spare parts, they would be able to control the speed of renewal of the car fleet. If maintenance costs became too high, consumers would be compelled to frequently replace their cars.[17] Considering that, at present, even in a competitive scenario, automakers tend to charge higher prices for "original" spare parts than those marketed by IMASPs, it is reasonable to expect that the costs of car maintenance will grow even more, as a result of the prohibition of competition in the secondary market.[18]

Although the complaint is silent about the environmental damage arising from the strategy followed by automakers, it is noteworthy that the reduction of the longevity of durable, expensive and highly polluting goods produces perverse and undesirable environmental effects in the current context, in which humanity faces the challenge of finding new ways to provide universal access to the material advances achieved during the twentieth century, without jeopardizing the future of the earth and of its inhabitants.

ANFAPE added that many of the registrations owned by the automakers could be null and void – notably, those which cover the design of bumpers, fenders, mirrors and headlights – because in its view, the plastic form of these parts is primarily determined by functional considerations. Accordingly they did not meet the legal requirement of being an ornamental plastic form or an ornamental arrangement of lines and colors that can be applied to a product (art. 95, LPI).[19]

Based on these arguments, ANFAPE concluded that the legal strategies implemented by the automakers constituted horizontal restraints on competition, as well as a violation against the economy because they created "difficulties for the establishment, operation or for the development of a competing company" (the IMASPs), in order to dominate the secondary market and to abuse their dominant position. In fact, in the absence of the competitive pressure exerted by the IMASPs, the defendant automakers would control 100 percent of the market for spare parts for the vehicles manufactured by them. In order to investigate and repress the allegedly illegal actions performed by the automakers to the detriment

15 See Araújo Jr. 2006, 2. 16 *Ibid.*, 6. 17 See Farina and Tormin 2007, 7.
18 See Araújo Jr. 2006, 7. 19 Farina and Tormin 2007, 13–14.

of the Brazilian economic order, ANFAPE requested SDE to immediately commence administrative proceedings. In addition, the Association requested the Brazilian Administrative Council for Economic Defense (CADE) to implement a number of sanctions against the automakers, among them, the application of a fine amounting to thirty percent of the gross revenue of the automakers achieved in 2006, and the compulsory licensing of the protected industrial designs misused by the automakers.

7.2.1 *SDE's ruling*

In response to ANFAPE's complaint, SDE commenced a preliminary inquiry, where it assessed the existence of evidence of anticompetitive conduct warranting the establishment of administrative proceedings and the application of sanctions against the automakers.[20] SDE interpreted the facts and the relevant Brazilian statutes in an unbalanced fashion: on the one hand, it overvalued the arguments raised by the automakers, associated with the need to shield IPRs as a means of protecting their investments in R&D and, on the other, overlooked the socio-economic impacts arising from this approach. It is noteworthy that SDE rejected the requests made by numerous labor unions, interested in taking part in the proceedings as third parties.[21] The labor unions intended to bring to the proceedings information about the prejudices caused to consumers, to the domestic industry and to local workers, should the legal stance adopted by the defendant automakers be endorsed.

SDE absorbed uncritically the arguments of the automakers and ruled there was no legal basis for an antitrust intervention, for the following reasons. To start with, SDE elucidated that "CADE's case law with regard to the automotive industry traditionally divided the relevant market from the point of view of the product as follows: (1) the market controlled by the manufacturers of new vehicles, (2) the retail market for new vehicles, (3) the wholesale market for spare parts [operated by the manufacturers of spare parts] and (4) the retail market for spare parts."[22] In the context of the complaint, SDE adopted the retail market for spare parts, where car dealerships and independent autopart retailers operate, as the relevant market in the case.[23]

SDE's report did not investigate the respective participation of automakers and of IMASPs in the retail market of spare parts.[24] It would be pertinent to investigate the participation of automakers in this market

[20] See SDE 2008 (proceedings no. 08012.002673/200 7–51). [21] *Ibid.*, 30.
[22] *Ibid.*, 31. [23] *Ibid.*, 32–33. [24] *Ibid.*, 38–39.

in order to clarify whether they hold a dominant position in this niche.[25] This is so because the case law of CADE makes having a dominant position a precondition for characterizing conduct, aimed to undermine free competition, as a violation of the economic order.[26]

Backed by antitrust decisions rendered by American and European authorities, SDE ruled that the primary and secondary markets are interdependent. Therefore, the preservation of free competition in the primary market of new vehicles was a suitable means of counteracting the market power of automakers in the secondary market.[27] In addition, SDE held that the continuous expansion of the net of businesses specialized in the sale of auto spare parts was enough to preserve competition in the secondary market, *although the suppliers of all these businesses occupy a monopolistic position in the market.*[28] In the process of building its position, SDE seems to have overlooked an investigation carried out by the Commission of the European Communities in 2004, which found that, in the European countries which extended design protection to spare parts, automakers charge for original spare parts prices between 6.4 and 10.3 percent higher than the ones they practice in the jurisdictions where this legal protection is not available.[29]

In respect of the argument brought by ANFAPE that the recognition of the right of automakers to control the primary and secondary markets would lead to the closure of IMASPs, SDE thought it empty of substance, because the legal protection conferred upon the owners of registered industrial designs is time-limited (up to twenty-five years).[30] So IMASPs could freely manufacture the spare parts in the public domain. In addition, these companies could still engage in the manufacture of tuning autoparts.[31] SDE seemed unaware that the average life cycle of a car model is about five years and that the average life of passenger cars is thirteen years.[32] Therefore, when the proprietary industrial designs move

[25] Pursuant to art. 20, § 3, Law no. 8.884/94, "The dominant position is presumed when a company or group of companies controls twenty percent (20%) of the relevant market; this percentage is subject to change by CADE for specific sectors of the economy."

[26] See Maciel Neto 2009, para. 81. [27] SDE 2008, 40. [28] *Ibid.*, 40–41.

[29] Commission of the European Communities 2004b, 4. The same study estimates the price differences between original and parallel auto spare parts in Germany and in the US: original spare parts are up to 223% more expensive than those provided by IMASPs (25–27).

[30] See SDE 2008, 42.

[31] According to Oliveira *et al.* (2009, 39) "tuning autoparts are those that have as a fundamental characteristic to be differentiated in respect to the original part of the car. Thus, consumers interested in tuning autoparts aim to personalize the cars with changes in the headlamps, bumpers, wheels, tires, mirrors, and various other car parts."

[32] See Commission of the European Communities 2004b, 21.

into the public domain, the market for the relevant spare parts is negligible or nonexistent. SDE also overlooked the fact that *tuning* parts should not be treated as a substitute for registered spare parts, because each category of autoparts serves "different interests and consumers' expectations." Since a consumer is usually motivated to purchase a vehicle for its external appearance, it is natural that when the time comes to repair it he chooses to restore its original appearance.

From the economic viewpoint, SDE held that the exclusive control of the secondary market by automakers is a legitimate means of ensuring the recovery of their "substantial" investment in R&D.[33] SDE embraced the standard mantra echoed by the holders of IPRs, without confirming whether the expenses incurred by carmakers in the development of the exterior body of a new car model are actually substantial. In actual fact, automakers invest the equivalent of 4.2 percent of their revenues on the research and development of a new car model (mechanics and design), but the development of the exterior of a new model consumes only 0.7 percent of their revenues In monetary terms, this means that between 50 and 60 euros of the price paid by the end consumer of a new *luxury* car is sufficient to cover the investments incurred by automakers in the development of its exterior body (body, glass, headlights, etc.).[34] It is therefore unnecessary to ensure such broad exclusive rights to automakers in order help them to recoup their investment in R&D.[35]

From the consumer's viewpoint, SDE considered as justifiable the exclusion of IMASPs from the secondary market and the high prices charged by automakers for the so-called "original" spare parts. In its view, the spare parts produced by automakers had a much higher quality compared to those manufactured by independent companies. In addition, the average consumers and service technicians struggle to differentiate the "original" spare parts from the parallels.[36] SDE's statements departed from the unproven premise that spare parts provided by IMASPs have inferior quality and also pose a danger to consumer's safety and free will. SDE's identification of a causal relationship between the lower prices charged by independent manufacturers and the low quality of their products represented a superficial examination of the issues. Even if the spare parts produced by IMASPs are of lower quality, it should be recalled that the issue of quality of the spare parts is irrelevant to the case, because "design protection is meant to reward the intellectual effort of the creator of a design, and not to safeguard its technical functions or quality . . . It follows that it is right to describe design protection and safety as being

[33] See SDE 2008, 43. [34] *Ibid.* [35] See European Union 2004.
[36] See SDE 2008, 46.

on two different conceptual levels."[37] In the intellectual property sphere, trademarks may play the role of performing quality control of the products that bear them and patents are the most appropriate legal tool to ensure protection for the technical features of patented goods.[38] The use of design protection for purposes not authorized by law – for example, ensuring the quality of spare parts – is an abuse of rights that should be resisted.[39]

Still from the consumerist perspective, SDE emphasized that automakers, after ceasing the production of any car model, are bound by the Brazilian Consumer Code (art. 32) to keep supplying the secondary market for a reasonable period of time, while IMASPs are not bound by this obligation. Recognition of the right of automakers to control the secondary market would be a fair means of recovering the investments made to meet a legal obligation.[40]

SDE held that nothing in the text of the Brazilian Industrial Property Act suggests that the rights conferred by registered industrial designs should extend only to the primary market for new products. Thus, automakers are entitled to control the use of their registered designs in *all* markets. In other words, "the legislature did not differentiate between primary market ("foremarket") and secondary market (aftermarket) for automotive spare parts. Once the INPI grants protection to a certain industrial design, the registration granted extends protection to both markets."[41]

As regards the argument raised by ANFAPE that automakers have been exercising their property rights at odds with their social function, SDE noted that "the fulfillment of the social function of property rights results from their full economic use, regardless of any other non-economic criteria."[42] There is no doubt that such an approach is unsustainable, basically because the social function of IPRs goes beyond their economic function.

Respect for the social function of IPRs comes from their application in carrying out their social purpose – that is, the reason that motivates their recognition – provided the limits set by third party rights (e.g. consumers) and by the legal order in general are observed. Design protection has "the sole purpose of... grant[ing] exclusive rights to the appearance of a product, but not a monopoly over the product as such;... protecting designs for which there is no practical alternative would lead in fact

[37] See Sigmund 2005, para. 4.6.
[38] See Commission of the European Communities 2004b, 33.
[39] See Comissão Europeia 2004b, 35. [40] See SDE 2008, 46.
[41] *Ibid.*, 2. [42] *Ibid.*, 53.

to a product monopoly; . . . if design protection is extended to spare parts . . . competition is eliminated and the holder of the design right is de facto given a product monopoly."[43] In other words, as stated by the European Economic and Social Committee "the essential precondition for a design premium – that a market exists and consumers can exercise preferences – does not apply if design protection is extended to the spare parts covered by the repair clause."[44]

Moreover, when a consumer buys a new car, the industrial design has completed its legal role, having served as a powerful marketing tool whose function was to entice the consumer to choose a particular vehicle, among those available in the market.[45] At the time of the purchase of a new car, the consumer satisfactorily remunerates the automaker for its investment in the development of the industrial design incorporated in the car body. If the secondary market for industrial designs is exclusively controlled by automakers, consumers will be paying a fresh amount for the industrial designs incorporated in their cars every time they purchase a spare part.[46] Recognition of the right of automakers to control the exploitation of their industrial designs in the primary and secondary markets allows them to be unjustly enriched on the secondary market. Therefore, there is no legal justification for being rewarded more than once for a single contribution, especially when it is recalled that the expenses associated with the design of a car body are low.[47] Consequently, the interpretation argued by automakers and endorsed by SDE violates the general principle that prohibits unjust enrichment and should be discarded.

Briefly, SDE dismissed the complaint filed by ANFAPE, as it considered that the automakers exercise their IPRs on a proper basis; so there was no legitimate reason for an antitrust intervention. According to SDE, there would be room for such intervention if automakers had abusively registered industrial designs ineligible for legal protection or if they had endeavored to exercise their rights in spheres not subject to their legitimate control.[48] Reflecting the view that IMASPs are free-riders that must be repelled,[49] SDE also decided to send the records of the administrative proceedings to the National Council against Piracy and Intellectual Property Crimes and to the National Department of Consumer Protection, so

[43] Comissão das Comunidades Europeias 2004, 1st recital of the Proposal for a Directive of the European Parliament and of the Council amending Directive 98/71/EC on the legal protection of designs.

[44] Sigmund 2005, para. 1.6.1.7. Along the same lines see Commission of the European Communities 2004b, 30.

[45] Commission of the European Communities 2004b, 45.

[46] Commission of the European Communities 2004a, 7.

[47] See ECAR 2009, 3.

[48] SDE 2008, 2.

[49] *Ibid.*, 47.

these governmental agencies could take the appropriate measures against IMASPs. The decision pronounced by SDE was appealed to the CADE board.[50] The CADE board is made up of a president, six counselors, a general-attorney and a member of the Federal Public Prosecution Office.

7.2.2 Efforts to reverse SDE's ruling

Since March 2008, when SDE decided to dismiss ANFAPE's complaint, ANFAPE has been trying to persuade the board of CADE to order the bringing of administrative proceedings against the three automakers referred to above. ANFAPE has sought to clarify the theoretical misconceptions used by SDE to ground its decision. In the arguments raised by ANFAPE there are five points of particular importance.

First, ANFAPE argued that "industrial designs are two- or three-dimensional creations conceived to give a new exterior aspect to the object to which they apply."[51] Design protection only affords protection to the full plastic form of a creation, but not to its individual parts. With regard to cars, automakers are only entitled to claim protection for the full body design of vehicles, but not for the component parts of the body design. Claiming protection for the constituent parts of the car body consists of an abusive act, not sanctioned by law. Therefore the registrations of industrial designs that cover isolated parts of a whole are legally invalid.[52] "Strictly speaking, taken in isolation the form of auto spare parts is essentially determined by their technical and functional purpose."[53] The form and appearance of must-match auto spare parts are devised to allow the restoration of the damaged appearance of the relevant complex product. Thus, spare parts are not eligible for design protection, pursuant to art. 100, II of the Brazilian Industrial Property Act, which provides "An industrial design is not registrable for: the necessary common or ordinary shape of an object or, further, that which is determined essential by technical or functional considerations."

Secondly, ANFAPE reiterated that design protection bestows on the automakers the right to control the primary market for new vehicles, but not the secondary market for spare parts, since the exclusive control of the latter "restricts the alternatives available to consumers, leads to the arbitrary increase of profits and reinforces the dominant position enjoyed by automakers."[54]

50 Pursuant to art. 7 (IV), Law no. 8.884/94, the CADE board is competent to "resolve *ex officio* appeals from the SDE Secretariat."

51 Silveira 2009, 19. 52 *Ibid.*, 25–33. 53 See Serrano and Tojal 2009, 7.

54 Oliveira *et al.* 2009, 8.

ANFAPE emphasized that in the Brazilian constitutional order, free competition and IPRs are legitimate concerns that share the same hierarchical status. In this context, the local antitrust authority should assess, according to the circumstances of the case, which concern should prevail by virtue of its greater relevance to society. In the specific case of auto spare parts the protection of free competition generates greater social welfare than the exclusive control of the secondary market by automakers, and thus the local antitrust authority has the duty to set limits on the exercise of the exclusive rights stemming from the registered industrial designs.[55]

Thirdly, ANFAPE refuted the view held by SDE that independent manufacturers produce poor quality "pirated" spare parts.[56] IMASPs pay taxes, "provide formal jobs and work, not infrequently, under ISO certified processes."[57] Many of these companies have been operating in Brazil for more than four decades.[58] ANFAPE also sought to prove with empirical data that the independent industries do not promote their businesses through the practice of acts of unfair competition, able to mislead consumers on the origin of spare parts, but through the affixation of their own trademarks on their spare parts and packaging.[59]

Fourthly, ANFAPE argued that it was incorrect to include in the same relevant market "car dealers, independent retailers of spare parts and the independent manufacturers of spare parts associated with ANFAPE [IMASPs]," since producing and distributing spare parts are different activities.[60] The approach adopted by the SDE "masks the dominant position of the automakers in several markets of spare parts and, accordingly, hides the negative competitive effects arising from the control of the secondary market by the holders of protected industrial designs."[61] When a consumer purchases a new car model, he may only purchase spare parts compatible with his car. Once the cars are highly differentiated, spare parts, in general, have no substitutes. Due to the specific characteristics of each autopart and the high costs involved in the setting-up of production lines, each independent manufacturer tends to be specialized in the production of a certain category of spare parts – e.g. door handles, locks, hoods or doors. Consequently, there are several relevant markets for auto spare parts, which should be considered by antitrust authorities when assessing whether automakers hold a dominant position in each of those markets and offend the economic order. There is no single relevant market, covering all categories of auto spare parts:

[55] *Ibid.*, 11, 60–61. [56] *Ibid.*, 11. [57] *Ibid.*, 15. [58] *Ibid.*, 17–18.
[59] *Ibid.*, 30–31. [60] *Ibid.*, 33. [61] *Ibid.*, 64.

Considering the characteristics of auto spare parts and the extreme differentiation adopted by automakers, the relevant market in terms of demand should be set according to the car model and vehicle part... Thus, as a general rule, we have the relevant market for left headlights for GM's Celta; the relevant market for Ford's K hoods, among others.[62]

Finally, ANFAPE argued that the position endorsed by SDE is highly detrimental to consumer interests, as the total abolition of free competition in the secondary market: confers on automakers the freedom to set prices in monopolistic conditions; reduces the availability of auto spare parts in more remote sites; and seriously endangers the future of independent repairers, which, in the absence of IMASPs, will have to resort to authorized dealers and distributors of spare parts.[63]

In January 2009, PROCADE, the office of the Attorney General of CADE, issued an opinion against the bringing of administrative proceedings against Fiat, Ford and Volkswagen. PROCADE basically adopted the same line of reasoning as SDE. In PROCADE's view, the preliminary investigation carried out by SDE provided insufficient proof that the automakers held a dominant market position in the secondary market for auto spare parts, guaranteed by their registered industrial designs,[64] even though a document submitted by ANFAPE pointed out that those automakers controlled about 80 percent of the market for spare body parts.[65]

Nevertheless, PROCADE adopted the presumption that the automakers held a dominant position in the market for auto spare parts, in order to prove that there was no justification for bringing administrative proceedings against them. PROCADE hastily concluded there were no legal grounds for such proceedings, for the following reasons. Firstly, the Brazilian Industrial Property Act did not exempt the manufacturing and marketing of spare parts for the restoration of the original appearance of complex products.[66] Secondly, CADE had already commenced three administrative proceedings devoted to investigating whether automakers employ excessively high prices for the autoparts supplied to their dealers, so there would be no reason to commence a new proceeding with a similar object.[67] Thirdly, the judicial and extrajudicial measures filed by automakers are not abusive since they rely on legitimate property titles, granted by INPI.[68]

From a competition law perspective, PROCADE deemed irrelevant the arguments put forward by ANFAPE in respect of the alleged practice

62 *Ibid.*, 34–35 (free translation). 63 *Ibid.*, 58–59.
64 Maciel Neto 2009, paras. 34, 38, 44 and 73. 65 ANFAPE 2008, 9.
66 Maciel Neto 2009, para. 86. 67 *Ibid.*, para. 88. 68 *Ibid.*, para. 90.

of abuse of rights by the automakers and the disrespect for the social function of design protection,[69] even though the Brazilian Competition Act (Law no. 8.884/94) is explicitly "driven by the constitutional dictates of free enterprise, free competition, social function of property, consumer protection and restraint of abuses of economic power" (art. 1). Despite the objectives pursued by Law no. 8.884/94, PROCADE overlooked the alleged negative economic impacts pointed out by ANFAPE that may arise from the confirmation of the legality of the control of the secondary market by the automakers, notably: the full control of a US$27 billion/year market, which employs nearly 1.5 million people; the potential closure of around 2,000 small Brazilian IMASPs, which not only supply the Brazilian market but also export their products to the US, South America, Europe, the Middle East and Asia; the possible arbitrary increase in the prices of autoparts and the maintenance costs of cars and the suppression of the freedom enjoyed by consumers in the secondary market.[70]

In March 2010, a member of the Federal Public Prosecution Office (MPF) issued an opinion in favor of the bringing of administrative proceedings to investigate the conduct of the automakers. In his view, SDE's report and the legal opinion issued by PROCADE overlooked the future impact on consumers' interests, resulting from the recognition of the right of automakers to monopolize the spare parts market. Moreover, SDE and PROCADE had failed to investigate whether the automakers, in fact, needed to control the secondary market in order to recoup the capital expenditures on R&D, and they wrongly endorsed the unproven assumption that non-original spare parts are of poor quality and are a source of insecurity to consumers.[71]

On December 15, 2010, CADE's board unanimously ordered SDE to initiate immediately an administrative proceeding, with the purpose of ascertaining whether Fiat, Ford and Volkswagen had committed a violation of the economic order, namely, an abuse of dominant position in order to hinder or impede the activities of competitors in the market for auto spare parts.[72] The rapporteur of the case, counselor Carlos Emmanuel Ragazzo, held that there were no legal, economic or

[69] *Ibid.*, para. 76. [70] See ANFAPE 2008.

[71] See Aras 2010, 6–8. On the issue of quality, the public prosecutor made an interesting observation: "Data collected . . . and submitted by ANFAPE . . . show that about 70% of the companies operating in the secondary market for spare parts were established before the 1980s. Even though, on average, these companies are small, they represent a significant number – about 2,000. Thus, in principle, it is unlikely that a consolidated segment with so much uptime and disseminated across the country, has an output that is subject to the quality issues suggested by SDE's report" (free translation).

[72] Ragazzo 2010, paras. 225 and 260.

consumerist grounds for the automakers to exercise the exclusive rights guaranteed by their registered industrial designs in the secondary market for spare parts:

> the exclusivity claimed by the automakers to the detriment of IMASPs is not justifiable by virtue of: (a) the need to recoup the investments incurred in the research and development of spare parts, the subject of the present proceedings, since such costs appear to be low and they are more than recovered at the time of sale of new vehicles. And even if IMASPs are allowed to operate in the secondary market, the profits gained by automakers in the aftermarket would remain significant; (b) the need to maintain incentives for innovation, because . . . the release of new products in the car industry focuses on the primary market for vehicle sales, and not on the secondary market for spare parts; (c) the need to ensure the quality and safety of autoparts, because . . . design protection is not intended to guarantee quality or safety of products; there are more suitable means of achieving these goals; (d) the need to prevent independent spare parts being falsely marketed as original ones, as this objective can be achieved through . . . other legal standards; and (e) the need to avoid "cream skimming" practices, since there is neither evidence that the maintenance of stocks of spare parts by automakers generates extra costs in relation to those borne by IMASPs, nor that these stocks are not profitable.[73]

Due to its deleterious social, economic and consumerist effects, Ragazzo held that the exercise of the exclusive rights conferred by registered industrial designs in the secondary market for auto spare parts constituted

> (a) an abusive exercise of the industrial property in question, insofar as it distorts its socio-economic goal, established by the Brazilian Constitution, namely, to foster "the social interest and the technological and economic development of the country" (art. 5, XXIX); (b) a legally disproportionate means [of protecting industrial designs], because it severely compromises the right to free competition, consumers rights and the repression of the abuse of economic power, and does not provide society with any consideration in terms of furthering the goals pursued by industrial property rights; and (c) a potential violation of the Brazilian Competition Act (Law no. 8884/94), as it represents an abuse of dominant position with the purpose of preventing or hindering the activities of competitors; such abuse can result in potentially damaging effects on the economic order.[74]

If SDE's investigations confirm that the automakers have committed an offense against the economic order, CADE has already stated that the necessary measure to be applied in the case, with the purpose of eliminating the prejudice to the economic order, would be to enjoin the

[73] *Ibid.*, para. 259, item (vi) (free translation).
[74] *Ibid.*, para. 259, item (viii) (free translation).

automakers from exercising their exclusive rights, guaranteed by registered industrial designs, against IMASPs, and to apply appropriate fines.[75]

Given the difficulties encountered in using, with efficiency and speed, competition law as an extrinsic limit to the exclusive rights enjoyed by automakers, in March 2009, ANFAPE filed a complaint with the Department of Consumer Rights and Economic Order of the Federal Prosecution Office of the state of Rio Grande do Sul, which was later forwarded to the Federal Prosecution Office of Rio de Janeiro (MPF). In this complaint, ANFAPE reiterated the same points raised in the complaint submitted to SDE, but emphasized the present and future losses inflicted on consumers by the exclusive control of the secondary market by automakers. According to ANFAPE, the practices carried out by automakers with the purpose of controlling the secondary market for spare parts engender the following prejudices to consumers' interests: "(i) the loss of savings and the decreasing household living standards; due to the high price of spare parts, many families will not be able to maintain their cars; (ii) the increase in unemployment rates due to closure or drastic reduction of the number of independent companies; (iii) the increase in violence due to increase in the number of burglaries and thefts of vehicles, spurred by a demand for cheaper spare parts, unmet by the automakers; (iv) the sharp increase in the costs of insurance resulting from the virtual increase in risks."[76] Based on this, ANFAPE requested the MPF to commence a public inquiry to investigate the alleged abusive actions committed by the automakers to the detriment of free competition, free enterprise and consumers' rights, and to take immediate legal action to ensure the freedom for IMASPs and other companies (e.g. retailers of spare parts) to operate in the secondary market for auto spare parts). In August 2010, the MPF began investigating the allegedly illegal practices carried out by Volkswagen, Fiat and Ford.[77]

In short, although competition law may function as an extrinsic limit on IPRs, the difficulties faced by ANFAPE in employing it for this purpose suggest that well-designed and clear legal exceptions explicitly incorporated into intellectual property statutes are more secure tools to safeguard the interests of a socio-economic nature, since their use is independent of case by case State interventions whose results are always uncertain. The only certainty is that administrative and judicial proceedings are expensive and complex. It is noteworthy that the difficulties related to the application of competition law as a tool for limiting IPRs are not

[75] *Ibid.*, para. 259, item (x). [76] See Fonseca and Monteiro 2009, 11–12.
[77] See Fontes 2010.

exclusive to Brazil. Regarding the issue of freedom of IMASPs to operate in the secondary market for auto spare parts, in *AB Volvo* v. *Erik Veng (UK) Ltd.* the European Court of Justice held:

> It must . . . be noted that the exercise of an exclusive right by the proprietor of a registered design in respect of car body panels may be prohibited by Article 86 if it involves, on the part of an undertaking holding a dominant position, certain abusive conduct such as the arbitrary refusal to supply spare parts to independent repairers, the fixing of prices for spare parts at an unfair level or a decision no longer to produce spare parts for a particular model even though many cars of that model are still in circulation, provided that such conduct is liable to affect trade between Member States.[78]

The first and third hypotheses rarely occur and the second one is difficult to prove.

The challenges faced by ANFAPE to ensure the right of IMASPs to keep operating in the secondary market for auto spare parts may emerge in any of the WTO Members. Bearing this in mind, the next section presents a repair exception proposed by the European Commission in 2004, which was designed to overcome the competition and consumerist problems identified in this chapter, arising from the unclear scope of the exclusive rights granted to the holders of industrial designs. The European repair exception will then be examined, to see whether it passes the test set out in art. 26(2) of the TRIPS Agreement.

7.3 European proposal for a repair exception

In October 1998, the EC adopted Directive 98/71/EC on the legal protection of industrial designs. At the time of its drafting, the EC unsuccessfully tried to include a repair exception in its text, whose object was to exclude the manufacture, sale and use of must-match spare parts from the scope of the rights conferred on the holders of industrial designs, such exclusion to begin to apply three years after the first marketing of complex products which embody protected industrial designs.[79] This proposal was rejected by automakers, who wanted more than three years of exclusivity in the secondary market.

A proposal for an exception was then submitted that would allow independent manufacturers to produce and market independent spare parts immediately after the registrations of industrial designs, provided they paid an equitable remuneration to right holders.[80] This proposal,

[78] ECJ, *AB Volvo* v. *Erik Veng (UK) Ltd* (Case 238/87), para. 9.
[79] See Sigmund 2005, para. 1.6. [80] *Ibid.*, paras. 1.8–1.9.

in turn, was rejected by independent producers of spare parts due to its operating costs.

Due to the lack of consensus, EC Member States compromised on introducing into the draft of what would become Directive 98/71/EC a transitional provision (art. 14), whereby the Member States of the EC whose legal orders already include a repair exception in that moment, are not entitled to revoke it. Legislative reforms may only be directed to liberalize the secondary market for spare parts. This solution is known as a "freeze-plus solution." The transitional arrangement produced the unintended effect of dividing the European market into two groups: the group that includes those countries which have enacted a repair exception (Belgium, Spain, the Netherlands, Hungary, Ireland, Italy, Latvia, Luxembourg and the UK) and the group of countries that extend design protection to spare parts (the other 16 EU Member States).[81]

With the firm intention of correcting this source of trade distortion and to restrict the participation of automakers in the market for spare parts – in 2004, 85 percent of this market was under the control of automakers[82] – Directive 98/71/EC obliged the European Commission to put forward, in 2004, a study on the effects produced by the Directive on Community industry, consumers, competition and on the functioning of the European market, and to submit it to the European Parliament. The Directive also dictates that the EU Council, no later than 2005, shall put forward a proposal for amendment of the referred Directive, with a view to adopting a unified solution to the problems created by the division of the European market for spare parts (art. 19).

In 2004, the European Commission commissioned an extended impact assessment from the French consulting company Technopolis, which investigated the pros and cons of four proposals for the amendment of art. 14 of Directive 98/71/EC,[83] which, in principle, seems able to overcome the problems created by the design protection of the component parts of complex products. The four alternatives examined by the study will be briefly outlined below, as well as the strengths and weaknesses identified by the Technopolis report.

Alternative 1: exclusive protection for a short period of time

The first alternative grants to the owners of protected industrial designs the exclusive control of the secondary market for a short period of time, e.g. three years. After the expiry of the term of protection, the owners

[81] See Sigmund 2005, para. 2.4.2.
[82] See Commission of the European Communities 2004b, 13. [83] *Ibid.*

of industrial designs applied to complex products retain the ability to exclusively control the use of their designs in the primary market of new products, while independent companies can freely produce and commercialize spare parts to supply the secondary market.[84]

Recalling that the life cycle of a car model is, on average, five years and that passenger cars have a lifespan of approximately thirteen years, this alternative was considered unable to promote the specific objectives pursued by the European Union, namely: removing the obstacles that prevent the creation of a single European internal market; generating new jobs within the European Union; strengthening small and medium-sized local businesses; increasing European exports of spare parts to markets that do not grant design protection to the component parts of complex products; reducing maintenance costs of automobiles and increasing consumers' welfare. This is so because, depending on the duration of the exclusive rights afforded to the holders of registered designs, it may be economically unfeasible for independent manufacturers to invest in the production of spare parts, as there is insufficient time to recover the investments incurred in the setting-up of new production lines. For these reasons, the holders of registered designs end up retaining de facto control of the secondary market.[85]

Alternative 2: Remuneration system

The second alternative examined by Technopolis ensures to independent manufacturers, immediately after the registration of industrial designs, the right to produce spare parts to supply the secondary market, against the payment of an equitable remuneration, whose calculation base is the sales results of spare parts.[86] If the remuneration system is associated with an efficient pricing mechanism, capable of setting a reasonable fee with no hassles, this option at first seems able to further the consumerist and competition objectives pursued by the EU.

Nevertheless, this option may involve not insignificant problems. First, setting up an administrative structure to manage the remuneration system and to monitor the payment of royalties is not cost-free. If these costs are borne by the independent manufacturers, they will be reflected in the prices of their products. This will certainly impact on their competitiveness and interest in operating in the secondary market.[87] Second, the task of setting royalties at a reasonable level is not an easy one. If a pricing system is established that involves the participation of the interested parties, the negotiation of acceptable royalties for all of them may

[84] *Ibid.*, 17. [85] *Ibid.*, 21. [86] *Ibid.*, 17. [87] *Ibid.*, 40.

consume too much time, and this can lead to the postponement of the introduction of competing spare parts in the secondary market. Third, depending on the structure of and powers vested in the management organization, the owners of industrial designs may resort to litigation to make the system inefficient and unattractive to independent industries, by arguing that the royalties due have not been paid or requesting an increase in the fees due. Such threats could produce inhibitory effects on the companies operating in the secondary market.[88]

Alternative 3: Combination of options 1 and 2

The third alternative examined by Technopolis grants to the owners of industrial designs the right to exploit them, exclusively, in the secondary market for a short period of time. After the expiry of this period of exclusivity, independent manufacturers can produce and commercialize spare parts to supply the secondary market upon payment of an equitable remuneration to the holders of the used designs.[89]

The problems created by the third option are the result of the association of the problems related to the other two alternatives discussed above: if independent manufacturers, besides enjoying a short period of time to recoup the investments incurred in the setting-up of new production lines, still have to pay fees to the owners of industrial designs, only a few companies will remain willing to operate in the spare parts market. In summary, this alternative also produces the impact of keeping the control of the spare parts market in the hands of the owners of protected industrial designs.[90]

Alternative 4: Non-onerous repair exception

The fourth alternative reviewed by Technopolis is a repair exception that allows independent manufacturers, without the need to pay any fees to the holders of registered designs, to produce and commercialize must-match spare parts and to exclusively supply the secondary market. The only obligation on independent manufacturers is to inform their customers of the origin of the spare parts supplied in order to avoid misunderstandings and unfair practices. The purpose of this alternative is to prevent the exercise of the exclusive rights conferred on the holders of protected industrial designs in a manner that prejudices free competition and consumers' welfare.

[88] *Ibid.*, 21. [89] *Ibid.*, 17. [90] *Ibid.*, 22.

Among the alternatives investigated, the fourth one was deemed the most suitable to promote free competition and the social interests pursued by the EU. In 2004, the European Commission, based on the results of the study carried by Technopolis, proposed to amend art. 14 of Directive 98/71/EC, with the purpose of enacting a non-onerous repair exception to the rights conferred on the holders of industrial designs. In December 2007, the European Parliament made some adjustments to the proposal originally put forward by the European Commission and approved it.[91] Approval of the amendment by the European Council is pending. As amended by the European Parliament, the proposed repair exception now has the following wording:

Article 14
Designs incorporated in component parts used for repair purposes

1. Protection as a design shall not exist for a design that is incorporated in or applied to a product which constitutes a component part of a complex product and is used within the meaning of Article 12(1) for the sole purpose of the repair of that complex product so as to restore its original appearance. This provision shall not apply where the primary purpose of putting the aforesaid component part on the market is other than the repair of the complex product.
2. Paragraph 1 shall apply provided that consumers are duly informed about the origin of the product used for the repair by the use of a marking, such as a trade mark or a trade name, or in another appropriate form so that they can make an informed choice between competing products offered for use in effecting the repair.
3. Paragraph 1 shall apply only in respect of visible component parts in the after market once the complex product is marketed in the primary market by the holder of the design right therein or with his consent.

There is no doubt that the introduction of a non-onerous repair exception, which prevents the holders of protected industrial designs from controlling the production and marketing of spare parts aimed at supplying the secondary market, is a satisfactory measure for promoting free competition, stimulating the growth of small and medium-sized enterprises, reducing maintenance costs of complex products and restricting the room available for the practice of economic abuses by the holders of industrial designs. In addition, it is clear that among the alternatives investigated by Technopolis, this is the one that most interferes with the economic interests of the owners of industrial designs – more specifically, with the interests of the automotive industry. The open question is whether the option embraced by the European Commission, which seems suitable to be transplanted to the legal orders of industrialized

[91] See European Parliament 2007.

and developing countries, complies with the requirements laid down by art. 26(2) of the TRIPS Agreement.

7.4 Assessment of the lawfulness of the European repair exception

7.4.1 First step

The exception under review will pass the scrutiny of the first step of the test if it presents limited character. As previously seen,[92] the assessment of the limited character of an exception to the rights conferred by industrial designs comprises a three-stage process. Firstly, the interpreter must evaluate whether the exception pursues any of the goals authorized by art. 8 TRIPS, including any of the general objectives pursued by the WTO system. Next, the interpreter must assess the suitability of the exception to accomplish the objectives that motivated its adoption. Finally, the interpreter must assess whether the exception observes the minimum obligations set out in the TRIPS Agreement.

The repair exception has as main objectives:

- strengthening free competition in the market for spare parts;
- strengthening outsourcing companies that manufacture autoparts for automakers: if the repair exception is enacted, the former can meet the demand from automakers and still supply the secondary market with the same products. With the expansion of the market available to these companies, their survival will no longer depend on the orders placed by automakers;[93]
- intensifying competition in the market of repair services. Since independent repairers will have access to a wider range of sources of supply of spare parts, they will enjoy greater chances of competing with authorized repairers, which as a rule, only deal with original spare parts;[94]
- encouraging small and medium-sized enterprises, given that independent manufacturers of spare parts are usually small and medium-sized companies; and
- reducing maintenance costs of complex products, notably of cars;[95] this, in turn, extends their lifespan.

[92] See Chapter 3, section 3.5.
[93] See Commission of the European Communities 2004b, 20. [94] *Ibid.*
[95] A report by ECAR (2009, 4) notes that "Many official investigations amply demonstrate that car manufacturers had to decrease their spare parts prices by at least 30–40% whenever competition arose or was admitted." The reduction of maintenance costs also leads to reduced auto insurance costs.

The objectives pursued by the repair exception have competitive, environmental and consumerist characteristics. There is nothing in the WTO/TRIPS system precluding the adoption of an exception aimed at accomplishing them. To prohibit the owners of industrial designs applied to complex products to exercise their exclusive rights in the secondary market of spare parts, as already seen, is an appropriate means to fulfill the objectives pursued by the repair exception.

Regarding the minimum obligations set by TRIPS, the repair exception fully observes them: the application of the repair exception does not prevent the protection of those categories of industrial designs that, pursuant to art. 25(1) and (3) TRIPS, should be eligible to receive legal protection, since it simply enjoins the holders of industrial designs to exercise their exclusive rights in the secondary market of spare parts. In addition, the repair exception affects in the same manner industrial designs owned by nationals and foreigners; so it does not create any kind of discrimination (arts. 3 and 4). Finally, the exception under review does not curtail the term of protection afforded to industrial designs (art.26 (3)). In view of the above, the repair exception should be considered as limited.

7.4.2 Second step

The second step of the test set out in art. 26(2) TRIPS has the function of assessing whether the proposed exception unreasonably interferes with the normal exploitation of the affected industrial designs. The repair exception will satisfy the second step of the test if the measure is one that, among the measures reasonably available to the proponent State, affects to a lesser extent the rights bestowed on the owners of industrial designs.

In this phase, the starting point is to investigate whether the exception affects any market that the owners of protected industrial designs have the *legitimacy* to control. In keeping with the view held by the WTO Panel in *Canada – Pharmaceutical Patents*, the only means of exploiting industrial designs that should be considered normal are those employed by all or most of the rights holders, with the purpose of adding value to functional products, differentiating them and making them more competitive.[96]

Despite the undeniable economic value of the secondary market, holders of protected industrial designs are not entitled to exercise their exclusive rights in this market for several reasons. First, if legitimacy for the

[96] WTO, WT/DS114/R, Panel Report, paras. 7.55 and 7.58.

owners of industrial designs to control the secondary market were recognized, the car industry would be the only sector to gain monopolistic control of the market for spare parts. An interpretation that produces the effect of ensuring discriminatory treatment in favor of one sector is not appropriate. And even in the automotive sector, not all automakers claim the right to control the production and marketing of auto spare parts. For example, in Brazil, out of the many automakers that operate in this market, so far only three (Fiat, Ford and Volkswagen) have claimed the right to control the secondary market for spare parts.

Second, the social function of design protection is fully met through the exercise of exclusive rights in the primary market for new products. So there is no valid reason to include in its scope the control of the secondary market.[97]

Third, it is not legally defensible to define "normal exploitation of industrial designs" so as to ensure for the car industry a dominant position in the secondary market. This would open up wide room for economic abuses, especially because TRIPS is not complemented by an agreement governing competition issues.

Fourth, in those countries that provide the holders of industrial designs with the right to control the secondary market, automakers tend to use the gains earned from the sale of auto spare parts to subsidize the prices of spare parts not protected by IPRs (mechanical parts, for example) and, consequently, are subject to free competition. In short, in this case the profits are used to undermine free competition, since independent manufacturers of autoparts do not have the same tool to keep their products competitive.[98]

Fifth, considering that the average lifespan of a car model is five years and that of passenger cars thirteen years, if the duration of the protection granted to industrial designs of spare parts is at least ten years – as required by art. 26(3) TRIPS – when these designs fall into the public domain, independent manufacturers will have no economic incentives to produce them, because the consumer demand will be very limited. In this context, in practical terms, the exclusive rights enjoyed by the automakers will not be time-bound, but eternal, in the sense that industrial designs will be kept in the private domain as long as they bear significant economic importance. Turning a time-limited right into a right of de facto unlimited duration attacks the foundations of intellectual property law.

Finally, the exercise of exclusive rights in the secondary market represents an abuse of rights, since it enables the holders of industrial designs

[97] Commission of the European Communities 2004b, 47.
[98] See ECAR 2009, 8.

to be unjustly enriched at the expense of consumers, who pay two or more times as much for the same design.

Briefly, the interpretation that produces discrimination among rights holders is not correct, that turns industrial designs into de facto patents, able to completely suppress competition in the market for spare parts; it gives the car industry the power to unjustly enrich itself at the expense of consumers; and it restricts the options for supply sources of spare parts.

For these reasons, the repair exception does *not* interfere with the normal exploitation of protected industrial designs, given that right holders are not entitled to control the use of their designs in the market for spare parts.[99] Consequently, it is unnecessary to evaluate the availability of alternative measures to the one under review.

Strictly speaking, the adoption of a non-onerous repair exception is not a condition for independent manufacturers to enjoy the freedom to produce and market independent spare parts aimed at supplying the secondary market. This exception is only necessary to create legal certainty for the economic actors, to prevent the commencement of costly and unnecessary disputes and industrial design being applied in a way that prejudices free competition and consumer interests.

7.4.3 Third step

The final step of the test in art. 26(2) TRIPS aims at assessing the reasonableness of the prejudices caused by the exception under review to the *legitimate* interests of the owners of industrial designs: that is, whether the total social benefits generated by the exception outweigh the prejudice to the legitimate interests of the holders of protected industrial designs.

The owners of protected industrial designs – in fact, the carmakers – might argue that the adoption of a non-onerous repair exception prevents the amortization of the expenses incurred on R&D activities. In response to the loss of exclusive control of the secondary market, they are forced to raise the prices of new vehicles and, accordingly, their sales suffer. This reasoning, however, is fraught with problems. First, as mentioned above, investment in the development of the outer appearance of cars is low, being easily recoverable through the high prices of new cars. Since investment incurred in the development of new car models is fully recoverable from the sales made in the primary market, there is no legal ground to confer on the holders of industrial designs monopolistic control of the secondary market.[100] Second, it is not the function of design

[99] See Commission of the European Communities 2004b, 28.
[100] See Drexl *et al.* 2005.

protection to turn the secondary market into a source of subsidies for the purchase of new cars. Third, the wide competition in the primary market ensures that the prices of new cars will not rise, by virtue of the enactment of the exception under analysis.[101] Fourth, the introduction of competition in the secondary market does not mean that automakers will be excluded from this market. Empirical data shows that in the European countries that do not grant design protection to spare parts, automakers control between 85 and 95 percent of the secondary market.[102] In view of the enactment of the repair exception, the only prejudice suffered by the holders of industrial designs is the loss of the right to charge monopoly prices for spare parts.[103]

Even if the liberalization of the market for spare parts causes automakers economic losses, the repair exception will successfully satisfy the third step of the test. Not only because the total social benefits engendered – consolidating free competition, increasing the welfare of consumers, creating new jobs, strengthening small and medium-sized enterprises, reducing maintenance costs of complex products and increasing the longevity of durable goods – far outweigh any losses suffered by the automakers; but above all, because the exception under review only affects a market that the owners of industrial designs are *not* entitled to control, while it keeps intact their right to control the use of their designs in the primary market for new products. Therefore, the exception does not prejudice any *legitimate* interest held by the owners of industrial designs.

The repair exception proposed by the European Commission, accordingly, complies with all the requirements set out in art. 26(2) of the TRIPS Agreement, and may indeed be adopted by any WTO Member. The fact that Australia, Belgium, Spain, the Netherlands, Hong Kong, Hungary, Ireland, Italy, Poland, Latvia, Luxembourg, Malaysia, the UK and Singapore have adopted non-onerous repair exceptions lends support to the analysis suggested here.[104]

[101] See Commission of the European Communities 2004b, 18. [102] *Ibid.*, 21.
[103] See Drexl *et al.* 2005. [104] See Aoki 2009, 301–302.

8 Copyright and the educational exception for underprivileged students and researchers

Everyone has the right to read
(Art. 1, Charter of the Book)

8.1 Introduction

The Berne Convention (BC) is one of the pillars of the TRIPS Agreement, which incorporates by reference its arts. 1–21 and annex (art. 9(1) TRIPS). In relation to the Berne regime, TRIPS has made some important updates, notably the inclusion of the obligation to protect computer programs and compilations of data or other materials as literary and artistic works (art. 10), and the obligation to ensure, at least to the holders of computer programs and cinematographic works, "the right to authorize or to prohibit the commercial rental to the public of originals or copies of their copyright works" (art. 11).

Although, in theory, the rationale for ensuring broad exclusive rights to copyright holders is to encourage creative activity and to widen the dissemination of works for the benefit of cultural progress, in practice contemporary copyright regimes, premised on the BC, over-protect the economic interests of copyright holders by affording to them the right to prevent the dissemination, transformation, adaptation, translation and parallel importation of copyrighted works during a absurdly long period of time. Contemporary copyright regimes have reached the point of preventing the production of photocopies of copyrighted works, even when they are sold out, as well as their translation to meet the demands of markets overlooked by copyright holders. In such cases, the public can only use them when they fall into the public domain. By then, potential users may no longer be alive or the works of interest may be outdated.

In response to the problems engendered by the BC, developing countries in the 1960s mobilized efforts to amend it in order to facilitate the dissemination of works in their countries and the sociocultural development of their peoples. These countries achieved very little. All they got was the appendix to the BC (Paris Act, 1971), which allows the contracting parties developing countries to grant compulsory licenses for the translation and/or reproduction of literary works for educational purposes. The procedures governing the compulsory licensing of these exclusive rights is so complex and intricate that they make the mechanism established by TRIPS to govern the compulsory licensing of patents seem a paragon of efficiency. Not surprisingly, the procedure introduced by the appendix of the BC has fallen into disuse.

In the face of the obstacles set by the BC to the socio-cultural progress of developing countries, one would expect that these countries would endeavor to make the best use of the flexibilities offered thereby. However, since the core of the BC was transplanted to the TRIPS Agreement, we witness the "updating" of the copyright regimes of developing countries, aimed exclusively at safeguarding the economic interests of copyright holders. As a result of this policy, according to a recent survey conducted by Consumers International, out of a group of thirty-four copyright laws, the eight laws that most limit access to knowledge belong to developing countries: Egypt, Zambia, Brazil, Argentina, Thailand, Kenya, Jordan and Chile.[1]

The *Copy/South Dossier*, edited by Alan Story, Colin Darch and Deborah Halbert, points out the main updates made by developing countries in their copyright laws, for the purpose of restricting access to knowledge: extending the term of copyright protection, expanding the list of works eligible for copyright protection, the curtailment of the roster and scope of copyright exceptions and the legal protection of technological measures.

Developing countries often extend the term of copyright protection beyond the period required by art. 7 (1) BC, which encompasses "the life of the author and fifty years after his death." Since the term of protection of copyrights is excessive, when a work finally falls into the public domain, it may be outdated. This observation is especially applicable to educational and scientific works.

Developing countries also tend to expand the list of exclusive rights granted to copyright holders, even when they are not legally required to do so. There are, for example, a growing number of developing countries, which are not parties to the WIPO Copyright Treaty (WCT), which provides copyright holders with the right of communication to the public as defined by art. 8 of the WCT. This right was designed to allow copyright holders to control the use of their works on the internet.

In parallel with the unnecessary expansion of the list of rights granted to copyright holders, copyright legislation in force in developing countries

[1] See Consumers International 2010.

tends to significantly restrict the scope of copyright exceptions. One of the ironies of international copyright regimes – and intellectual property regimes in general – is that copyright holders enjoy a certain minimum level of protection on a global scale, while users of works, whose interests are protected by, inter alia, copyright exceptions, enjoy a strictly national protection: within the limits permitted by international intellectual property law, each State is free to adopt the exceptions it deems appropriate.[2] Within the freedom guaranteed to them, developing countries tend to adopt few copyright exceptions, which not infrequently have little practical relevance to users of protected works.

If the narrow scope of the copyright exceptions incorporated into the legal orders of developing countries was not already problematic enough, one is faced with their being deprived of any force by copyright holders. In respect of works in digital format, copyright holders tend to protect them through the adoption of technological measures designed to prevent access to or the unauthorized copying of copyrighted works. The WCT and the WPPT[3] require its Contracting States to adopt legal measures of a civil and/or criminal nature, in order to deter users from circumventing technological measures added to copyrighted works.[4] These measures not only serve to protect the legitimate rights of copyright holders. They also interfere with the rights of users to make use of the exceptions provided by law. Thus, they constitute an instrument for practicing abuse of rights. This is so because the States that choose to ensure legal protection for technological measures tend to overlook their statutory duty to compel copyright holders to offer users effective means to enforce the rights guaranteed by copyright exceptions, when access to their works is hindered by technological measures.[5]

The legal measures indicated, often adopted by developing countries, have retroactive effect; thus they benefit pre-existing works. It is hard to believe that these amendments could create incentives for creativity, when many of the benefitted works were created prior to their enactment.[6]

Although the social benefits resulting from these legislative amendments are possibly insubstantial, its evils are concrete. According to the Copy/South Dossier and the final report of the Commission on Intellectual Property Rights, contemporary copyright regimes impose many obstacles on the progress of developing countries. Among those identified, six are noteworthy.

[2] See Story *et al.* 2006, 133. [3] Art. 11 WCT; art. 18 WPPT.
[4] See Story *et al.* 2003, 104–118. [5] See Ricketson 2003, 83–84.
[6] See Story *et al.* 2006, 93–94.

First, copyright regimes hinder the proper functioning of educational programs (including distance-learning programs) designed to meet the needs of poor students. The reproduction and distribution of copyrighted works (textbooks, scientific articles, illustrations, pictures, etc.) is a *sine qua non* for the success of any education program.[7] If access to these materials depends on the approval of copyright holders and, therefore, on the payment of fees, possibly only a small proportion of students will have the means to attend these courses, since the costs associated with copyright are generally borne by students.[8]

Second, copyrights impede the translation of foreign works into the languages of developing countries, impoverishing cultural diversity. By opposing the translation of their works into the languages spoken in developing countries, copyright holders encourage the perpetuation of the inequitable character of these societies, since their decision produces the undesirable effect of giving exclusive access to those individuals that master the languages spoken in industrialized countries.[9] By virtue of the obstacles created by copyrights, many copyrighted works do not circulate on a global scale.[10] If the circulation of works is limited, because of language barriers, cultural prejudices tend to perpetuate.

Third, copyright hinders access to works by the visually impaired and by those with other physical disabilities. In many countries, the conversion of protected works to Braille or to other accessible formats for people with physical disabilities depends on the authorization of copyright holders and therefore on the payment of a remuneration.[11] As the conversion process to other formats is quite expensive, any additional cost dramatically impacts on its accessibility by people with disabilities, which, in most cases, have scarce resources to meet their basic needs.[12] Moreover, the adoption of the principle of national exhaustion of IPRs prevents the lawful importation of works produced in other markets, under the aegis of a copyright exception or under the protection of a license granted by the copyright holders. This means, for example, that the expenses already incurred in country A to convert a given work to Braille will be incurred again in country B, if it adopts the principle of national exhaustion of rights.[13]

7 *Ibid.*, 95. 8 See Commission on Intellectual Property Rights 2002, pp. 102–103.
9 See Story *et al.* 2006, 99. 10 *Ibid.*, 136. 11 *Ibid.*, 106.
12 According to the World Health Organization, in 2009 there were approximately 314 million visually impaired people worldwide. 87% of this group live in developing countries. 85% of the cases of visual impairment and 75% of the cases of blindness could have been prevented if these people had had access to health services and medicines (WHO 2009).
13 Story *et al.* 2006, 130.

Fourth, copyright interferes with the conservation of cultural heritage. Libraries, public or private, are facing problems in the digitization of their collections of works in order to perpetuate them for the benefit of future generations. This is so since any reproduction of copyrighted works, even for non-commercial purposes, generally depends on the authorization of copyright holders.[14] Furthermore, today it is an ordinary practice for libraries to purchase subscriptions to digital libraries and databases. As a rule, the licenses governing access to these databases prohibit subscribers from making copies of the works comprised in the electronic collections. Once the subscription expires, library users can no longer access the works of the digital library.[15]

Fifth, copyrights impair the quality of teaching. With the high prices of copyrighted works, public schools and libraries are struggling to obtain many of the resources demanded by students, teachers and researchers. And when they manage to get the needed materials, they do not have enough copies to meet the needs of the public.[16] Teachers try to compensate for the lack of copies through the organization of "teacher´s folders" made up of all mandatory course readings, which are made available in libraries or copyshops, located in the vicinity of educational institutions. However, as the possibility of resorting to photocopying in many poor countries has been restricted by modern copyright laws, the demand for books and other educational materials remains unmet.[17] Even if educational institutions agree to obtain onerous licenses, which confers on them the right to photocopy copyrighted works to meet the needs of their faculty and students, this task may not be easy to carry out. When the relevant country hosts a copyright collective management organization (CMO) for reprographic rights, responsible for granting licenses on behalf of its members, this organization may represent a small spectrum of copyright holders. If the CMO does not represent the owners of the works of interest, the interested party will have to make Herculean efforts to identify and locate each of the relevant copyrights holders and try to negotiate individual reprographic licenses. When the relevant copyrights holders are foreign individuals or companies, the task becomes even harder. After the identification and location of the relevant copyright holders, the difficulties may persist, since they can always demand the payment of too costly fees. Ultimately, the process of obtaining licenses on reasonable terms may be too time-consuming and expensive, undermining the activities of educational and research institutions.[18]

[14] Commission on Intellectual Property Rights 2002, 103–104.

[15] Story *et al.* 2006, 108.

[16] *Ibid.*, p.110; Commission on Intellectual Property Rights 2002, 103–104.

[17] See Story *et al.* 2006.

[18] *Ibid.*, 112–113.

Finally, copyrights may restrict freedom of expression. As a result of the ongoing expansion of the scope of copyrights, accompanied by the parallel decline of the diversity and scope of copyright exceptions, libraries, educational institutions and individuals from developing countries face difficulties in obtaining updated works in satisfactory quantity and variety. This state of affairs restricts the ability of individuals to access, create and disseminate new knowledge and ideas and to hone their intellectual skills and critical capacity. Even the moral rights of authors (art. 6 *bis*, BC), secured to them to protect their reputation and honor, may be exercised so as to restrict the freedom of expression of others. Holders of moral rights may impede the circulation of translations of their works, or the changing of their format of presentation or the detachment of a book chapter from the whole, by arguing that these activities prejudice their honor and reputation.[19]

This chapter illustrates the recent changes suffered by the copyright laws of developing countries with a case study taken from Brazil.[20] It shows how the Brazilian legislature, as has happened in other developing countries, has chosen to focus excessively on the economic interests of copyright holders to the detriment of the rights to education and freedom of scientific and creative expression of other sectors of society. In the second part of this chapter, an educational exception is proposed, specifically designed to overcome the obstacles created by contemporary copyright regimes to the realization of the rights to education and freedom of expression vested in underprivileged students and researchers based in developing countries. Finally, the legality of the proposed exception in light of the TRIPS Agreement is examined.

8.2 The broadening of exclusive rights and the Brazilian Copyright Act of 1998

Despite the recent progress, Brazil still has many social challenges ahead. According to recent data, 35 percent of its population lacks access to enough food to meet their needs;[21] the 10 percent richest Brazilians hold 75.4 percent of the total wealth of the country and only 5,000 local families control 45 percent of all national wealth.[22] The imbalance in income distribution is reflected in the field of education: on the one hand, Brazil is already the seventh largest economy in the world, on the other hand, in 2006, among 129 countries assessed, it occupied the 80th

19 *Ibid.*, 134.
20 For a similar study about the legal-political situation in South Africa, Ghana, Senegal, Morocco, Egypt, Uganda, Kenya and Mozambique, see Armstrong *et al.* 2010.
21 Farid 2010.
22 Pochmann 2007, 16–18.

place in the UNESCO Education Index;[23] and in 2010, it occupied the 53rd position in the Programme for International Student Assessment, out of a group of 65 countries evaluated. In the cultural field, the situation is no different: a recent survey by the Ministry of Culture on access to cultural goods in Brazil pointed out that "only 14% of the Brazilians go to the movies once a month, 92% have never attended museums, 93% have never been in an art exhibition and 78% have never attended a dance performance."[24]

From the perspective of the needs of underprivileged sectors of a country like Brazil, the Copyright Act in force in Brazil in the pre-WTO period (Law 5988 of December 14, 1973) was very favorable to the legitimate interests of resource-poor students, researchers and educational institutions, once it freed "the reproduction in a single copy of any work," provided the copies produced were not for profit (art. 49, II). That is, under the umbrella of the old Copyright Act, any work could be photocopied in full by any individual for their own use, regardless of obtaining any authorization or paying any fee to copyright holders. This legal landscape has changed substantially since the enactment of the new Copyright Act of Brazil (LDA) (Law no. 9610 of February 19, 1998), passed in order to comply with the obligations taken on by Brazil before the WTO.

The new LDA goes far beyond the minimum obligations set by TRIPS. Regarding the term of protection of the economic rights enjoyed by copyright holders, the new law confers protection on the successors of authors for 70 years counted from their death (art. 41, chapeau). Regarding the list of exclusive rights granted to copyright holders, although Brazil is not a Contracting Party to the WCT or to the WPPT, it has behaved as if it were, as it bestows on copyright holders the right of communication to the public as defined by arts. 8 of the WCT and 10 of the WPPT.[25]

The Brazilian legal order gives copyright holders the residual right to control "any other form of use that exists at present or might be devised in the future" (Art. 29, X), and the right to prevent the parallel importation of original works, lawfully produced abroad by copyright holders or their licensees. Thus, if a particular book published in Brazil costs twice what the same book costs in Portugal, a Brazilian book distributor is not authorized to import this product with the purpose of increasing competition. And if a local organization tries to circumvent the ban, it

23 UNESCO 2009, 249. The UNESCO Education Index assesses the situation of a country in respect of the achievement of four goals: universal access to primary education, adult literacy, good quality of education and gender equality.

24 Ministério da Cultura 2010c, 3.

25 Art. 29 (VII) LDA.

will be subject to civil[26] and criminal penalties[27] and the imported copies may be seized and destroyed.

The substantial expansion of the scope and duration of copyrights was accompanied by an excessive restriction on the scope of the exceptions devised to further access to knowledge for research and educational purposes. The LDA does not provide any exception for the benefit of libraries in order to facilitate the conservation of its collections for present and future generations. Quite the opposite. The library director who orders the reproduction of works contained in the library's collection, in any medium or format without the permission of the relevant rights holders, will be subject to a prison sentence of up to four years,[28] to a fine, and to the payment of compensation for damages to the aggrieved rights holders. In addition, any copies produced with the aim of perpetuating the collection of the institution may be seized and destroyed.[29]

So far the LDA does not provide an exception that allows the use of copyrighted works in the realm of online distance-learning programs, even if promoted for the benefit of underprivileged students. The Brazilian legal system makes anyone responsible for managing a course of this nature, which reproduces copyrighted literary works without authorization, subject to a prison sentence of up to four years,[30] to a fine, to the payment of compensation to the aggrieved right holders, and to the confiscation of any computers and equipment used to perform acts of copyright infringement (arts. 103, 105 and 106, LDA).The disproportionate nature of the criminal penalties applicable to copyright infringements can be better understood by comparing those penalties with the penalties under art. 38 of the Environmental Crimes Act (Law 9.605/98), which punishes the act of destroying or damaging a forest located in an area of permanent preservation with a prison sentence of one to three years *or* a fine. This means that up to this point in Brazil, the unauthorized reproduction of a copyrighted work is subject to a harsher punishment than is the destruction of a part of the Amazon rainforest.

In the education field, the LDA is limited to providing two exceptions: a quotation exception (art. 46, III), which in fact is a matter of mandatory adoption by all Contracting Parties to the BC (art. 10(1)), and a private copying exception, which permits "the reproduction in one copy of short extracts from a work for the private use of the copier, provided that it is done by him without gainful intent" (art. 46, II). Because of the

[26] Art. 102 LDA. [27] Art. 184 § 2°, Brazilian Penal Code (Decree-Law 2848/40).
[28] Art. 184 §§ 1° e 2°, Brazilian Penal Code. [29] Art. 103 LDA.
[30] Art. 184 §3°, Brazilian Penal Code.

ambiguous wording of the latter provision, doubts remain about the activities that are exempted thereby.

Although the scope of the private copying exception seems too limited, in particular when it is compared to the private copying exception provided by the Brazilian Copyright Act of 1973, it seems that it has not been able to satisfy the demands of copyright holders. In this regard, it is noteworthy that, between 2007 and 2011, Brazil ranked annually in the Special 301 Watch List prepared by the United States Trade Representative (USTR), for not combating "book piracy appropriately."[31] In line with the demands of copyright holders, who strongly demand the combating of "book piracy," in May 2007, the then-Congressman Bilac Pinto submitted to the House of Representatives Bill 1197/2007. If approved, it will forbid *all* "operation in higher education institutions, of photocopying machines or any other mechanical or electronic device capable of reproducing literary works." In case of violation of this prohibition, the legal representative of the pertinent institution will be subject to civil penalties and to a prison sentence of up to 4 years.[32]

If the scope of the private copying exception were not sufficiently prejudicial to the interests of the underprivileged sectors of the Brazilian society, the LDA has an aggravating factor: it imposes civil penalties on anyone who "alters, removes, modifies or in any way disables technical devices that have been incorporated in copies of protected works and productions to prevent or restrict reproduction" (art. 107, I), even if the author of the offense has done so in order to make use of any of the copyright exceptions enshrined in the LDA. This implies that the copyright exceptions provided by the LDA may be waived by copyright holders, as they develop technical mechanisms to prevent the unauthorized use of their works. The civil penalty applicable to the act of altering/removing/modifying technical devices is so disproportionate that it possibly deters anyone who tries to make use of copyrighted works protected by the technical devices: the *minimum* indemnity to be paid by the violator corresponds to the market price of the number of copies made without authorization. When this figure is unknown, the offender shall pay an amount corresponding to 3,000 copies of the reproduced work (art. 103).

In short, the LDA has created an inhospitable environment for the promotion of the cultural rights of that part of the local population which has few resources to invest in its education and intellectual enlightenment. The difficulties created by the LDA can be illustrated by the conflicts

[31] See Office of the United States Trade Representative 2007, 2008, 2009, 2010 and 2011.
[32] See Pinto 2007.

experienced in Brazil stemming from the ambiguous private copying exception (art. 46, II).

8.2.1 The cumbersome Brazilian private copying exception

As already indicated, the private copying exception set out in the LDA frees "the reproduction in one copy of short extracts from a work for the private use of the copier, provided that it is done by him without gainful intent" (art. 46, II). This provision sets five cumulative conditions that must be met by the beneficiaries of the exception: (i) the individual may only reproduce "small extracts" of a copyrighted work; (ii) only a single copy of the extracts may be produced; (iii) the copy reproduced may only be used for private purposes; (iv) the reproduction should be made by the recipient of the exception; and (v) the individual shall not have any gainful intent.

In the absence of a clear limit on how much of a work may be reproduced under this exception, copyright holders seek to advocate a restrictive interpretation of the ambiguous terms of art. 46 (II), LDA. On this point, it is interesting to refer to the interpretation supported by the Brazilian Association of Reprographic Rights (ABDR or Association) of the five conditions that shall be met by beneficiaries of the private copying exception.[33]

Before moving on to the normative meaning of the five conditions according to the ABDR's view, it is essential to clarify the institutional objectives pursued by this association. The ABDR is a private non-profit organization, established in the 1990s to defend the economic interests of several private publishing houses involved in publishing technical and scientific books. Its institutional objectives are: to defend the copyrights held by its members by fighting "book piracy"; to administer a system of management of reprographic rights, which includes the licensing of reprographic licenses in favor of educational institutions and companies, and the collection and transfer of royalties to its members; to promote public awareness campaigns about the need to respect copyrights; and to represent, in and out of court, its members.[34] Although the ABDR has as one of its institutional missions to act as a CMO, through the licensing

[33] The information used in this work in respect of the interpretation supported by the ABDR has been drawn from the ABDR's website www.abdr.org.br; from the legal defense submitted by the ABDR's lawyer to the district court of São Paulo, in the context of a public civil lawsuit filed by IDCID against the ABDR in June 2006 (Morato Filho 2007); and from the legal opinion by Professor Manoel J. Pereira dos Santos (Pereira dos Santos 2007), used by the ABDR to support its defense in the context of that lawsuit.

[34] ABDR 1993[?], art.1.

of reprographic rights upon payment of fees, the association states on its website that "since December 2003, the ABDR's members have decided to no longer provide onerous licenses for the reproduction of their works due to the enormous difficulties associated with the monitoring of the effective implementation of the licenses granted."[35]

Let us now turn to the five conditions for the exercise of the Brazilian private copying exception, as interpreted according to the ABDR´s view.

Condition I: Reproduction of short extracts the ABDR argues that in Brazil copyright holders enjoy the right to full control of their works.[36] They may prohibit, inter alia: the partial or total reproduction of out of print works by students;[37] the reproduction of an illustration or a few pages of a work for the purposes of teaching in the classroom;[38] the organization of "teacher´s folders";[39] the reproduction of works by needy underprivileged students (i.e. those who are not part of the consumer market).[40] In this vein, the ABDR argues that art. 46 (II), LDA allows the reproduction of short *extracts* of a work, provided they *do not comprise* the core of the work. Consequently, any extract that reflects the core of the work can not be reproduced without the authorization of the relevant copyright holder:

> It is important to note that short extracts of a work *do not entail its substance.* "Short extract" does not refer to the extent of the reproduced extract, but to its content. Thus, any intention to associate "short extracts" with 10% or 15% of a work is absolutely inappropriate. This is so because it is possible that 10% or 15% of a work contains the core of the protected work.[41]

If the ABDR's understanding were correct, the manager of a copyshop could only reproduce a certain chapter of a copyrighted work, at the request of a college student, after examining the whole contents of the work and confirming that the chapter does not encompass the core thereof. How should a Brazilian who only speaks Portuguese, assess whether a certain chapter of a book written in a foreign language entails the core of the latter? Even if the realization of the prior assessment were viable, what would be the relevance to a student, researcher or teacher to reproduce unimportant extracts of a work, in terms of substance? In other words, the ABDR seems to argue that the Brazilian private copying exception only allows the reproduction of *qualitatively and quantitatively* insignificant extracts of a work, as a way of ensuring that copyright holders control all forms of reproduction of their works. This interpretive

[35] See ABDR 2010[?], item no. 23. [36] See Frasson 2010.
[37] See ABDR 2010[?], item no. 21. [38] *Ibid.*, item no. 22.
[39] *Ibid.*, item no. 16. [40] *Ibid.*, item no. 18. [41] *Ibid.*, item no. 5 (free translation).

alternative is impossible to implement and, therefore, has the effect of making the private copying exception devoid of any practical applicability.

In the alternative, the ABDR also considers it reasonable to interpret the expression "short extracts" as synonymous with an extract amounting to up to 3 percent of the whole work.[42] Although this alternative brings greater legal certainty than the first one, it is quite limiting of the rights of third parties to access copyrighted materials for educational purposes.

Condition II: Only a single copy of the extracts may be produced The beneficiary of the exception may only request a single copy of the extracts of interest. Thus, he is not entitled to request multiple copies thereof and share them with others, even if he does not have a gainful intent. This implies that a teacher is not entitled to make copies of an extract of a book and to distribute them to her students for classroom use, even if the school is public and is located in a marginalized neighborhood.[43]

Nor do copyshops enjoy the prerogative of printing excerpts of protected works, in advance of requests made by students. In Brazil, there are copyshops that, as soon as the syllabus prepared by the academic institutions located in their vicinity are made available, produce and store numerous copies of the reading materials listed in the syllabus, in order to meet the students' demands more rapidly. In the ABDR's opinion, this practice breaches one of the conditions laid down by the Brazilian private copying exception, as copyshops, under in these circumstances, behave as a publisher-bookstore.[44]

Condition III: Private use of the copies reproduced Copies should only be made for the personal use of end-users. They shall not be produced for commercial purposes – for example, to meet the demands of third parties – nor may they be distributed to third parties – for example, in classrooms.[45]

Condition IV: Reproduction should be made by the beneficiary. The LDA is not clear about the identity of who can reproduce short extracts of a copyrighted work. The association seems to understand that the beneficiaries of the exception must make their copies on their own initiative – e.g. the beneficiary would have to personally

[42] See Morato Filho 2007, item III.2.3., para. 26. [43] See Pereira dos Santos 2007, 23.
[44] Ibid., 22–23. [45] See Morato Filho 2007, item III.2.3, para. 21.

handle the photocopy machine.[46] This understanding reflects the current practice in research institutions and universities based in industrialized countries, where students and researchers manage photocopy machines to make their own copies. Nevertheless, this is not the reality in Brazil, where small copyshops provide reprographic services to students upon payment of small fees, directed to cover the expenses associated with printing supplies and human resources. If students, teachers and researchers are not allowed to resort to copyshops, reprography may be banned as an instrument of access to knowledge in Brazil.

In the alternative, the Association also considers as acceptable the view that copies made by copyshops at the request of the *direct* beneficiary of the private copying exception are lawful, provided the other four conditions set forth by the exception are met.[47]

Condition V: Lack of gainful intent The Association argues that both end-user and the copyshop have duties to fulfill. An individual may benefit from the private copying exception if he uses the copy made "in a private setting and if he has no gainful intent."[48] In the case of copyshops, only those acting in "good faith" may reproduce copies for others.[49] In the opinion of the Association, copyshops act in bad faith and, therefore, outside the ambit authorized by the exception for private copying, if they: reproduce and store copies of copyrighted works, in order to meet more easily third parties' demands; make copies beyond the limits set by the LDA; have as their *primary* economic activity the reproduction of copyrighted works on demand.[50] According to this view, possibly many copyshops operating within the premises of universities and in their vicinity have no legitimacy to make copies of copyrighted works under art. 46 (II) of the LDA. In summary, the interpretation argued by the ABDR reflects the traditional understanding that copyright exceptions must be construed narrowly; after all they are only "exceptions."[51]

Armed with the above interpretation of the private copying exception, the ABDR promotes public awareness campaigns,[52] files complaints before police departments that specialize in combating crimes against IPRs and brings lawsuits against copyshops operating inside and outside the realm of student associations, universities and research

[46] *Ibid.*, item III.2.3, paras. 30 and 36. [47] See Pereira dos Santos 2007, 22.
[48] See Morato Filho 2007, item III.2.3.1, para. 21.
[49] See Pereira dos Santos 2007, 20. [50] See Pereira dos Santos 2007, 20–21.
[51] See Pereira dos Santos 2007, 13–14.
[52] See ABDR 2010[?], items no. 13, 15 and 19.

institutions, which have allegedly violated copyrights associated with literary and scientific works.[53]

In response to the ABDR's view of the scope of the private copying exception, some of the most prestigious universities in Brazil have approved internal resolutions addressed to the copyshops operating within their premises, with the aim of clarifying how much of copyrighted works may be freely reproduced. Thus, the University of São Paulo (USP), through Resolution no. 5213, of June 2, 2005, authorized, within its premises: the production of photocopies of book chapters and articles published by scientific journals; the reproduction of whole works which are out of print and have not been republished for more than ten years; foreign works unavailable in the domestic market; works in the public domain and copyrighted works bearing express permission to reproduce. In addition, the resolution authorizes the USP's faculty to reproduce and distribute copyrighted works to the students regularly enrolled at USP, provided the copies are essential background materials for the courses taught at the university (art. 4).[54] Also in 2005, the president of the Getúlio Vargas Foundation (FGV), through Ordinance 55/2005, adopted an internal resolution modeled on the USP's Resolution no. 5213.[55] Finally, in the same year, the Pontifical Catholic University of São Paulo, after a brief period with a total ban on reprographic activities,[56] issued a resolution which freed the reproduction of up to 10 percent of copyrighted works.

Quite possibly the USP's resolution fully meets the requirements set by the three-step test set out in art. 9(2) of the BC. Despite this fact, it drew the ire of copyright holders. In 2010, the International Intellectual Property Alliance (IIPA) submitted to the USTR a report recommending that Brazil is kept on the Special 301 Watch List because of, inter alia, the USP's Resolution no. 5213. In IIPA's view, this resolution is harmful to the interests of copyright holders once it frees the reproduction of a wide array of copyrighted works, and also serves as a role-model for other local educational institutions.[57] It is noteworthy that the IIPA report,

[53] The objective pursued by these lawsuits is the seizure of materials allegedly reproduced in violation of copyrights. Once seized, these materials are examined by experts, who will prepare a report (arts. 524–530, Brazilian Code of Criminal Procedure). This report serves as support for the filing of a lawsuit for damages. If there is enough evidence about the practice of a copyright infringement and of its authorship, the person responsible for the alleged violation will be charged for the crime of copyright infringement.

[54] See Universidade de São Paulo 2005.

[55] See Magrani 2006.

[56] See Hiche *et al.* 2005, 1.

[57] IIPA 2010, 2 (recommends that Brazil "have the State of São Paulo University (USP) reverse its harmful administrative rule which allows widespread reprographic copying of portions of books by commercial, for-profit copy centers, and institute guidance for other universities that have followed in USP's footsteps.")

while expressing concern that a wide array of copyrighted works have been reproduced without the payment of any fees, omitted to say that a possible reason for copyshops not paying fees to copyright holders is that publishers seem to oppose the granting of reprographic licenses. It is because of these licenses that students and researchers based in highly industrialized countries can make photocopies of the materials they consider necessary, without bureaucracy.

In addition to universities, student associations and civil society organizations also mobilized against the narrow exception. In February 2006, students from universities based in Rio de Janeiro and in São Paulo launched a manifesto titled "Copying Books is a Right," where the signatories expressed their dissatisfaction with narrow interpretations of the scope of the Brazilian private copying exception that put into jeopardy their right to make copies of copyrighted works. In the manifesto, the signatories also emphasized the need to amend the LDA, in order to allow the practical reconciliation between the rights to education and to freedom of expression and the legitimate economic interests of copyright holders.[58]

In line with the manifesto, on June 1, 2006, the Institute for International Trade Law and Development (IDCID or Institute), a private non-profit organization, filed a public civil lawsuit against the ABDR before a district court of São Paulo.[59] The two main objectives pursued by the lawsuit were to enjoin the ABDR from: (i) prejudicing the right of copyshops in general and of the general public to reproduce "short extracts" of copyrighted works for private purposes; and (ii) taking any actions focused on curbing the underprivileged sectors of Brazilian society, that do not have the means for purchasing books and other copyrighted works, to fully reproduce these works, since these individuals are not part of the consumer market of literary works.[60]

Out of the two claims, without doubt, the second one is more controversial. This claim was clearly inspired by the Dutch Supreme Court's ruling in *Dior* v. *Evora*. In that case, the Supreme Court of the Netherlands recognized its prerogative to devise and implement new copyright exceptions, beyond those expressly provided for in local statutes, provided the "court exceptions" reflect the same kind of balancing of competing interests enshrined in the exceptions provided for in statutes.[61] In line with this ruling, the Institute argued that the Brazilian copyright regime contains intrinsic and extrinsic copyright exceptions. The former

[58] Manifesto Copiar Livro é Direito, 2006.
[59] 5th Civil Court of São Paulo, Judicial Power of the State of São Paulo, Judicial Proceedings no. 583.00.2006.158832.
[60] Rodrigues Jr.and Carboni 2006, 48.
[61] See Hugenholtz 1996, 17–18.

are explicitly provided in the text of the Brazilian Copyright Act, while the latter stem from other norms of the Brazilian legal system, notably the constitutional norms that recognize the rights to education[62] and of access to information and knowledge,[63] the principle of the social function of property[64] and the principle prohibiting abuse of rights.[65]

In order to prove the legality of the second claim vis-à-vis the international copyright framework, the IDCID in addition argued that a recognition of the right of the underprivileged sectors of Brazilian society to make full copies of copyrighted works complies with the conditions laid down in art. 9(2) BC. According to the IDCID, this is so because these activities pursue a compelling public interest (the cultural rights of large sectors of the Brazilian population) and they do not conflict with the normal exploitation of the affected works, since resource-poor individuals are not part of the consumer market for literary works. Therefore, the potential economic prejudice imposed on copyright holders by the exempted activities are, at worst, tiny and, therefore, justified in the face of the social benefits produced thereby. In its defense, the ABDR took the view presented above regarding the scope of the Brazilian private copying exception.

The first instance judgment found that the IDCID had no *locus standi* to bring a public civil lawsuit against the ABDR, since the institute did not have as an institutional mission the defense of consumers' interests. The first instance ruling was confirmed by the Court of Justice of São Paulo.

Despite all the criticism echoed by civil society organizations, the truth is that the actions taken by publishers to defend copyrights are backed by the Brazilian legal order. These actions are premised on the idea that "book piracy" generates losses of R$ 1 billion per year. This figure is based on the "average consumption of unauthorized copies, made annually by higher education students." It is possible that this figure is inflated since its calculation seems to assume that the students who take photocopies of copyrighted works would consume books instead, if they were no longer authorized to have recourse to reprography.[66] But possibly there are many individuals, in particular those with a modest income, who will not have enough resources to purchase all the works needed to complete their studies if they are no longer entitled to make copies of scientific and technical works. The figure also overlooks the fact that many of the works frequently photocopied by higher education

62 Art. 205 FCB. 63 See arts. 5, XIV and 215, chapeau, FCB.
64 See arts. 5°, XXIII and 170, III, FCB.
65 See art. 187, Brazilian Civil Code (Law no. 10.406/2002).
66 See ABDR 2010, item no. 9.

students are unavailable locally, either because they are out of print or because they are foreign.

Even if the figure referred to is correct, copyright holders seem to ignore the annual aids amounting to hundreds of millions of dollars granted by Brazilian society to the publishing industry. According to a recent study compiled by the University of São Paulo's Research Group on Public Policy for Access to Information (GPOPAI), in 2006 the book industry did not contribute to the state coffers, by virtue of the tax immunities devised to benefit it, about R$ 978 million. This figure corresponded to 34 percent of the revenues of the book industry for that year (R$ 2,880 million).[67] The Brazilian government is also responsible for heavily subsidizing the production of contents of a substantial number of technical and scientific works, through the payment of salaries of professors and researchers, working full-time at public universities and research institutions,[68] the offer of places in graduate programs at public universities and the granting of scholarships.[69] Finally, the Brazilian state contributes to the publishing industry through the channeling of direct and indirect investments for the maintenance of dozens of university presses.[70] Therefore, in the Brazilian context, the royalties paid by publishers to the authors of technical-scientific works are not the only driving force behind the local creation of these works. Thus, even if the publishing industry suffers losses of R$ 1 billion per year due to the unauthorized reproduction of technical and scientific works, the direct and indirect investments made by the Brazilian state in this sector on behalf of its people exceed that figure.

The difficulties stemming from the absence of a functional private copying exception are not theoretical. In the study cited above, GPOPAI investigated the impact of the ban on reprography on access to educational materials by the students enrolled on ten courses at USP. Based on the acquisition costs of the obligatory bibliography for the first year of ten undergraduate courses, and on the average income of the students enrolled in these courses, the Group reached the conclusion that "in *all* courses, for more than three quarters of the students, the annual costs for the purchase of the mandatory bibliography is very close to the

[67] See Craveiro *et al.* 2008, 21.

[68] The study prepared by GPOPAI indicated that up to 86% of the books adopted by the university courses evaluated were authored by researchers and lecturers working full-time in Brazilian public institutions (*ibid.*, 28–29).

[69] Many of the technical-scientific works published by Brazilian publishers are the output of research conducted within graduate programs of public universities and funded by scholarships granted by governmental agencies (*ibid.*, 32).

[70] *Ibid.*, 41–42.

monthly family income of these students."[71] And even if these students had sufficient economic resources to purchase all the required works, about 30 percent of the works included in the basic bibliography were out of print.[72] It is undeniable that, if such students are prevented from resorting to reprography, future professionals will be increasingly less prepared in overcoming daily challenges. This is surely a severe disadvantage for people who aspire to intellectual and material progress.

It is also possible that excessive restriction of the scope of the private copying exception causes deleterious effects on governmental programs aimed at democratizing access to higher education, such as the Scholarship Program University for All (ProUni)[73] and the system of quotas at public universities. It is pointless to facilitate the access of underprivileged students to higher education if they have no guarantee of access to the intellectual tools necessary to complete their studies with success and quality. If an increasing number of students rely on works available in public libraries to complete their courses, many may not succeed since these libraries are unable to meet the huge demand.[74] Bearing in mind the social, economic and environmental objectives Brazil wishes to achieve in the coming decades, the copyright exceptions provided by the LDA should be radically amended.

8.2.2 The response of the Brazilian government

After a decade of problems engendered by the LDA of 1998, during the Lula administration the Brazilian government acknowledged publicly that this piece of legislation is "completely at odds with the Brazilian socio-economic and cultural reality and [is] considered by local and foreign specialists as one of the most restrictive in the world."[75] In order to prevent access to copyrighted works by the underprivileged sectors of Brazilian society becoming a sort of "clandestine joy,"[76] the Federal Government decided to take action. In 2007, the Ministry of Culture of Brazil launched the National Copyright Forum, which organized eight workshops and meetings, attended by representatives of copyright-dependent businesses, authors, artists and associations representing users and consumers. The main objective of these meetings and

[71] *Ibid.*, 35. [72] *Ibid.*

[73] ProUni is a scholarship program devised to benefit low-income higher education students.

[74] Craveiro *et al.* 2008, 35. [75] See Ministério da Cultura 2010b.

[76] Lispector (1971 [?]), in "Felicidade Clandestina" ("Clandestine Joy") recounts the indignities she faced, in her impoverished childhood in the city of Recife, in satisfying her urge to read the book "Reinações de Narizinho," by Monteiro Lobato.

workshops was to identify the real problems generated by the LDA and to raise suggestions as to how to overcome or mitigate them.

The main result from the process of public consultations is a bill drafted by the Ministry of Culture and released on June 15, 2010 for public consultation. The bill not only aims to "ensure effective protection and encouragement to authors and their creations," but in particular to "promote the balance of rights amongst all interested parties; broaden and democratize the population's access to cultural goods and services; to harmonize the local legislation with the new paradigms established by the digital environment; and to enable the State to formulate public policies oriented towards the promotion, supervision, regulation and defense of the interests of society and of the country."[77] Because of the breadth of its goals and its favorable orientation towards access to knowledge, the bill has been strongly opposed with the aim of blocking its submission in its present form to the National Congress.[78]

Among the proposed amendments put forward by the bill, those of interest to this work refer to the establishment of new copyright exceptions, devised to further access to knowledge for educational purposes. Under the bill, the new version of art. 46 of the LDA exempts, inter alia, the following activities, without the payment of any remuneration to copyright holders:[79]

> IX – the reproduction, distribution, communication and the making available to the public of works for the exclusive use of people with physical disabilities, provided that the disability requires, for the enjoyment of the work by impaired people, the use of a particular process or an adaptation of the work, provided that the reproduction or adaptation has no commercial purpose;
>
> XIII – the reproduction necessary for conservation, preservation and archiving of any work with no commercial intent, provided the reproduction is made by libraries, archives, documentation centers, museums, cinematheques and other institutions to the extent required to meet the referred goals;
>
> XVII – the reproduction without commercial purpose of literary, sound recording or audiovisual work, provided its latest publication is no longer available for sale in sufficient quantity to meet market demands, and there is no stock available of such work for sale;
>
> Sole Paragraph: in addition to the cases expressly provided in this article, the reproduction, distribution and communication to the public of a copyrighted work, without the prior written consent of the copyright holder and the payment of fees, does not constitute a copyright violation provided such use: I – is performed for educational, instructional, informational or research purposes, or for

[77] See Ministério da Cultura 2010a.
[78] See Dias and Cabral 2011.
[79] See Ministério da Cultura 2010b.

use as a creative input and II – is made to the extent required to reach the end pursued and without prejudicing the normal exploitation of the work used and the legitimate interests of the author.[80]

From the perspective of the urgent need to expand the access to educational materials, the most significant exceptions are those enshrined in art. 46 (XVII) and in its sole paragraph. The former allows the full reproduction of works that are out of print. The latter authorizes the reproduction of copyrighted works for educational purposes – e.g. the reproduction of supporting materials for students enrolled in an educational program, the use of works in distance-learning programs in general, including online courses, and the reproduction of copyrighted works for research purposes. However, the exercise of the latter exception is a complicated task, since it embodies the three-step test of the BC. If the Brazilian courts construe the terms of the proposed exception in harmony with the interpretation endorsed in *US – Section 110(5) Copyright Act*, the list of exempted activities will be narrow. But in case the local courts construe them in accordance with the interpretation proposed in the first part of the present study, there will be enough room for widening the access to knowledge by underprivileged people. In any event, it is not possible, a priori, to predict the interpretive approach to be adopted by the courts and, accordingly, it is not possible to predict the activities that are, in fact, exempted by the proposed provision. In any case, the safeguard clause included in the sole paragraph benefits the public, since it allows courts to apply it, in a subsidiary manner, to guarantee access to copyrighted works, as long as the conditions set by the three-step test are met.

With regard to reprography, the photocopying of copyrighted works by commercial copyshops will be subject to the payment of a remuneration to copyright holders.[81] The bill drafted by the Ministry of Culture does not make clear whether the making of copies of copyrighted works by public and other non-profit institutions, for use by their students, researchers and staff, would be subject to the payment of any remuneration to copyright holders. On this point, the bill does not create an actual exception, since copyshops will only be allowed to make copies of the works whose copyrights holders directly or through a CMO have authorized them to do so. Therefore, rights holders will not obliged to grant reprographic licenses to copyshops. If a copyright holder refuses to grant a voluntary reprographic license on reasonable terms to a

[80] Ministério da Cultura 2010c (free translation).

[81] Ministério da Cultura 2010b.

copyshop or educational institution, the latter may request a non-voluntary license from the President of Brazil.[82] Having as a precedent the Brazilian experience in the patents field, marked by the under-utilization of the compulsory licensing mechanism,[83] it is unlikely that such a mechanism will be able to repress, effectively, the abuses committed by copyrights holders. As far as reprography is concerned, the proposed amendment of the LDA seems more detrimental to access to knowledge than the private copying exception currently in force, given the ambiguous terms of art. 46 (II). The LDA at least offers some room for educational institutions to adopt internal measures aimed at furthering access to knowledge. A case in point is Resolution no. 5213 approved by the USP. If the amendment proposed by the Ministry of Culture is enacted, this room for maneuver will be removed.

In summary, some of the amendments enshrined in the bill drafted by the Ministry of Culture still require adjustment, with a view to better protecting the right of access to knowledge. It is possible that through the process of public consultations, the problems identified above can be overcome.

8.3 Proposal for an educational exception for underprivileged students and researchers

A huge number of people live in precarious conditions in developing countries, but this does not stop them looking for a better future. Freeing these people from the bondage of poverty is the task of education. For that to happen, governments in those countries shall promote, among other things, policies oriented to widen access to educational materials.

To put to the test the ability of art. 9(2) BC to foster the overriding public interests of the WTO Members, especially those of the most vulnerable countries, an exception is proposed that is devised to enhance access to educational materials in developing countries. The proposed exception is in line with the always timely demand of developing countries to ensure facilitated access to copyrighted technical and scientific works by their populations.

The proposed exception allows the free reproduction of works of an educational character (e.g. technical and scientific books, textbooks, scientific articles, case studies, drawings, tables), published in any medium and in any language, provided the reproduction has no commercial

[82] Art. 52-B, IV, Ministério da Cultura 2010c.

[83] Since the enactment of the LPI, the Brazilian government compulsorily licensed a single patent for the production of an antiretroviral drug.

intent. The exception is devised to benefit exclusively underprivileged students and researchers based in developing countries, as well as public and private educational institutions that serve this public through the provision of educational or capacity building programs at any level. This implies that the copies produced may neither be sold nor distributed to students and researchers who do not qualify as resource-poor. The sole obligation on the beneficiaries of the exception is to mention, in all forms of use of the affected works, the author's name, if it is indicated on the work. There are seven exempted activities, namely:

(a) Production of copies, by resource-poor students or researchers, of any literary or artistic work in circulation,[84] exclusively for private non-commercial purposes. This component of the exception does not authorize the full reproduction of copyrighted works, but only of book chapters, journal articles and excerpts of works.
(b) Production of full copies of locally unavailable (e.g. foreign works) or out of print works, directly by resource-poor students or researchers for private non-commercial purposes, or by libraries that serve this public. The beneficiaries of this component of the exception may only fully reproduce an out of print work when its latest edition is sold out for at least one year.
(c) Production of copies of book chapters, journal articles or excerpts of any works by educational institutions, for subsequent distribution to resource-poor students, provided that the copies are employed as supporting material for the courses offered by these institutions, and they bear a notice indicating that their commercial distribution is prohibited. Equally exempted are compilations by educational institutions and their distribution to the resource-poor students enrolled in these institutions, provided that the distribution is made free of charge.
(d) Reproduction of works in new formats made by educational institutions or by students/researchers themselves in order to meet the educational and cultural needs of visually impaired persons and of persons with other disabilities.
(e) Reproduction of works, within the framework of distance-learning courses made available by correspondence or online, by educational institutions, public or private, provided that the courses are addressed to resource-poor students. This component of the exception supports exclusively the reproduction of extracts of works, book chapters, journal articles and compilations. The exception authorizes: the making available of these works in an electronic environment, their

[84] See art. 3(3) BC.

transmission by wire or wireless means, their reception (display on screen) and printing by resource-poor students. A benefitted institution is only authorized to exercise this component of the exception in the realm of the internet so long as it adopts effective technological measures, able to prevent or to substantially reduce the chances that the works made available online will be spread in an uncontrolled manner.[85]

(f) Translation of copyrighted works to the extent strictly necessary to make use of the prerogatives guaranteed by paragraphs (c), (d) and (e) above.

(g) The beneficiaries of the exception are allowed to circumvent technological measures, employed by copyright holders to restrict unauthorized access and reproduction of their works, to the extent necessary to carry out the activities indicated in paragraphs (a) – (f) above.[86]

Defining "resource-poor students and researchers" is the most difficult aspect of the realization of the proposed exception. The difficulty lies in the lack of a universal set of criteria devised to characterize the state of poverty. Reference could be made to the UN's Human Development Index (HDI). Nevertheless, it does not seem sufficiently precise to reflect reality. Brazil, in 2010, occupied the 73rd place in the HDI; such placement is sufficient to characterize Brazil as a country with advanced human development. However, the same country is home to several resource-poor regions. Among them are the Brazilian semi-arid regions, where many locals fight against starvation, droughts and unemployment, and suffer a lack of water, education and means of livelihood on a daily basis. Seen in isolation from the rest of Brazil, this region would probably rank very low in the HDI. Thus the ideal situation is to delegate to each State the power to determine the criteria for identifying the beneficiaries of the exception, namely, those students and researchers who actually have no means of acquiring literary and artistic works, without compromising their right to an adequate standard of living, which includes the right to food, clothing and adequate housing.[87]

[85] Element based on Xalabarder 2003, 166.

[86] This element mirrors a recommendation made by Consumers International (2010, 9). Although the analysis of the WCT falls outside the scope of the present work, as its provisions are not part of the TRIPS Agreement, it is unwise to overlook it. Art. 11 of the WCT requires its Contracting Parties to "provide adequate legal protection and effective legal remedies against the circumvention of effective technological measures" to prevent the unauthorized use of their works, provided that such measures are selective, in the sense that they do not prevent third parties from exercising the copyright exceptions. If the technical measure hinders the exercise of copyright exceptions, third parties may circumvent it in order to enforce their users' rights.

[87] See art. 11(1) ICESCR.

For those countries that have reached a certain level of socio-economic development, but still retain very impoverished municipalities or regions, the proposed exception would benefit the entire population of these places, since the number of wealthy people in these regions that could unfairly take advantage of the exception would be negligible. In other words, in those locations, individuals and educational institutions would be free to rely on the exception, regardless of any state control of the identity and living standards of the beneficiaries of the exception. The exercise of the proposed exception in impoverished regions, however, is not always a simple task, since even today there are many regions in developing countries that are not served by electric power grids. In these circumstances, the exception provides teachers and educational institutions with the right to commission the production of the needed copies by copyshops located in other regions, provided they submit a formal statement, issued by the institution where the copies will be employed, ensuring that the copies will exclusively benefit resource-poor students.

For those cities where there is poverty and also prosperous areas, the adoption of more stringent control mechanisms is essential. In those cities, the only people who should benefit from the exception would be the demonstrably resource-poor students and researchers, enrolled in educational programs, official or otherwise, offered by public or private institutions. In the case of private institutions, only resource-poor students awarded with scholarships would benefit from the exception. The educational institutions would be responsible for requiring from their students and researchers proof of their resource-poor economic situation, for example, an individual or family income tax declaration. Those who manage to prove their poor living standard would be granted a non-transferable document of personal use, which would allow them to make copies of the works they need within the premises of the institution where they are enrolled, as well as in copyshops in general. Copyshops would be obliged to set two different rates for their services: a fee to be paid by the non-beneficiaries of the exception, to be used to cover printing- and copyright-related costs, and a fee to be paid by the beneficiaries of the exception, directed to cover exclusively printing-related costs.

8.3.1 Assessment of the legality of the proposed educational exception

8.3.1.1 Assessment of the special character of the exception At first sight, it seems that the exception under review affects the right of communication to the public provided in art. 8 WCT, which states that "authors of literary and artistic works shall enjoy the exclusive right of authorizing any communication to the public of their works, by wire or wireless means, including the making available to the public of their works in such a way that members of the public may access these works from a place and at a time individually chosen by them." Nevertheless, the right of communication to the public, as provided for by art. 8 WCT, is neither guaranteed by the BC nor by TRIPS. Thus, the proposed exception only affects the exclusive right of reproduction, guaranteed by art. 9(1) BC, which bestows on authors of literary and artistic works "the exclusive right of authorizing the reproduction of these works, in any manner or form." The lawfulness of the proposed exception is then exclusively controlled by the three-step test set out in art. 9(2) BC.

The exception under review will satisfy the first step of the test if it fully complies with four conditions, namely: (1) it is devised to foster any of the goals of a public nature provided by art. 8 of TRIPS; (2) it is a suitable means to promote the achievement of the goals that motivated its adoption; (3) it is the least restrictive means of the right to reproduction, among the alternative means reasonably available to the proponent State; (4) it observes the minimum obligations set by TRIPS. The latter obligation requires that the exception shall: not prevent the protection of any of the categories of works eligible to receive protection in the territories of WTO Members; observe the clauses on national and most-favored-nation treatment; have no impact on the term of copyright protection; and respect the area occupied by the compulsory licensing system governed by the appendix to the BC. Does the proposed exception meet all those requirements?

The exception meets the first condition, since it is designed to promote, to the greatest extent possible, the rights to education, to participate in cultural life and to the freedom of scientific and creative expression of low-income students and researchers based in developing countries, including those with disabilities. Its ultimate goal is to eliminate or at least reduce the cultural gap that separates the more privileged classes from underprivileged ones. Thus the exception fosters public interests of vital importance to the socio-economic and technological development of developing countries.

The proposed exception also meets the second requirement, as the substantial reduction of the acquisition costs of educational materials borne by educational institutions and low-income students and researchers is a suitable means of realizing the goals behind the exception; support for this view can be seen in the fact that the Contracting States to the ICESCR recognize that the full realization of the right of *everyone* to education depends on, among other measures, the continuous improvement of the material conditions of teaching staff (art. 13(2)(e)). The Contracting Parties to this covenant also recognize that the full realization of the right to participate in cultural life depends on the adoption of measures "necessary for the conservation, the development and the diffusion of science and culture" and for promoting "freedom indispensable for scientific research and creative activity" (art. 15 (2) and (3)). The ICCPR, in turn, stresses that the right to freedom of expression includes the "freedom to seek, receive and impart information and ideas of all kinds," including those of an artistic, literary and scientific nature (art. 19(2)). These provisions confirm that the full realization of the rights to education, to participate in cultural life and to freedom of expression is premised on increasing access to literary and artistic works by students, researchers and education and research institutions.

The exception under review meets the third requirement set by the first step of the test, as it is the least restrictive means of the right of reproduction granted to the affected copyright holders, among the alternatives reasonably available to developing countries, which are capable of promoting to the same extent the same goals as those pursued by the proposed exception. At first, a plausible alternative to the proposed exception, equally capable of expanding access to copyrighted works for educational and scientific purposes, is to vest a governmental agency with the power to receive applications for compulsory licenses and to grant them to resource-poor students, researchers and educational institutions. Once granted, the non-voluntary licenses would authorize the applicants to reproduce portions or the entirety of certain works, without the payment of any fees. This alternative measure would seem to be a more effective means of preventing fraud, as there would be greater state control over who may reproduce a copyrighted work without the right holder's permission. However, it is contended that such a measure should not be regarded as a satisfactory alternative to the exception proposed in this chapter. This is so because obtaining a compulsory license depends on the establishment of a bureaucratic procedure that could consume too much time to achieve its ultimate goal. The problem is especially pertinent when it is borne in mind that the number of potential beneficiaries of a compulsory licensing scheme is very high in developing countries, quite apart from the economic costs of such a procedure and the social costs of delay. In addition, it is always possible that applicants who actually meet all the legal requirements for obtaining a license, would not succeed in their applications, because the granting of licenses would depend on the judgement of the competent authority regarding the fulfillment of the legal requirements, notably proof of the applicant's state of poverty.

Another possible alternative to the proposed exception would be the fair use-type defense as provided for in section 107 of the US Copyright Act. However, as seen previously, the fair use defense brings uncertainty to its potential beneficiaries, as it is usually not possible to predict positively the opinion the court will reach about the legality of a particular unauthorized use.[88] Considering that underprivileged students, researchers and educational institutions tend not to have enough resources to purchase the works required for their daily activities, it is obvious that neither will they have enough resources to fund expensive and time-consuming litigation against conglomerates. On these grounds, a fair use defense would lead to the under-use of literary and artistic works by underprivileged individuals and institutions. In the end, no copyright exception, whose exercise relies on case-by-case State interventions, can be regarded as an alternative to the exception proposed in this chapter.

Finally, the proposed exception complies with the minimum standards set by TRIPS. It does not have the practical effect of preventing the protection of any of the categories of literary and artistic works which, pursuant to art. 2 BC and art. 10 TRIPS, should be eligible to receive copyright protection. It also does not curtail the minimum term of protection to be given to copyright holders. It also complies with the clauses on national treatment and most-favored-nation, because it affects both the works of nationals of the proponent State and those of nationals of other WTO Members. Finally, the exception respects the area occupied by the compulsory licensing system governed by the Annex to the BC, since it does not allow third parties to produce and distribute copies of works of others, or to translate foreign works, produce and distribute copies of the translation, in order to meet the reasonable demands of students and researchers *in general.* The proposed exception only allows *resource-poor* students and researchers to make copies of copyrighted works to meet their *individual* needs (paragraphs (a), (b), (d) and (e) of the proposed exception), and allows educational institutions to reproduce copyrighted works, including those in the virtual environment, to *exclusively* meet the needs of *resource-poor* students enrolled in these institutions (paragraphs (c), (d), (e) and (f) of the exception). The exception should therefore be regarded as having a "special" character.

8.3.1.2 Assessment of the ability of the exception to conflict with the normal exploitation of the affected works The proposed exception does not interfere with the normal exploitation of the affected works. This is because the beneficiaries – low-income students and researchers based in developing countries, including those with disabilities, and educational institutions that serve this public – do not possess sufficient resources to purchase

[88] See Chapter 5, section 5.6.2.2.

books and other intellectual products to meet their needs without harming, in the case of students and researchers, their fundamental human rights and, in the case of institutions, the full realization of their educational missions. In other words, the recognition of the right of those individuals and institutions to reproduce copyrighted works does not conflict with the normal exploitation of the affected works, since the beneficiaries of the exception are outside the consumer market for the works affected thereby. Thus, the exception under review does not lead to what Hardin calls "bibliocide,"[89] as its application does not affect the sales of the affected works. It is not legitimate to give copyright holders the right to receive compensation and/or control the reproduction of works by individuals and institutions that do not have sufficient resources to acquire them in the market, because the exercise of the right would, in these circumstances, amount to an abuse of the right: on the one hand, its exercise with respect to this group of individuals and institutions does not further in any way the legitimate economic interests of copyright holders and, on the other hand, it hinders the cultural and scientific development of the marginalized sectors of society, as well as the creation of new works, the dissemination of knowledge and the democratization of culture.

8.3.1.3 Assessment of the unreasonable character of the prejudice caused by the exception to the legitimate interests of copyright holders The proposed exception satisfies the third step of the test in art. 9(2) BC, inasmuch as it engenders social benefits outweighing the prejudice caused to the legitimate economic interests of copyright holders (e.g. authors and publishers).

The exception under review catalyzes the realization of the rights to education, to participate in cultural life and to freedom of scientific and artistic expression, as it facilitates the access to works which are useful to the advancement of education, culture and science. Furthermore, the exception extends the ability of educational institutions that serve low-income individuals to fully realize their institutional mission. Those interests hold a position of the highest importance in any civilized society; so much so they are all safeguarded by the International Bill of Human Rights.[90]

With regard to the social weight of the individual losses caused by the proposed exception to the legitimate interests of copyright holders,

[89] Hardin 1977, 883.

[90] The right to education is guaranteed by art. 13(1) ICESCR. The right to freedom of expression is recognized by art. XIX UDHR and art. 19(2) ICCPR.

it is, at best, negligible: the exception does not create any economic harm to the *legitimate* interests of copyright holders, as the beneficiaries of the exception are not part of the consumer market for the affected works, by reason of the socio-economic context in which they live (in the case of individuals) or operate (in the case of educational institutions). Even if, by a failure of control, the exception benefits some individuals with economic capacity to acquire the required works in the market, the number of individuals unjustly benefitted would be insignificant, since the exception is designed to truly benefit impoverished municipalities, individuals and institutions that serve underprivileged individuals. And should copyright holders manage to identify cases of fraud, they can always resort to the courts to claim damages for their loss.

Consequently, considering that the exception under review promotes individual and social interests of the highest degree of importance to the material and cultural progress of any society and to the preservation of democracy, while it causes negligible prejudice to the economic interests of copyright holders, it fully complies with the requirements set by the test of art. 9(2) BC.

Concluding remarks on Part II

All the hypothetical exceptions proposed to assess the ability of the general exception clauses of TRIPS to support the adoption of measures directed at furthering the legitimate interests underpinning the ideal of sustainable development have succeeded in satisfying the tests contained in those clauses.

In Chapter 5 we saw that art. 30 of TRIPS allows WTO members to harmonize the economic interests of patent holders with the greater interests of society, by adopting bold patent exceptions. The R&D exception and that for diagnostic tests can jointly promote socio-economic interests that are highly valued by any society, notably the rights to life, health and freedom of scientific expression, free competition and free enterprise. The following are the main advantages offered by the exceptions proposed here:

- The exceptions constitute an easier instrument – legally and politically – to handle than the control performed by patent authorities over the quality of granted patents, or the exclusion of certain controversial subject matters from the list of inventions eligible for patent protection. One should not ignore the fact that the clientele of patent offices are the companies investing in innovation. Thus, it is unlikely that these agencies will opt to enrich the public domain, rather than safeguard the private interests held by the business sector. Regardless of how extensive the list of inventions eligible for patent protection in a given State is, there remains plenty of space for scientific and technological research, provided it adopts exceptions like those proposed in Chapter 5.

- They restrain abusive and anticompetitive practices, such as refusal to license, excessively high royalty fees, and include reach-through clauses in licensing agreements.
- They prevent tragedies of the anti-commons and excessive royalty stacking, opening a long road which innovators have to tread to develop and launch new products and technologies in the market, as well as for humanitarian purposes.
- They are a type of "active" technology transfer, in the sense that third parties may only enjoy the technological contributions of others if they embark on transformative uses of that technology. This is the most appropriate means of transferring technologies to developing countries, because it involves active participation from local business and scientific communities to adapt them to the local needs and context. In the course of the adaptation process, scientists acquire new skills and knowledge that can help them solve unforeseen problems and develop new technologies more independently.
- They foster scientific and technological, academic and philanthropic activities within institutions and weaken the brain drain process. The patent exceptions proposed here offer indirect incentives for talented scientists to continue their work in public institutions and universities either because non-profit research projects or those with humanitarian purposes would pay no fees, or because projects with economic purposes could be carried out without running the risk of being unable to market their results at reasonable prices.
- They attract investments to scientific and technological fields in the countries that adopt them, provided they also have the basic staff and infrastructure to carry out scientific and technological research. As industrialized countries tend to adopt ever more limited research exceptions, it becomes even more urgent that developing countries should embrace exceptions such as the ones analyzed in this work. Institutions based in industrialized countries may then be more prepared to outsource scientific tasks to organizations based in countries with innovation systems that are more willing to foster innovation.
- They save scarce resources that are no longer spent on bureaucratic activities, such as: (i), the "reinvention of the wheel," when third parties do not obtain an authorization to use an invention that is essential for their activities; (ii) protracted negotiations with uncertain results; (iii) costly and sluggish proceedings, launched with the

purpose of obtaining compulsory licenses or to prove the fair character of a particular use.
- They efficiently protect higher public interests such as public health, freedom of expression in science and free competition.
- R&D and diagnostic tests exceptions may be immediately adopted by any WTO Member, including those that have committed themselves to new obligations in accordance with TRIPS-plus norms.

In Chapter 6, it was sought to demonstrate that art. 17 TRIPS bestows on WTO Members the discretion to adopt exceptions to the exclusive rights granted by trademarks, devoted to ensuring, within certain limits, the freedom of others to create and disseminate parodies of trademarks and critical messages involving trademarks in speeches and publications. In other words, the test in art. 17, if well employed, supports the adoption of protective measures of one of the most important pillars of democracy, the right to freedom of expression.

In Chapter 7, it was sought to demonstrate that art. 26(2) TRIPS provides enough space for WTO Members to devise exceptions to the rights conferred by protected industrial designs, able to safeguard the freedom of competition, freedom of consumer choice, the right to work of countless individuals and, indirectly, the preservation of scarce natural resources.[91] The tested repair exception, in addition to not putting at risk the future of multinational car companies, also encourages the growth of the business sector in developing countries, since, in the context of these countries, the greatest beneficiaries of the exception referred to tend to be local small and medium-sized companies. This effect is essential for the achievement of sustainable development, because, under principle 6 of the Rio Declaration, policies truly directed at fostering sustainable development should not be limited to promoting economic growth, social development and environmental conservation in a given country, while they prejudice the economy, nature and the society of third countries. They must be tailored to meet the social, economic and environmental needs of *all* countries.

Finally, in Chapter 8, it was sought to show that, although the BC and TRIPS have as their central focus maximization of the protection afforded to the economic interests of copyright holders,[92] art. 9(2) BC and art. 13 TRIPS ensure that WTO Members have enough room to design exceptions to copyrights that are able to promote interests

91 In the opposite direction, de Borja (2008, 508), when assessing the legality of the repair exception proposed by the EU in view of art. 26(2) TRIPS, concluded that this exception, quite possibly, is not TRIPS-compliant.

92 See Yu 2003, 12–14.

of the highest value: the rights of all to education, to freedom of expression and to participate in cultural life, both as consumers of cultural goods and as producers of new intellectual products.[93]

Thus, contrary to what many authors have been arguing in recent years, in its current state TRIPS provides legal scope wide enough to enable the adoption of exceptions to IPRs that aim to reconcile the economic interests of the holders of IPRs with the legitimate demands of other sectors of society.[94] This does not mean that there is no room for improvement. With the purpose of turning into reality the wide array of social, economic and environmental objectives of the WTO, it is highly advisable to complement the general exception clauses of TRIPS with a set of mandatory exceptions for every WTO Member to incorporate within its legal order.[95]

This is especially relevant because of the belief that the general exception clauses of TRIPS only offer prerogatives that may or may not be exercised by WTO Members. If they are under-used, it is clear that intellectual property regimes will remain unbalanced in favor of the demands – sometimes unreasonable – of the holders of IPRs.

Nevertheless, the discretion offered by TRIPS to WTO Members not to utilize the general exception clauses is, in fact, quite limited; national parliaments may not even adopt explicit exceptions to IPRs.

[93] In the opposite direction, Story (2009, 3–12) argues that the international regime of copyright protection, whose central axis is represented by the Berne Convention, is an inherently unbalanced system and unable to be balanced, basically because historically it has been constructed to protect exclusively the economic interests of copyright holders, through the continued expansion of the term of copyright protection and the roster of exclusive rights. In the opinion of this author, the interests of users to widely access literary and scientific works are overlooked by the BC, because it does not impose social obligations on the holders of copyrights and the only areas in which users' interests can be safeguarded are called "exceptions," and also because adoption of exceptions is not mandatory.

[94] In general, proposals for reforming the general exception clauses of the TRIPS Agreement with a view to widening the possibilities available to WTO Members to adopt socially efficient exceptions to IPRs, are concentrated in the realm of copyright: see, e.g., Sun 2007, 302–303 (proposes a test with the following wording to replace art. 13 of the TRIPS: "Members may provide limitations on the exclusive rights, provided that such limitations take account of the legitimate interests of right holders and of third parties."); Okediji 2000, 168–171 (proposes an "international fair use doctrine" to check the legality of copyright exceptions); Koelman 2006, 410 (proposes to transform the test in art. 13 of TRIPS into a fair use test; alternatively, he proposes to replace the text of the second step of the test in art. 13 with the wording of the second step of the test in art. 30); Ricketson 2008, 65 (proposes to replace the three-step test of copyright law with a four-step test, which seems to incorporate the constituent elements of the principle of proportionality).

[95] In this sense, it is worth noting the proposal of amendment of the TRIPS Agreement, designed under the auspices of the project "IP in Transition Research Programme" (Kur and Levin 2006).

However, WTO Members, represented by their judicial bodies and antitrust authorities, whenever necessary, have the power/duty to directly apply the general exception clauses to resolve private disputes. Should they not do so, they will prevent the WTO system and TRIPS from meeting their goals and principles, enshrined in the preamble of the Marrakesh Agreement in arts. 7 and 8 TRIPS.

When one recalls the social, economic and environmental goals pursued by the WTO system and by the TRIPS Agreement, as well as the customary international obligations of the international community crystallized in the Universal Declaration of Human Rights, one is bound to conclude that WTO Members will fail to achieve those goals and will not observe these customary obligations, whenever their national parliaments fail to adopt domestic normative instruments which enshrine exceptions to IPRs, designed to promote, effectively, those legitimate interests. To avoid the emergence of this problem, WTO Members, through their courts and antitrust authorities should, whenever necessary, directly apply the general exception clauses of TRIPS to determine, on a case-by-case basis, whether a particular use of an intangible asset protected by an IPR, which prima facie seems not to be authorized by law, is exempted by the pertinent general exception clause. One of the great benefits brought about by the direct application of the general exception clauses of TRIPS is the setting of a tacit absolute limit to IPRs: IPRs holders are not entitled to control abnormal forms of exploitation of their intangible assets.

The direct application of the general exception clauses of TRIPS implies that many of the hypothetical exceptions examined in the second part of this study are already tacitly incorporated into the legal systems of WTO Members, even if not provided verbatim in national statutes, namely: (i) parts 1 and 2 of the R&D exception (Chapter 5 on patents); (ii) the parody and criticism exception (Chapter 6 on trademarks); (iii) the repair exception (Chapter 7 on industrial designs); (iv) the educational exception for underprivileged students and researchers (Chapter 8 on copyrights). Because of its details and complexity, the transposition of the other hypothetical exceptions examined – parts 3 and 4 of the R&D exception and the diagnostic test exception – into the national legal orders of WTO Members requires legislative action to be taken by national parliaments. Undoubtedly, it brings greater legal certainty for users, if the examined exceptions and other IPR exceptions are explicitly provided in national statutes. And even if these and other exceptions to IPRs have not been made explicit in the domestic legal order by national parliaments, what really matters is that the protection of vital legitimate interests whose realization depends on access to knowledge is not held hostage by the absence of textually explicit exceptions to IPRs.

In summary: the direct application of the general exception clauses of TRIPS by judicial and antitrust authorities of WTO Members is essential in order to realize, to the fullest extent possible, the multitude of social, economic and environmental goals of TRIPS and the WTO, and to effect the international customary obligations of the international community, crystallized in the UDHR. The essentiality of the general clauses of the TRIPS Agreement in achieving these legitimate interests stems from the fact that legislators may not be able to determine ex ante explicit exceptions robust enough to resolve any conflict between such interests and IPRs. By virtue of the principle of effective interpretation, which requires the interpreter to seek the interpretation of TRIPS provisions that maximizes the effectiveness of its goals, WTO Members should either allow the direct application of the general exception clauses of TRIPS by local courts and antitrust authorities, or, at least, include in their domestic legal order general safeguarding clauses, to reflect the normative contents of the general exception clauses of TRIPS and to operate whenever the exceptions expressly provided for by the legislation are insufficient to protect the vital interests of society at large.

Final remarks

The sustainability of a society is measured by the ability of the present generation to bequeath to the next one economic, natural and human capital, at least on the same qualitative and quantitative levels as that received from the previous generation.[1] To achieve this, there is no other way than the direction of public and private investment and public policy towards the reduction of society's carbon footprint, the expansion of the freedoms enjoyed by individuals and the improvement of the conditions of the (natural, cultural and artificial) environment.

Even though IPRs play a relevant role in the material progress of contemporary societies, freedom of access to the diverse forms of knowledge – e.g. literary and scientific works, the various expressions of the arts, scientific and technological knowledge, research tools, brands – is a *sine qua non* for setting up the supporting pillars of the ideal of sustainable development. In other words, what is dependent on free access to the various forms of knowledge is the realization of interests of the utmost social importance: the rights to health and life, the right to freedom of expression, the right to food, the right to a healthy environment, the right to work, the protection of free competition, the right to education and the right to participate in cultural life.[2]

Given the present context, characterized by the substantial expansion of the list of subject matters eligible for intellectual property protection and the relaxation of the protection criteria, the exceptions to IPRs – whether they be modeled by courts, administrative bodies or the legislature – appear as an effective means of neutralizing many of the potential deleterious social effects engendered by contemporary intellectual property regimes. That is so because, on the one hand, they partially restore the public good character of proprietary intangible goods, with the specific purpose of promoting relevant public interests, and, on the other

[1] See Veiga 2010, 18.

[2] See, e.g., Committee on Economic, Social and Cultural Rights 2009, para. 2; UNGA, Resolution A/RES/60/205, 1st recital.

hand, they do not prejudice unreasonably the economic incentives to perform creative and inventive activities.

Moreover, considering that, at present, the overwhelming majority of the holders of IPRs are concentrated in industrialized countries, the transfer of knowledge from industrialized to developing countries, driven by robust exceptions to IPRs, is a means of fulfilling two major obligations owed by them. The first one is the commitment made by the members of the international community, enshrined in art. 55(a) of the Charter of the United Nations, to support each other to achieve "higher standards of living, full employment, and conditions of economic and social progress and development." The second one stems from the principle of common but differentiated responsibilities, inscribed in principle 7 of the Rio Declaration, whereby although all states "shall cooperate in a spirit of global partnership to conserve, protect and restore the health and integrity of the Earth's ecosystem," industrialized countries contributed to a greater extent to the deterioration of the global environment and control major economic and intellectual resources and, accordingly, they bear greater responsibilities in the solution of these problems than developing countries.

TRIPS, in its current configuration, has created uncontested difficulties to many WTO Members, by requiring them to warrant a wide range of exclusive rights to the holders of IPRs and to substantially expand the list of subject matters eligible for legal protection. That does not represent an insurmountable obstacle to the establishment of public policy measures aimed at promoting the ideal of sustainable development. The general exception clauses of the TRIPS Agreement, when interpreted through the strict observance of the customary rules of treaty interpretation provided in the VCLT, allows parliaments, courts and other public organs of WTO Members, such as antitrust authorities, to introduce exceptions to IPRs, suitable to accomplish the multiple social, economic and environmental objectives pursued by the WTO system, including the core interests safeguarded by human rights treaties and MEAs. The fact that the TRIPS Agreement allows the adoption of exceptions as robust as those suggested in the second part of this work, raises the question of the necessity of reforming TRIPS to make room for the adoption of public policies built on the curtailment of the scope of IPRs. It is therefore not advisable to confuse absence of local technical capacity to use the tools offered by the TRIPS Agreement with the lack of legal leeway to protect vital public interests. When WTO Members opt for intellectual property regimes exclusively centered on safeguarding the economic interests of the holders of IPRs, they do so through ignorance or because of other political interests. At all events, what is clear is that the enactment of regimes with such characteristics is not a legal requirement imposed by TRIPS.

Those who consider that the presence of a wide legal capacity that embraces the adoption of socially efficient exceptions to IPRs is highly harmful not only to the economic interests of the holders of IPRs, but also to the scientific and cultural progress of humanity, are overlooking the fact that this capacity ensures the sustainability of the TRIPS Agreement.[3] A system that fosters the prosperity of a small group of States, companies and individuals at the expense of the well-being of the majority of mankind and of the health of the Earth is undoubtedly indefensible and, accordingly, illegitimate. At no time should one forget that the fundamental premise of sustainable development is "improving the quality of life of *all* the world's people, both today and for future generations, without increasing the use of our natural resources beyond the earth's carrying capacity."[4]

At first, the realization of the socio-environmental goals of the multilateral trading system would seem much simpler, were TRIPS to indicate, unambiguously, a minimum set of exceptions to IPRs that all WTO Members should have to incorporate into their legal orders. This approach has been lately supported by civil society organizations,[5] developing countries[6] and academics.[7] However, we must recognize that, at present, it is unlikely that industrialized countries will agree to include a package of minimum mandatory exceptions in TRIPS or in any other special agreement which binds all WTO Members. In the end, what actually matters is that TRIPS, though it affects the sovereignty of its contracting parties, ensures that each WTO Member has the freedom to adopt human rights-based intellectual property regimes, through the enactment of robust exceptions to IPRs directed at widening and facilitating access to proprietary intellectual goods for legitimate goals.

Yet WTO Members should remain vigilant of the fact that the only way to preserve the prerogatives currently provided by the general exception

3 See OHCHR 2005, 13.

4 Johannesburg Declaration on Health and Sustainable Development 2002, para. 2.

5 In 2005, civil society organizations released a treaty proposal titled "Treaty on Access to Knowledge," whose goal is to expand the public domain (CPTECH 2005). The proposal includes several exceptions to IPRs, which should be adopted by the contracting parties to the treaty.

6 See, e.g., the draft international treaty, put forward by the African Group in 2010 before the WIPO Standing Committee on Copyright and Related Rights, that comprises a roster of minimum copyright exceptions of mandatory adoption by the contracting parties, with a view to debureaucratizing access to works by the visually impaired and for educational purposes (African Group 2010).

7 See, e.g., Hugenholtz and Okediji 2008 (who propose an international treaty that comprises copyright exceptions for mandatory adoption).

clauses of TRIPS is by putting them into practice. Not only because it is the only means for domestic intellectual property regimes to promote the multitude of non-commercial goals of the WTO and TRIPS, but also because if WTO Members support – explicitly or otherwise – the interpretations put forward in the panel reports adopted by the DSB on the terms of arts. 13, 17 and 30 TRIPS, in future they may lose legal ground to adopt more efficient exceptions to IPRs, from the socio-environmental perspective. This is due to the fact that, in the terms of art. 31(3)(b) VCLT, the interpreter of the general exception clauses of TRIPS will have to consider "any subsequent practice in the application of the treaty which establishes the agreement of the parties regarding its interpretation." Should the interpretation of the general exception clauses proposed in *US – Section 110(5) US Copyright Act*, *EC – Trademarks and Geographical Indications* and in *Canada – Pharmaceutical Patents* receive over time unanimous consent because many WTO Members follow it while no other Members of the organization challenge it, it will no longer be legally possible to read these provisions as a *sui generis* test of proportionality. And this would undoubtedly prejudice the most fragile WTO Members. This proves that least developed and developing countries should urgently strive to adopt in the coming years socially efficient exceptions to IPRs, whose force would witness the rejection of those socially unbalanced and legally misguided interpretations embraced by the WTO at the expense of pressing social and environmental interests.

Bibliography

Abbott, F. M. (2002), "WTO TRIPS Agreement and Its Implications for Access to Medicines in Developing Countries", Study Paper 2a, Commission on Intellectual Property Rights (2002), 80. Available at: www.iprcommission.org/papers/pdfs/study_papers/sp2a_abbott_study.pdf

ABDR (1993 [?]), "Estatuto da Associação Brasileira de Direitos Reprográficos", Associação Brasileira de Direitos Reprográficos (1993). Available at: www.abdr.org.br/site/estatuto.asp

ABDR (2008), "Revisão da Lei de Direitos Autorais: uma ameaça à Educação", Associação Brasileira de Direitos Reprográficos (2008), p. 6. Available at: www.linhaselaudas.com.br/site/imgmateriasmidia/Cartilha_bx.pdf

ABDR (2010 [?]), "Perguntas e respostas", Associação Brasileira de Direitos Reprográficos (2010). Available at: www.abdr.org.br/site/perguntas_respostas.asp

Abramovay, R. (2010), "Desenvolvimento sustentável: qual a estratégia para o Brasil?" (2010) 87 *Novos Estudos CEBRAP* 97–113

Adhikari, R. (2005), "Patents, Royalty Stacking and Management" (2005) 8 *World Pharmaceutical Frontiers* 25–26

Advisory Council on Intellectual Property (2005), "Patents and Experimental Use", Australian Government (October 2005)

Advocacia Geral da União (2007), "NOTA/INPI/PROC/CJCONS/N° 023/2006", Procuradoria-Geral Federal do Instituto Nacional da Propriedade Industrial (2007)

Afonso da Silva, L. V. (2005a), "O conteúdo essencial dos direitos fundamentais e a eficácia das normas constitucionais", Full Professorial Thesis, Law School of the University of São Paulo (2005), p. 370

Afonso da Silva, L.V. (2005b), *A constitucionalização do direito: os direitos fundamentais nas relações entre particulares* (São Paulo: Malheiros Editores, 2005)

African Group, *Draft WIPO Treaty on Exceptions and Limitations for the Disabled, Educational and Research Institutions, Libraries and Archive Centers* (SCCR/20/11), WIPO Standing Committee on Copyright and Related Rights, Geneva (June 21–24, 2010)

Alexy, R. (2009), *Teoria dos direitos fundamentais*, translated by Virgílio Afonso da Silva (São Paulo: Malheiros, 2009), p. 669

Amaral Jr., A. (2011), *Do comércio internacional e a proteção do meio ambiente* (São Paulo: Atlas, 2011)

American College of Medical Genetics (1999), "Position Statement on Gene Patents and Accessibility of Gene Testing" (August 2, 1999). Available at: www.acmg.net/StaticContent/StaticPages/Gene_Patents.pdf

American Intellectual Property Law Association (2004), "AIPLA Response to the National Academies Report entitled A Patent System for the 21st Century". Available at: www.aipla.org/advocacy/executive/Pages/National-Academy-of-Sciences.aspx

Andenas, M. and Zleptnig, S. (2007), "Proportionality: WTO Law in Comparative Perspective" (2007) 42 *Texas International Law Journal* 370–427

ANFAPE (2008), "Considerações sobre o mercado independente de autopeças brasileiro e as consequências de um possível monopólio sobre peças de reposição". Available at: www.anfape.org.br/imagens/Memorial%20ProCade%2030-09-2008.pdf

Aoki, H. (2009), "Design Protection of Spare Parts from a Global Perspective: Types of Protection among Countries, and Trends in the EU and USA" (September 2009) *AIPPI Journal* 295–319

Aras, A. (2010), "Parecer do Procurador da República Augusto Aras MPF/CADE no. 23/2009 no âmbito da averiguação preliminar no. 08012.002673/2007-51", CADE, March 8, 2010. Available at: www.anfape.org.br/imagens/Parecer_do_MPF_08-03-10.pdf

Araújo Jr., J. T. (2006), "Restrições verticais no mercado brasileiro de autopeças: impactos anticompetitivos", Ecostrat Consultores, December 2006. Available at: www.anfape.org.br/imagens/Nota%20tecnica%20Jose%20Tavares%2012-2006.pdf

Armstrong, C. *et al.* (2010), *Access to Knowledge in Africa: The Role of Copyright* (Claremont: UCT Press, 2010)

Association of University Technology Managers (2007), "In the Public Interest: Nine Points to Consider in Licensing University Technology". Available at: www.fptt-pftt.gc.ca/eng/resources/articles/2007/03/InthePublicInterest.html

Aust, A. (2000), *Modern Treaty Law and Practice* (Cambridge University Press, 2000)

Aymé, S., Matthijs, G. and Soini, S. (2008), "Patenting and Licensing in Genetic Testing: Recommendations of the European Society of Human Genetics" (2008) 16 *European Journal of Human Genetics* 3–9

Baca, M. R., "Barriers to Innovation: Intellectual Property Transaction Costs in Scientific Collaboration" (2006) 4 *Duke Law & Technology Review*. Available at: www.law.duke.edu/journals/dltr/articles/2006dltr0004.html

Bandeira de Mello, C. A. (2004), *Curso de direito administrativo*, 17th edn (São Paulo: Malheiros, 2004)

Barbosa, D. and Grau-Kuntz, K. (2010), *Exclusions from Patentable Subject Matter and Exceptions and Limitations to the Rights: Biotechnology* (SCP/15/3 – Annex III) (Geneva: WIPO, 2010)

Basheer, S. (2005), "Block Me Not: How 'Essential' are Patented Genes?" (2005) 1 *Journal of Law, Technology & Policy* 55–96

Basheer, S., Purohit, S. and Reddy, P. (2010), *Patent Exclusions that Promote Public Health Objectives* (SCP/15/3, Annex IV) (Geneva: WIPO, 2010)

Bauer, R. J. (2005), "Why Not Try the Experiment and Stop Pointing the Finger? Modern University Unaffected by a Narrow Experimental Use Exception" (2005) 34 *Temple Journal of Science and Technology & Environmental Law* 121–142

Bederman, D. J. (2001), *Classical Canons: Rhetoric, classicism and treaty interpretation* (Aldershot: Ashgate, 2001)

Bently, L. (2010), *Exclusions from Patentability and Exceptions and Limitations to Patentees' Rights* (SCP/15/3, Annex I) (Geneva: WIPO, 2010)

Bergström, S. (1967) "Report on the Work of Main Committee I (Substantive Provisions of the Berne Convention: Articles 1 to 20)", in BIRPI, *Records of the Intellectual Property Conference of Stockholm, June 11 to July 14*, vol. II (Geneva: BIRPI, 1967)

BIRPI (1967a), *Reports on the Work of the Five Main Committees of the Intellectual Property Conference of Stockholm, 1967* (Geneva: BIRPI, 1967)

BIRPI (1967b), *General Report of the Swedish/BIRPI Study Group Established on July 1, 1964: Diplomatic Conference of Stockholm, 1967* (DA/22/2) (Geneva: BIRPI, 1967)

Bostyn, S. J. R. (2004), *Patenting DNA Sequences (Polynucleotides) and Scope of Protection in the European Union: An Evaluation – Background Study for the European Commission within the Framework of the Expert Group on Biotechnological Inventions* (Brussels: European Commission, 2004)

Botero, C. (2009), *Informe Anual de la Comisión Interamericana de Derechos Humanos 2009: informe de la relatoria especial para la libertad de expresión* (OEA/Ser.L/V/II. Doc. 51) (Washington, DC: Comisión Interamericana de Derechos Humanos, 2009)

Bradley, W. (2003), "Supertropical", NIFCA, 2003. Available at: http://superflex.net/text/articles/supertropical.shtmlt

Brennan, D. J. (2002), "The Three-step Test Frenzy: Why the TRIPS Panel Decision Might be Considered per incuriam" (2002) 2 *Intellectual Property Quarterly* 221–225

Brownlie, I. (1998), *Principles of Public International Law* (Oxford: Clarendon Press, 1998)

Bruzzone, L. C. (1993), "The Research Exemption: A Proposal" (1993) 21 American *Intellectual Property Law Association Quarterly Journal* 52–69

Byers, M. (2002), "Abuse of Rights: An Old Principle, a New Age" (2002) 47 *McGill Law Journal* 390–431

Byström, M and Einarsson, P. (2001), *Consequences for Developing Countries: Implications for Swedish Development Cooperation* (Stockholm: Swedish International Development Cooperation Agency, 2001)

Cambridge University Press (2011), *The Cambridge Advanced Learner's Dictionary* (Cambridge, 2011). Available at: http://dictionary.cambridge.org/dictionary/british

Caruso, A. J. (2003), "The Experimental Use Exception: An Experimentalist's View" (2003) 14 *Albany Law Journal of Science & Technology* 215–244

Cheng, B. (1953), *General Principles of Law as Applied by International Courts and Tribunals* (London: Stevens & Sons Limited, 1953)

Clark, V. (2004), "Pitfalls in Drafting Royalty Provisions in Patent Licences" (2004) *Bio-Science Law Review*. Available at: http://pharmalicensing.com/public/articles/view/1087832097_40d70021d738c

Clift, C. (2007), "Patenting and Licensing Research Tools", in Krattiger, A. *et al.* (eds.), *Intellectual Property Management in Health and Agricultural Innovation: A Handbook of Best Practices*, vol. 1 (Oxford and Davis, CA: MIHR and PIPRA, 2007), pp. 79–88

Commission of the European Communities (2004a), *Proposal for a Directive of the European Parliament and of the Council amending Directive 98/71/EC on the legal protection of designs* (COM(2004) 582 final) (Brussels: European Commission, 2004)

Commission of the European Communities (2004b), *Proposal for a Directive of the European Parliament and of the Council Amending Directive 98/71/EC on the Legal Protection of Designs: Extended Impact Assessment* (Brussels, European Commission, 2004) Available at: www.europanu.nl/9353000/1/j4nvgs5kjg27kof_j9vvh6nf08temv0/vi7jgsymsdz3/f=/.pdf

Commission on Human Rights (2001), *Globalization and its Impact on the Full Enjoyment of Human Rights: Progress Report Submitted by J. Oloka-Onyango and Deepika Udagama, in accordance with Sub-Commission Resolution 1999/8 and Commission on Human Rights Decision 2000/102* (E/CN.4/Sub.2/2001/10) (Geneva: Commission on Human Rights, 2001)

Commission on Intellectual Property Rights (2002), *Integrating Intellectual Property Rights and Development Policy* (London: CIPR, 2002)

Committee on Civil and Political Rights (2001), "General Comment on Article 4" (CCPR/C/21/Rev.1/Add.11), adopted at the 1950th meeting, July 24, 2001

Committee on Economic, Social and Cultural Rights (2009), *General Comment No. 21: Right of Everyone to Take Part in Cultural Life (Art. 15, para. 1(a), of the International Covenant on Economic, Social and Cultural Rights)* (E/C.12/GC/21). Economic and Social Council, Geneva (December 21, 2009)

Conceição, P., Heitor, M. V., Sirilli, G. and Wilson, R. (2004), "The 'Swing of the Pendulum' from Public to Market Support for Science and Technology: Is the US Leading the Way?" (2004) 71 *Technological Forecasting and Social Change* 553–578

Consumers International (2010), *IP Watchlist, 2010*. Available at: http://a2knetwork.org/sites/default/files/IPWatchList-2010-ENG.pdf

Cook, T. (2006), *A European Perspective as to the Extent to which Experimental Use, and Certain Other, Defences to Patent Infringement Apply to Differing Types of Research* (London: Intellectual Property Institute, 2006). Available at: www.ipeg.com/_UPLOAD%20BLOG/Experimental%20Use%20for%20IPI%20Chapters%201%20to%209%20Final.pdf

Correa, C. M. (2007), *Trade Related Aspects of Intellectual Property Rights: A Commentary on the TRIPS Agreement* (Oxford University Press, 2007)

Council of the European Union (2009), "Revised Proposal for a Council Regulation on the Community Patent", Council of the European Union, Brussels

(September 29, 2009). Available at: http://register.consilium.europa.eu/pdf/en/09/st13/st13706.en09.pdf

CPTECH (Consumer Project on Technology) (2005), "Treaty on Access to Knowledge", May 2005. Available at: www.cptech.org/a2k/a2k_treaty_may9.pdf

Craveiro, G., Machado, J. and Ortellado, P. (2008), *O mercado de livros técnicos e científicos no Brasil:subsídio público e acesso ao conhecimento* (São Paulo: Grupo de Pesquisa em Políticas Públicas para o Acesso à Informação da Universidade de São Paulo, 2008)

Creative Commons Brazil, "Coletivo dinamarquês acusa Fundação Bienal de censura", October 16, 2006. Available at: www.creativecommons.org.br/index.php?option=com_content&task=view&id=66&Itemid=51

Crespi, R. S. (2001), "Patents on Genes: Can the Issues be Clarified?" 3 (5) (2001) *Bio-Science Law Review* 199–204

Cypriano, F. (2006), "Grupo acusa Fundação Bienal de censurar obra", *Folha de São Paulo*, October 5, 2006. Available at: www1.folha.uol.com.br/folha/ilustrada/ult90u64886.shtml

D'Amato, A. (1992), "Good Faith", in Bernhardt, R. (ed.), *Encyclopedia of Public International Law* (Amsterdam: Elsevier, 1992), pp. 599–601

Danish Council of Ethics, *Patenting Human Genes and Stem Cells: A Report* (Copenhagen: The Danish Council of Ethics, 2004). Available at: http://etiskraad.synkron.com/graphics/03_udgivelser/engelske_publikationer/patenting_human_genes/patents04/patenting_human_genes.pdf

De Borja, A. G. (2008), "Exceptions to Design Rights: The Potential Impact of Article 26(2) TRIPS" (2008) 30 *European Intellectual Property Review* 500–508

De Larena, L. R. (2005), "What Copyright Teaches Patent Law About 'Fair Use' and Why Universities Are Ignoring the Lesson" (2005) 84 *Oregon Law Review* 779–819

De Schutter, O. (2009), *Seed Policies and the Right to Food: Enhancing Agrobiodiversity, Encouraging Innovation. Background Document to the Report (A/64/170) Presented by Prof. Olivier De Schutter, Special Rapporteur on the Right to Food, at the 64th Session of the UN General Assembly (October 2009)* (Geneva: OHCHR, 2009)

De Franco, D. W., Levy, C. M. and Pogach, M. L. (2006), "The Experimental Use Exception: Looking towards a Legislative Alternative" (2006) 6 Journal of High Technology Law 93–111

Dennis, C. (2003), "Geneticists Question Fees for use of Patented 'Junk' DNA" (May 2003) 423 *Nature* 105

Derzko, N. M. (2003), "In Search of a Compromised Solution to the Problem Arising from Patenting Biomedical Research Tools" (2003) 20 *Santa Clara Computer & High Technology Law Journal* 347–409

Desmedt, A. (2001), "Proportionality in WTO Law" (2001) 4 *Journal of International Economic Law* 441–480

Dias, T. M. and Cabral, R. (2011), "Quem tem medo da mudança?", *O Estado de São Paulo*, March 20, 2011. Available at: http://blogs.estadao.com.br/link/quem-tem-medo-da-mudanca/

Dinwoodie, G. B. and Dreyfuss, R. C. (2004), "International Intellectual Property Law and the Public Domain of Science" (2004) 7 *Journal of International Economic Law* 431–448

Dinwoodie, G. B. and Dreyfuss, R. C. (2007), "Diversifying Without Discriminating: Complying with the Mandates of the TRIPS Agreement" (2007) 13 *Michigan Telecommunications and Technology Law Review* 445–456

Doctors Without Borders (2002), "Why Article 30 Will Work. Why Article 31 Will Not', MSF, June 24, 2002. Available at: www.accessmed-msf.org/prod/publications.asp?scntid=24920041455473&contenttype=PARA&

Dreier, T. (2005), "Interpreting International IP Law: Some Observations Regarding WTO Dispute Resolution", in Kur, A., Luginbuhl, S. and Waage, E. (eds.), "*. . . und sie bewegt sich doch!*" – *Patent Law on the Move* (Cologne: Carl Heymanns Verlag, 2005), pp. 45–62

Drexl, J., Hilty, R. and Kur, A. (2005), "Design Protection for Spare Parts and the Commission's Proposal for a Repairs Clause" (2005) 36 *International Review of Intellectual Property and Competition Law* 448–457

Dreyfuss, R. C. (2003), "Varying the Course in Patenting Genetic Material: A Counter-Proposal to Richard Epstein's Steady Course", Public Law and Legal Theory Research Paper Series, Research Paper No. 59, New York University School of Law (April 2003)

Dreyfuss, R. C. (2004), "Protecting the Public Domain of Science: Has the Time for an Experimental Use Defense Arrived?" (2004) 46 *Arizona Law Review* 457–472

Dreyfuss, R. C. (2005), "Unique Works/Unique Challenges at the Intellectual Property/Competition Law Interface", Law and Economics Research Paper No. 05–13, European Competition Law Annual, New York University (2005). Available at SSRN: http://ssrn.com/abstract=763688

ECAR (2006), "The 'spare parts' Issue: The Position of ECAR". Available at: www.ecar-eu.com/documents/ECARPositionPaperonEurodesign05–2007.pdf

ECAR (2009), *Why a Few Member States Should No Longer Block the Liberalization of the Vehicle Spare Parts Market: ECAR – Analysis of the Legal, Economic and Political Status of the "Repairs Clause"* (Brussels: ECAR, 2009)

Eisenberg, R. S. (1989), "Patents and the Progress of Science: Exclusive Rights and Experimental Use" (1989) 56 *University of Chicago Law Review* 1017–1086

Eisenberg, R. S. (2003), "Science and the Law: Patent Swords and Shields" (2003) 299 [5609] *Science* 1018–1019

Eisenberg, R. S., Marks, A. and Annas, G. (2002), "Molecule vs. Information: Should Patents Protect Both? Symposium on Bioinformatics and Intellectual Property Law, April 27, 2001, Boston, Massachusetts" (2002) 8 *Boston University Journal of Science & Technology* 190–217

Elkind, J. B. (1976), "Footnote to the Nuclear Test Cases: Abuse of Right – A Blind Alley for Environmentalists" (1976) 9 *Vanderbilt Journal of Transnational Law* 57–98

Engle, E. (2009), "The History of the General Principle of Proportionality: An Overview", SSRN (2009). Available at: http://ssrn.com/abstract=1431179

European Commission (2009), "Communication from the Commission: Executive Summary of the Pharmaceutical Sector Inquiry Report". European Commission, Brussels (July 8, 2009). Available at: http://ec.europa.eu/competition/sectors/pharmaceuticals/inquiry/communication_en.pdf

European Parliament (2005), "European Parliament Resolution on Patents for Biotechnological Inventions", October 26, 2005

European Parliament (2007), "Legislative Resolution of 12 December 2007 on the Proposal for a Directive of the European Parliament and of the Council amending Directive 98/71/EC on the Legal Protection of Designs (COM(2004)0582 – C 6–0119/2004 – 2004/0203(COD))"

European Union (2004), "Commission Proposes Enhancing Competition in the Market for Replacement Parts for Cars: Frequently Asked Questions" (MEMO/04/215), September 14, 2004

Farid, J. (2010), "35% dos brasileiros ainda não se alimentam o suficiente", *O Estado de São Paulo*, June 23, 2010. Available at: http://economia.estadao.com.br/noticias/economia+brasil,35-dos-brasileiros-ainda-nao-se-alimentam-o-suficiente,not_24382,0.htm

Farina, L. N. and Tormin, R. S. (2007), "Representação apresentada em nome da Associação Nacional dos Fabricantes de Autopeças (ANFAPE), perante a Secretaria de Direito Econômico do Ministério da Justiça do Brasil", ANFAPE (2007). Available at: www.anfape.org.br/imagens/Representação%20%20SDE-CADE%2004–04–2007.pdf

Federal Trade Commission (2003), "To Promote Innovation: The Proper Balance of Competition and Patent Law and Policy". Available at: www.ftc.gov/os/2003/10/innovationrpt.pdf

Feldman, M. P., Colaianni, A. and Liu Kang, C. (2007), "Lessons from the Commercialization of the Cohen-Boyer Patents: The Stanford University Licensing Program", in Krattiger, A. *et al.* (eds.), *Intellectual Property Management in Health and Agricultural Innovation: A Handbook of Best Practices*, vol. 2. (Oxford and Davis, CA: MIHR and PIPRA, 2007), pp. 1797–1808

Ficsor, M. (2003), *Guide to the Copyright and Related Rights Treaties Administered by WIPO and Glossary of Copyright and Related Rights Terms* (Geneva: WIPO, 2003)

Fitzmaurice, G. G. (1950), "The Law and Procedure of the International Court of Justice: General Principles and Substantive Law" (1950) 27 *British Yearbook of International Law* 1–41

Fonseca, R. A. and Monteiro, R. S. (2009), "Representação da ANPAPE apresentada perante o Ministério Público Federal do Rio Grande do Sul", ANFAPE (2009). Available at: www.anfape.org.br/imagens/Representação-Consumidor%20MPF-RS%2013–03–2009.pdf

Fontes, S. (2010), "MPF vai investigar ação de montadoras na área de reposição" *Valor Econômico*, September 1, 2010, B9.

Franck, T. M. (2008), "On Proportionality of Countermeasures in International Law" (2008) 102 *The American Journal of International Law* 715–767

Frankel, S. (2005), "WTO Application of 'the Customary Rules of Interpretation of Public International Law'" (2005) 46 *Virginia Journal of International Law* 365–431

Frankel, S. (2010), "The Applicability of GATT Jurisprudence to the Interpretation of the TRIPS Agreement", in Correa, C. M. (ed.), *Research Handbook on Intellectual Property Law and the WTO* (Cheltenham: Edward Elgar Publishing, 2010), pp. 3–23

Frasson, A. (2010), "Cópia ilegal na Unicamp gera apreensão de livros: Ação realizada pela DIG combate violação de direitos autorais; a Unicamp afirma seguir a lei de direitos", *Correio Popular*, March 30, 2010. Available at: http://blog.vilage.com.br/copia-ilegal-na-unicamp-gera-apreensao-de-livros

Freeburg, R. E. (2005), "No Safe Harbor and No Experimental Use: Is It Time for Compulsory Licensing of Biotech Tools?" (2005) 53 *Buffalo Law Review* 351–408

Friedmann, W. (1963), "The Uses of 'General Principles' in the Development of International Law" (1963) 57 *American Journal of International Law* 279–299

García, F. V. (1960), "State Responsibility: Fifth Report on International Responsibility" (A/CN.4/125 and Corr. 1) (1960) II *Yearbook of the International Law Commission* 41–68

Gardiner, R. K. (2008), *Treaty Interpretation* (Oxford University Press, 2008)

Geiger, C. (2004), "Fundamental Rights, a Safeguard for the Coherence of Intellectual Property Law?" (2004) 35 *International Review of Intellectual Property and Competition Law* 269–280

Geiger, C. (2005), "Right to Copy v. Three-Step Test: The Future of the Private Copy Exception in the Digital Environment" (2005) 1 *Computer Law Review International* 7–13

Geiger, C. (2006a), "Copyright and Free Access to Information: For a Fair Balance of Interests in a Globalised World" (2006) *European Intellectual Property Review* 366–373

Geiger, C. (2006b), "The Private Copy Exception, an Area of Freedom (Temporarily) Preserved in the Digital Environment" (2006) 37 *International Review of Intellectual Property and Competition Law* 74–81

Geiger, C. (2006c), "The Three-Step Test, a Threat to a Balanced Copyright?" (2006c) 37 *International Review of Intellectual Property and Competition Law* 683–699

Geiger, C. (2007a), "The Role of the Three-Step Test in the Adaptation of Copyright Law to the Information Society" (2007) *UNESCO e-Copyright Bulletin*, January–March. Available at: http://portal.unesco.org/culture/en/files/34481/11883823381test_trois_etapes_en.pdf/test_trois_etapes_en.pdf

Geiger, C. (2007b), "Trade Marks and Freedom of Expression: The Proportionality of Criticism" (2007) 38 *International Review of Intellectual Property and Competition Law* 317–327

Geiger, C. (2008a), "Flexibilising Copyright: Remedies to the Privatisation of Information by Copyright Law" (2008) 39 *International Review of Intellectual Property and Competition Law* 178–197

Geiger, C. (2008b), "Rethinking Copyright Limitations in the Information Society: The Supreme Court Leads the Way" (2008) 39 *International Review of Intellectual Property and Competition Law* 943–950

Gervais, D. (1998), *The TRIPS Agreement: Drafting History and Analysis* (London: Sweet & Maxwell, 1998)

Gervais, D. (2005), "Towards a New Core International Copyright Norm: The Reverse Three-Step Test" (2005) 9 *Marquette Intellectual Property Law Review* 1–35

Ghidini, G. (2006), *Intellectual Property and Competition Law: The Innovation Nexus* (Cheltenham: Edward Elgar, 2006)

Ginsburg, J. C. (2001), "Toward Supranational Copyright Law? The WTO Panel Decision and the 'Three-Step Test' for Copyright Exceptions", Center for Law and Economic Studies Working Paper No. 181, Columbia Law School (2001)

Gitter, D. M. (2001), "International Conflicts over Patenting Human DNA Sequences in The United States and The European Union: An Argument for Compulsory Licensing and a Fair-Use Exemption" (2001) 76 *New York University Law Review* 1623–1691

Gold, E. R. and Carbone, J. (2008), "Myriad Genetics: In the Eye of the Policy Storm", International Expert Group on Biotechnology, Innovation and Intellectual Property (2008). Available at: http://papers.ssrn.com/sol3/papers.cfm?abstract_id=1260098

Gold, E. R. and Joly, Y. (2010), *The Patent System and Research Freedom: A Comparative Study (SCP/15/3 – Annex VI)* (Geneva: WIPO, 2010)

Gold, E. R., Joly, Y. and Caulfield, T. (2005), "Genetic Research Tools, the Research Exception and Open Science" (2005) 3(2) *GenEdit* 1–11

Goldscheider, R. (1995), "The Negotiation of Royalties and Other Sources of Income from Licensing" (1995) 36 *IDEA* 1–17

Goldstein, P. (2001), *International Copyright: Principles, Law and Practice* (Oxford University Press, 2001)

Greenpeace UK (2010), "Greenpeace rebrands BP", May 24, 2010. Available at: http://members.greenpeace.org/blog/greenwashing/2010/05/24/greenpeace_rebrands_bp

Grubb, P. (2002), "How Real are Patent Thickets, Reach-Through Rights, Royalty Stacking and Dependency, and Freedom-to-Operate Restrictions?", OECD Berlin Workshop (2002). Available at: www.oecd.org/dataoecd/16/4/1817832.pdf

Hagelin, T. (2006), "The Experimental Use Exemption to Patent Infringement: Information on Ice, Competition on Hold" (2006) 58 *Florida Law Review* 483–560.

Hamilton, D. P., "Silent Treatment: How Genentech, Novartis Stifled A Promising Drug: Biotech Firm Tried to Pursue Peanut-Allergy Injection but Contract Got in Way", *Wall Street Journal*, April 5, 2005, p. A1

Hardin, G. (1968), "The Tragedy of the Commons" (1968) 162 *Science*, 1243–1248

Hardin, G. (1977), "Will Xerox kill Gutenberg?" (1977) 198 (4320) *Science*, 883

Heide, T. (1999), "The Berne Three-Step Test and the Proposed Copyright Directive" (1999) 21 *European Intellectual Property Review* 105–109

Heller, M. A. and Eisenberg, R. (1998), "Can Patents Deter Innovation? The Anticommons in Biomedical Research" (1998) 280 (5364) *Science* 698–701

Hestermeyer, H. (2007), *Human Rights and the WTO: The Case of Patents and Access to Medicines* (Oxford University Press, 2007)

Hiche, B., Condini, A. and Jabur, G. (2005), "Crítica ao Direito de Autor e a Questão das Copiadoras nas Universidades". Available at: www.migalhas.com.br/mostra_noticia.aspx?cod=12617

Hilf, M. (2001), "Power, Rules and Principles – Which Orientation for WTO/GATT Law?" (2001) *Journal of International Economic Law* 111–130

Hilf, M. and Goetz, J. G. (2003), "The Relation of Economic and Non-Economic Principles in International Law", in Griller, S. (ed.), *International Economic Governance and Non-Economic Concerns: New Challenges for the International Legal Order* (Vienna, New York: Springer, 2003), pp. 5–46

Hilf, M. and Puth, S. (2002), "The Principle of Proportionality on its Way into WTO/GATT Law", in Bogdandy, A. von and Mavroidis, P. C. (eds.), *European Integration and International Coordination: Studies in Transnational Economic Law in Honour of Claus-Dieter Ehlermann* (The Hague: Kluwer Law International, 2002), pp. 199–218

Hindle, A. (2005), "Reach-Through Claims", Hindle Lowther (2005). Available at: www.hindlelowther.com/article_reach.htm

Hiraki, Y. (2000), "Problems Regarding the Patentability of Genomics and Scope of Protection of ESTs in Japan" (2000) *CASRIP Newsletter* 17–26

Hoffman, D. C. (2003), "A Modest Proposal: Toward Improved Access to Biotechnology Research Tools by Implementing a Broad Experimental Use Exception" (2003) 89 *Cornell Law Review* 993–1043

Houghton Mifflin (2004), *American Heritage Dictionary of the English Language*, 4th edn (Houghton Mifflin Company, 2004). Available at: www.answers.com

Howse, R. (2004), "Mainstreaming the Right to Development into International Trade Law and Policy at the World Trade Organization – Note by the Secretariat" (E/CN.4/Sub.2/2004/17). Commission on Human Rights, Sub-Commission on the Promotion and Protection of Human Rights, Geneva (June 9, 2004)

Hu, J. (2004), "The Role of International Law in the Development of WTO Law" (2004) 7 *Journal of International Economic Law* 143–167

Hugenholtz, P. B. (1996), "Chronicle of The Netherlands: Dutch Copyright Law, 1990–1995" (1996) 169 *Revue internationale du droit d'auteur* 128–195

Hugenholtz, P. B. (1997), "Fierce Creatures – Copyright Exemptions: Towards Extinction?", IFLA/IMPRIMATUR Conference 1997

Hugenholtz, P. B., "Copyright and Freedom of Expression in Europe", in Dreyfuss, R. C., First, H. and Zimmerman, D. L. (eds.), *Innovation Policy in an Information Age* (Oxford University Press, 2000)

Hugenholtz, P. B. and Okediji, R. L. (2008), *Conceiving an International Instrument on Limitations and Exceptions to Copyright: Final Report* (Amsterdam and Minnesota: Institute for Information Law University of Amsterdam and University of Minnesota, 2008)

Hughes, J. (1997), "The Philosophy of Intellectual Property", in Moore, A. D. (ed.), *Intellectual Property: Moral, Legal, and International Dilemmas* (Lanham: Rowman & Littlefield Publishers, 1997), pp. 107–177

HUGO Intellectual Property Committee (2003), "Statement on the Scope of Gene Patents Research Exemption, and Licensing of Patented Gene

Sequences for Diagnostics", Human Genome Organisation (December 2003). Available at: www.hugo-international.org/img/ip_gene_2003.pdf

ICTSD (2010) (International Centre on Trade and Sustainable Development), "Litigating Environmental Protection and Public Health at the WTO: The Brazil-Retreaded Tyres Case", ICTSD Information Note No. 1 (September 2010)

Iluyomade, B. O. (1975), "The Scope and Content of a Complaint of Abuse of Right in International Law" (1975) 16 *Harvard International Law Journal* 47–92

International Intellectual Property Alliance (2010) "Brazil: Special 301 Report on Copyright Protection and Enforcement". Available at: www.iipa.com/rbc/2010/2010SPEC301BRAZIL.pdf

International Law Commission (1966), "Draft Articles on the Law of Treaties with Commentaries" (1966) 2 *Yearbook of the International Law Commission*, 187–274

International Law Commission (2001), "Draft Articles on Responsibility of States for Internationally Wrongful Acts", adopted by the International Law Commission at its Fifty-Third Session (2001). http://www.ilsa.org/jessup/jessup06/basicmats2/DASR.pdf

International Law Commission (2006), "Expulsion of Aliens: Memorandum by the Secretariat" (A/CN.4/565), International Law Commission, Fifty-Eighth Session (1 May–9 June and 3 July–11 August 2006)

International Law Commission (2008), *Draft Articles on Responsibility of States for Internationally Wrongful Acts, with Commentaries* (New York: United Nations, 2008). Available at: http://untreaty.un.org/ilc/texts/instruments/english/commentaries/9_6_2001.pdf

IP Australia (2009), "Exemptions to Patent Infringement: Towards a Stronger and More Efficient IP Rights System", Consultation Paper, Australian Government (2009)

Jalet, F. T. (1962), "The Quest for the General Principles of Law Recognized by Civilized Nations: A Study" (1962) 10 *UCLA Law Review* 1041–1086

Jehoram, H. C. (2005), "Restrictions on Copyright and their Abuse" (2005) 27 *European Intellectual Property Review* 359–364

Jensen, K. and Murray, F. (2005), "Intellectual Property Landscape of the Human Genome" (2005) 310 *Science* 239–240

Johnson, J. A. (2003), "The Experimental Use Exception in Japan: A Model for US Patent Law?" (2003) 12 *Pacific Rim Law & Policy Journal* 499–533

Jones, K. J., Whitham, M. E. and Handler, P. S. (2007), "Problems with Royalty Rates, Royalty Stacking, and Royalty Packing Issues", in Krattiger, A. *et al.* (eds.), *Intellectual Property Management in Health and Agricultural Innovation: A handbook of Best Practices*, vol. 2 (Oxford and Davis, CA: MIHR and PIPRA, 2007), pp. 1121–1126

Kang, K., Ryu, T. and Lee, Y. (2009), "Effects of Research Tool Patents on Biotechnology Innovation in a Developing Country: A Case Study of South Korea" (2009) *BMC Biotechnology* 9–25

Kingsbury, B. and Schill, S. (2009), "Investor-State Arbitration as Governance: Fair and Equitable Treatment, Proportionality and the Emerging Global

Administrative Law", IILJ Working Paper 2009/6 (Global Administrative Law Series), New York University School of Law

Kiss, A. (2009), "Abuse of Rights", in Wolfrum, R. (ed.), *Max Planck Encyclopedia of Public International Law* (Heidelberg and Oxford: Max Planck Institute for Comparative Public Law and International Law and Oxford University Press, 2009)

Koelman, K. J. (2006), "Fixing the Three-Step Test" (2006) 28 *European Intellectual Property Review* 407–412

Kolb, R. (2006), "Principles as Sources of International Law (with Special Reference to Good Faith)" (2006) 53 *Netherlands International Law Review* 1–36

Koskenniemi, M. (2006), *Fragmentation of International Law: Difficulties Arising from the Diversification and Expansion of International Law* (A/CN.4/L.682) (Geneva: International Law Commission, 2006)

Kratiger, A. (2007), "Freedom to Operate, Public Sector Research, and Product-Development Partnerships: Strategies and Risk-Management Options", in KRATTIGER, A., *et al.* (eds.), *Intellectual Property Management in Health and Agricultural Innovation: A Handbook of Best Practices*, vol. 2 (Oxford and Davis, CA: MIHR and PIPRA, 2007), pp. 1317–1327

Kur, A. (2008), "Of Oceans, Islands, and Inland Water: How Much Room for Exceptions and Limitations under the Three Step-Test?", Research Paper Series No. 08–04, Max Planck Institute for Intellectual Property, Competition and Tax Law (2008), p. 48

Kur, A. and Levin, M. (2006), "Agreement on Trade-related Aspects of Intellectual Property Rights: Synopsis of Original Version and Proposals for Amendment", ATRIP conference, Parma (2006)

Kur, A. and Ruse-Khan, H. G. (2009), *Enough is Enough: The Notion of Binding Ceilings in International Intellectual Property Protection* (Munich: Max Planck Institute, 2009)

Lauterpacht, H. (1949), "Restrictive Interpretation and the Principle of Effectiveness in the Interpretation of Treaties" (1949) 26 *British Yearbook of International Law* 48–85

Lewinski, S. von (2008), *International Copyright Law and Policy* (Oxford University Press, 2008)

Lichtman, D. G. (1999), "Property Rights in Emerging Platform Technologies", John M. Olin Law & Economics Working Paper No. 97, University of Chicago Law School (1999). Available at SSRN: http://ssrn.com/abstract=216533

Lipszyc, D. (2001), *Derecho de autor y derechos conexos* (Buenos Aires: Ediciones UNESCO, CERLALC and Zavalia, 2001)

Lispector, C. (1971 [?]), "Felicidade Clandestina" (1971). Available at: http://intervox.nce.ufrj.br/~valdenit/felicida.htm

Maciel Neto, A. R. (2009), "Parecer da PROCADE no. 853/2008 no processo no. 08012.002673/2007–51", CADE (2009). Available at: www.anfape.org.br/imagens/Parecer%20ProCADE%2008–01–2009.pdf

Macmillan, F. (1999), "Striking the Copyright Balance in the Digital Environment" (1999) 10 *International Company and Commercial Law Review* 350–360

Magrani, B. (2006), "Copiar livro é direito! Entrevista com Fernando Oshima", April 12, 2006. Available at: www.culturalivre.org.br/index.php?Itemid=48&id=53&option=com_content&task=view

Manifesto Copiar Livro é Direito (2006). Available at: www.midiaindependente.org/pt/blue/2006/03/347085.shtml

Mara, K. (2010), "WTO Members to Consider Review of TRIPS Public Health Amendment", IP Watch, February 11, 2010. Available at: www.ip-watch.org/weblog/2010/02/11/wto-members-to-consider-review-of-trips-public-health-amendment/

Masouyé, C. (1978), *Guía del Convenio de Berna para la Protección de las Obras Literarias y Artística (Acta de París, 1971)* (Geneva: OMPI, 1978)

Matthijs, G. (2004), "Patenting Genes: May Slow Down Innovation and Delay Availability of Cheaper Genetic Tests" (2004) 329 *BMJ* 1358–1360

Max Planck Institute and Queen Mary, University of London (2008), "Declaration on a Balanced Interpretation of the 'Three-Step Test' in Copyright Law" (2008). Available at: www.ip.mpg.de/shared/data/pdf/declaration_three_step_test_final_english.pdf

McGrady, B. (2009), "Necessity Exceptions in WTO Law: Retreated Tyres, Regulatory Purpose and Cumulative Regulatory Measures" (2009) 12 *Journal of International Economic Law* 1–21

McMullen, J. A. and Halprin, D. A. (1993), "New Technique for Quantifying Reasonable Royalty from Appropriate Case Law" (1993) 75 *Journal of the Patent and Trademark Office Society* 843–847

McNair, L. (1961), *The Law of Treaties* (Oxford: Clarendon Press, 1961)

Merriam-Webster Online Dictionary (Merriam-Webster, Inc.). Available at: http://mw.com/

Merton, R. K. (1977), "La estructura normativa de la ciencia", in Storer, N. W. (ed.), *La sociología de la ciencia, 2: investigaciones teóricas y empíricas* (Madrid: Alianza Editorial, 1977), pp. 355–368

Merz, J. F., Kriss, A. T., Leonard, D. G. B. and Cho, M. K. (2002), "Diagnostic Testing Fails the Test: The Pitfalls of Patents Are Illustrated by the Case of Hemochromatosis", University of Pennsylvania, Center for Bioethics (2002). Available at: http://repository.upenn.edu/cgi/viewcontent.cgi?article=1047&context=bioethics_papers

Ministério da Cultura (2010a), "Esclarecimentos à sociedade sobre a revisão da Lei de Direito Autoral", Ministério da Cultura do Brasil. Available at http://www.cultura.gov.br/site/2010/04/12/nota-a-sociedade-sobre-a-revisao-da-lei-de-direito-autoral/

Ministério da Cultura (2010b), "Revisão da Lei de Direito Autoral (N° 9610/98)" Available at: http://www.cultura.gov.br/site/2010/04/12/pontos-revisao-lda/

Ministério da Cultura (2010c), "Projeto de Lei: Altera e acresce dispositivos à Lei n° 9.610, de 19 de fevereiro de 1998, que altera, atualiza e consolida a legislação sobre direitos autorais e dá outras providências". Available at: http://www.cultura.gov.br/consultadireitoautoral/consulta/

Ministério da Cultura (2010d), "De A a Z: Todos Ganham – Consulta Pública para Modernização da Lei de Direito Autoral". Available at: http://www.cultura.gov.br/consultadireitoautoral/wp-content/uploads/2010/06/Cartilha.pdf

Mitchell, A. D. (2007), "The Legal Basis for Using Principles in WTO Dispute" (2007) 10 *Journal of International Economic Law* 795–835

Morato Filho, D. S. (2007), "Contestação da Associação Brasileira de Direitos Reprográficos", Ação Civil Pública no. 583.00.2006.158832 proposta pelo Instituto de Direito do Comércio Internacional e Desenvolvimento, March 27, 2007

Mueller, J. M. (2001), "No 'Dilettante Affair': Rethinking the Experimental Use Exception to Patent Infringement form Biomedical Research Tools" (2001) 76 *Washington Law Review* 1–66

Murray Neto, A., Mazieiro, E., Sesina, E. and Polido, F. P. (2010), "Contra-notificação extrajudicial – Professora Dra. Kátia Rubio – Uso de expressão 'Olímpicos' – Obra 'Esporte, Educação e Valores Olímpicos'", February 2, 2010

National Research Council (2006), *Reaping the Benefits of Genomic and Proteomic Research: Intellectual Property Rights, Innovation, and Public Health* (Washington, DC: National Academies Press, 2006)

Neumann, J. and Turk, E. (2003), "Necessity Revisited: Proportionality in World Trade Organization Law after *Korea–Beef, EC–Asbestos* and *EC–Sardines*" (2003) 37 *Journal of World Trade* 199–233

NIH (1998), "Report of the National Institutes of Health Working Group on Research Tools", presented to the Advisory Committee to the Director on June 4, 1998. Available at: www.nih.gov/news/researchtools/

NIH – Office of Technology Transfer (1999), "Sharing Biomedical Research Resources: Principles and Guidelines for Recipients of NIH Research Grants and Contracts" (1999) 64 *Federal Register*, 100, 28205–28209

NIH – Department of Health and Human Services (2005), "Best Practices for the Licensing of Genomic Inventions: Final Notice", April 11, 2005. Available at: http://ott.od.nih.gov/policy/lic_gen.html

Nordemann, W., Vinck, K. and Hertin, P. W. (1983), *Droit d'Auteur international et droits voisins dans les pays de langue allemande et les Etats membres de la Communauté européenne* (Brussels: Bruylant, 1983)

Nuffield Council on Bioethics (2002), *The Ethics of Patenting DNA: A Discussion Paper* (London: Nuffield Council on Bioethics, 2002)

Okediji, R. (2000), "Towards an International Fair Use Doctrine" (2000) 39 *Columbia Journal of Transnational Law* 75–175

O'Rourke, M. A. (2000), "Toward a Doctrine of Fair Use in Patent Law" (2000) 100 *Columbia Law Review* 1177–1249

Ost, F. (1990), *Droit et intérêt: entre droit et non-droit: l'intérêt*, vol. 2 (Brussels: Publications des facultés universitaires Saint-Louis Bruxelles, 1990)

OECD (2002), *Genetic Inventions, Intellectual Property Rights and Licensing Practices: Evidence and Policies* (Paris: OECD, 2002)

OECD (2006), *Guidelines for the Licensing of Genetic Inventions* (Paris: OECD, 2006)

Office of the Associate Minister of Commerce (2006), "An Experimental Use Exception for New Zealand's Patent Legislation". Government of New Zealand. Available at: www.med.govt.nz/upload/36358/cab-paper-200606.pdf

OHCHR (2001), *The Impact of the Agreement on Trade-Related Aspects of Intellectual Property Rights on Human Rights*, UN Doc. E/CN.4/Sub.2/2001/13 (Geneva, June 27, 2001)

OHCHR (2005), *Human Rights and World Trade Agreements: Using General Exception Clauses to Protect Human Rights* (New York and Geneva, United Nations, 2005)

Office of the United States Trade Representative (2007), "2007 Special 301 Report". Available at: www.ustr.gov/sites/default/files/asset_upload_file60_11126.pdf

Office of the United States Trade Representative (2008), "2008 Special 301 Report". Available at: www.ustr.gov/sites/default/files/asset_upload_file193_14872.pdf

Office of the United States Trade Representative (2009), "2009 Special 301 Report". Available at: www.ustr.gov/sites/default/files/Watch%20List.pdf

Office of the United States Trade Representative (2010), "2010 Special 301 Report", April 30, 2010. Available at: www.ustr.gov/webfm_send/1906

Office of the United States Trade Representative (2011), "2011 Special 301 Report", April 2011. Available at: http://www.ustr.gov/webfm_send/2841

Oliveira, G., Prado, L. and Scazufca, P. (2009), "Aspectos concorrenciais do mercado de peças de reposição", ANFAPE. Available at: www.anfape.org.br/imagens/PARECER%20ECONÔMICO%2009–0 6–09.pdf

Ortino, F. (2005), "From 'Non-discrimination' to 'Reasonableness': A Paradigm Shift in International Economic Law?", Jean Monnet Working Paper 01/05, New York University (2005)

Ostrom, E. and Hess, C. (2003), "Artifacts, Facilities, and Content: Information as a Common-pool Resource" (2003) 66 *Law & Contemporary Problems* 44–79

Ostrom, E. and Hess, C., *Understanding Knowledge as a Commons: From Theory to Practice* (Cambridge, MA, MIT: 2007)

Oxford University Press, *Compact Oxford English Dictionary of Current English*, 3rd edn rev. (Oxford University Press, 2009). Available at: www.askoxford.com/dictionaries/compact_oed/?view=uk

Palma, A. J. C., Ribas, L. and Malard, N. T. (2010), "Memorial da ANFAPE dirigida ao Conselheiro do CADE Carlos Emmanuel Joppert Ragazzo, no âmbito da Averiguação Preliminar n° 08012.002673/2007–51", ANFAPE, April 8, 2010. Available at: www.anfape.org.br/imagens/Memorial-ao-Conselheiro-do-CADE-Dr.Ragazzo-08–04–2010

Pals, F. (2010), "BP Shareholders Protest Canadian Oil Sands Project (Update1)", Bloomberg, February 8, 2010. Available at: www.bloomberg.com/apps/news?pid=newsarchive&sid=agncUeKHmHJo

Paradise, J. and Janson, C. (2006), "Decoding the research exemption" (2006) 7 *Nature Reviews Genetics* 148–154

Pereira, C. J. (2006), "Proteção jurídica penal, estado democrático de direito e bens jurídicos universais", Doctoral thesis, Pontifical Catholic University of São Paulo (2006). Available at: www.dominiopublico.gov.br/download/texto/cp011650.pdf

Pereira dos Santos, M. J. (2007), "Parecer: consulta realizada pela Associação Brasileira de Direitos Reprográficos a respeito da interpretação e aplicação do art. 46, II da Lei no. 9.610, de 19 de fevereiro de 1998", ABDR, March 20, 2007

Pinto, B. (2007), "Projeto de Lei 1197/2007, de 30 de maio de 2007", Câmara dos Deputados do Brasil. Available at: www.camara.gov.br/sileg/integras/464956.pdf

Pochmann, P. (2007), "O país dos desiguais" *Le monde diplomatique Brasil* (October 2007) 16–18

Ragazzo, C. E. J. (2010), "Voto – Averiguação Preliminar no. 08012.002673/2007-51 – Representante: Associação Nacional dos Fabricantes de Autopeças; Representadas: Volkswagen do Brasil Indústria de Veículos Automotivos Ltda; Fiat Automóveis S.A. e Ford Motor Company Brasil Ltda", Conselho Administrativo de Defesa Econômica (December 15, 2010)

Rai, A. K. and Eisenberg, R. S. (2003), "The Public and the Private in Biopharmaceutical Research", in Boyle, J. (ed.), *Collected Papers: Conference on the Public Domain* (Durham: Center for the Study of the Public Domain, 2003), pp. 157–175. Available at: www.law.duke.edu/pd/papers/raieisen.pdf

Razgaitis, R. (2007), "Pricing the Intellectual Property of Early-Stage Technologies: A Primer of Basic Valuation Tools and Considerations", in Krattiger, A. *et al.* (eds.), *Intellectual Property Management in Health and Agricultural Innovation: A Handbook of Best Practices*, vol. 1 (Oxford and Davis, CA: MIHR and PIPRA, 2007), pp. 813–860

Reichman, J. H. (2000), "Of Green Tulips and Legal Kudzu: Repacking Rights in Subpatentable Innovation" (2000) 53 *Vanderbilt Law Review* 1743–1798

Richer, A. G. (2010), "Carta do Comitê Olímpico Brasileiro, datada de 15 de janeiro de 2010, endereçada à Profa. Kátia Rubio" – Ofício 2887/2009/AGR/tcs, Comitê Olímpico Brasileiro, January 15, 2010

Ricketson, S. (1987), *The Berne Convention for the Protection of Literary and Artistic Works: 1886–1986* (The Hague: Kluwer Law International, 1987)

Ricketson, S. (2003), *WIPO Study on Limitations and Exceptions of Copyright and Related Rights in the Digital Environment (SCCR/9/7)* (Geneva: WIPO, 2003)

Ricketson, S. (2008), "WIPO Study on Limitations and Exceptions of Copyright and Related Rights in the Digital Environment", WIPO (2008). Available at: www.wipo.int/edocs/mdocs/copyright/en/sccr_17/sccr_17_www_111472.pdf

Ricketson, S. and Ginsburg, J. C. (2006), *International Copyright and Neighbouring Rights: The Berne Convention and Beyond*, vol. 1 (Oxford University Press, 2006)

Rivers, L. N. (2002), "Introduction of the 'Genomic Research and Diagnostic Accessibility Act of 2002' H.R. 3967 and the 'Genomic Science and Technology Innovation Act of 2002' H.R. 3966", US House of Representatives, March 14, 2002. Available at: http://thomas.loc.gov/cgi-bin/query/z?r107:E14MR 2-0020

Rodrigues Jr., E. B. and Carboni, G. (2006), "Ação Civil Pública proposta pelo Instituto de Direito do Comércio Internacional e Desenvolvimento, em 1° de junho de 2006, em face da Associação Brasileira de Direitos

Reprográficos", Poder Judiciário de São Paulo, June 1, 2006 (on file with author)

Royal Society (2003), "Keeping Science Open: The Effects of Intellectual Property Policy on the Conduct of Science", The Royal Society Working Group on Intellectual Property. Available at http://royalsociety.org/uploadedFiles/Royal_Society_Content/policy/publications/2003/9845.pdf

Rubio, K. (2010), "Pelo Direito Olímpico de se estudar e pesquisar estudos olímpicos no Brasil", open letter, January 29, 2010. Available at: http://blog.cev.org.br/novidades/2010/cob-versus-katia-rubio/

Ruse-Khan, H. G. (2008), "A Comparative Analysis of Policy Space in WTO Law", Research Paper Series no. 08–02, Max Planck Institute for Intellectual Property, Competition and Tax Law, p. 68

Sachs, I. (2007), "Em busca de novas estratégias de desenvolvimento", in Sachs, I. and Vieira, P. F. (eds.), *Rumo à ecossocioeconomia: teoria e prática do desenvolvimento* (São Paulo: Cortez, 2007), pp. 247–284

Schmieder, S. (2004), "Scope of Biotechnology Inventions in the United States and in Europe – Compulsory Licensing, Experimental Use and Arbitration: A Study of Patentability of DNA-Related Inventions with Special Emphasis on the Establishment of an Arbitration-Based Compulsory Licensing System" (2004) 21 *Santa Clara Computer & High Technology Law Journal* 163–234

Schreuer, C. H. (1974), "Unjustified Enrichment in International Law" (1974) 22 *American Journal of Comparative Law* 281–301

Scotchmer, S., "Standing on the Shoulders of Giants: Cumulative Research and the Patent Law" (1991) 5 *Journal of Economic Perspectives* 29–41

SACGHS (2009), *Public Consultation Draft Report on Gene Patents and Licensing Practices and Their Impact on Patient Access to Genetic Tests (SACGHS Public Consultation Draft Report for Public Comment from March 9 to May 15, 2009)*

SDE (2008), "Relatório da averiguação preliminar – Autos no. 08012.002673/200 7–51. Representante: Associação Nacional dos Fabricantes de Autopeças (ANFAPE); representada: Volkswagen do Brasil Indústria de Veículos Automotivos Ltda.; Fiat Automóveis S/A; Ford Motor Company Brasil Ltda.", Ministério da Justiça da República Federativa do Brasil (March 10, 2008). Available at: www.anfape.org.br/imagens/Nota%20Tecnica%20Final%20-%20SDE%201 0–0 3–2008.pdf

Senftleben, M. (2004), *Copyright, Limitations and the Three-Step Test: An Analysis of the Three-Step Test in International and EC Copyright Law* (The Hague: Kluwer Law International, 2004)

Senftleben, M. (2006), "Towards a Horizontal Standard for Limiting Intellectual Property Rights? WTO Panel Reports Shed Light on the Three-Step Test in Copyright Law and Related Tests in Patent and Trade Mark Law" (2006) 37 *IIC* 407–438

Serrano, P. and Tojal, S. (2009), "Esclarecimentos prestados pela ANFAPE ao Ministério Público Federal do Rio de Janeiro – Procedimento Administrativo MPF/RJ n°. 1.30.012.000388/200 9–61", ANFAPE (2009). Available at: http://www.anfape.org.br/imagens/Manifestacao%20a%20resposta%20do%20INPI%201 0–0 9–2009.pdf

Shapiro, R. J. (2005), "AIDS Drug Patent Uproar Brazil Attacks Foundations of American Prosperity", *San Francisco Chronicle*, July 14, 2005

Sheremeta, L. and Gold, E. R. (2003), "Creating a Patent Clearinghouse in Canada: A Solution to Problems of Equity and Access" (2003) 11 *Health Law Review* 17–21

Sherman, B. (2010), *Computer Programs as Excluded Patentable Subject Matter (SCP/15/3 – ANNEX II)* (Geneva: WIPO, 2010)

Sigmund, A. M. (2005), "Opinion of the European Economic and Social Committee on the Proposal for a Directive of the European Parliament and of the Council Amending Directive 98/71/EC on the Legal Protection of Designs", COM(2004) 582 final, 2004/0203 (COD), European Economic and Social Committee (June 8, 2005). Available at: http://eur-lex.europa.eu/LexUriServ/LexUriServ.do?uri=OJ:C:2005:286:0008:01:EN:HTML

Silveira, N. (2009), "Parecer: O abuso das montadoras face às fabricantes independentes de autopeças", ANFAPE (2009). Available at: www.anfape.org.br/imagens/Parecer%20Jurídico%20Dr.%20Newron%20Silveira%2004–0 5–2009.pdf

Simma, B. and Paulus, A. L. (1999), "The Responsibility of Individuals for Human Rights Abuses in Internal Conflicts: A Positivist View" (1999) 93 *American Journal of International Law* 291–423

Simmons, B. (2010), *Patents and Clean Energy: Overview and Main Findings* (Geneva: UNEP, EPO and ICTSD, 2010). Available at: http://ictsd.org/downloads/2010/07/presentation_simmons.pdf

Sinclair, I. (1984), *The Vienna Convention on the Law of Treaties*, 2nd edn (Manchester University Press, 1984)

Soares, G. F. S. (2001), *Direito internacional do meio ambiente: emergência, obrigações e responsabilidades* (São Paulo: Atlas, 2001)

Stiglitz, J. E. (1995), *The Theory of International Public Goods and the Architecture of International Organizations* (New York: United Nations Department for Economic and Social Information and Policy Analysis, 1995)

Stix, G. (2006), "Genoma humano: propriedade privada" (2006) 46 *Scientific American Brasil*. Available at: www2.uol.com.br/sciam/reportagens/genoma_humano_propriedade_privada_imprimir.html

Story, A. (2009), "The Global Copyright System: Unbalanced and Unbalanceable for Educational Access in the Global South", South Centre Third International Symposium, 2009

Story, A., Darch, C. and Halbert, D. (2006), *The Copy/South Dossier: Issues in the Economics, Politics, and Ideology of Copyright in the Global South* (Copy/South, 2006)

Strandburg, K. J. (2004), "What Does the Public Get? Experimental Use and the Patent Bargain" (2004) *Wisconsin Law Review* 81–155

Sun, H. (2007), "Overcoming the Achilles Heel of Copyright Law" (2007) 5 *Northwestern Journal of Technology and Intellectual Property* 267–331

Sweet, A. S. and Mathews, J. (2008), "Proportionality Balancing and Global Constitutionalism" (2008) 47 *Columbia Journal of Transnational Law* 72–164

Taubman, A. (2007), "TRIPS Jurisprudence in the Balance: Between the Realist Defense of Policy Space and a Shared Utilitarian Ethic", in Lenk, C., Hoppe, N. and Andorno, R., *Ethics and Law of Intellectual Property: Current Problems in Politics, Science and Technology* (Aldershot: Ashgate, 2007), pp. 89–122

Taylor, G. D. S. (1972), "The Content of the Rule Against Abuse of Rights in International Law" (1972) 46 *British Yearbook of International Law* 323–352

Then, C. and Tippe, R. (2009), "The Future of Seeds and Food under the Growing Threat of Patents and Market Concentration", "No Patents on Seeds" campaign. Available at: www.misereor.org/fileadmin/redaktion/2009_e_report_future_of_seed.pdf

Thumm, N. (2004), *Research and Patenting in Biotechnology: A Survey in Switzerland* (Bern: Swiss Federal Institute of Intellectual Property, 2004)

Thursby, J. and Thursby, M. (2003), "University Licensing and the Bayh–Dole Act" (2003) 301 *Science* 1052

UNCTAD–ICTSD (2005), *Resource Book on TRIPS and Development* (Cambridge University Press, 2005)

UNDP (1999), *Human Development Report 1999* (Oxford University Press, 1999). Available at: http://hdr.undp.org/en/media/HDR_1999_EN.pdf

UNDP (2000). *Human Development Report 2000* (Oxford University Press, 2000). Available at: http://hdr.undp.org/en/media/HDR_2000_EN.pdf

UNEP (2010) (*The Economics of Ecosystems and Biodiversity – TEEB for Business: Executive Summary* (United Nations Environment Programme, 2010)

UNESCO 2009, *Education for All: Global Monitoring Report* (Paris: UNESCO, 2009). Available at: www.unesco.org/education/gmr2009/press/efagmr2009_Annex1_EDI.pdf

UNFCCC (2009), "Non-paper No. 36 – Proposed by the Co-Chairs", Ad Hoc Working Group on Long-Term Cooperative Action Under the Convention, Barcelona, November 2–6, 2009

United Kingdom Intellectual Property Office (2009), "The Patent Research Exception Consultation: Summary of Responses". Available at www.ipo.gov.uk/response-patresearch.pdf

Universidade de São Paulo (2005), "Parecer – Sugestões para a revisão do parecer normativo CJP 1158/98 – Questão da extração de cópias reprográficas para fins de estudo de pesquisa" (2005). Available at: http://reformadireitoautoral.org/files/2010/03/parecer_xerox.pdf.

US Department of Justice (2010), "Brief for the United States as Amicus Curiae in Support of Neither Party: In the United States Court of Appeals for the Federal Circuit: *The Association for Molecular Pathology* et al. *v. United States Patent and Trademark Office, Myriad Genetics, Inc.*", October 29, 2010. Available at: http://graphics8.nytimes.com/packages/pdf/business/genepatents-USamicusbrief.pdf

Van Overwalle, G. (2006), "The Implementation of the Biotechnology Directive in Belgium and its After-Effects: The Introduction of a New Research Exemption and a Compulsory Licence for Public Health" (2006) 37 *IIC* 889–920

Van Overwalle, G., Van Zimmeren, E., Verbeure, B. and Matthijs, G. (2006), "Models for Facilitating Access to Patents on Genetic Inventions" (2006) 7 *Nature Reviews Genetics* 143–148

Veiga, J. E. da (2010), *Sustentabilidade: A legitimação de um novo valor* (São Paulo: Editora Senac, 2010)

Verschuuren, J., *Principles of Environmental Law: The Ideal of Sustainable Development and the Role of Principles of International, European and National Environmental Law* (Baden-Baden: Nomos Verlagsgesellschaft, 2003)

Virally, M. (2000), "Fuentes del derecho internacional", in Sorensen, M. (ed.), *Manual de derecho internacional público* (México, D.F., Fondo de Cultura Económica, 2000), pp. 172–176

Visser, C. (2011), Patent Exceptions and Limitations in the Health Context (SCP/15/3 – Annex V) (Geneva: WIPO, 2011)

Waldeck und Pyrmont, W. Prinz zu (2008), "Research Tool Patents after *Integra v Merck*: Have They Reached a Safe Harbor?" (2008) 14 *Michigan Telecommunications and Technology Law Review* 367–446

Waldock, H. (1964), 'Third Report on the Law of Treaties (A/CN.4/167 and Add. 1–3). 3 March, 9 June, 12 June and 7 July 1964" (1964) 2 *Yearbook of the International Law Commission* 5–65. Available at: http://untreaty.un.org/ilc/documentation/english/a_cn4_167.pdf

Walljasper, J. (2010), *All That We Share: A Field Guide to the Commons* (New York: New Press, 2010)

Walsh, J. P., Arora, A. and Cohen, W. M. (2003), "Effects of Research Tool Patents and Licensing on Biomedical Innovation", in Cohen, W. M. and Merrill, S. A. (eds.), *Patents in the Knowledge-Based Economy* (Washington, DC.: National Academy of Sciences, 2003)

Weber, D. (2004), "Abuse of Law: European Court of Justice, 14 December 2000, Case C-110/99, *Emsland-Stärke*" (2004) 31 *Legal Issues of Economic Integration* 43–55

Weschler, C. (2004), "The Informal Experimental Use Exception: University Research after *Madey v. Duke University*" (2004) 79 *NYU Law Review* 1536–1569

WHO (2008), *Global Strategy and Plan of Action on Public Health, Innovation and Intellectual Property* (WHA61.21) (Geneva: WHO, 2008)

WHO (2009), "Visual Impairment and Blindness", Fact Sheet No. 282, May 2009. Available at: http://www.who.int/mediacentre/factsheets/fs282/en/print.html

WIPO (1971a), *Records of the Intellectual Property Conference of Stockholm (June 11 to July 14, 1967)*, vol. I (Geneva: WIPO, 1971)

WIPO (1971b), *Records of the Intellectual Property Conference of Stockholm (June 11 to July 14, 1967)*, vol. II (Geneva: WIPO, 1971)

WIPO (2007), "The 45 Adopted Recommendations under the WIPO Development Agenda", October 2007. Available at: www.wipo.int/export/sites/www/ip-development/en/agenda/recommendations.pdf

WIPO (2010), "Proposal from Brazil" (SCP/14/7), Standing Committee on the Law of Patents, January 25 to 29, 2010

WIPO (2010), "Conclusiones del SCCR/21", Comité Permanente de Derecho de Autor y Derechos Conexos, November 8–12, 2010

World Commission on Environment and Development (1987), *Our Common Future: Report of the World Commission on Environment and Development* (A/42/427) (New York: United Nations, 1987)

WTO (2005), *WTO Appellate Body Repertory of Reports and Awards 1995–2005*, 3rd edn (Geneva: WTO, 2005). Available at: www.wto.org/english/tratop_e/dispu_e/repertory_e/repertory_e.htm

WTO (2001), "Submission by the African Group, Barbados, Bolivia, Brazil, Cuba, Dominican Republic, Ecuador, Honduras, India, Indonesia, Jamaica, Pakistan, Paraguay, Philippines, Peru, Sri Lanka, Thailand and Venezuela" (IP/C/W/296), Council for Trade-Related Aspects of Intellectual Property Rights, June 29, 2001

WTO (2002), *GATT/WTO Dispute Settlement Practice Relating to GATT Article XX, paragraphs (b), (d) and (g)* (WT/CTE/W/203) (Geneva: Committee on Trade and Environment, 2002)

WTO (2003), *Working Party on Domestic Regulation: "Necessity Tests" in the WTO: Note by the Secretariat* (S/WPDR/W/27) (Geneva: WTO, 2003)

WTO and UNEP (2009), *Trade and Climate Change: A WTO–UNEP Report* (Geneva: WTO and UNEP, 2009)

Xalabarder, R. (2003), "Copyright and Digital Distance Learning Education: The Use of Pre-Existing Works in Distance Education Through the Internet" (2003) 26 *The Columbia Journal of Law & Arts* 101–178

Xavier, F. C. (2008), *Justiça Divina: estudos e dissertações em torno da substância religiosa de O Céu e O Inferno/ pelo Espírito Emmanuel*, 13th edn (Rio de Janeiro: Federação Espírita Brasileira, 2008)

Xiuli, H. (2007), "The Application of the Principle of Proportionality in *Tecmed v. Mexico*" (2007) 6 *Chinese Journal of International Law* 635–652

Yambrusic, E. S. (1987), *Treaty Interpretation: Theory and Reality* (Lanham: University Press of America, 1987)

Yu, P. K. (2003), "The Copyright Divide", Public Law & Legal Theory Working Paper Series – Research Paper no. 10–21 (2003)

Zeitler, H. E. (2005), "'Good Faith' in the WTO Jurisprudence: Necessary Balancing Element or an Open Door to Judicial Activism?" (2005) 8 *Journal of International Economic Law* 721–758

Zhang, N. (2007), "Treaty Interpretation of the WTO Dispute Settlement" (2007) *US–China Law Review* 22–31

Zovko, N. M. (2006), "Nanotechnology and the Experimental Use Defense to Patent Infringement" (2006) 37 *McGeorge Law Review* 129–156

Index

Lightning Source UK Ltd.
Milton Keynes UK
UKOW041857290312

822UK00001B/4/P

9 781107 017481